Accounting, Legal and Tax Aspects of Corporate Acquisitions

Joseph R. Guardino

Prentice-Hall, Inc. / Englewood Cliffs, N.J.

Library of Congress Cataloging in Publication Data

Guardino, Joseph R   (date)
    Accounting, legal, and tax aspects of corporate
acquisitions.

    1. Consolidation and merger of corporations--
United States. I. Title.
KF1477.G8   346'.73'0662   72-5394
ISBN 0-13-002105-9

This publication is designed to provide accurate and authoritative information in regard to the subject matter covered. It is sold with the understanding that the publisher is not engaged in rendering legal, accounting or other professional service. If legal advice or other expert assistance is required, the services of a competent professional person should be sought.

–From a Declaration of Principles jointly adopted by a Committee of the American Bar Association and a Committee of Publishers and Associations.

Printed in the United States of America

About the Author

Joseph R. Guardino is Tax Manager with Hurdman and Cranstoun, Penney and Company. He is a licensed CPA and attorney in New York State, with extensive experience in tax research, tax planning, compliance with corporate reorganizations, liquidations, mergers, acquisitions, and negotiations before the Internal Revenue Service.

Mr. Guardino has contributed articles to professional journals, covering tax and business aspects of subjects treated in this book. He has lectured before professional societies and taught accounting, tax, and law on the college level.

The author has a B.B.A. in accounting and an M.B.A. in taxation from City College in New York. He also received a J.D. Degree from New York Law School.

Mr. Guardino is a member of the American Institute of CPA's, the New York State Society of CPA's, the American Bar, the New York State Bar, and the American Arbitration Association.

To my wife Mary Ann and our families

Foreword

This book deals with corporate reorganizations, mergers, consolidations and acquisitions. Section 368 of the Internal Revenue Code, which affects such transactions, is, to many tax practitioners, the most complex area of the Code. The section specifies the rules through which various types of reorganizations may be effected tax free. Because the tax-free aspect is derived from Congressional privilege, the rules must be applied literally or the transactions will be deemed taxable.

The complexity of the tax considerations is aggravated by a number of other factors; such as, the Securities Exchange Act, applicable state laws, and the equitable realignment of diverse stockholders' interests. The dollar amounts are generally large and the need for immediate decision is almost always urgent. The Internal Revenue Service eases some of the pressure by its willingness to issue prior rulings on proposed reorganizations. However, excessive litigation relative to the tax effects of reorganizations has pointed up the need for a better understanding of the application of Section 368.

The author has made a substantial contribution to the published literature on this subject by incorporating and reviewing the tax, legal and accounting aspects of each type of reorganization. Accordingly, this more inclusive approach offers a broader dimension for evaluation of a contemplated merger or acquisition.

From the functional viewpoint, the book contains many useful tools, including checklists, tax planning suggestions, charts, forms and numerous illustrations. To facilitate further research, the text provides citations of court decisions and I.R.S. rulings. The book is written in an easily readable style and will appeal to both the general practitioner and the specialist.

Milton Zipper, CPA

What This Book Will Do for You

This book is a storehouse of tax planning ideas and information on corporate realignments, acquisitions, liquidations, and reorganizations. Here in one volume is a complete library which will be beneficial to every lawyer, businessman, and accountant as a guide to handling a reorganization or liquidation from A to Z.

There are specific approaches to: (1) the acquisition team and mutually overlapping areas of responsibility; (2) the legal problems inherent in the amalgamation of corporations; (3) accounting aspects such as valuation of corporate and noncorporate businesses and financing along with illustrations of the purchase and pooling of interest methods of accounting; (4) the various types of reorganization and whether it will be treated as a taxable or tax-free acquisition with its concomitant tax treatment for both the corporation and shareholders; and, (5) various overlooked areas such as carryovers, deductibility of reorganization expenses, consolidated returns, state legal and tax problems. Basic principles and rules of general application are emphasized throughout the book with exceptions of minor importance noted.

This practical guide will give the reader a single source from which to pinpoint answers to legal, SEC, tax and accounting problems in acquiring another corporation -- from beginning to end. Each type of reorganization includes forms and illustrations with a discussion of the legal problem, whether it be SEC, federal, or state law. In addition, the accounting problems inherent in such reorganization are discussed. This integrated approach utilized throughout the book obviates the need to search through various other sources for solutions to particular factual situations.

The lawyer will find the legal checklists along with the drafted agreements for each type of reorganization beneficial in advising and assisting their clients, and also find useful the detailed analysis of tax and SEC problems. The accountant will find the book helpful in valuing corporations and accounting for such amalgamation under either the purchase or pooling method, determining which method to utilize from the various tax types of reorganization discussed.

This book, along with serving the professional specialist, whether he be attorney or accountant, will be useful to the general practitioner who would like to become knowledgeable in the area without having to refer to other sources to get an overall view of the problems involved. Similarly, it should help the businessman recognize the tax aspects of the business transaction, outline a deal or an approach to a negotiation with the financial factors in mind, and, in general, focus on the areas in which he should seek professional advice.

The material in this book is presented in a manner that takes the reader through the thought processes of every problem. Sometimes there may seem to be distinctions without differences; however, numerous examples supplement the simplest possible language consistent with accuracy and completeness. Those undertaking transactions of the type discussed herein must know the tax consequences thereof. Knowing the route with the most favorable tax effects leads to proper tax planning. Only by proper tax planning can a businessman be certain that his tax is no more than the government requires it to be.

Joseph R. Guardino

Acknowledgments

I wish to thank the following for granting permission to reproduce excerpts from materials published by them:

- Accounting Principles Board Opinions No. 15, copyright 1969; No. 16, copyright 1970; and Accounting Research Bulletin No. 48, copyright 1957, by the American Institute of Certified Public Accountants.

- Chapter 10, "Corporate Redemptions and Liquidations," is reprinted with some minor adjustments from the author's articles in *Tax Counselor's Quarterly,* Volume 9, No. 1, 1965, pages 1-23, Volume 9, No. 3, 1965, pages 225-254, published by Callaghan and Company, 6141 North Cicero Avenue, Chicago, Illinois, 61646.

- "Corporate Liquidations: Which Method Offers Your Client the Best Treatment?" by Joseph R. Guardino. *Taxation for Accountants,* September-October 1969, page 248.

- Chapter 2, "Solving Legal Problems of Corporate Acquisitions," appeared in slightly different form in *The Nassau Lawyer,* Volume 18, No. 8, page 263, under the title "Some Legal Problems of Corporate Acquisitions."

I am sincerely indebted to numerous people who have helped me bring this book into existence, especially my wife, Mary Ann, for her patience, love, understanding and encouragement; my parents, Mr. and Mrs. Richard Guardino; and Maryann Morea and Kathleen Leonard for their typing prowess.

Contents

2 Solving Legal Problems of Corporate Acquisitions, *cont.*

3 Accounting Aspects of Corporate Acquisitions 49

4 Statutory Merger or Consolidation 69

6   The Stock for Assets and Recapitalization Type of Tax-Free Reorganization, *cont.*

7   Pitfalls to Avoid in Divisive Reorganizations **165**

8   Managing Tax Loss Carryovers with Expertise **181**

8   Managing Tax Loss Carryovers with Expertise, *cont.*

9   Typical Situations Resulting in Reduced Tax Liability **191**

10   Corporate Redemptions and Liquidations **215**

Setting the Stage for Successful Acquisition

1

The most significant economic phenomenon arising during this Age of Aquarius has been the increasing number of corporate marriages. One need only read the pages of any financial magazine or newspaper to see that this trend will continue unabated irrespective of obstacles like the tight money market, depressed stock prices and the government's arsenal of antitrust laws (see Table I at the end of this chapter). The role of federal income taxation has added greater impetus toward the amalgamation of corporations by providing statutory deferral rules to postpone the recognized gain until a subsequent taxable disposition of the securities occurs.

Business combinations offer corporate management a chance to expand into new product lines rapidly by acquisitions rather than the more tedious and sometimes unsuccessful method of internal growth. Another principal motive of corporate acquisitions is basically the desire to increase profits for stockholders by increasing earnings per share or the enhancement of earnings stability or both.

Other factors which have stimulated the trend toward business combinations are the following: (1) development of a stronger organization having better production facilities and managerial talent, (2) reduction of costs through efficient operations being conducted on a larger scale, (3) increased market control thereby improving its competitive position, (4) greater access to capital for growth and lower financing costs, (5) diversification into new fields and (6) income tax advantages.

PRELIMINARY CONSIDERATIONS

Business combinations are born in an economic context which has corporate, tax, regulatory and financial aspects. Each of these factors is so intertwined that it is difficult to separate one from the other since a successful acquisition depends upon each of the factors enumerated. The following checklist will highlight some of the problems involved and skills required to consummate the business combination:

A. Corporation Law
    1. Charter
    2. Bylaws
    3. Appraisal rights
    4. Contract restrictions
    5. Bulk sales
    6. Pension and profit-sharing agreements

B. Tax Factors
   1. Tax-free acquisitions
   2. Taxable acquisitions
   3. State tax problems
   4. Documentary stamps
   5. Ruling request
C. Regulatory Factors
   1. Sherman and Clayton Antitrust Acts
   2. The Securities Act of 1933
   3. The general rules and regulations under the Securities Act of 1933
   4. The Securities Exchange Act of 1934
   5. The general rules and regulations under the Securities Exchange Act of 1934.
   6. New York Stock Exchange requirements
   7. American Stock Exchange requirements
D. Financial Factors
   1. Latest audited financial statements
   2. Federal income tax returns including any revenue agent reports
   3. Federal tax carryover attributes
   4. State and local tax returns
   5. Purchase versus the pooling method of accounting for the business combination.

THE ACQUISITION TEAM

The acquisition team is invariably made up of attorneys, certified public accountants, investment bankers, and corporate financial analysts. This is not to say that no other specialists are part of the acquisition team, but these four are chiefly necessary to consummate a corporate acquisition. Other specialists involved may be appraisers, registrars, and transfer agents.

Each member brings to the team his own professional competence and skills. The attorney has the technical competence to negotiate and draft the various legal instruments to consummate the business combination. The public accountant brings to the task the full range of knowledge of his client's business affairs including his reservoir of accounting and tax expertise. The role of the investment banker is essentially one of financing the acquisition which may take the form of cash, or issuance of stock or debt instruments, or any combination of the foregoing. The financial analyst plays a key role in effectuating the acquisition by implementing his employer corporation guidelines in the program.

The role of any of these advisors should not be restricted to the aforementioned skills since each of these specialists is competent to advise his clients on most aspects of this highly technical field. On the other hand, there are certain functions which should be restricted to certain members of the team. For example, the drafting of legal instruments is the function of the practice of law, and is a matter restricted by law to the attorney. As a further example, the certified public accountant is the party to conduct audits of corporate financial statements and to advise on the tax consequences of the transaction. Accordingly, some measure of teamwork is required within the team as a consequence of their individual specializations and because of their overlapping functions. The members of the team should always remember that their basic purpose is to serve the best interest of the corporation.

CORPORATE LEGAL PROBLEMS

The function of the attorney as previously stated is to assist in all negotiations relating to the acquisition. After all the terms have been agreed to orally, he must draft the legal instruments incorporating all the previously agreed to terms necessary to effectuate the business combination.

Some of the other functions which an attorney must perform consist of fulfilling his responsibilities in the following areas:

1. *State Statutes.* The attorney must determine whether or not a particular state permits a business combination. Without the permissive statutory authority, such transactions are impossible to effectuate. Many states prohibit the acquisition of banks, insurance companies, and public utilities except by companies engaged in the same or similar lines of business because of the public interest vested in these businesses.

2. *Shareholders' Rights.* The laws of many states (including New York) require the consent of shareholders to effectuate such a business combination. Similarly, many states have appraisal rights for minority shareholders who are opposed to the merger. Thus, such shareholders may tender their stock to the corporation and receive payment for it. This usually presents a valuation problem and also poses a cash drain to the acquiring corporation.

3. *SEC and Blue Sky Laws.* Federal laws may require a registration statement if the acquisition is to be accomplished through the issuance of additional stock which is frequently an expensive and time-consuming process. Various states have also imposed state securities laws which must be complied with before stock can be issued to such shareholders.

4. *Antitrust Problems.* The attorney must frequently study a corporation's pricing policies to see that it does not violate the Clayton Act. Similarly, it is against public policy for an acquisition to occur between companies which will tend to lessen competition. Thus, a violation of the Clayton Act will occur in the acquisition between a manufacturer and its chief distributor, or between Ford and Chrysler. The attorney should also be familiar with the Sherman Act and the Robinson-Patman Act.

5. *Stock Exchange Requirements.* The issuance of additional shares by the acquiring corporation in a stock acquisition may necessitate the listing of such shares with the various stock exchanges, or, more specifically, the New York and the American Stock Exchanges. Furthermore, a requirement of the stock exchange is that shareholder approval may be required before the listing of the additional shares. This is so irrespective of the fact that no such approval may be required pursuant to state law. For example, the New York Stock Exchange rules require shareholder approval before the acquisition of a company if the amount of the additional stock to be issued increases the outstanding stock by more than twenty percent of the market value of the outstanding common shares.[1]

ACCOUNTING PROBLEMS

The accounting problems arising from a business combination can be categorized into three areas: (1) valuation problems; (2) goodwill attributable to a business, if any; (3) purchase or pooling of interest method being utilized to account for the acquisition.

A major problem in agreeing to a merger or acquisition is the establishment of a value for a cash purchase, or an exchange ratio, if payment is to be accomplished by using stock or securities. Some of the methods frequently used to establish a value are the book value of a company or the market value of securities with a payout over a period of time if certain earnings tests are met.

Some acquisitions give rise to goodwill or intangible asset classifications on the new balance sheet and other difficult problems in the valuation of the assets acquired.

The purchase concept versus the pooling of interest concept of handling business combinations has caused great divergence of opinion among accountants as to which method should be utilized. Basically, a purchase is a business combination of two or more corporations in which an important part of the ownership interests in the acquired corporation or corporations is eliminated or in which other factors requisite to a pooling of interests are not present.[2]

A pooling of interest occurs when two or more firms combine to carry out their business functions as a single enterprise. The general interpretation of Bulletin 48 of the Accounting Research Bulletin is that a business combination involving the exchange of stock can generally be considered to be a pooling of interests unless the circumstances indicate to the contrary. By this is meant that if cash is the consideration used to effectuate the combination, then the purchase method of accounting is called for. These problems will be discussed in greater detail in the chapter dealing with accounting problems.

TAX PROBLEMS

Probably the most important factor in casting the terms of the deal is attributable to the tax consequences, but this should not be the controlling factor. Rather business considerations should control, but in actual practice this is not usually the case. Each of the factors previously mentioned, that is, business, legal and financial considerations, should be given equal weight in arriving at the decision to acquire a corporation, but few of these considerations are as significant as the tax cost of the transaction. Accordingly, tax considerations play the key factor in acquiring corporations which should not be the case since many acquisitions turn sour. This can readily be seen by a company's earnings declining radically after the acquisition with the result that the acquired corporation is usually disposed of within a few years.

The tax laws permit corporate acquisitions to be arranged either as a taxable sale of assets or a tax-free transaction.[3] In a taxable sale of stock or assets, the seller has a recognized gain or loss, either capital or ordinary depending upon the character of the assets disposed of. The seller could also have unfavorable tax consequences in the sale of assets whenever part of the gain may be taxable as ordinary rather than capital gain. This is attributable to the depreciation recapture rules applicable to the disposition of tangible personal and real property. Similarly, it is possible that investment credit recapture could arise by disposing of the asset prior to the statutory lives of the assets previously determined. This means a dollar for dollar recapture rather than a dollar of income arising as in depreciation recapture which is taxed at approximately fifty percent.

The purchaser of the assets for cash in a taxable transaction will have a new basis equal to the consideration exchanged for them. Thus, the higher basis for the assets will be recovered through depreciation deductions.

A tax-free reorganization is a misnomer since the realized gain or loss is only deferred until a future taxable disposition occurs. Thus, in a B-type reorganization in which solely voting stock is exchanged between the corporations, the shareholders of the acquired corporation have a tax basis of $10 for the stock and a fair market value of $25 but receive listed stock from the acquiring corporation worth $50. Their paper gain is $40 and no tax is imposed until they subsequently sell it. If it is sold for $60, the capital gain is $50 ($60 - 10) and not $10 ($60 - 50) since the basis of stock received is the same as the basis for the stock exchanged or given up. Thus, the basis of stock given up is the same as the basis of the stock received, or, a substituted basis.

Section 368 of the 1954 Internal Revenue Code provides for only six types of exchanges which qualify for this privileged tax treatment. They are as follows:

A. *Statutory Merger or Consolidation.* The only requirement necessary to effectuate such a transaction is that state corporation laws permit it.

B. *Stock Exchanged Solely for Voting Stock.* This requirement requires literal compliance with its terms since anything else used as consideration to effectuate the business combination will cause the transaction to be a taxable transaction. After the acquisition, the acquired corporation is usually operated as a subsidiary of the acquiring corporation.

C. *Stock Used to Acquire Assets.* This requirement is met when stock is exchanged for assets of the acquiring corporation. After the exchange, the shareholders of the acquired corporation receive stock from the acquiring corporation in exchange for their stock. The acquired corporation usually has few assets left, or enough assets remaining, to pay off certain liabilities after which it is usually liquidated in a tax-free liquidation under either Sections 331 or 337 of the 1954 Internal Revenue Code.

D. *Corporate Separations.* This is the least desirable method of achieving a tax-free acquisition, since it is usually a trap to the unwary because of the statutory conditions stating there must be an active business and not a device to distribute its earnings and profits requirements.

E. *Recapitalization.* This type usually involves a reorganization of the capital structure by issuing other classes of stock, such as, preferred or Class A and B common or debt instruments for the stock interest.

F. *Change in Identity or Form.* This type is the simplest method and can arise by an incorporation in another state.

These various types enumerated above are often designated in tax literature according to the subparagraph that they refer to. Thus, a C-type is stock exchanged for assets.

The consideration involved in choosing between taxable and tax-free acquisitions depends on the consideration being exchanged by the purchaser. The seller and the purchaser have various motives in such a transaction.

The seller ordinarily seeks to arrange for a tax-free reorganization in order to postpone the gain or loss until a subsequent disposition. But if a loss will occur, the seller will arrange the transaction to be taxable so that the loss can be deducted immediately.

A taxable sale of assets requires the allocation of purchase price among the assets acquired to determine the gain or loss and a basis for depreciation of the assets for the purchaser. This leads logically to two basic problems. One problem is that the seller desires to allocate the purchase price among the assets to maximize his capital gain and minimize the portions applicable to the ordinary income portions. The purchaser, on the other hand, will seek to allocate as much to receivables and inventory to reduce ordinary income, and as much as possible to fixed assets in order to recover the purchase price by higher depreciation allowances. Thus, the Treasury Department would in effect be financing the acquisitions.

Other nonbusiness factors enter into how the transaction is to be cast. Frequently, a seller wishes to retire and would like to receive cash rather than stock for his business. Thus, a taxable transaction will be the form utilized. Sometimes, as it frequently happens, the owner of a closely held corporation has no children interested in the business and would like to sell. On the other hand, the owner would like to receive stock in a tax-free transaction which could be distributed to his children.

The acquiring corporation is concerned with the carryover of tax attributes, such as, net operating loss carryovers, earnings and profits, and depreciation and accounting methods.

FINANCING THE ACQUISITION

The method of financing the acquisition is determined early in the negotiations stage. It is probably the most crucial factor in determining whether a business combination can be effectuated successfully. This is usually the stage at which most contemplated transactions "fizzle out."

The plan as finally adopted depends upon the intent of the parties concerned as to what they will accomplish by completing the acquisition. If the intent of the parties is to postpone tax, then the acquisition exchange will be accomplished by an exchange of voting common stock rather than cash and/or other property being exchanged. A taxable acquisition, if desired by the parties, gives rise to greater flexibility regarding the consideration being exchanged since the mode of payment can be with the use of cash, nonvoting preferred stock, convertible debt instrument, warrants or any combination of the foregoing.

The increased use of convertible instruments in the past decade as a method of financing the corporate acquisition has caused these types of paper instruments to be referred to as "funny money." The Treasury has also been concerned with the transaction being cast in the form of a taxable transaction by using convertible type instruments since the interest paid on debt is a tax deduction whereas a dividend paid on stock is nondeductible. The Tax Reform Act of 1969 as enacted restricts the interest that can be deducted in financing corporate acquisitions to five million dollars.

The most widely used method of financing acquisitions is that of exchanging the stock of the acquiring firm for the stock of the acquired corporation or corporations. However, other methods are also frequently employed. Some acquisitions are commonly effected through acquiring stock or purchasing assets from individual persons or companies at a private sale or in the open market. If a firm has a substantial amount of surplus cash on hand, it has both the means and the incentive to acquisition activities, and may acquire assets outright or the stock claims behind them. Borrowed funds and other bank loans are also used in many instances for such purposes.

In an asset acquisition, a corporation may (1) purchase all the assets of a going concern, (2) purchase only a portion of the firm's assets or business such as a division, or (3) purchase the assets of a firm in bankruptcy reorganization.

THE TREND OF MERGER ACTIVITY

There is no question that the United States economy is in the midst of an usually large period of acquisition, consolidation, and merger. This can be readily seen by the following table showing large acquisitions made by firms classified among the 200 largest companies from 1948-1967.

Year	Total Large Acquisitions[a]		Total Acquired by 200 Largest Firms[b]	
	Number	Assets (millions)	Number	Assets (millions)
1948	4	$66	4	$66
1949	5	67	5	67
1950	4	173	2	107
1951	9	201	5	125
1952	13	327	6	187
1953	23	679	17	561
1954	35	1,425	17	906
1955	68	2,129	33	1,412
1956	58	2,037	37	1,527
1957	50	1,472	29	1,104
1958	38	1,107	24	707
1959	64	1,960	36	1,425
1960	62	1,710	33	978
1961	59	2,129	25	1,240
1962	72	2,194	31	1,095
1963	68	2,917	34	1,843
1964	91	2,798	37	1,221
1965	93	3,900	29	2,601
1966	101	4,100	31	2,215
1967	170	8,246	66	5,392
TOTAL	1087	39,584	601	24,239
1968 estimate	188	12,366	70[c]	6,755[c]

Source: Bureau of Economics, Federal Trade Commission

---

[a]Acquired units with assets of $10 million or more.

[b]For years 1948-1965, 200 largest firms ranked by 1965 assets, for 1966 and 1967, acquirers are 200 largest firms ranked by 1966 assets, excluding those firms acquired in 1967.

[c]Estimate of the 1968 acquisitions by the 200 largest companies of 1967.

The Federal Trade Commission recently announced that there were 4,550 mergers during 1969. But the gain in the number of mergers during the year—up 618 from 1968—fell far short of the increase of 1,548 between 1967 and 1968. Included in the companies disappearing in 1967 were three corporations with assets of more than $1 billion each.

FOOTNOTES

[1] New York Stock Exchange Company Manual, Sec. A-284.

[2] Accounting Research Bulletin No. 48.

[3] IRC—1954—Sec. 368 (a).

Solving Legal Problems of Corporate Acquisitions

2

The legal problems arising from business combinations involve such factors as state law, shareholder approval, and the rights of dissenting shareholders to receive payment for their shares. In addition, other legal considerations involved are an awareness of the problems that could arise under the federal Sherman, and Clayton Acts, Securities regulations, and state and local tax laws. It is no wonder that the attorney is a key member of the acquisition team during both the negotiation and consummation of such acquisition because of the complexity of the laws.

The term "business combinations" involves both mergers and consolidations. A "merger" is a transaction in which the "surviving corporation" is one of the "constituent corporations." A "consolidation" is a transaction in which a new "consolidated corporation" is organized to take over the assets subject to the liabilities of the "constituent corporations." Basically, the difference is that upon consolidation, a new corporation comes into existence, and the prior corporation ceases to exist; whereas upon merger, the existence of one of the corporations is continued without the formation of a new corporation, the other being merged into it. For example, a merger would be deemed to occur where A Corporation and B Corporation are joined together with A Corporation as the surviving corporation. A consolidation would occur where A Corporation and B Corporation are joined together and C Corporation comes into existence. The term "constituent corporation" means an existing corporation that is participating in the merger or consolidation with one or more other corporations. A "surviving corporation" means that constituent corporation into which one or more other constituent corporations are merged. A "consolidated corporation" means the new corporation into which two or more constituent corporations are consolidated.

As one reads the statute, it can readily be seen that the terms "reorganization" or "business combination" are nowhere to be found. This is because a reorganization is peculiar to federal income taxation while a business combination is a work of art attributable to the accounting profession. Thus, it can readily be seen that a statutory consolidation involves the formation of a new corporation and the payment of the organization tax on all its shares. On the other hand, a merger would not require the payment of any organizational taxes unless the authorized shares of the surviving corporation exceeds those paid by the constituent corporations. For example, if Corporations A and B have 1,000 shares outstanding and agree to merge into Corporation C having outstanding shares of 2,500, the organization tax will be paid on the excess number of shares or 500 [2,500 (C) - 1,000 (A) - 1000 (B)].

The statutory law of New York permits the merger of any domestic corporation which owns at least ninety-five percent of the outstanding shares of each class of another domestic corporation into itself without shareholder approval. This type of merger is usually referred to as a short merger, because of the absence of the requirement of shareholder approval as in other types of merger. This type of merger can occur by the approval of the board of directors of the parent corporation.

PLAN OF MERGER OR CONSOLIDATION

The first legal requirement for consummating a merger or a consolidation is a plan which must be approved by the board of directors of each corporation before submission to the shareholders. Such a plan should[5] include the following information:

1. The name of each constituent corporation, and if the name of any of them has been changed, the name under which it was formed, and the name of the surviving corporation, or method of determining it, of the consolidated corporation.

2. As to each constituent corporation, the designation and number of outstanding shares of each class and series, specifying the class and series, if any, entitled to vote as a class, and, if the number of any such shares is subject to change prior to the effective date of the merger or consolidation, the manner in which such change may occur.

3. The terms and conditions of the proposed merger or consolidation, including the manner and basis of converting the shares of each constituent corporation into shares, bonds or other securities of the surviving corporation, or the cash or other consideration to be paid or delivered in exchange for shares of each constituent corporation, or a combination thereof.

4. In case of merger, a statement of any amendments or changes in the certificate of incorporation of the surviving corporation to be affected by such merger; in case of consolidation, all statements required to be included in a certificate of incorporation for a corporation formed under Article 9 of the Business Corporation Law, except statements as to facts not available at the time the plan of consolidation is approved by the board.

5. Any other provisions with respect to the proposed merger or consolidation as the board considers necessary or desirable.

APPROVAL BY SHAREHOLDERS

The plan of merger must be submitted to the shareholders after approval by the board of directors of each of the constituent corporations. The procedure for this is as follows:[6]

1. Notice of meeting shall be given to each shareholder of record, whether or not entitled to vote. A copy of the plan for merger or consolidation or an outline of the material features of the plan shall accompany such notice to the shareholders.

2. The plan for merger or consolidation shall be authorized by a meeting of shareholders by vote of the holders of two-thirds of all outstanding shares entitled to vote thereon. Notwithstanding any provision of certificate of incorporation, the holders of shares of a class or series shall be entitled to vote

and to vote as a class if the plan of merger or consolidation contains any provisions which, if contained in an amendment to the certificate of incorporation, would entitle the holders of shares of such class or series to vote and to vote as a class thereon.

3. Notwithstanding, shareholder authorization and at any time prior to the filing of the certificate of merger or consolidation, the plan of merger or consolidation may be abandoned pursuant to a provision for such abandonment, if any, contained in the plan of merger or consolidation.

CERTIFICATE OF MERGER OR CONSOLIDATION

After approval of the plan of merger or consolidation by the board of directors and two-thirds of the shareholders of the constituent corporation, the certificate must be prepared. The certificate of merger or consolidation must be signed and verified on behalf of each constituent corporation and delivered to the Department of State. The contents of such certificate must[7] include the following:

1. The plan of merger or consolidation, and, in case of consolidation, any statement required to be included in a certificate of incorporation for a corporation formed under this chapter but omitted under the plan since it was not available at the time of the plan of consolidation, is approved by the board.

2. The date when the certificate of incorporation of each constituent corporation was filed by the Department of State.

3. The manner in which the merger or consolidation was authorized with respect to each constituent corporation.

Thereafter, the surviving or consolidated corporation shall cause a copy of such certificate, certified by the Department of State, to be filed in the office of the clerk of each county in which the office of a constituent corporation, other than the surviving corporation, is located, and in the office of the official who is the recording officer of each county in this state in which real property of a constituent corporation, other than the surviving corporation, is situated.

MERGER OF SUBSIDIARY CORPORATION

By statute,[8] any domestic corporation owning at least ninety-five percent of the outstanding shares of each class of another domestic corporation or corporations may merge such other corporation or corporations into itself without the authorization of the shareholders of any such corporation. In actual practice, this "short merger" is used frequently to realign corporate structures without the necessity of requiring the approval of the shareholders of the parent corporation.

The board of directors shall approve a plan, setting forth:

1. The name of each subsidiary corporation to be merged and the name of the surviving corporation, and if the name of any of them has been changed, the name under which it was formed.

2. The designation and number of outstanding shares of each subsidiary corporation to be merged and the number of such shares of each class owned by the surviving corporation; and if the number of any such shares is subject to change prior to the effective date of the merger, the manner in which such change may occur.

3. The terms and conditions of the proposed merger, including the manner and basis of converting the shares of each subsidiary corporation to be merged and not owned by the surviving corporation, or the cash or other consideration to be paid or delivered in exchange for shares of each such subsidiary corporation, or a combination thereof.

4. a. Any other provision with respect to the proposed merger as the board considers necessary or desirable.

   b. A copy of such plan of merger or an outline of the materials shall be given, personally or by mail, to all holders of shares of each subsidiary corporation to be merged, not owned by the surviving corporation, unless the giving of such copy or outline has been waived by such holders.

   c. "A certificate of merger" shall be signed, verified and delivered to the Department of State by the surviving corporation. If the surviving corporation does not own all shares of each subsidiary corporation to be merged, such certificate shall be delivered not less than thirty days after the giving of the copy or outline of the material features of the plan of merger to shareholders of each subsidiary corporation, or at any time after the waiving thereof by the holders of corporation not owned by the surviving corporation. The certificate shall set forth:

   i. The plan of merger

   ii. The date when the certificate of incorporation of each constituent corporation was filed by the Department of State

   iii. If the surviving corporation does not own all the shares of each subsidiary corporation to be merged, either the date of the giving to the holders of shares of each such subsidiary corporation not owned by the surviving corporation a copy of the plan of merger or an outline of the material features thereof, or a statement that the giving of such copy or outline has been waived, if such is the case.

   d. The surviving corporation shall thereafter cause a copy of such certificate, certified by the Department of State, to be filed in the office of the official who is the recording officer of each county in this state in which real property of a constituent corporation is situated.

   e. The right of merger granted by this section to certain corporations shall not preclude the exercise by such corporations of any other right of merger or consolidation under this article.

A fee of thirty dollars is to paid to the Department of State upon filing of a certificate of merger or consolidation.[9] Similarly, an organization tax will be assessed if the aggregate number of shares of the new corporation exceeds the aggregate number of shares of the constituent corporation. The tax is five cents a share, but in no case shall the tax be less than $10.[10]

A minority shareholder is entitled to have his shares appraised or valued according to law and to receive cash in payment thereof. In a short merger, a minority shareholder is one or more holders of the remaining five percent of the stock.

EFFECT OF MERGER OR CONSOLIDATION

The merger or consolidation becomes effective thirty days after filing of the certificate of merger or consolidation with the Department of State and paying the prescribed $30 filing fee. The certificate of incorporation of the surviving corporation is automatically amended by operation of law to give effect to the merger. In the case of a consolidation, the certificate of consolidation becomes its certificate of incorporation. The consent of the State Tax Commissioner to the merger or consolidation is to be affixed to such certificate at the time of filing with the Department of State. Thus, the merger or consolidation becomes effective upon filing the certificate or on such date subsequent thereto, but not later than thirty days after the filing.

After the merger or consolidation has been effected:

1. Such surviving or consolidated corporation shall possess all the rights, privileges, immunities, powers and purposes of each of the constituent corporations.[11]

2. All the property, real and personal, including subscription to shares, causes of action and every other asset of each of the constituent corporations, shall vest in such surviving or consolidated corporation without further act or deed.[12]

3. The surviving or consolidated corporations shall assume and be liable for all the liabilities, obligations and penalties of each of the constituent corporations. No liability or obligation due or to become due, claim or demand for any cause existing against any such corporation, or any shareholder, officer or director thereof, shall abate or be discontinued by such merger or consolidation, but may be enforced, prosecuted, settled or compromised as if such merger or consolidation had not occurred, or such surviving consolidated corporation may be substituted in such action or special proceeding in place of any constituent corporation.[13]

4. In the case of a merger, the certificate of incorporation of the surviving corporation shall be automatically amended to the extent, if any, that changes in the certificate of incorporation are set forth in the plan of merger; and, in the case of consolidation, the statements set forth in the certificate of consolidation and which are required or permitted to be set forth in a certificate of incorporation of a corporation formed under this chapter shall be its certificate of incorporation.

The language of the statute is sufficiently broad to cover all liabilities, both existing and contingent. Furthermore, liabilities arising after the merger or consolidation which are attributable to the premerger activities are binding on the surviving corporation.

MERGER OR CONSOLIDATION OF
DOMESTIC AND FOREIGN CORPORATIONS

By statute,[14] one or more foreign corporations could be merged or consolidated with one or more domestic corporations, if such merger or consolidation is permitted by the laws of the jurisdiction under which each such foreign corporation is incorporated. As regards the procedure to consummate such a merger or consolidation, the only statutory requirement is that the domestic corporation comply with the laws of New York, and each foreign corporation shall comply with the applicable law of the jurisdiction under which it is incorporated.[15] The rules applicable to short merger are also available where either the subsidiary corporation or the parent corporation owns at least ninety-five percent of the corporation, and the merger is permitted under the laws of the jurisdiction under which the foreign corporation is incorporated. If a domestic corporation is to be the surviving or consolidated corporation, the certificate of merger or consolidation should be signed, verified and delivered to the Department of State. The contents of the certificate shall set forth the jurisdiction and date of incorporation of each of the constituent foreign corporations, and the date when its certificate of authority to do business in this state was filed by the Department of State, or if no application was filed, a statement to that effect.[16] The consent of the State Tax Commission is to be attached to the certificate.[17]

SALE, LEASE, EXCHANGE OR
OTHER DISPOSITION OF ASSETS

Sometimes it is difficult to obtain the necessary two-thirds vote of the shareholders to ratify a merger. One method used to get around the shareholder approval is to sell the assets to a purchaser followed by a liquidation of the corporation. As it will be seen later, this result can be achieved tax free under Section 337 of the Internal Revenue Code.

In actual practice, this sale, exchange, or lease of assets is referred to as a de facto merger. The basis for this term is that it is another method of obtaining assets from one corporation to another without the imposition of any federal income tax liability.

By statute,[18] a sale, lease, exchange or other disposition of all or substantially all of the assets of a corporation, is not made in the usual or regular course of the business actually conducted by such corporation, and shall be authorized only in accordance with the following procedure:

1. The sale, lease, exchange or other disposition shall be approved by the board of directors prior to submission to a vote of the shareholders.
2. Notice of meeting to dispose of the assets of the corporation is to be submitted to each shareholder, whether or not entitled to vote.
3. The shareholders shall authorize such sale, lease, exchange or other disposition and may vest the board with the authority to fix terms and conditions for such disposition. Furthermore, the consideration to be received by the corporation may consist of cash or other property, real or personal, including intangibles such as stocks, bonds or other securities from the acquiring corporation whether it be domestic or foreign. In tax terminology, this would be a C-type tax-free reorganization since it is an exchange of stock for assets.

Whenever a transaction involves sale, exchange, lease or other disposition of all or substantially all the assets of the corporation, including the name, to a new corporation formed under the same name as the existing corporation, then upon the expiration of thirty days from the filing of the certificate of incorporation of the new corporation, with the consent of the State Tax Commission attached, the existing corporation shall be automatically dissolved, unless, before the end of the thirty-day period, such corporation has changed its name. The adjustment and winding up of the affairs of such dissolved corporation shall proceed pursuant to the laws applicable to a nonjudicial dissolution.

The board of directors reserves its right to abandon the proposed sale, lease, exchange or other disposition without further action by the shareholders. The only reservation is that such withdrawal is subject to the rights of third parties, if any, under contract relating thereto.

APPRAISAL RIGHTS OF MINORITY SHAREHOLDERS

As it frequently happens in business combinations, certain shareholders are not content with the terms of a merger. By statute,[19] the dissenting or minority shareholders have a right to receive payment for shares upon merger, consolidation or sale, lease, exchange or other disposition of assets. This can present a cash drain to the corporation along with other problems because of time factors.

The shareholder of a domestic corporation shall have the right to receive payment for the fair value of his shares and other rights and benefits. Such right exists in the following cases: (1) a shareholder entitled to vote who does not assent to any plan of merger or consolidation to which the corporation is a party; and, (2) any sale, lease, exchange or other disposition of all or substantially all of the assets of a corporation which requires shareholder approval other than a cash transaction where the approval by the shareholders is conditioned upon the dissolution of the corporation and the distribution of substantially all of its net respective interests within one year after the date of such transaction.[20]

In a merger or consolidation, such right to receive payment of the fair value of the shares is not available to the shareholders of the surviving corporation in a parent-subsidiary merger or a merger or consolidation of a domestic and foreign corporation.[21] Similarly, such right is not available to a shareholder of the surviving corporation unless the merger affects the rights of the shares held by such shareholders in the following situations: (1) the preferential right of the shareholder is altered or abolished; (2) creates, alters or abolishes any provision or right in respect of redemption of any sinking fund; (3) excludes or limits the right to vote. The right to receive payment for such shares is not an absolute and unconditional one, but one arising if the aforementioned conditions are met.

The procedure to enforce such rights are as follows:[22] (1) Written objection by shareholders to proposed corporation action to be filed with corporation, before meeting of shareholders at which action is submitted to vote, or at such meeting but before vote. (2) Written notice by corporation to be sent by registered mail to each objecting shareholder and each shareholder from whom written objection is not required, of shareholders' authorization of or consent to proposed corporate action within ten days thereafter. (3) Written notice of election to dissent by objecting shareholders to be filed with corporation within twenty days after giving of notice to him. (4) Stock certificates are to be submitted by dissenting shareholders to corporation for notation at time of filing of notice of election to dissent or within one month thereafter. (5) Written offer by corporation to be sent by registered mail to all dissenting shareholders to pay for shares at specified price, within seven days after expiration of period within which shareholders may file their notices of election to dissent or within seven days after proposed corporate action is consummated, whichever is later. (6) Payments for shares to be made within sixty days after shareholders' authorization date upon surrender of certificates representing such shares, if corporation and shareholder agree upon price within thirty days after mailing of written offer by corporation.

The only question remaining is how the shares are to be valued. The statutory valuation standard in New York is "fair value as of the close of business on the day prior to the shareholders' authorization date, excluding any appreciation or depreciation directly or indirectly induced by such corporate action or its proposal."[23] One point that must be remembered before leaving this section is that the dissenting shareholder must dissent as to *all* his shares and not just a part of them.

DISSOLUTION

The term "dissolution" is used interchangeably with "liquidation," but they are not the same. A dissolution is a legal concept meaning that the corporation ceases to exist as a matter of law. Since it is created by the State, it logically follows that only state law can cause its termination. On the other hand, a corporate liquidation is concerned with the winding-up of the affairs of a corporation. This is usually accomplished by selling the assets, paying off creditors and distributing the proceeds to the shareholders.

There are two types of legal dissolution in New York. They are: (1) judicial or nonvoluntary and (2) nonjudicial or voluntary dissolution. A judicial dissolution can be brought by the attorney-general because the formation was produced through fraud or concealment of a material fact, or that it has exceeded its authority (ultra vires) or carried on its business in a fraudulent manner.[24] Another ground for the attorney-general to bring an action to dissolve a corporation is that it has not filed reports or paid franchise taxes for three years.[25] The board of directors or the shareholders may petition the court for a judicial dissolution where the assets of a corporation are not sufficient to discharge its liabilities or that a dissolution will be beneficial to the shareholders.

A voluntary dissolution may be authorized at a meeting of shareholders by vote of the holders of two-thirds of all outstanding shares entitled to vote thereon or by their unanimous written consent without a meeting.[26] The original certificate of incorporation may contain a provision that any shareholder or the holders of any specified number or portion of outstanding shares or class or series of shares may require dissolution at will or upon the recurrence of any specified event. Each stock certificate must bear conspicuously on its face or back, a reference to such provision. If it is desired to amend the certificate of incorporation to include such provision, or if it includes it, to change or strike it out, it must be authorized at a meeting by vote of all the holders of all outstanding shares, voting or nonvoting shares or by such lesser portion of shares, class (but not less than a majority) of all outstanding shares entitled to vote on any amendments as the certificate provides for such purpose.[27]

After dissolution, the corporate status is one in which no business is to be carried on except to wind up its affairs (liquidation). It has the power to fulfill or discharge its contracts, collect or sell assets, pay its liabilities and do other acts appropriate to liquidation after adequately providing for the payment of its liabilities. The corporation may, if authorized at a shareholder's meeting by a vote of the majority of all outstanding shares entitled to vote thereon, sell all or part of its remaining assets for cash and/or securities and distribute them among the shareholders.

The corporation may give notice to all creditors, including those with unliquidated or contingent claims or having unfulfilled contracts, to present their claims in writing at a specified place and by a specified day, which must not be less than six months after the first publication of the notice to be published once a week for two consecutive weeks. A copy of it is to submitted to every person believed to be a creditor. If such a creditor does not submit his claim timely as provided in the notice, the statute of limitations is reduced.[28]

STATE AND LOCAL TAX PROBLEMS

New York State imposes a tax on every domestic corporation possessing a franchise rather than a corporate income tax. Thus, it is not a tax on doing business, but rather the mere possession of a franchise which forms the basis for taxation. Accordingly, a domestic corporation formed in New York which is not doing business, or is merely dormant, or is a name-saving corporation, is subject to the corporate franchise tax.

A domestic corporation which ceases to possess a franchise through dissolution, merger or consolidation into another corporation, must pay a tax measured by its entire net income (federal taxable income plus adjustments) up to the date on which it ceases to possess a franchise. Similarly, a foreign corporation authorized to do business in New York must also pay a franchise tax when it ceases to do business in New York.

There are two ways of handling the last franchise tax report for a dissolving corporation. The first method is to file a report on an estimated basis. Thereafter, a final report is to be filed within thirty days with the State Tax Commission after the Certificate of Dissolution is filed with the Secretary of State.

FEDERAL SECURITIES LAW

The number of "corporate marriages" which occur annually arise between listed companies. For this reason, the role of the Securities and Exchange Commission (S.E.C.) may play a prominent role in the consummation of mergers.

The Federal Securities Laws were enacted to protect the rights of public investors by providing them with adequate disclosure of all relevant facts to base a decision upon the investment merits of the securities. The laws which were enacted to provide such information were attributable to the excessive public speculation compounded by fraudulent and unethical practices in the sale of securities. This led to the stock market crash in October 1929, and the Great Depression.

The Securities Act of 1933 was the first piece of remedial legislation enacted by Congress to provide investors with knowledge concerning new issues of securities. The underlying purpose of this Act is full disclosure rather than regulatory measures.

The Securities Exchange Act of 1934 established the Securities and Exchange Commission. It deals chiefly with securities listed on national securities exchanges and in the over-the-counter markets. It is regulatory in scope and, for this reason, differs from the 1933 Act which is a disclosure statute.

In addition, four other statutes are administered by the Securities and Exchange Commission. The Public Utility Holding Company Act of 1935 is concerned with the regulation of public utilities. The Federal Trust Indenture Act of 1939 relates to the issuance of bonds and other evidences of indebtedness. The Investment Company Act of 1940 provides for the regulation of investment companies. Lastly, the Investment Advisors Act of 1940 is concerned with the regulation of investment advisors who advise concerning the investment merits of securities in return for a fee.

SECURITIES ACT OF 1933

The Securities Act of 1933 was enacted with a twofold purpose. The first objective was to protect investors by requiring full disclosure of all financial material and other information concerning the sale of new security issues offered for sale to the public. The second objective was to prohibit fraud, misrepresentation and other practices in the sale of securities. To accomplish these objectives, Section 5 of the Act provides that a registration statement be in effect whenever any instrument of interstate commerce or the mails is used to offer to sell a security. It is unlawful to sell a security or to deliver a security after sale unless a registration statement is in effect. Furthermore, no security can be delivered unless a statutory prospectus accompanies or precedes such delivery.

A registration statement contains the following information: (1) description of issuer's business, (2) description of stock to be offered, (3) information about management of company, (4) certified financial statements by an independent public accountant, and, (5) an opinion by legal counsel considering the validity of the stock offering. Stock which is required to be registered under the Act can be offered for sale twenty days after the registration statement is filed, unless accelerated by the Commissioner.[28]

DEFINITION OF SECURITY

Section 2 (i) of the Act defines the term "securities" so broadly as to embrace not only securities, bonds, notes, debentures, warrants, and rights, but any other type of instrument which provides for a profit participation to be achieved through the efforts of others. For Section 5 to become operative, there must be a "sale" or "offer to sell" of a security. The term "sale" includes "every contract of sale or disposition of a security for value."[29] The term "offer" includes every attempt or offer to dispose of, or solicitation of an offer to buy a security or interest in a security for value. The "value" referred to in the definition of "sale" or "offer" need not be cash. Thus, the concept of sale becomes important when a corporate merger should occur between two companies where securities are to be distributed to shareholders since a registration statement may be required in the absence of a specific exemption.

EXEMPT SECURITIES

The Securities Act of 1933 provides three exceptions to the general rule requiring a registration statement when securities are to be sold. These exemptions are as follows: (1) intrastate offerings; (2) Regulation A offerings, and (3) private offerings.

Section 3(a) (ii) of the Securities Act of 1933 exempts from its registration statement and prospectus requirements "any security which is a part of an issue offered and sold only to persons resident within a single state or territory, or to a corporation, incorporated and doing business within, such sale or territory. Thus, if all the statutory conditions are complied with, no registration statement is required, but if a sale is made to one offeree who is a resident of another state, the exemption is nullified for the entire issue. Hence, it can readily be seen that strict compliance is required.

A Regulation A, or Small Offering Exemption, provides an exemption from Section 5 registration statement provisions when the maximum offering is $300,000. There is a proposal to pass legislation to raise the maximum amount to $500,000. The Regulation only applies to United States or Canadian corporations having their principal business activities in the United States or Canada. The dollar limitation is based upon the market value or the offering price, whichever is higher. Furthermore, the aggregate offering price must not have exceeded $300,000 during the preceding two years.

Such offerings are usually preceded by an offering circular. No offering circular is required if the offering is less than $50,000.

The $300,000 limitation is reduced to $100,000 if the shareholder rather than the issuer is making the offering.

The last exemption[30] provides that "any security exchanged by the issuer with its existing security holders exclusively where no commission or other remuneration is paid or given directly or indirectly for soliciting such exchange" is exempt. Thus, no registration statement will be required when a stock split occurs, stock for stock being exchanged (a "B-type" tax-free reorganization) or an exchange of stock for debentures (an "E-type" tax-free reorganization).

RULE 144

Rule 144 under the 1933 Securities Act would preclude the necessity for a ruling on individual transactions concerning the public sale of letter stock by specifying the conditions under which the shares may be resold to the public. Generally, resales could be made after a two-year holding period if the shares were fully paid for and owned for the entire period and if the issuer had filed current financial statements with SEC. A one percent selling limitation would be imposed upon the issuer's outstanding shares or of the average of four weeks' trading volume to prevent a substantial effect on the market price of the outstanding shares. Failure to meet this rule would allow such stockholders to sell such stock in limited amounts in private transactions after a five-year holding period.

PRIVATE OFFERING

A "private offering"[31] exempts transactions by an issuer not involving any public offering. The term "public offering" is a work of art which is incapable of definition, but depends upon all the facts and circumstances involved. Among the facts that have been considered determinative are: (1) the need for information which the offerees would obtain from a registration statement; (2) the number of offerees involved and their relationship to the issuer; (3) the size of the offering; (4) the number of units involved; and (5) the manner of the offering. The aforementioned tests have been used in determining whether a registration statement would be required in a public offering or if a private offering has occurred. This area is usually fraught with dangers and is used sparingly.

In case of "private offerings," it has become customary to obtain from each purchaser an investment letter. The investment letter usually provides restrictions on the security whenever the purchaser is purchasing the security for investment purposes with no present intention to redistribute them.

RULE 133

Rule 133 of the General Rules and Regulations of the Securities Act, (it is sometimes referred to as the "no sale" rule), provides an important exemption from the registration statement provisions of the Act. Were it not for this Rule, a tender of stock from the buyer to the seller's stockholders would give rise to a public offering and all its attendant provisions.

Rule 133 applies to any statutory merger or consolidation (an "A-type" tax-free reorganization) or the buyer acquires the assets of another corporation in consideration of the issuance of securities of such other person (the "C-type" of tax-free reorganization). It provides that "no offer" or "sale" of the securities of the surviving corporation shall be deemed to have been made and, accordingly, no registration statement is required pursuant to Section 5 of the Act. The theory underlying this is that securities are not being offered for sale, but rather a corporate act is being conducted pursuant to state law.

Rule 133 comes into play if the statutory provisions of the state of incorporation of the seller require a vote of the majority shareholders which will authorize the proposed transaction and bind all the shareholders of such a corporation, except to the extent that dissenting shareholders may be entitled, under statutory provisions or provisions contained in the certificate of incorporation, to receive the appraised or fair value of their holdings. Thus, this rule permits a buyer to deliver his shares in an acquisition without satisfying the registration statement requirements of the Act. The basis underlying this is that the vote of shareholders as a group authorizes the corporate act and the individual consent required for sales is lacking.

An exception to the "no sale" rule exists when there is a previous binding commitment to redistribute the securities acquired in the reorganization. Rule 133 is inapplicable to such security distribution and adherence to the registration statement provisions of the Act is required.

Another situation in which Rule 133 is inapplicable is where a person is in a control relationship with one of the constituent corporations and proposes to redistribute the securities received in the reorganization. Rule 133 restricts the right of any shareholder of the seller to sell the buyers' stock as such seller is deemed an "affiliate" of the seller. An affiliate[32] is defined as one who is in "control" of the seller attributable to the "provision, direct or indirect, of the power to direct or cause the direction of the management and policies of a person, whether through the ownership of voting securities by contract, or otherwise." Thus, if an affiliate redistributes such securities, a technical violation of the Act occurs.

Such a violation occurs when the selling shareholder sells the stock acquired from the buyer during a six-month period which exceeds the permissible number of shares legally permitted to be sold. Rule 133 permits one percent of the number of outstanding shares of the buyer's stock to be sold within a six-month period if such stock is not listed on any exchange. On the other hand, if the shares are listed, then the maximum number which is permitted to be disposed of is the lesser of: (1) one percent of the number of outstanding shares of the buyer's stock, or (2) the largest reported volume of trading in the buyer's stock during any one week within four calendar weeks preceding the receipt by the broker of the order to sell the buyer's stock.[33]

CIVIL LIABILITIES OF THE ACT

If the Act is violated, then civil liabilities will arise whereby the purchaser may obtain money damages. In addition, the S.E.C. may terminate the effectiveness of a registration statement and may obtain injunctions to prohibit the further distribution of securities.

Section 11 of the Act provides that any material misstatements or omissions in a registration statement impose liability for damages on the suit of a person acquiring the security, upon persons who signed the registration statement, including directors of the issuer, experts (C.P.A.'s or attorneys) who are with their consent named in the registration statement as having prepared certified material contained in or used in connection with the registration statement, and underwriters of the securities.

Section 12 of the Act provides that a person who uses interstate commerce or the mails to offer or sell securities that were not (but should have been) registered, or who offer or sell securities by written material or oral communications that contain an untrue statement of a material fact or omit to state a material fact may be liable to purchasers of the securities unless the seller sustains the burden of proof that he is not and could not in the exercise of reasonable care have known of the omission or untruth. Thus, a successful claimant may rescind the transaction and recover the consideration he paid with interest (less any income received on the security), or, if he is no longer owner of the securities, he may recover damages.

THE SECURITIES EXCHANGE ACT OF 1934

Registration under the 1934 Securities Exchange Act differs materially than under the 1933 Act. The former is concerned with postdistribution trading of securities or listed exchanges or in the over-the-counter market where the issuer has total assets in excess of one million dollars and its stock is held by more than 500 shareholders. The latter is concerned chiefly with the initial distribution of securities.

The 1934 Act comes into force after a registration statement has become effective. Thereafter, it requires periodic reports whether they be annual, semiannual, or current, which are to be filed to keep the information current and be distributed to its shareholders.[34] The Act,[35] including the regulations which implement it, regulates the solicitation of proxies by registered corporations. Section 16 of the Act provides for the recapture of certain short-swing profits made in the securities of their companies by officers, directors, and ten percent shareholders of registered corporations within any six-month period. The purpose of this section is to prevent insiders from profiting at the expense of any public shareholder.

In addition to the above, the Commission has other weapons in its arsenal to prevent fraud, misrepresentation, deceit and other fraudulent practices in connection with the purchase and sale of any security. The weapons are Section 10 and Rule 10b 5 which apply not only to companies and insiders, but to any person engaged in the purchase and sale of any security.

PROCEDURAL REQUIREMENTS OF S.E.C.

The Securities and Exchange Commission requires that Form 8-k be filed if a company acquires a significant amount of assets not in the ordinary course of business or if it disposes of a significant amount of its assets.

An acquisition or disposition includes mergers, consolidations or acquisition of stock and securities which is deemed to be the indirect acquisition or disposition of the assets represented by such securities. The term "significant amount of assets" is defined as the acquisition of more than fifteen percent of the total assets of the transferee corporation. This term is also applied when a transfer of business occurs in which gross revenue exceeds fifteen percent of the total revenue of the transferee corporation.[36] Form 8-k must be filed within ten (10) days after the close of the month during which any of the aforementioned transactions occurred.[37]

PROXY SOLICITATION RULES

The solicitation of proxy is an act requiring the vote of shareholders upon a corporate matter. Regulation 14 of the Exchange act of 1934 requires certain information to be disclosed in the proxy. The proxy statement must contain the following information:

1. Description of the business and properties of each company involved;
2. Explanation of the proposed acquisition;
3. The rights of shareholders including those of dissenting shareholders;
4. The recommendations of the Board of Directors;
5. Detailed financial statements.

TENDER OFFER ACQUISITIONS

One corporate phenomenon occurring during the soaring sixties was the trend to use a tender offer to acquire publicly-owned corporations. Basically, the modus operandis of tender offers is as follows. A corporation makes an offer in the newspapers to stockholders of another corporation at a price substantially in excess of the current market value (usually fifteen percent) with the condition that the offer must be accepted within a certain specific period of time, usually less than a month. The tendering or acquiring corporation only wishes to acquire a specific number of shares necessary to effectuate control. The tendering corporation usually reserves the option to reject when more or less than the specific number of shares is tendered. Another condition is that the offeror corporation can terminate its offer if there should occur conditions which will adversely affect the acquisition.

The key feature of such an acquisition is that no violation of any Securities Act is involved. The reason for this is that the Securities Act only applies to sales and not the purchase of securities. Furthermore, such tender offers were outside the disclosure requirements of the 1934 Exchange Act.

The Williams Bill amended the Securities Exchange Act of 1934 on July 29, 1968, to regulate the acquisition of more than a ten (10) percent stock interest. The amendments to the Act regulate the acquisition of such an interest not only when the tender offer is first made, but also when more than ten percent of any class of stock is acquired.

The offeror must file Schedule 13 D with the Securities Exchange Commission prior to publication of the offer and furnish all soliciting material to the offeree company. The tender offer to security holders must include the following information:

1. Name and address of issuer of such securities.
2. Identity of persons making the tender offer.
3. Time in which security holders have the right to withdraw their securities after deposit.

   In addition, if less than all the outstanding stock is sought, and if a greater number of shares are deposited within ten days after the offer is first published, then the offeror must take the shares on a pro rata basis.

STATE BLUE SKY LAWS

Many states have their own "Blue Sky Laws" regulating the distribution of securities. The Securities Act of 1933 expressly reserves the right of such states to regulate the sale of securities in addition to the requirements of the federal act. However, state regulation takes a variety of forms, ranging from New York, which only requires a one page form called "Further State Notice" requiring practically no information about the issue nor any affirmative action by the state officials, to California, which has the most cumbersome registration requirements of any state.

New York has a "dealer registration" statute which prohibits the offering of securities within the state except by a dealer licensed with the State authorities. In registering securities, the statute[38] requires that an offering prospectus must be filed which makes full and fair disclosure of all material facts with the Department of Law. Such a prospectus becomes effective sixteen days after it has been filed. The prospectus must accompany an offer to sell or a sale to a prospective purchaser.

The statute[39] provides that the following exemptions apply to securities from state registration:

1. Offerings pursuant to which a registration statement has become effective under the Securities Act of 1933.
2. Offerings where a registration statement is not required to be filed other than the exemption provided in Section 3 (a) (11) of the Act.
3. Securities subject to Section 352 (e), 359 (d), (e), (f) and (m) of the general business law. This covers real estate syndication offerings, state bank or trust company, educational organization, and sales by or for the account or of a pledgee or mortgagee selling or offering for sale or delivery to liquidate a bona fide debt.

The Attorney General by statute,[40] exempts the following from filing of state notice:

1. Securities of corporations which have been in existence for a period of not less than ten years or which are attributable to a consolidation, merger, or successor of one or more corporations which have been in existence for a period of not less than ten years, and which have not defaulted in the payment of principal or interest.
2. Securities which are fully listed on any securities exchange located in this state so long as the same shall remain so listed.
3. Securities which are to be sold in a limited offering to not more than forty persons.
4. Securities issued in connection with employees' stock purchase, pension or profit-sharing plans.

STOCK EXCHANGE LISTING PROCEDURE

The Securities Act of 1934[41] requires the registering of securities on a national securities exchange concurrently with their listing upon that exchange. Registration is required pursuant to that statute, but the exchange will usually require that a separate listing application be filed.

Among the advantages of listing of securities on a national securities exchange are the following:

1. It creates a market for the corporation's securities.
2. It provides a readily ascertainable market value for corporate securities.

There are seven major stock exchanges in the United States. The largest is the New York Stock Exchange, which lists securities of approximately 1,500 corporations. Many corporations list their securities on more than one exchange in order to increase their marketability, and at the same time, enhance the public interest in the distribution of such securities.

Each of the various stock exchanges prescribes certain conditions which must be met before they will list a corporation's securities. The items which a securities exchange will consider before they will list a corporation's securities include the following:

1. Number of shares publicly held
2. Market value of such shares
3. Number of shareholders
4. Income of the corporation
5. Net tangible assets of the corporation

The following chart will illustrate the listing requirements of both the New York Stock Exchange and the American Stock Exchange, the second largest exchange in the United States.

Item	New York	American (Amex)
Number of shares publicly held	800,000	300,000
Market value	$14,000,000	$2,000,000
Number of shareholders	2,000	900
Earnings before tax	$2,500,000	300,000
Net tangible assets	$14,000,000	$3,000,000

The listing arrangement with the securities exchange prescribes certain standards which the listed company must adhere to in order to maintain its listing. Basically, it is an agreement between the corporation and the Exchange requiring timely disclosure of financial information and regular publication of current and annual reports which must be submitted to shareholders.

A listing fee is required to be paid to the New York Stock Exchange when the securities are first listed, ranging from one cent to one-eighth of a cent per share times the number of shares being listed. The minimum initial fee cannot be less than $250. In addition to the listing fee, there is a continuing annual fee required to be paid which is $1,000 per annum, or $250 per stock issue, whichever is higher. Similar fees are prescribed in registering bonds and other securities.

The New York Stock Exchange Company Manual[42] requires that when an acquisition is contemplated by a listed corporation, it must obtain shareholder approval when the amount of stock to be issued represents an increase in the number of outstanding shares by twenty percent or more of the outstanding common stock or when the combined value of stock and all other considerations approximates twenty percent or more of the market value of the outstanding common stock. For example, if a listed corporation has 1,000,000 shares outstanding and plans to acquire another corporation by issuing an additional 200,000 shares, then the approval of the shareholders is required prior to listing. The manual further states that shareholder approval is required in the following circumstances:

1. "Options granted to or special remuneration plans for directors, officer, or key employees.
2. Acquisition of a company or property in which directors, officers or substantial security holders have an interest.
3. Actions resulting in a change in the control of the company."

FEDERAL ANTITRUST LAWS

No discussion of mergers and acquisitions would be complete without an understanding of the weapons which the federal government has to prevent corporate take-overs. They fall into four areas: (1) the Clayton Act, (2) the Sherman Act, (3) the Federal Trade Commission Act, and (4) the Robinson-Patman Act. Consequently, no corporate acquisition should be undertaken without reviewing its possibilities for violation of the antitrust laws by legal counsel.

The Sherman Act

The Sherman Act, as enacted in 1890, is the basic source of the antitrust law. Its purpose as stated in Section 1 is as follows:

> Every contract, combination in the form of a trust or otherwise, or conspiracy, in restraint of trade or commerce among the several states, or with foreign nations, is declared to be illegal.

Section 2 provides as follows:

> Every person who shall monopolize or attempt to monopolize, or combine or conspire with any other person or persons, to monopolize any part of the trade or commerce among the several States, or with foreign nations, shall be guilty of a misdemeanor, and, on conviction thereof, shall be punished by fine not exceeding fifty thousand dollars, or by imprisonment not exceeding one year, or by both said punishments, in the discretion of the court.

From the foregoing two sections, it can readily be seen that there must be a combination in restraint of trade which shall attempt to create a monopoly to violate the statute. Thus, the sections have been interpreted by the courts to prohibit price-fixing, boycotts and allocation of territories through concert of action by corporate competitors.

Federal Trade Commission Act

Section 5 of the Federal Trade Commission Act forbids "unfair methods of competition in commerce, and unfair or deceptive acts or practices in commerce."

This act overlaps with the Sherman Act in the sense that its prohibition of unfair methods of competition reaches unreasonable restraints of trade in interstate and foreign commerce. Basically, this act has been interpreted to prohibit false advertisement and unfair methods of competition which might enable a company to become a monopoly in a particular industry.

Robinson-Patman Act

The Robinson-Patman Act of 1936 is an amendment to Section 2 of the Clayton Act. It imposes civil and criminal sanctions.

Subsection (a) declares generally that it is unlawful for any person, in interstate or foreign commerce, to discriminate in price between purchasers of commodities of like grade and quality sold for use, consumption or resale within the United States and its territories:

> Where the effect of such discrimination may be substantially to lessen competition or tend to create a monopoly in any line of commerce, or to injure, destroy, or prevent competition with any person who either grants or knowingly receives the benefit of such discrimination, or with customers of either of them.

Section 2(b) of the Act sets forth defenses to a violation of the statute. In essence, it provides that a charge of price discrimination is not unlawful if made in good faith to meet the price of a competitor.

Subsection (c) forbids the "payment or acceptance of brokerage by a person engaged in interstate or foreign commerce, in connection with the sale or purchase of merchandise, either to the other party to such transaction, or to agent, representative, or other intermediary."

Section 2(d) prohibits payment for services or facilities by a person engaged in interstate or foreign commerce, in connection with the sale of commodities unless such payment or consideration is available on proportionally equal terms to all other customers competing in the distribution of such . . . commodities."

From the foregoing, it can be seen that the purpose of the act is to prohibit price discrimination and practices which have the effect of lessening competition or creating monopoly in any line of commerce.

The Clayton Act

The Clayton Act was passed to complement the Sherman Act by prohibiting specifically enumerated practices. Among the statutory practices prohibited are those dealing with price discrimination, exclusive dealing and mergers. It is this last area which we are concerned with in planning a prospective acquisition, since it is the only statute specifically directed toward acquisitions.

Section 7 of the Clayton Act provides as follows:

> That no corporation engaged in commerce shall acquire, directly or indirectly, the whole or any part of the stock or other share capital and no corporation subject to the jurisdiction of the Federal Trade Commission shall acquire the whole or any part of the assets of another corporation engaged also in commerce, where in any line of commerce in any section of the country, the effect of such acquisition may be substantially to lessen competition, or to create a monopoly.

Thus, the antitrust laws do not prohibit all mergers and acquisitions, but only those which tend to lessen competition or are later found to be illegal. It need not be a definite proven fact that the acquisition actually lessened competition, but a reasonable probability that such an effect could result.

There are three types of corporate acquisition which may violate the Clayton Act. They are referred to as "horizontal," "vertical," or "conglomerate" mergers. A horizontal merger involves the acquisition by one company of all or part of the stock or assets of a competitor which offers the same goods or services in the same market area. For example, if Radio Corporation of America would seek to acquire Motorola Corporation, this horizontal merger would violate the Clayton Act. The effect of this merger would tend to lessen competition since the merged companies would control a greater percentage of the market for their goods after the merger.

A vertical merger is one in which the acquiring corporation merges with a supplier or a customer. For example, if Consolidated Edison, a public utility, would acquire General Electric, their chief supplier of power equipment, a violation of the Act would occur.

A conglomerate merger involves the acquisition by one corporation engaged in an unrelated business to that of the acquiring corporation. A real estate corporation which acquires an insurance company is an example of a conglomerate merger.

Let us now turn to an analysis of Section 7 of the Clayton Act to understand its application.

Acquisition

An acquisition in whole or part of the assets or stock of another corporation is the first prerequisite that must be met before a violation of the statute can be found. Such an acquisition can be made directly or indirectly by the acquiring corporation. An indirect acquisition would occur where a subsidiary acquires the assets or stock of another corporation.

Line of Commerce

The phrase "line of commerce" does not refer to an industry but rather the product and geographical market. The product market consists of products or services to be offered by either the acquiring or acquired company. The geographical market is the area in which the acquiring, the acquired company, or both conduct operations. Thus, it is not dollar figures which determine if the act is violated.[43] The judicial trend has been toward a facts and circumstances test in determining whether a given acquisition violates the Act.

Any Section of the Country

The statutory phrase "section of the country" has been interpreted to mean any area and not necessarily the entire country as a whole. The language of the section requires merely that the government prove the merger has a substantial anti-competitive effect somewhere in the United States—"in *any* section" of the United States.[44]

Tendency to Lessen Competition

One of the requirements is that the acquisition must have the effect of substantially lessening competition, or to tend to create a monopoly. Thus, an acquisition need not be proven to have actually reduced competition, but a reasonable expectation that such a result could occur is all that is necessary to invoke the Act.

DEPARTMENT OF JUSTICE MERGER GUIDELINES

On May 30, 1968, the Department of Justice issued guidelines as to when they will seek to challenge a corporate acquisition as being in violation of Section 7 of the Clayton Act.

Horizontal Merger

In the area of horizontal mergers, the primary test to be applied is the size of the market held by both the acquiring and the acquired companies. In a highly concentrated market—one in which the four largest firms control approximately seventy-five percent of the market—they will challenge the following acquisitions occurring between companies having the following percentage of the market:

Acquiring Firm	Acquired Firm
4%	4% or more
10%	2% or more
15%	1% or more

On the other hand, in a less concentrated market, the following types of acquisitions will be subject to attack:

Acquiring Firm	Acquired Firm
5%	5% or more
10%	4% or more
15%	3% or more
20%	2% or more
25%	1% or more

Vertical Mergers

The Department will challenge any merger between a supplying firm with ten percent or more of the market, and a company which is purchasing at least six percent of that market. Furthermore, such merger should not confer on the purchasing firm a significant source of supply over its competitors.

Conglomerate Merger

A merger occurring between a firm having at least twenty-five percent of the market, or one in which it is one of the two largest firms in a market will be challenged.

ANTITRUST SANCTIONS

The antitrust statutes can be used to prevent violations of the Act in various ways. The Federal Trade Commission can seek legal redress in the courts to dissolve the merger or injunctive remedies to prohibit such a merger. Private parties can maintain a private suit to enjoin or dissolve the merger. In addition, Section 7 of the Clayton Act permits an action for treble damages for injury arising from the merger.

BULK TRANSFER OF ASSETS
(BULK SALES LAW)

To protect creditors from a transfer of assets not in the ordinary course of business, New York has provided that public notice[45] of such transfer must be given. The purpose of the statute is not to secure for creditors the proceeds of the transfer, but to require that they have notice of it before it takes place, so that they can proceed to use their remedies given them by the statute. A bulk transfer[46] is defined as a transfer in bulk, not in the ordinary course of the transferor's business, of a major part of the material merchandise or other inventories of an enterprise, whose principal business is the sale of merchandise from stock, including those who manufacture what they sell.

A transfer to a new business enterprise organized to take over and continue the business, if public notice thereof is given and the new enterprise assumes the debts of the transferor and received only an interest in the business junior to the claims of creditors, is not subject to the bulk sales law[47] Thus, business combinations are not subject to the bulk transfer law if public notice is given, and the liabilities are assumed by the acquiring company.

The public notification requirement of the statute may be complied with by publishing an advertisement once a week for two consecutive weeks in a newspaper of general circulation where the transferor had his principal place of business in New York, which notice should include the name and address of the transferor and transferee and the effective date of the transfer.[48]

One of the most overlooked items in considering a merger or acquisition is the legal obligations flowing from labor laws and contractual obligations from bargaining agreements of the predecessor company.

The Supreme Court has previously ruled[49] that a corporation must notify the collective bargaining representative regarding any proposed merger or decision to sell assets. Thus, such representative will have an opportunity to bargain concerning the operations attributable to the union contract.

The National Labor Regulations Board recently decided four landmark cases relating to corporate acquisitions. The effect of these provisions is that the broad principles of contract law are not applicable to collective bargaining.[50] Furthermore, all the terms of a collective bargaining agreement negotiated between a union and a predecessor company become binding upon a successor or acquiring company. Thus, by operation of law, all the terms of the original labor contract are binding upon a successor company which continues the operations of the predecessor company.

The National Labor Relations Board with court approval have held that where there is a substantial continuity of the employing industry, the successor must assume the former employer's obligation to bargain with a labor organization representing a majority of the employees.[51] This rule is applicable to merger,[52] and a purchase of assets where there is a substantial similarity of operation and continuity of identity of the business enterprise before and after the change in ownership. The entire collective bargaining agreement is binding upon the predecessor employer.

In any acquisition, it is now incumbent upon legal counsel to examine closely the union contracts since the acquiring company is bound by operation of law to employ the predecessor's employees and remedy all unfair law practices committed by the predecessor. One solution to any unascertained legal contingency is to provide for indemnification in the acquisition agreement together with escrow moneys sufficient to guarantee such provisions.

LEGAL CHECKLIST

A. *New York Statutory Law*

   I. *Types*

      a) Merger

      b) Consolidation

      c) Parent-subsidiary merger, ninety-five percent of stock is owned

      d) Merger of domestic and foreign corporation permitted

      e) De facto merger–sale, lease, exchange or another disposition of assets

  II. *Procedure*

      a) Plan of merger or consolidation

      b) Approval of Board of Directors

      c) Approval by shareholders after a meeting–two-thirds vote

      d) Certificate of merger or consolidation signed and verified

      e) Department of State filing along with $30 fee

      f) File Certificate in County Clerk's office

      g) Pay organization tax to State Tax Commission, if required

 III. *Effect of Merger or Consolidation*

      a) Effective thirty days after filing

      b) Surviving or consolidated corporation is transferred to all rights of constituent corporation

      c) Assumes all liabilities by operation of law

      d) No charges required for real property deeds

 IV. *Minority Shareholders' Rights*

      a) No approval of merger or consolidation by shareholder

      b) No approval to sale, lease, exchange of other asset disposition

      c) Written objection filed with corporation

      d) Stock certificates tendered to corporation

      e) Payment of fair value by corporation within sixty days

  V. *Dissolution*

      a) Judicial by Attorney General

      b) Voluntary–two-thirds vote of shareholders

      c) Liquidation–wind-up of corporate affairs

      d) No requirement that it be done in a merger

 VI. *State and Local Tax Problems*

      a) Filing of final franchise tax reports for state and local tax purposes

VII. *Bulk-Sale Law*

      a) Public notification requirement

B. *Federal Securities Laws*

   I. Securities Act of 1933–disclosure statute

      a) Definition of security

      b) Offer or sale

      c) Exempt security

         i. Intrastate offering

        ii. Regulation A

        iii. Private offering

      d) Rule 133 and mergers

      e) Civil liabilities

  II. Securities Exchange Act of 1934–postdistribution regulations

      a) Proxy requirement

      b) Shareholder reports

      c) Form 8-K in connection with mergers, consolidation or asset acquisition

      d) Tender offer requirements

  III. State Blue Sky Laws

      a) New York–Further State Notice

      b) Exemption from filing if federal registration statement in effect

  IV. *Stock Exchange Listing Requirement*

      a) Listing requirement

      b) Effect on acquisitions where additional stock is to be listed.

C. *Federal Antitrust Laws*

  I. Sherman Act–combinations in restraint of trade

  II. Federal Trade Commission Act–unfair methods of competition

  III. Robinson-Patman Act–price fixing

  IV. Clayton Act–horizontal, vertical and conglomerate mergers

---

FOOTNOTES

[1] New York Business Corporation Law (BCL), Sec. 901(a)(1)&(2).

[2] Ibid., Sec. 901(b)(3).

[3] Ibid., Sec. 901(b)(4).

[4] Ibid., Sec. 901(b)(5).

[5] Ibid., Sec. 902.

[6] Ibid., Sec. 903.

[7] Ibid., Sec. 904.

[8] Ibid., Sec. 905.

[9] New York Executive Law, Sec.96(9)(b).

[10] New York Tax Law, Sec. 180.

[11] New York Business Corporation Law (BCL), Sec. 906(b)(1).

[12] New York Business Corporation Law, Sec. 906(b)(2).

[13] Ibid., Sec. 906(b)(3).

[14] Ibid., Sec. 907(a)

[15] Ibid., Sec. 907(b).

[16] Ibid., Sec. 907(d).

[17] Ibid., Sec. 907(f).

[18] Ibid., Sec. 909.

[19] Ibid., Sec. 910.

[20]Ibid., Sec 910(a)(1)(A)&(B).

[21]Ibid., Sec. 910(a)(1)(A)(i)&(ii).

[22]Ibid., Sec. 623.

[23]Ibid., Sec. 623(b)(4).

[24]Ibid., Sec. 1001,1111-b(1).

[25]New York Tax Law, Sec. 293, 203-a

[26]New York BCL, Sec. 1001.

[27]Ibid., Sec. 1002.

[28]Ibid., Sec. 1007.

[29]Securities Act of 1933, Sec. 8.

[30]Ibid., Sec. 2(3).

[31]Ibid., Sec. 3(a)(9).

[32]Ibid., Sec. 4.

[33]Ibid., Rule 405.

[34]Securities Exchange Act of 1934, Sec. 13.

[35]Ibid., Sec. 14.

[36]Instructions to Form 8K.

[37]Securities Exchange Act of 1934, Rule 15d-11.

[38]New York General Business Law, Sec. 359(e).

[39]Ibid Sec. 359(f).

[40]Ibid., Sec. 359(2).

[41]Securities Exchange Act of 1934, Sec. 12(b).

[42]New York Stock Exchange Company Manual, Sec. A-284.

[43]Brown Shoe Co. v. United States, 370 U.S. 294(1962).

[44]U.S. v. Pabst Brewing Co., 384 U.S. at 349(1966).

[45]Uniform Commercial Code, Sec. 6-102.

[46]Ibid., Sec. 6-103.

[47]Ibid., Sec.6-103(7).

[48]Ibid., Sec. 6-103; 9-111.

[49]Fibreboard Paper Products v. N. L. R. B., 379 U.S. 203 (1964).

[50]The William J. Burns International Detective Agency, Inc., 182 N.L.R.B. No. 50; Hackney Iron and Steel Co., 182 N.L.R.B. No. 52; Kota Division of Dura Corporation, 182 N.L.R.B. No. 41; and Travelodge Corporation, 182 N.L.R.B. No. 52 (1970).

[51]John Wiley & Sons v. Livingston, 376 U.S. 543 (1964).

[52]Wackenhut Corp. v. International Union, 332 F (2D) 954, (1964).

Accounting Aspects of Corporate Acquisitions **3**

Some of the most perplexing problems arising with business combinations are attributable to the accounting aspects of such transactions. The accounting problems inherent in such an acquisition can be divided into four areas: (1) valuation factors; (2) purchase versus pooling of interest; (3) goodwill; and (4) earnings per share (EPS).

VALUATION FACTORS

A major factor in effectuating a merger or other type of acquisition is establishing a value for a purchase whether the consideration to be utilized is cash or stock, or an appropriate exchange ratio if payment is to be made in stock or other securities in a stock transaction. In some situations, a "goodwill" or other intangible asset classification can arise on the balance sheet if the consideration exchanged is more than the value of the assets acquired.

Generally speaking, the problem of evaluation of a going business sought to be acquired is a matter of judgment or, as it is sometimes referred to, a "guesstimate." Every acquisition agreement is the result of negotiation and compromise, particularly on price. It is the general consensus that valuation of companies should be based on earnings which are attributable to the assets being acquired. The higher the earnings of a particular company, the higher the consideration to be paid for the company.

The earnings to be used in establishing a criterion for price negotiations are the future earnings and not the past earnings. This is not to say that past earnings of a corporation are immaterial as regards the price to be paid, but they are significant only insofar as establishing a floor from which to "guess" future earnings. It is at this time that any increases or decreases of future earnings should be given effect, such as, an effective market campaign in connection with a new product or a new union contract providing for a substantial pay increase.

One of the most difficult factors in creating such an estimate is that the earnings of a business can vary with the type of business involved, particularly with cyclical industries. Since projected earnings are a matter of judgment and no one can predict the future with a fair amount of certainty, it is desirable that the income statements of the company being acquired for the past five years, and preferably for at least ten years, be utilized.

The next step is to average the earnings for a certain period, which is usually a five-year period. After the average earnings have been determined, a capitalization ratio is applied to the average earnings in order to determine an initial price to be paid for the company. The capitalization ratio ranges from eight to fifteen percent. But the actual price to be paid will vary depending upon certain factors which can never be accounted for and reflected in the financial statements. These factors may relate to the acquired company's position in the industry, favorable location and "know-how."

The capitalization ratio that is applied to the average earnings of the business may vary with the business. Among the sources frequently used in determining a capitalization ratio are industry trade associations, the sale of a business in the same industry, or the Department of Commerce. The rate that is determined usually depends upon the stability of earnings, the rate of earnings-per-share increase per year, and other factors which affect the long-term and short-term outlook for the company.

If the company sought to be acquired is listed on a major securities exchange, or in the over-the-counter market, a readily ascertainable market value can be determined for its stock. The market price of its stock will readily lead to a price-earnings ratio or P/E ratio. For example, a stock earning $2 a share and selling at $30 a share is deemed to have a P/E ratio of fifteen to one. Thus, a capitalization ratio will be approximately fifteen times earnings. The more speculative the business, the higher the capitalization ratio will be, and vice versa.

The capitalization ratio will usually be discounted for factors such as market or industry position, short-term trends and growth of earnings. The converse of the situation also holds true.

Tax Valuation

One area in which valuation plays a great part is in the valuation of stock of closely held corporations for purposes of the federal estate or gift tax. This is attributable to the lack of a market for the stock.

Where sales price and bid and asked prices are unavailable or unreliable, valuation of closely held or other inactive stocks must rest upon "the company's net worth, prospective earning power and dividend paying capacity and other relevant factors."[1] The Service has used one value, the estate another value and the courts a value somewhere in the middle.

There are usually two well-recognized valuation techniques, both of which involve the appraisal of the underlying corporate enterprise as a whole. These may conveniently be referred to the "asset" and "income" approaches to valuation. The asset approach looks toward liquidating value and the income approach looks to value as a continuing business enterprise.

The asset approach places its chief reliance upon the net realizable value of the separate assets of the corporation which can be liquidated. The net realizable value is determined by adjusting book values to bring them into accord with the fair market value of such assets.

The income approach to valuation relies heavily upon the earnings of the corporation as a measure of the value of the business as a going concern. Then, a capitalization ratio is applied to the earnings to arrive at the potential future earnings. Past earnings is the most significant guide to future earnings. Greater weight is given to a long favorable earnings experience than to a brief one, to a stable earnings record than to unstable one, and, lastly to an upward trend of earnings rather than to the converse.

An excess of earnings over a fair return on the net tangible assets usually is regarded as indicative of goodwill.[2] This goodwill is often valued by capitalizing the excess earnings at an appropriate rate.[3] The application of this formula usually depends upon the nature of the business. There are various ways to determine goodwill such as the following: (1) years' purchase of past annual earnings; (2) years' purchase of average past earnings; (3) years' purchase of excess earnings; (4) capitalized earnings, minus net assets; and (5) excess earnings capitalized.

Under the first method, the goodwill will be valued at an amount equal to the total net income of, say, five years. This is illogical since goodwill is not dependent upon total earnings but upon the relation of the earnings to the net assets, and no goodwill exists unless the earnings are in excess of normal income.

The second method is to average earnings for a number of years and to apply a number of years' purchase of the average earnings. For example, if the average earnings is $10,000 and the number of years' purchase is 3, the goodwill will be $30,000.

The third method consists of applying a ratio to the net tangible assets of the business and offsetting it against the net income. The excess for the number of years' purchase will be the goodwill. For example, assume that net income for a three-year period is $10,000, $15,000 and $20,000. The net assets are capitalized at 10 percent of $100,000. The goodwill will be $15,000, determined as follows:

Year	Net Income	10%	Excess
1	10,000	10,000	—
2	25,000	10,000	3,000
3	20,000	10,000	10,000
		Total Payment for Goodwill	15,000

The fourth method will be determined by subtracting the value of the assets from the earnings which are capitalized for a number of years. For example, if the earnings of the business are $25,000, and are capitalized at 20 percent, the goodwill will be computed as follows:

Capitalized Value of Business	$125,000
Value of Assets	100,000
Goodwill	$ 25,000

The last method can be determined by applying a capitalization ratio to the earnings without offsetting the net assets. In the fourth method, as illustrated above, the value of the business will be $125,000.

Market Value of Stock

In acquisitions involving listed companies, the acquiring company will use the average market value of their stock for a number of days, usually ten days, prior to the announcement of the acquisition. This is to avoid the substantial fluctuations which usually arise in the price of a stock involving listed companies. The price paid for the stock of the acquired company will usually be determined by the same method.

Book Value

Another method used in determining the purchase price of a company is the use of book value. This is the least desirable method because the values used for financial reporting purposes have no relationship to the current realizable value. This may be due to the fact that different methods of inventory pricing may be used, such as, the last-in—first out (LIFO) or in the first-in—first-out (FIFO) method, or the accelerated method of depreciation rather than the straight-line method is being used. Both methods are in accordance with generally accepted accounting principles.

The book value method can be used as a starting point in the negotiation stage if adjustments are made to compute a rate of return for resulting earnings. But the results obtainable can be significantly lower than produced by other methods.

Appraisal of Assets

There are numerous companies engaged in the appraisal of assets for the purpose of corporate acquisitions. Such a method can be useful if problems of "goodwill" are existent. But, generally speaking, methods of appraisal are inadequate because the value of assets may bear no relationship to their ability to produce earnings.

The chief advantage of an appraisal is to determine the market or replacement cost of each asset. Another advantage of a professional appraisal is that it can serve as a basis for an allocation of the purchase price for the "basket of assets" acquired in a cash purchase.

Goodwill or Going Concern Value

Another method which is used infrequently of late is the value of a going concern. This method is used by taking the average annual earnings of the company for a specific period of years and reducing it by the rate of return produced on tangible assets. The remainder represents the company's excess earning power which is capitalized usually at ten percent to give the value of goodwill. The value of the goodwill is added to the value of the tangible assets to determine the value of the company as a going concern.

RECENT DEVELOPMENTS

Many acquisitions taking place today use all kinds of considerations to finance the acquisition. Using Ling-Temco-Vought (LTV) as an example, it will be found that LTV includes cash, notes, debentures, warrants and various forms of convertible debentures and preferred stock to finance acquisitions. In its acquisitions of Wilson & Company they used a recapitalization procedure whereby the acquired company was divided into three separate companies having their own common stock. Each company was then liable for a portion of the debt used to acquire the company. This had the effect of the acquired company paying off the consideration used in acquiring them. In other words, the acquired company was acquired for nothing.

The recent tender offer for Amerada Petroleum Corporation stock by Phillips Petroleum Company illustrated the market value exchange ratio to be used in the acquisition.

Hess Oil had proposed a merger with Amerada Petroleum. Before the stockholders of both companies could approve the merger, Phillips announced that their directors had made an offer to the board of Amerada Petroleum to enter into a merger agreement. The terms were as follows:

Each share of Amerada would be exchanged for an amount of Phillips stock having not less than a $135 market value and a maximum value of $144, depending upon the market value of Phillips stock for a given period prior to the merger.

Before the merger becomes effective, determination would be made of the weighted average price per share of Phillips Common Stock sold on the New York Stock Exchange during the twenty-day trading period which precedes the ten-day period before the meeting of Amerada stockholders which would be held to approve the agreement. If such average price is less than $75, then each share of Amerada would be exchanged for $135 of Phillips stock based on the average price. If the average price is $75 up to and including $80, each share of Amerada would be exchanged for 1.8 shares of Phillips. If the average price is more than $80, each share of Amerada would be exchanged for $144 of Phillips stock.

The merger would be subject to the approval by Phillips shareholders and a ruling from the Internal Revenue Service that the exchange of stock would be a tax-free reorganization to the shareholders of Amerada.

While both Phillips and Hess Oil were fighting over the merger of Amerada, the stock jumped from $80 to $115 a share. Although Hess held some 14% of Amerada common stock, they offered $125 a share for 2,000,000 shares if good faith.

The tender offer by Phillips encompassed the following:

It would take the average price of Phillips stock on twenty days of trading. If the average price on the twenty days was less than $75 a share, Amerada shareholders would receive $135 worth of Phillips stock at the average price. If the average price was 72 for Amerada, shareholders would get 1.875 shares of Phillips stock for each share of Amerada. If the average price was 79 a share, they would receive 1.8 shares of Phillips, and if the average price was 84, they would receive 1.714 shares of Phillips.

Subsequently, the Phillips offer was turned down by Amerada stockholders and they merged with Hess Oil into a new company called Amerada Hess Corporation (which was a consolidation). For each share of common, the shareholders received a $3.50 con. pfd. stock convertible into 2.2 shares of Amerada Hess common stock.

FINANCING THE ACQUISITION

One of the first steps that is used for corporate expansion is increasing the authorized number of common shares. Such shares may be offered to the public after the stock has been registered with the Securities and Exchange Commission. This public stock offering will increase the amount of cash in the Company's treasury.

Common Stock Offering

The most frequently used method of corporate acquisition is the issuance of common stock. The chief advantage of this method is that of its being tax free if the statutory requirements of the 1954 Code are met. The seller may not want stock because of a lack of marketability for the stock especially if it is not listed (letter stock). Another reason is a lack of diversification when the holder's investment is in only one corporation.

Cash Offering

If cash is used to finance the acquisition few problems arise. The seller will recognize gain on the difference between his basis for the stock and what he received. Assume that the sole shareholder receives three million dollars for his stock with a value or basis to him of one million dollars. The seller would have a long-term capital gain of two million dollars. On the other hand, if the consideration paid to the shareholder was solely stock, then no gain would be recognized in this tax-free reorganization.

Convertible Debentures and/or Securities

The recent trend in financing corporate expansion is to issue convertible debentures and/or stock. The chief advantage of issuing convertible stock is to reduce the problem of dilution in per share earnings. The dilution problem arises in that the earnings of the two companies might not cover the additional common shares issued. Thus, the dilution aspects of the convertible issues can be minimized.

Accounting Principles Board's Opinion No. 15 required that convertible preferred stock be considered the equivalent of common stock in computing primary earnings per share if it has a cash yield based on market price at issue of less than 66-2/3 percent of the current prime rate (8-1/2%). Fully diluted earnings per share arise when all types of convertible issues are deemed to be converted.

Cash Purchase of Assets

In many situations, the assets are purchased under various conditions in order to effect a combination of two or more concerns. A new company may be formed to purchase the assets of several companies or the assets purchased may be transferred to the new company. The legal procedure to effectuate such transfer of title is by ordinary methods of conveyance, such as a bill of sale. The acquiring company usually assumes some or all of the selling company's liabilities.

The selling company is usually "stripped" of all its assets. It may then liquidate and distribute the cash to its shareholders. The chief advantage of this method is that legal procedures are not as detailed as the formation of a new corporation. Another reason is that it is the only practical method of combining corporations organized under state laws that prohibit mergers.

The chief disadvantage is that a substantial federal tax liability may result to the selling corporation on the gain unless the twelve-month liquidation method has been utilized. Another disadvantage is the rights of dissenting shareholders to avail themselves of the statutory appraisal rights.

In New York, Section 909 of the Business Corporation Law provides that a sale, lease, exchange or other disposition of substantially all the assets of a corporation can be disposed of only if there is a vote by both the Board of Directors and two-thirds vote of the shareholders, if such disposition is not made in the usual or regular course of the business of the corporation.

Installment Purchase of Business

One of the most frequently used methods of acquiring a business of late is through the use of the installment method. This method has the effect of either increasing or decreasing the purchase price paid.

It is chiefly used when an acquiring company cannot determine with any degree of accuracy what the future earnings of the business would be. Accordingly, the acquiring company obligates itself to pay a price based on the acquired company being able to meet reasonable earnings after taxes in the future. The consideration to the acquiring company usually takes the form of a straight stock deal or cash plus stock. Another reason for a corporation to avail themselves of this method is that it is difficult to determine how much the acquired business will contribute to or reduce the earnings.

Generally speaking, the purchase price is being financed through the earnings realized by the acquired business. This method is sometimes referred to as a "boot-strap" acquisition. The mechanics of such a method are as follows. The buyer will pay ten million dollars in stock, five million down and one million each year if certain target amounts are met for earnings after considering income taxes.

For purpose of illustration, assume the following:

Calendar Year	Target Amount
1972	$5,000,000
1973	6,000,000
1974	7,000,000
1975	8,000,000
1976	9,000,000

Thus, it can be readily ascertained that if the earnings after taxes equal or exceed the target amounts, then additional stock is due to the seller. On the other hand, if such amounts are not met, then the purchase price is to be reduced by a certain formula specified in the acquisition agreement. This method also works with cash acquisitions.

The negative provisions of the agreement could provide that the purchase price be reduced by a dollar for every two dollars of earnings never met. Such agreements frequently provide that excess earnings realized over target amounts could be carried forward to offset subsequent years earnings "deficiencies." This provision has the effect of averaging the target amounts and preventing an off year from substantially reducing the total consideration to be paid.

ACCOUNTING FOR CORPORATE ACQUISITIONS

A business combination brings the assets of two or more companies under single ownership and control. In certain instances, there is a change in original ownership, as, for example, when the assets of one company are sold for cash to another. However, some combinations provide for a continuation of the original ownership, as, for example, when assets of one company are transferred to another company in exchange for stock which offers the original ownership a continuing interest in the assets via a stock interest.

Generally speaking, there are two ways of handling a business combination. The first type is a combination that involves the elimination of an important part of the original ownership and is commonly referred to as a pooling of interest.

In a purchase, the net assets of the acquired company are recorded at cost for financial reporting purposes. Such cost is measured by the cash securities or other property consideration given or at the fair market value of the property acquired, whichever is the more evident. Fair market value is the price at which a willing buyer and a willing seller would agree upon, both being under no compulsion to do so.

In a pooling of interest, the financial position of the constituent companies is treated as they were previously affiliated. Thus, no "goodwill" (as hereinafter discussed) is created. The net book assets of the constituent companies are combined and carried forward. Adjustments are made for the stock.

Perplexing problems arise as to which method is to be used. Compounding such state of affairs are the various legal and tax considerations to be met before the acquisition can be made.

The Committee on Accounting Procedure of the American Institute of Certified Public Accountants in Accounting Research Bulletin No. 48 has stated:

> For accounting purposes, the distinction between a purchase and a pooling of interests is to be found in the attendant circumstances rather than in the designation of the transaction according to its legal form (such as a merger, an exchange of shares, a consolidation, or an issuance of stock for assets and businesses), or in the number of corporations which survive or emerge, or in other legal or tax considerations (such as the availability of surplus for dividends).

The purchase method has been used basically in cash deals or those involving consideration other than voting stock. The pooling method has been used chiefly when there has been an exchange of securities or other voting stock which has resulted in one business owning the assets of another business either directly or through one or more subsidiaries.

This has created numerous problems since pooling has been used with greater frequency when the exchange should have been treated for accounting purposes as a purchase.

Some of the criteria used in determining when the purchase method is to be utilized are as follows: (1) ninety to ninety-five percent of the voting stock is acquired and (2) management of one of the constituents is eliminated. The criteria to be used in accounting for the acquisition as a pooling of interest are as follows: (1) continuity of management; (2) continuity of stock interest by former owners; (3) relative size and (4) similar activities. But such criteria have been violated in practice since many accountants hold such guidelines as unworkable.

Pooling has been used for companies which are disproportionate in size and have created instant earnings through the use of "accounting magic" by retroactively reporting the earnings of the acquired company in their consolidated income statement. Another objection is that the assets are misstated because they don't reflect current values.

The criticism ascribed to the purchase method is that excess price paid over the value of the assets is never reflected in the earnings per share. Another objection is that the assets reflected on the books have different values.

ACCOUNTING AS A PURCHASE

In the purchase method, the legal life of the acquired company is deemed at an end. The assets of the acquired company are recorded as cost giving rise to a new basis of accountability. It is here where the appraisal of assets has its greatest significance.

The assets acquired are recorded at the cash price paid. If other consideration is involved, the net assets (assets less liabilities) are recorded at either the fair value of such consideration given or the fair value of the net assets acquired, whichever is more clearly evident.

As it invariably happens, the consideration passing between the parties exceeds the assets being acquired. This excess of cost of consideration given over the net assets acquired is commonly referred to as "goodwill." There is no generally accepted accounting principle that such excess, or "goodwill," be amortized in the income statement. Goodwill is not amortizable for tax purposes. Goodwill is basically an intangible asset. This excess of amount paid over assets acquired has been assigned to tangible and to intangible assets where possible. Accounting procedures have provided for amortization of intangible assets when the life can be ascertained. But good will defies the ascertainment of a life like patents and copyrights which have been amortized over seventeen and twenty-eight years respectively based on their legal life. Since no life can be ascertained, it has been reflected on the financial statements at values such as $1.

On the other hand, favorable negotiations may result in a company being acquired for less than book value. This will give rise to a negative goodwill. The solution in that case is to write down the assets acquired to their current realizable values through the use of competent professional appraisers. This negative goodwill is similarly not subject to amortization. It has been shown as a deferred credit on the liability side of the balance sheet for financial reporting purposes.

Miscellaneous Purchase Problems

In a purchase, the shareholders' equity of the acquired company is eliminated. This includes the retained earnings section too. There is no restatement of prior years' net income since the net income of the acquired business is only from the date of acquisition. Some accountants reflect the retained earnings into the capital surplus account and report only earnings of the acquiring company. This is a questionable practice since state law may provide for a dividend to be paid from such account.

The cash purchase price is allocated among tangible assets and other intangibles. The excess is designated and allocated to goodwill. The new values of the tangible assets are usually higher than the current historical costs recorded by the acquiring company. Thus, lesser earnings arise since increased depreciation and amortization costs exist for the new business than earned by the old business prior to the acquisition. This is illogical since the assets of both the old and new business should be adjusted.

For example, assume the following condensed balance sheet of two companies, X and Y, who are desirous of effectuating a merger. The purchase price of the shares of Y will be $4,000, in terms of X stock at market value. The book value of Y is $2,000, X is paying for $2,000 excess of cost over assets acquired. This excess, or $2,000 will be goodwill. X will issue additional shares to effectuate the merger.

	X	Y
Assets	$8,000	$4,000
Liabilities	$4,000	$2,000
Capital	4,000	2,000
	$8,000	$8,000

BEFORE MERGER	X
Assets	$ 8,000
Investment in Y	4,000
	$12,000
Liabilities	$ 4,000
Capital	8,000
	$12,000

Y's balance sheet remains unchanged. The combination of X and Y into one entity, C, is accomplished by adding Y's net assets of $2,000 to X's net assets. The investment in Y of $4,000 is netted against Y's capital of $2,000 and results in goodwill of $2,000.

AFTER THE MERGER

	X	Y	Elimination	C
Assets	$ 8,000	$4,000		$12,000
Investment in Y	4,000		(2,000)	2,000
	$12,000	$4,000		$14,000
Liabilities	4,000	2,000		6,000
Capital	8,000	2,000	(2,000)	8,000
	$12,000	$4,000		$14,000

POOLING OF INTEREST

As previously stated, a new basis of accountability does not arise. Under the pooling of interest concept of accounting, the business combination is not viewed as the purchase of one company by another, but as a joining or pooling of the companies. The assets and liabilities of the acquired or merged companies are carried forward at historical costs into the surviving entity. The stockholders' equity, after adjustments, and revenue and expenses are combined, giving effect to the concept of a single entity basis for financial reporting.

Goodwill does not arise under this method. Thus, no goodwill is reflected in this type of transaction. Although goodwill is difficult to value and usually attaches to the business as a whole, interesting problems can arise. Thus, one company may use its stock having a value of ten million to acquire another company having a book value of five million. Under the pooling method, this excess five million dollars is not recorded anywhere. Thus, goodwill arises from the exchange transaction itself and not on factors which normally create goodwill, such as, a favorable business location, product lines and competent management.

Adjustments that arise can be classified into three areas, namely, capital stock, capital surplus and retained earnings.

As regards capital stock, adjustments are made to reflect the new combined stated capital of the constituent companies.

Any upward or downward adjustments should be reflected as a charge or credit to the capital surplus account. If the account is inadequate to absorb such amount, then the excess should be reflected in the retained earnings account. On the other hand, if the stated capital after the pooling is less than that of the constituents, the difference is credited to capital surplus.

The income statements of the continuing enterprise should reflect the combined results of operations of the constituent companies for the entire period and not just from the date of pooling. This differs from the purchase method which records result of operations only from the date of acquisition. For comparative reporting purposes, prior income statements should be adjusted to reflect the pooling.

For example, using the same illustration as above before the acquisition, the results would be as follows:

AFTER THE COMBINATION

	X	Y	C
Assets	8,000	4,000	12,000
	8,000	4,000	12,000
Liabilities	4,000	2,000	6,000
Capital	4,000	2,000	6,000
	8,000	4,000	$12,000

The perceptive reader may wonder about the $4,000 of the market value of the X stock issued to pay the Y shareholders. Since X issued with $4,000 of capital and issued $4,000 worth of additional shares suggests a capital of $8,000. But the pooled capital is only $6,000. The excess, or $2,000 (goodwill in a purchase) is ignored.

PART-PURCHASE AND PART-POOLING

A third or hybrid method used to account for a business combination is the part-purchase, part-pooling. This method is utilized when the cash portion of a corporate acquisition is more than ten percent of the total consideration. If the cash and/or debt securities are less than ten percent of the total consideration, the business combination may be accounted for as a pooling of interest.

Under the partial pooling concept, an allocation is required when the cash portion of the consideration exceeds the corresponding percentage of the book value of the net assets of the acquired company; such excess is allocated to tangible assets and goodwill. The carrying values are then brought forward as in pooling of interest accounting, except for this recording of goodwill. Similarly, the percentage of the retained earnings of the acquired company corresponding to the cash portion of the consideration is eliminated and the remainder of the retained earnings is carried forward. As regards the other stockholders' accounts, such as paid-in surplus, part of the consideration attributable to the cash portion is eliminated and the remainder is carried over or pooled.

As regards the income statement, the combined results of operations of the constituent companies for the entire period are included. However, under the partial pooling concept, the percentage of preacquisition net income attributable to the cash portion of the consideration is shown as a minority interest deduction in arriving at reported net income.

EARNINGS PER SHARE (EPS)

Earnings per share were defined as net income less preferred dividends divided by the number of shares of common stock outstanding. Thus, merger-minded companies noted that if other forms of consideration were used such as debentures, there would be no dilution of the EPS ratio. And, in addition, if the acquisition was accounted for as a pooling, there would be an increase in per share earnings since the "excess consideration" paid was never reflected in the income statement. Furthermore, such a method could shelter a poor performance by a subsidiary.

Thus, the pooling concept was used to show instant earnings and thereby, a growth situation. It was also used when a company wanted to add results of operations before and after the combination. On the other hand, the purchase method was used to step up the basis of assets in a taxable transaction or when the combined earnings before the merger are more than they will be immediately after the combination.

For example, assume the following earnings record:

	Earnings	
	Year 1	Year 2
Parent	50	20
Subsidiary	30	80

The parent acquired the subsidiary in a B-type reorganization. Utilizing the pooling method of accounting for the business combination would show the following earnings:

	Year 1	Year 2
Earnings	80	100

Thus, there would be a twenty-five percent increase in earnings rather than a sixty percent drop in the earnings of the parent.

The aforementioned abuses led to changes by the American Institute of Certified Public Accountants. Opinion No. 15 now provides for two types of earnings per share which should be reported for corporations having capital structures which include securities having a potentially dilutive effect on earnings per common share. These two amounts are referred to as primary and fully diluted earnings per share.

Primary earnings per share are the amount of earnings attributable to each share of outstanding common stock, including common stock equivalents. By common stock equivalents are meant securities which, because of the terms under which they were issued, are, in substance, equivalent to common stock. They may take the form of convertible preferred stock, convertible debentures, and options or warrants to purchase common stock.

These common stock equivalents participate in the appreciation or other economic benefits resulting from the underlying earnings and earnings potential of the corporation, if the value of the common stock rises. The only difference is such a security has a specified dividend or interest rate different from that of the common stock. Its value is derived from the value of the common stock to which it is related or into which it is convertible. The actual calculations of primary earnings per share are the amount of earnings attributable to each share of common stock outstanding plus dilutive common stock equivalents. Convertible securities which yield less than two-thirds of the prime interest rate at the time of issuance are classified as common stock equivalents. Convertible securities issued with the same terms as those of an outstanding common stock equivalent are classified as common stock equivalents regardless of their yield.

Fully diluted earnings per share data are based on outstanding common stock, and common stock assumed to be outstanding to reflect the maximum dilutive effect of common stock equivalents and other potentially dilutive securities. Thus, convertible securities, options, warrants, stock purchase contracts and agreements to issue stock in the future are included in such computation. The basic difference between the primary and fully diluted earnings per share amounts is the additional dilution resulting from other potentially dilutive securities outstanding.

The term "dilution" results in either an increase in earnings per share or an increase in net loss per share, based on the assumption that convertible securities have been converted or that options and warrants have been exercised or that other shares have been issued.

Opinion No. 15 now requires the presentation on the income statement of two types of earnings per share data—primary and fully diluted—both reflecting any adjustments for potential dilution. The only time that a single presentation will be used is if a corporation's capital structure is simple, that is, it has no potentially dilutive security outstanding during the accounting period. If there are dilutive securities outstanding, dual presentation will not be required if the computation of both primary and fully diluted EPS results in less than three percent dilutive. Another condition for this single presentation is that each and every potentially dilutive security is anti-dilutive, that is, would increase earnings per share.

As applied to the purchase method of business combination, a weighted number of shares should be used to give effect to additional securities issued only from the date of acquisition. The results of operations of the acquired business are also included in the statement of income only from the acquisition date.

In a pooling of interest accounting for a business combination, the weighted average of outstanding securities of the constituent corporations is adjusted to the equivalent securities of the surviving corporation used in determining the EPS computation for all periods presented.

For purposes of illustration, assume the following:

	Company	
	X	Y
Net Income	$2,000,000	$1,000,000
Common Stock Outstanding	1,000,000	800,000
EPS	2	1.25

X's stock has a market value of $80 per share. X acquires B by issuing $10,000,000 of eight percent convertible debentures, each $1,000 bond convertible into twenty shares of common stock. Also assume further that there is no change in operating results.

If no effect is given to potential dilution, the following would be the results.

Consolidated Net Income	$3,000,000
Interest Expense—Net of taxes	400,000
Net Consolidated Net Income	$2,600,000
Common Stock	1,000,000
EPS	$2.60

If conversion occurs and no change in results occur, the following will be the results.

Consolidated Net Income	$3,000,000	
Interest expense—Net of taxes	400,000	
Net Consolidated Net Income		$2,000,000
Common stock	1,000,000	
Converted	200,000	1,200,000
EPS		$1.67

CURRENT ACCOUNTING TRENDS IN CORPORATE ACQUISITIONS

Due to the widespread abuses inherent in the pooling method, the Accounting Principles Board released an exposure draft of its opinion on Business Combinations on February 23, 1970. The Board concluded that the purchase method and the pooling of interests method are both acceptable in accounting for business combinations, although not as alternative procedures which have existed in the past.

Opinion No. 16 of the Accounting Principles Opinion issued in August 1970[4] provides that both the purchase and pooling methods are acceptable in accounting for business combinations, but *not* as alternatives in accounting for the *same* business combinations. If certain specified conditions are met, then the pooling of interests method must be utilized. All other business combinations should be accounted for as an acquisition of one or more companies by a corporation, that is, by the purchase method. The cost of an acquired company should be determined by the accounting principles relating to the acquisition of an asset. Such cost should be allocated to the individual assets acquired and liabilities assumed based on their fair values. Any excess or cost which cannot be allocated should be recorded as goodwill and amortized over a period not in excess of forty years.

PURCHASE METHOD

The purchase method of accounting for a business combination should employ the historical cost basis of accounting for an asset. An asset acquired by issuing cash or other assets is recorded at cost. Any liability incurred by issuing assets is to be recorded at the present value of the amounts to be paid. If an asset is acquired by issuing stock of the acquiring corporation, then the asset is to be recorded at the fair value of the asset acquired.

In a purchase of a "bundle of assets," cost allocation problems arise. The cost of acquiring a company utilizing the purchase method includes the direct costs of acquisition. Such costs include the cost of registering and transferring securities which are a reduction of the fair value of the securities. All other indirect costs and expenses are deductible in arriving at the net income.

If the deferred stock distribution method is to be used in acquiring a company, all contingent stock should be included in determining the cost of an acquired company at the time when the contingency is resolved and the consideration is issued.

After all identifiable assets acquired have been accorded a value, any excess of cost of the acquired company over the sums of the amounts assigned to identifiable assets acquired less liabilities assumed, should be recorded as goodwill. If the assets acquired exceed the cost of an acquired company, such excess is referred to as negative goodwill, which should not be recorded unless those assets (except long-term investments in marketable securities) are reduced to zero values.

The following guides are to be used in assigning values to the individual assets acquired and liabilities assumed, except goodwill:

1. Marketable securities	current net realizable values
2. Receivables	present value of amounts to be received at current interest rate less allowance for uncollectibility
3. Inventories	
Finished goods	estimated selling price less disposal costs and a reasonable profit
Work in process	estimated selling prices of finished goods less sum of costs to complete, disposal and a reasonable profit
Raw materials	current replacement costs
4. Fixed Assets	current replacement costs
5. Intangible assets	appraisal values
6. Land, nonmarketable securities	appraisal values
7. Accounts and notes payable, long-term debt	present values of amounts to be paid at appropriate current interest rates
Liabilities and accruals	present values of amounts to be paid determined at appropriate current interest rates
Other liabilities	present values of amounts to be paid determined at appropriate current interest rates

The excess of acquired net assets over cost is referred to as goodwill.[5] Such excess should be allocated to reduce proportionately the values assigned to noncurrent assets, except long-term investments in marketable securities. After allocating such excess, the remainder should be allocated systematically (straight-line method) to income over a period estimated to be benefited, but not in excess of forty years. Such method and period of amortization should be disclosed.

The date of acquisition is the date assets are received and other assets are given or securities are issued. Another date for the acquisition could be agreed upon by the parties in a written agreement.

Disclosure by way of footnote should indicate results of operations for the current and prior period as though the companies had combined at the beginning of these periods.

POOLING OF INTEREST METHOD

The pooling of interest method of accounting for a business combination should be employed when voting common stock is issued to acquire voting common stock. All other combinations which use cash should use the purchase method. The part-purchase, part-pooling method is not to be used in accounting for a business combination.

Opinion No. 16 permits combination of unincorporated companies. This type of combination does not have legal significance since it is not a constituent corporation. Neither do the tax-free reorganization provisions of the Code apply to unincorporated companies since its provisions are only applicable to corporations. After the pooling method has been utilized, any subsequent acquisition of stock held by minority shareholders should be accounted for under the purchase method.

The purpose of the pooling of interest method of accounting is to present as a single entity two or more corporations which were previously independent.

There are two conditions for combining companies. They are:

1. Each of the combining companies is autonomous and has not been a subsidiary or division of another corporation within two years before the plan is initiated
2. Each of the combining companies is independent of the other combining companies

A plan of combination is initiated on either the date the stockholders are notified in writing of an exchange offer or the date the terms of an offer are announced publicly. Thus, a plan of combination may be initiated even if shareholder approval is required.

By "independent" is meant that the acquiring company does not own more than ten percent of the total outstanding common stock of the company to be acquired. Stock acquired in exchange for stock after the date on which the plan of combination is announced does count in determining this ten percent requirement. There is no prohibition of combining a wholly-owned subsidiary. However, it is not deemed a business combination for accounting purposes and therefore is not subject to Opinion No. 16.

If stock to be issued for voting common stock is not voting common stock, (for example if debt and preferred stock are to be issued for the voting common stock of the combining company) the purchase method of accounting for the business combination is required rather than the pooling of interest method. The reason for this is that combining requires a sharing of all risks and rights which is lacking when securities are issued having different rights.

There are seven conditions required for combining of interests. They are as follows:

1. The combination is effected in a single transaction or is completed in accordance with a specific plan within one year after the plan is initiated.
2. A corporation offers and issues only common stock with rights identical to those of the majority of its outstanding voting common stock in exchange for substantially all of the voting common stock interest of another company at the date the plan of combination is consummated.
3. None of the combining companies changes the equity interest of the voting common stock in contemplation of effecting the combination either within two years before the plan of combination is initiated or between the dates the combination is initiated and consummated; changes in contemplation of effecting the combination may include distributions to stockholders and additional issuances, exchanges, and retirements of securities.
4. Each of the combining companies reacquires shares of voting common stock only for purposes other than business combinations, and no company re-

acquires more than a normal number of shares between the dates the plan of combination is initiated and consummated.

5. The ratio of the interest of an individual common stockholder to those of other common stockholders in a combining company remains the same as a result of the exchange of stock to effect the combination.

6. The voting rights to which the common stock ownership interests in the resulting combined corporation are entitled are exercisable by the stockholders; the stockholders are neither deprived of nor restricted in exercising those rights for a period.

7. The combination is resolved at the date the plan is consummated and no provisions of the plan relating to the issue of securities or other considerations are pending.

The first condition is self-explanatory. The only exception is governmental authority or litigation which prevents consummating the combination within one year after the plan is initiated.

The second condition would not be violated if a small proportion of cash or other consideration is issued for fractional shares or to dissenting shareholders. But a pro rata distribution of cash is not within the purview of this rule since cash as the consideration requires the purchase method. Thus, a de minimis rule for cash can be used in a pooling. The term "substantially all the voting stock" means at least ninety percent of the voting stock of the acquired. In a B-type exchange, that is stock for stock, the statutory requirement is that at least eighty percent of the voting stock must be acquired. Thus, the accounting requirement is more than the tax requirement.

The third condition states that any distribution to shareholders which are not greater than normal dividends are not changes for this condition.

The fourth condition provides that any shares reacquired (treasury stock) for purposes of stock options and compensation plans do not violate the pooling method.

The fifth condition indicates that the stock received by the shareholder who exchanges his stock does not violate his interest which he held before the stock exchange.

The sixth condition would be violated if stock is transferred to a voting trust.

The seventh and last condition is that no stock will be issued at a subsequent date. This refers to contingent or a delayed distribution of stock to satisfy an earnings at market price contingency. The purchase method is to be used for combinations providing for contingent stock distributions.

Utilizing the pooling method does not require the dissolution of a combining company. The pooling method can be utilized if the combining company becomes a subsidiary after the combination is consummated.

The recorded assets and liabilities of the separate companies become the recorded assets and liabilities of the combined corporation.

If there is to be a change in the accounting method to conform the combining companies, such change should be applied retroactively. Similarly, the financial statements should be restated for prior periods.

The stockholders' equities of the separate companies should be combined as part of the pooling of interest method of accounting. This includes the capital stock, capital contributed in excess of par, and retained earnings. If the outstanding stock on a combined basis exceeds the total amount of capital stock of the separate combining companies, then the excess should be deducted first from the combined other contributed capital. If any excess is left after the contributed capital excess is exhausted, it should be applied to the combined retained earnings.

The operations of the combined companies should be reported as if the combination had occurred as of the first day of the accounting period to the end of such period. Any intercompany transactions between the two companies prior to the combination should be eliminated. A footnote should show the revenue extraordinary items and net income of the two companies before the combination is consummated. Similarly, balance sheets and other financial information of the separate companies should be presented as though the companies had been combined at that date.

Any expenses related to the combination should be deducted in determining the net income of the resulting combined corporation for the period in which the expenses are incurred.

The business combination should be recorded as of the date the combination is consummated. The pooling of interest method should be disclosed in its financial statements.

ILLUSTRATION

Assume that a corporation is desirous of going public. It is desirous of "pumping up" its financial statements. An individual owns three properties with a cost basis of $500,000 and a fair market value of $1,000,000. The corporation wishes to acquire such properties.

The question arises: how should such assets be acquired and reflected on the books of the acquiring corporation with a basis of $1,000,000?

One proposal was to incorporate under I.R.C. Section 351. It provides that no gain or loss will be recognized if one or more persons transfer property to a newly formed corporation and immediately after the exchange such transferor is in control of the corporation. Thus, from a tax point of view, the incorporation presents no tax problem. The basis of the stock to the shareholder would be a cost basis. The cost basis of the shareholder would be the same in the hands of the corporation (Section 362).

Subsequently, it would have a tax-free reorganization under either Section 368(a)(1)(A) or Section 368(a)(1)(B). The A-type is a merger and presents no problem. The basis to the acquired corporation for the assets would be the same as in the hands of the corporation which would be the transferor's basis. Thus, the acquiring corporation would have a basis for the assets of $4,500,000. If the B-type reorganization is used, the newly formed corporation would become a subsidiary of the acquiring. The acquiring would issue voting stock in return for the stock of New. The shareholder of the New would have a basis of $500,000 for the stock. Thus, the only problem is the basis of the assets in the hands of the subsidiary is still $500,000. Since there would no longer be any need to keep the New in existence, it would probably be liquidated. This would change the B-type of tax-free reorganization into a C-type stock for assets and the statutory requirements must be met.

From an accounting point of view, neither the A nor B-type would give the assets acquired a stepped-up basis.

As an alternative, the acquiring could acquire ninety percent of the stock of the New corporation since the realty may have liabilities which they would not want to subject themselves to. Thus, the acquiring could acquire control ninety percent of New in a taxable transaction. Subsequently, the acquiring could merge the New into them tax free, pursuant to Section 332. But this would give a substituted basis. Section 334(b)(3) provides that the term "purchase" means a taxable transaction rather than one having a basis determined in whole or in part in the hands of the person from whom acquired. Thus, a substituted basis transaction (tax-free reorganization) would not work to step up the basis of the parcels to $100,000.

The merger of a parent and subsidiary is deemed to be a liquidation rather than a tax-free reorganization. Thus, Section 332 would apply. If the requirements of Section 334(b)(2) apply, then the basis of the stock would be adjusted to equal the basis of the assets. Section 334(b)(2) provides that a liquidation occurring within two years after the date of purchase of control within a twelve-month period would result in a step-up in the basis of the assets which is usually the purchase price of the stock. Thus, Section 334(b)(2) would give us the step-up of $1,000,000.

From an accounting point of view, the pooling of interest method results in a carryover of assets. On the other hand, a purchase would result in the price paid (fair market value of stock) being attributable to the assets. An asset acquired by issuing shares of stock of the acquiring corporation is recorded at the fair value of the asset, that is, shares of stock issued are recorded at the fair value of the consideration received for the stock. Furthermore, no goodwill would arise since stock is only issued for the value of the assets. No excess of consideration paid over the assets acquired would arise (goodwill).

The taxable transaction could result in cash plus stock being issued, thereby avoiding the transaction as being deemed a tax-free "B" reorganization. Instead of cash being issued, notes could be used with stock.

As regards the shareholder of the New, the stock issued and the notes would be compared with the $1,000,000 basis to determine gain or loss on the taxable transaction. The stock received would be letter stock. Thus, gain would be recognized on the transaction because of the case which would entitle the stockholder of the New to pay the tax. Thus, this transaction will be deemed taxable and upon liquidation, a step-up in basis would occur.

Section 1031 provides that no gain or loss is recognized if property is exchanged solely for like kind qualifying property. Property qualifying for nonrecognition includes property held for productive use in trade or business or for investment and excludes stock in trade, stocks, bonds or notes. Thus, an exchange by the corporation of cash and stock for the three parcels would also result in a step-up in the basis since gain would be recognized on the exchange. Furthermore, Section 1031 would be avoided, and gain would be recognized on the difference between the cash and value of the stock and the basis of the three parcels. The gain would be taxed as a long-term capital gain unless the individual was a real estate dealer.

FOOTNOTES

[1] Revenue Ruling 59-60; 1959-1 C.B. 237.

[2] Ibid.

[3] A.R.M. 34, 2 C.B. 31 (1920).

[4] Accounting Principles Opinion No. 16.

[5] Accounting Principles Opinion No. 17.

Statutory Merger
or Consolidation

4

Basically, a corporate reorganization is undertaken to simplify existing corporate structures. It has a different connotation in tax terminology than readjustment of corporate structure of a corporation in financial distress. In tax parlance, it usually refers to a corporation which acquires the stock or assets or another corporation, readjusts its capital structure by issuing equity instruments for debt obligations or changes its name or place of incorporation. The term "reorganization" is to be strictly limited to the specific transactions specified in Section 368(a) of the 1954 Internal Revenue Code. The term does not embrace the mere purchase by one corporation of the properties of another corporation, for it imports continuity of interest on the part of the transferor or its shareholders in the properties transferred. If the properties are transferred for cash and deferred payment obligations of the transferee are evidenced by short-term notes, the transaction is a sale and not an exchange in which no gain or loss is recognized.

A reorganization, generally speaking, occurs between corporations and their shareholders. Ordinarily, if the statutory conditions are complied with, there will be no gain or loss recognized to the shareholders upon the exchange of equity instruments, that is, only stock or securities. Similarly, both corporations, parties to a reorganization, will be able to effectuate the exchange of stock or securities tax-free. The concept of tax-free is a misnomer. Rather, it is called tax deferral, for until the stock or securities are disposed of in a taxable transaction, it is an exchange.

The tax-free reorganization provisions of the Internal Revenue Code are probably among the most difficult in the entire Code. There is a complex body of case law in addition to the regulations and revenue rulings which one must be cognizant of in planning such a reorganization. Lurking in the background are obscure little provisions which may turn a tax-free transaction into a taxable one. The Courts have enunciated judicial doctrines, such as, "business purpose," and "continuity of stock interest" which must be adhered to in consummating such a transaction. Obviously, the area is replete with traps for the unwary.

STATUTORY MERGERS OR CONSOLIDATIONS

Section 368(a)(1)(A) provides that the term "reorganization" means a statutory merger or consolidation. This is all the statute specifies is necessary to accomplish the A-type of reorganization. The Regulations[1] provide that a "statutory merger or consolidation" refers to a merger or consolidation effected pursuant to the corporation laws of the United States or a State or Territory or the District of Columbia.

Accordingly, the only requirement necessary to effectuate the A-type of reorganization is that it must be accomplished under state law. Thus, if state law does not permit a merger or consolidation, then the A-type cannot be effectuated in that particular state.

Since state law is necessary to accomplish the A-type of reorganization, a merger of two foreign corporations under foreign law could not be accomplished within the purview of Section 368. However, a merger of a domestic and foreign corporation could be accomplished tax-free if state law permits such a merger.

Some of the advantages of the A-type of reorganization are as follows: (1) it is the simplest method to use because the only requirement is that it be accomplished under state law, (2) the use of nonvoting stock and other property can be used without disqualifying the merger in its entirety: (3) minority stockholders cannot prevent the consummation of a merger. Some of the disadvantages of the A-type of reorganization are as follows: (1) practical problems of complying with state law may exist; (2) the vote of the shareholders of both corporations is required; (3) all liabilities, existing or unknown, are automatically assumed by the surviving corporation by operation of law.

MECHANICS

A merger is a transaction which occurs between two corporations, whereby one corporation is amalgamated into another corporation with the survival of one of the companies. For example, X Corporation and Y Corporation are two separate conditions. Pursuant to state law, X Corporation is merged into Y Corporation. Y Corporation becomes the surviving corporation and X Corporation ceases to exist by operation of the law. The shareholders of X Corporation exchange their stock for stock in Y. The transaction constitutes an "A" reorganization.

A consolidation is a transaction which occurs between two corporations whereby they are combined into a newly formed third corporation with the two corporations ceasing to exist as a matter of law. For example, Corporations A and B are separate corporations. Pursuant to state law, Corporations A and B are consolidated into a newly formed corporation, C Corporation. The shareholders of Corporation A and Corporation B exchange their stock for stock of C Corporation. The transaction is an "A" reorganization.

The A-type is the most flexible of all the reorganization provisions of the Code. It can occur in other types of situations. For example, Corporation P, the parent, can merge downstairs into Corporation S, its subsidiary, with Corporation S as the surviving corporation. This is often referred to as a downstream merger. On the other hand, Corporation S, the subsidiary, can merge upstairs into Corporation P, the parent, with Corporation P as the surviving corporation. This is referred to as an upstream merger.

Prior to October 22, 1968, a subsidiary could not use the stock of its parent to effectuate an A-type of reorganization. Such was not the case as regards the B-type, stock for stock exchange, or the C-type, stock for assets. In both the B and C type of exchanges, the subsidiary could use the stock of its parent in exchange for either stock or assets without disqualifying the exchange from being tax-free. On October 22, 1968,[2] the statute was amended to permit a subsidiary to use the stock of its parent in a statutory merger. The amendment provides that the acquisition by one corporation, in exchange for stock of a corporation (the controlling corporation) which is in control of the acquiring corporation, of substantially all of the properties of another corporation which in the transaction is merged into the acquiring corporation shall not disqualify a transaction as a merger if such transaction would have qualified if the merger had been into the controlling corporation, and no stock of the acquiring corporation is used in the transaction. In other words, the merger of a corporation with a subsidiary corporation would qualify if the merger was undertaken by its parent, and, no stock of the acquiring corporation, the subsidiary, is used. Thus, the amendment now puts both the A, B and C types of reorganizations on an equal footing when the subsidiary is the acquiring corporation.

In a merger, as previously stated, only one corporation survives. The acquired company usually transfers all of its assets to the acquiring corporation in return for the stock of the surviving corporation. The acquired corporation is legally dissolved as a matter of law. The stock of the acquiring corporation is distributed to the shareholders of the acquired corporation who now become the shareholders of the acquiring corporation.

In a consolidation, a new corporation is formed which distributes its stock to the acquired companies in exchange for their assets. The acquired companies then distribute the stock to its shareholders who become shareholders of the "new" corporation.

CONSIDERATION UTILIZED IN A-TYPE EXCHANGES

The A-type is the most flexible of all the reorganization exchanges as far as the consideration involved. The only requirement is that voting stock be used in the exchange. The B-type of exchange has been strictly construed to mean that only voting stock must be exchanged. Thus, cash, nonvoting stock and other property including cash can be utilized in the exchange without disqualifying the transaction in its entirety. If such other forms of consideration are exchanged, the corporations involved will still have a tax-free reorganization, but the shareholders will recognize a gain or loss on the distribution of such other property. On the other hand, such a distribution will disqualify a stock-for-stock (B-type) and stock-for-assets exchange in its entirety.

Another advantage of the A-type is that the assets received from the acquired company can be transferred to a subsidiary without disqualifying the reorganization exchange. Furthermore, such subsidiary could be newly formed. It is also possible that the acquiring corporation could transfer only a portion of the assets acquired from the acquiring corporation to a new subsidiary. If some of the assets of the acquired corporation are disposed of, such disposal will not negate the A-type.

Section 351 of the Internal Revenue Code provides that there can be a tax-free incorporation if certain statutory conditions are met. It provides that "no gain or loss is recognized when one or more persons transfer property to a corporation solely in exchange for its stock or securities, if immediately after the exchange they control the corporation."[3] Services are not considered property. Gain or loss may be recognized if stock or securities are issued for property of relatively small value as compared to the value of the stock and securities already owned by the transferor.[4] There can be no tax-free exchange involving a foreign corporation without a "toll-charge" being prepaid. By this is meant that an advance ruling from the Internal Revenue Serivce that the transfer was not for tax avoidance purposes[5] is required before such exchange can be consummated.

The term "control" means the ownership of at least eighty percent of the voting stock, and at least eighty percent of all other classes of stock of the corporation.[6] For example, M owns 3,000 of 4,000 shares of the voting common stock of the A Corporation and 8,000 of its 10,000 nonvoting preferred stock. M transfers property to A Corporation in exchange for 1,000 additional common shares. There is no gain recognized to M because M is in control of the corporation immediately after the exchange. M owned stock with at least eighty percent of the total voting power (4,000 out of 5,000 common) and at least eighty percent of all other classes of stock, or more specifically 8,000 out of 10,000 preferred.

When more than one person transfers property, the stock and securities each received need not be in the same proportion as his interest in the property. But a gift will result or compensation being deemed paid to those who receive more than they transferred. Both the transferor and corporation must file information about the transfer with their income tax returns for the year the exchange is made. Permanent records must be kept from which gain or loss on the later sale of the stock or securities and other property received in exchange can be determined.[7]

The substance of the transfer of the assets of the acquired company to a newly formed subsidiary has the effect of casting the reorganization exchange as a B-type, since the B-type results in a parent-subsidiary relationship after the transfer.

EFFECT OF LIABILITIES
IN A REORGANIZATION EXCHANGE

Practically every merger involves the acquisition of assets of an acquired corporation which will be assumed subject to its liabilities. Sometimes the acquiring corporation will take part of the liabilities of an acquired corporation. In the area of corporate mergers, liabilities usually present few problems. The term "liabilities" includes those presently recorded on the books and all those subsequently arising, such as, a contingent liability for notes guaranteed or any future federal tax liability arising from a tax examination.

Generally speaking, if a corporation acquires property subject to a liability, or assumes a liability, the transaction can still be effectuated tax free. It is only where the purpose of such assumption is to avoid taxes, or if the transaction does not have a real business purpose, that the transaction is not tax free. It is only where the purpose of such assumption is to avoid taxes, or if the transaction does not have a real business purpose, that the transaction is not tax free. In that case, the total liability assumed or acquired is considered as money received by the transferor[8] and taxable as "boot" (hereinafter to be discussed).

BUSINESS PURPOSE DOCTRINE

Irrespective of strict adherence to the literal requirements of the reorganization provisions, this still may not be enough in order for the reorganization exchange to be afforded tax-free status. The Regulations[9] provide that there must be a business purpose for every reorganization. In fact, the Internal Revenue Service will not rule upon a prospective reorganization unless there is a business purpose specified in it.

This doctrine is an outgrowth of the most cited case[10] in tax literature, the Gregory case.

In the Gregory case, Mrs. Gregory was the sole stockholder of United Mortgage Corporation which owned 100 percent of the shares of stock in the Monitor Corporation. She devised a plan to avoid the tax that would be payable if the Monitor shares were first distributed to her as a dividend. The plan involved the formation of a corporation, Averill, which transferred its stock to United Mortgage in return for Monitor's stock. Averill distributed stock to Mrs. Gregory as a liquidating dividend, and three days later Averill was dissolved. She sold the stock and paid a capital gains tax.

The Supreme Court held for the Commissioner on the theory that, although the form met the literal requirements of the statute, the substance was tax avoidance, and this was improper.

Thus, a transaction, even though it literally complies with the requirements of the Code so as to qualify as a tax-free reorganization, will not be considered as such if there is no business purpose. Accordingly, there is a general requirement that a reorganization, to be tax free, must have a bona fide corporate business purpose. The reorganization cannot be used merely as a tax avoidance device.

It should be noted that a substantial, valid business purpose, the tax-free nature of a reorganization, will not be disregarded merely because there is also incidently a tax-saving motive.

The Regulations[11] have incorporated this doctrine as follows:

> The purpose of the reorganization provisions of the Code is to except from the general rule certain specifically described exchanges incident to such readjustment of corporate structures made in one of the particular ways specified in the Code, as are required by business exigencies and which effect only a readjustment of continuing interest in property under modified corporate forms.

They further state:

> A scheme, which involves an abrupt departure from normal reorganization procedure in connection with a transaction on which the imposition of tax is imminent, such as a mere device that puts on the form of a corporation reorganization as a disguise for concealing its real character, and the object and accomplishment of which is the consummation of a preconceived plan having no business or corporate purposes, is not a plan of reorganization.

From the above it is apparent that every tax reorganization must be founded upon a business basis.

Since corporation reorganizations involve many tax dollars, it is advisable that a favorable tax ruling be secured in advance as to how the Internal Revenue Service will treat the transaction from a tax standpoint. As previously stated, the ruling should include the business purpose for the transaction. Such business purpose must not be subordinate to the resultant tax savings that can occur in the exchange. In other words, the business purpose should be the reason why the transaction is being effectuated, rather than any tax benefits which may inure from the transaction.

THE CONTINUITY OF INTEREST REQUIREMENT

Another doctrine which must be met before a reorganization exchange can be considered tax free is that there must be a continuity of interest. The Regulations[12] provide:

> The application of the term "reorganization" is to be strictly limited to the specific transaction set forth in Section 368(a). The term does not embrace the mere purchase by one corporation of the properties of another corporation, for it imports a continuity of interest on the part of the transferor or its shareholders in the property transferred. If the properties are transferred for cash and deferred payment obligations of the transferee evidenced by short-term notes, the transaction is a sale and not an exchange in which gain or loss is not recognized.

This can be illustrated as follows: The A Corporation and B Corporation, separate and unrelated corporations, pursuant to state law, effectuate a statutory merger with B as the surviving corporation. As part of the exchange, the shareholders of A Corporation receive cash and short-term notes. Although the literal definition of the statute was met, the transaction is not deemed a tax-free reorganization. The continuity of interest requirement was not met since the shareholders of A Corporation do not have a proprietary interest in B Corporation, the surviving corporation.

By proprietary interest is meant that the shareholders of A Corporation have an equity or stock interest in B Corporation. Thus, the continuity of interest requirement is twofold. The first is that the shareholders of the acquired corporation must have an equity or stock interest in the acquiring corporation. The second is that there must be a continuity of business enterprise. This interest exists when a substantial part of the consideration received constitutes an equity interest in the surviving corporation.

The courts have held that the interest must be in the nature of a proprietary or stock interest as distinguished from an interest held by a creditor. Thus, the use of notes[13] and bonds[14] do not satisfy this requirement.

A question arises as to whether all the shareholders of an acquired corporation must receive stock upon the exchange. The Service has stated[15] that the test is not applied to each shareholder, but, rather is complied with if one or more of the acquired corporation's shareholders have such a proprietary interest in the continuing or acquiring corporation. Furthermore, the Service has dropped the percentage-in-number test in favor of a more practical one. It now[16] requires that as long as one or more shareholders of the transferor or acquired corporation have a continuing interest in the transferee's stock equal in value to fifty percent of all the transferor's outstanding stock at the date of the reorganization, the test is met. On the other hand, if the fifty percent test is not met, the Service will hold that a taxable liquidation has occurred when the shareholders of the acquired corporation receive less than twenty percent of the value of the stock of the acquiring corporation.[17]

The equity securities which satisfy the continuity of interest rule must represent a substantial and material portion of the overall consideration paid by the transferee.[18]

The shareholders of the acquired corporation who receive cash for their shares rather than stock will have a capital gain under Section 302(b)(3) dealing with a complete termination of a shareholder's interest since every merger in effect involves a stock redemption.

Regulations 1.368-1(b),(c) state that the "continuity of business enterprise" must be met. Its requirement is that a reorganization transaction must be an ordinary and necessary incident of the conduct of the enterprise and must provide for a continuation of the enterprise under a modified corporate form.

STEP TRANSACTION DOCTRINE

A problem usually arises when the reorganization exchange is simply one step in a scheme which has no substance other than tax avoidance. The Treasury has invoked the "step transaction doctrine" to prevent the fragmentation of an exchange into a series of transactions which have both taxable and nontaxable factors. For example, an individual acquired all the stock of A Corporation. The same individual subsequently acquired a controlling interest in both B and C Corporations. A Corporation then acquired all of the shares of B and C in return for A stock. B and C Corporations were then liquidated. The Commissioner looked at all the steps of the transaction, including the liquidation, to produce a tax-free reorganization. The taxpayer argued for a taxable purchase of assets. The Court[19] in this factual situation held for the taxpayer.

Thus, it can be seen that a step transaction rationale may be used to integrate a series of independently taxable transactions into a nontaxable whole to form a reorganization.[20] Alternatively, integration of transactions completed before and after a step, which itself would be a reorganization, may result in taxable treatment.[21] The important point is that the steps taken to effectuate a transaction will not be construed in a vacuum but will be aggregated.

The Supreme Court has held[22] that the doctrine will be applied whenever a first step has occurred, and there is a binding commitment to take the later steps. Basically, this means that a transaction will be aggregated into a single plan to see if the statutory provisions have been met. For example, a tax-free merger was held to be a redemption of minority situations.[23]

In a recent case,[24] the Court refused to apply the step transaction and held that a tax-free merger had occurred. The taxpayer, King Enterprises, was a holding company which possessed a substantial interest in another company, Tenco. The directors ratified an agreement which obligated the taxpayer and Tenco to transfer their Tenco shares to Minute Maid in exchange for cash, promissory notes and stock of Minute Maid. Tenco shareholders received over fifty percent of the total consideration, including over fifteen percent of the total of Minute Maid's shares. Minute Maid, which was the the sole shareholder of Tenco, voted to merge Tenco and other subsidiaries into Minute Maid. The Commissioner in a private ruling held that the adjusted basis of Tenco stock would be determined pursuant to Section 334(b)(2) of the 1954 Code. The Commissioner held that a valid merger had occurred but refused to integrate the earlier exchange and hold it to be nontaxable. The taxpayer argued that the gain received by King should not be recognized since the transaction was consummated pursuant to a plan of reorganization. The Court held for the taxpayer and held that the binding commitment test is relevant only as to the issue of control and not continuity. Thus, a fine distinction is being made.

REQUIREMENTS OF A REORGANIZATION EXCHANGE

One of the requirements of a reorganization exchange is that there must be a plan of reorganization adopted in advance by each of the constituent corporations involved, that is, parties to a reorganization.

The term "plan of reorganization" is not defined in either the Code or the

Regulations. The only requirement is that such an exchange must be consummated pursuant to this "plan." There is no requirement that such a plan even be in writing. The Regulations[25] provide that a certified copy of the plan shall be filed by each corporation that is a party to a reorganization. A plan of reorganization is an enumeration of all the steps necessary to consummate a reorganization exchange.

PARTY TO A REORGANIZATION

Section 368(b) provides that "a party to a reorganization" includes: (1) a corporation resulting from a reorganization and (2) both corporations, in the case of a reorganization resulting from the acquisition by one corporation of stock or properties of another.[26]

The corporation controlling the acquiring corporation is also a party to a reorganization when their stock is used in the exchange for stock (B-type) or for substantially all the assets (C-type). Similarly, a corporation remains a party to the reorganization although it transfers all or part of the stock or assets acquired to a controlled subsidiary. For example, all three corporations are parties to a reorganization if Corporation A transfers substantially all its assets to Corporation B in exchange for all or part of the voting stock of Corporation X, which is in control of Corporation B. On the other hand, both Corporation A and B, but not Corporation C, are parties to the reorganization if Corporation A acquires stock of Corporation B from Corporation C in exchange solely for a part of the voting stock of Corporation A, if (1) the stock of Corporation B does not constitute substantially all of the assets of Corporation C, (2) Corporation C is not in control of Corporation A immediately after the acquisition, and (3) Corporation A is in control of Corporation B immediately after the exchange. Thus, both corporations in a statutory merger and all three corporations in a statutory consolidation are parties to the reorganization.

All of the steps of the plan must be germane to the continuance of the business of a corporation—a party to the reorganization.[27] All of the consideration exchanged between the parties to the reorganization must be pursuant to the plan of reorganization.

RECORD REQUIREMENTS OF A REORGANIZATION

The regulations[28] require certain information to be included and filed with the tax returns as follows:

(a) The plan of reorganization must be adopted by each of the corporations parties thereto. An adoption must be shown by the acts of its responsible corporate officers. Each corporation shall file as a part of its return for its taxable year within which the reorganization occurred a complete statement of all the facts pertinent to the reorganization including a certified copy of the plan of reorganization. The cost of all property, including all stock or securities transferred, incident to the plan must be stated. A statement must be similarly attached as to the amount of stock or other securities and other property or money received from the exchange including all distributions. The amount and nature of all liabilities, including property subject to a liability, should be included in such statement.

(b) Every taxpayer, other than a corporate party to the reorganization, who receives stock or securities and other property or money should disclose such in his income tax return for the taxable year in which the exchange occurred. The statement should include the cost or other basis of the stock exchanged and the money or other property received including the fair market value of the stock or securities received.

(c) Permanent records in substantial form shall be kept by every taxpayer who participates in a tax-free exchange in connection with the reorganization.

CORPORATE PARTIES TO A REORGANIZATION

One must turn to other statutory provisions of the Code to determine the tax consequences to the shareholders and corporate parties to a reorganization. Section 354 provides generally that no gain or loss shall be recognized if stock or securities in a corporation, a party to a reorganization, are exchanged solely for stock or securities in a corporation or in another corporation, a party to a reorganization, if undertaken pursuant to a party to the reorganization. Section 361 provides generally that no gain or loss shall be recognized if a corporation, a party to a reorganization, exchanges property solely for stock or securities in another corporation, a party to the reorganization, if it is pursuant to a plan of reorganization.

For example, if a statutory merger should occur between Corporation A and B, and the stock of Corporation B is distributed to the shareholders of Corporation A in exchange for their stock, such exchange is tax free. Similarly, if Corporation B received all of the assets of Corporation A pursuant to the plan of reorganization, such property can be received without any tax consequences to the surviving corporation.

"Boot" Problems

As previously stated, the specification of the reorganization provisions of the law are precise. Both the terms of the specifications and their underlying assumptions and purposes must be satisfied in order to entitle the taxpayer to the benefits of the tax-free provisions.

The A-type is the most flexible of all the reorganization provisions. Basically, this means that if other property, such as, cash, notes, etc., are used in the exchange, such an exchange will not affect the tax-free status of the merger type. But the shareholders will realize some adverse tax consequences.

The corporation receiving such property (referred to as boot) will have the effect of making the transaction partially taxable. The taxation of such boot may be either as ordinary income or capital gains depending upon the circumstances involved.

Basis Problems for Assets or Stock

Section 362(b) provides that "if property was acquired by a corporation in connection with a reorganization then the basis shall be the same as it would be in the hands of the transferor, increased in the amount of gain recognized to the transferor on such transfer." Thus, the basis to the transferee is a carryover basis, that is, the basis for the property in the hands of the acquiring corporation is the same as in the hands of the acquired corporation.

Recapture of Depreciation

Section 1245 provides that all depreciation occurring after December 31, 1961 is recaptured and reduces the capital gains recognized on the sale of property. It is applicable to tangible personal property. Section 1250 is applicable to real property, and it provides that depreciation to the extent an accelerated method such as double declining balance or sum of the digits method exceed the straight line method after December 31, 1963, the capital gain recognized on such sale will be offset by the depreciation recaptured. The amendments made by the Tax Reform Act of 1969 will be discussed in another chapter.

These provisions are inapplicable to an A reorganization since the acquiring corporation takes a carryover basis for the property received from the transferor corporation. On the other hand, if tangible personal property or real property is the "boot" in such a reorganization, the shareholders of the disappearing corporation will realize ordinary income to the extent of depreciation recaptured.

Carryovers in a Statutory Merger

In the A-type of reorganization, the tax attributes of the disappearing corporation are carried over to the surviving corporation.[29] Among the more important carryover provisions are the following: net operating losses, capital losses, earnings and profits, depreciation, accounting and inventory methods. They will be discussed in greater detail in a subsequent chapter.

SHAREHOLDER PROBLEMS

Section 358 provides for the nonrecognition of loss or gain to shareholders who exchange their stock or securities for stock or securities of the acquiring corporation. Thus, there is a substituted basis for the new stock or securities received equal to the basis of the old. Similarly the holding period of the "old" carried over to the new stock or securities received.

As previously stated, it is permissible for shareholders in an A type of reorganization to receive additional forms of consideration without disqualifying the tax-free nature of the reorganization. Such consideration is referred to as boot.

Boot is money or property received in an otherwise nontaxable exchange. It has the effect of making the exchange partially taxable, that is, to the extent of boot received. The gain to be recognized will be an amount not in excess of the value of the property received. For example, if A, a shareholder, exchanges his stock with a basis of $1,000 for stock with a value of $500 and a bond with a value of $750, the bond is boot. The actual gain is $250 ($500 + $750 received - $1,000 exchanged). But only $250 is taxed, either as a dividend or capital gain depending upon the circumstances.

The basis of the stock or securities received in a nontaxable reorganization exchange is the same as the basis of the stock or securities exchanged. This basis must be reduced by (1) any money received, (2) the fair market value of any other property received, and (3) any loss that was recognized. The basis must be increased by any amount treated as a dividend and any gain recognized on the exchange. Using the previous example, A would have a basis of $500 for the new stock determined as follows: $1,000 (basis of old stock) less $750 (value of bond) plus $250 gain recognized. The basis of the bond is $750, its fair market value.

When distributee shareholder receives several kinds of stock or securities, the basis must be allocated among the properties received in proportion to the fair market values of the stock of each class.

The problem arising with boot is whether it should be afforded capital gain rather than dividend income treatment. Section 356(a)(2) provides that if such an exchange has the effect of the distribution of a dividend, the gain shall be treated as a dividend to the extent of the distributee's share of the undistributed earnings of the corporation. This statutory provision is nebulous since no rules have been given as to when a distribution has the effect of a dividend. Accordingly, it would seem that individual shareholders should report it as capital gains. The Service's position has been strengthened by a case[30] which seems to imply automatic dividend treatment in all cases where boot is involved in an exchange. On the other hand, if the shareholder receives only cash, an argument could be made for capital gains treatment on the theory that there has been a complete termination of the shareholders' interest pursuant to Section 302(b)(2).

Liabilities assumed are not treated as "other property or money" for the purpose of determining the amount of recognized gain, except when tax avoidance was the principal purpose for the assumption or when the liabilities assumed exceed the adjusted basis of the property transferred. As applied to an A-type of reorganization exchange, the assumption of liabilities by a surviving corporation is not relevant since such assumption arises by operation of law.

RELATIONSHIP OF REORGANIZATION TYPES AND REDEMPTION AND LIQUIDATIONS

If the transaction fails to constitute a tax-free merger, then gain will be recognized to the shareholders equal to the difference between the shareholder's cost basis for his stock and the liquidating dividend to the corporation. The gain should be non-recognized to the dissolving corporation under Section 337, which permits the nonrecognition of gain or loss being recognized to a corporation upon sale or exchange of its assets within the twelve-month period. This result will convert a "plan of reorganization" into a "plan of complete liquidation."

There seems to be no problems arising in a type A reorganization if some of the stock is redeemed prior to the reorganization as long as there is an equity continuing interest on the part of at least fifty percent of the shareholders.

It sometimes occurs that a merger may meet the C or D type of reorganization. It follows then that the details of those reorganizations must be met. There is no answer to the above but it seems reasonable that the A type will prevail. As regards a C or D type which overlap, the D type provisions prevail.[31]

If a reorganization can also qualify as an intercorporate liquidation under Section 332, then it shall be treated as a liquidation by the parent corporation.[32] Thus, it has been held by the Service[33] that a parent cannot liquidate an insolvent subsidiary. Similarly, the liquidation provisions precede the reorganization rules.[34]

An interesting interplay arises between the liquidation and reorganization provisions when a corporation purchases at least eighty percent of the stock of another corporation and then liquidates the newly acquired subsidiary within a two-year period; the provisions of Section 334(b)(2) will generally apply. Under these provisions, the assets of the acquired corporation will obtain a new basis equal to the cost of the stock. This new basis may be lower than the old basis of the assets. In addition, there will be depreciation recapture under Sections 1245 and 1250, as well as investment credit recapture under Section 47. Further, certain carryovers are lost, as for example, a net operating loss carryover or a capital loss carryover. Thus, obviously there are times when it is most desirable to avoid the provisions of Section 334(b)(2). However, the Section is not elective; if the liquidation falls within its scope, the provisions automatically apply.

The question then is how the provisions of Section 334(b)(2) can be avoided when it is desired to immediately combine the parent and the newly acquired subsidiary. A merger of the subsidiary will not work. Such a merger is deemed to be the same as liquidating the subsidiary. The Service recently ruled[35] that the merger of the parent into the subsidiary will be treated as a reorganization under the provisions of Section 368(a)(1)(A). Thus, the existing basis of the assets will not be changed and, further, the ruling provides that there will be no recapture under Sections 47, 1245 or 1250. But the ruling is silent as to whether a net operating loss of a subsidiary could be carried over under Section 381. It seems that it could be utilized absent a violation of Section 269 which will be discussed in greater detail in a subsequent chapter.

One of the disadvantages of the merger route is that consent of shareholders is required under state law including the rights of minority shareholders to have their shares appraised for cash. Furthermore, the SEC rules generally provide that whenever a publicly held acquiring corporation obtains its shareholders' consent to a merger, it must distribute to its shareholders a proxy statement containing information about both companies. Thus, most companies have avoided the merger type reorganization.

In October 1968, Congress amended the law to make the parent a party to the reorganization when an acquired corporation A merges into a subsidiary S in exchange for S's stock. The requirements provide that only voting stock of the parent can be used; none of the subsidiary corporation stock can be used. It would have been a tax-free reorganization if it could have merged into the parent.

The stock of the parent received by the subsidiary would be a capital contribution to them. Their basis for the stock would be the transferor's basis for the assets.[36] A problem arises as to its basis in subsidiary stock. There is no Code provision dealing with such stock. This leads to the unrealistic result that it has a zero basis for the S stock it received in the Section 351 tax-free exchange. The same problem arises in connection with the B and C type of reorganization.

SEC PROBLEMS

Rule 133, as previously discussed, would have the effect of requiring no registration statement to be filed in connection with stock issued in a merger or consolidation since no stock is being sold. Furthermore, the plan of reorganization must be submitted to the shareholders of both corporations to be voted upon. All shareholders will be bound by such vote, except dissenting shareholders who perfect their appraisal rights.

The New York Stock Exchange requirement of shareholder approval to list the additional securities would present no complicated compliance problem since state law automatically requires such voting approval.

ACCOUNTING PROBLEMS

The purchase method of business combinations would result in the purchase price being allocated among the assets being acquired. For this reason, it is not the appropriate method to be utilized in such a merger.

The pooling method, as previously illustrated, would be the type to be utilized. Since there is usually an adjustment of the stockholder's equity section, it would have to be readjusted for tax purposes since the retained earnings or the earnings and profits are carried forward in the statutory merger.

CONTINGENT STOCK REORGANIZATIONS

A recent trend in the statutory type of merger has been the issuance of Certificates of Contingent Interests. They are issued rather than stock when there is difficulty in determining a purchase price to be paid in an acquisition. Basically, they provide that additional stock is to be issued over a period of time if the acquired company's earnings materialize according to designated levels.

If the purchase type of acquisition is used, the additional payments made must be based upon the attained earnings in excess of a minimum level and are to be allocated to the purchased assets. In some situations, such payment may be allocated to goodwill if the original purchase price was fully allocated to the tangible assets.

In the pooling of interest concept in accounting for corporate acquisitions, the additional payments should be accounted for by transferring amounts to stated capital from capital surplus, or if inadequate for this purpose, then from retained earnings.

The Service has provided[37] that contingent stock can be used in an A, B or C type of reorganization if the following conditions are met:

(1) All of the stock must be issued within five years from the date of the transfer of the assets in the case of (A) and (C) reorganization or within five years from the date of the initial exchange in the case of (B) reorganizations.

(2) There is a valid business reason for not issuing all of the stock immediately, such as the difficulty in determining the value of one or both of the corporations involved in the reorganization.

(3) The maximum number of shares which may be issued in the exchange is stated.

(4) At least fifty percent of the maximum number of shares of each class of stock which may be issued is actually issued in the initial distribution.

(5) The agreement evidencing the right to receive stock in the future prohibits assignment except by operation of law.

(6) Only the receipt of additional stock of the acquiring corporation can be used.

Thus, the receipt of such certificates in the reorganization type previously enumerated will constitute stock rather than boot.

MISCELLANEOUS CONTINGENT STOCK PROBLEMS

It sometimes happens that a corporation acquires another corporation by utilizing contingent stock. Subsequently, the acquiring corporation is itself the acquired corporation in another reorganization. If the five-year payout provision is not met, serious problems arise. These problems can be avoided by providing in the merger agreement that any subsequent acquisition shall accelerate the payout provision.

Another problem would arise when the acquiring corporation wishes to modify its original agreement to issue stock because of dilution in earnings problems, and substitute cash for the certificates. There is no answer to this problem. The tax consequences should be as follows. The corporate parties to the reorganization should suffer no adverse tax consequences since cash can be utilized in a tax-free merger. The shareholders receiving cash would probably realize dividend income upon the distribution equal to the acquiring and acquired corporation's earnings and profits. The Treasury could invoke the step transaction doctrine and find that the original reorganization was nothing more than a liquidation. Hence, the plan or reorganization would be converted to a plan of liquidation.

Another problem is the holding period of deferred stock received by a shareholder who subsequently disposes of it at a capital gain. Such gain will be presumed to relate to the same period that the original stock was held.[38]

Section 483 provides for imputed interest rules being applicable to corporate reorganizations. This will be discussed in greater detail in a subsequent chapter.

MISCELLANEOUS EXCHANGE CONSIDERATIONS
IN A-TYPE REORGANIZATIONS

The Convertible Debenture Problem

Many reorganizations have involved the use of convertible debentures. Since a debenture is not a proprietary interest, the reorganization was taxable because of a lack of meeting the continuity of interest rules.

The chief advantage besides allowing the seller to elect to use the installment sales method of reporting income was the ability of the seller to "ride the market" and convert it into stock. From a buyer's point of view, the interest paid on the debentures was a tax-deductible expense. If the buyer had issued stock in the acquisition, the dividends paid were of course nondeductible to the corporation.

A potential tax problem in the use of debentures, whether or not convertible, is the original issue discount. Original issue discount [39] is the difference between the face amount of the debenture and the price paid for it. Then to the extent that such discount exists, it is taxed as ordinary income to the seller at maturity. The Tax Reform Act of 1969 changed the provisions to require the holder to include in his income the ratably monthly portion of the original issue discount multiplied by the number of complete months thereof that he has held such debenture or other evidence of indebtedness during the taxable year. The holder's basis is correspondingly increased by the amount of such original issue discount required to be included in his income.

Warrants

Warrants are another type of this "funny money" currently being used as a method to finance a corporate acquisition. They are often used with cash in acquiring a company. The seller will, if he meets the thirty percent rule of installment sales method of reporting income, use it.[40]

Warrants have been held[41] by the Supreme Court as not the equivalent of voting stock and cannot be given tax free in a reorganization. Therefore, they have been used primarily in taxable acquisitions.

Use of Preferred Stock

Another method used to finance corporate acquisitions is convertible preferred stock. Such stock usually carries full voting rights, a fixed dividend rate with priority over common stock dividends, and a preferred liquidation value. The convertibility feature of such stock is the right to convert it into common stock of the acquiring corporation at a specified date and a lower price. This permits the holder to "ride the market."

A significant tax disadvantage inherent in such stock is that it may be deemed "Section 306 stock." Such stock does not affect the tax-free nature of the reorganization exchange in which the convertible preferred was received. The amount realized upon a subsequent sale of the stock may be treated as a gain from the sale of property which is not a capital asset.[42] The proceeds, to the extent they exceed the basis for the stock, will be taxed as dividend income. The purpose of this provision is to prevent a "bail out" of corporate earnings at long-term capital gains.

The definition of "Section 306 stock"[43] includes any stock received in pursuance to a plan of reorganization if:

1. It is not "common stock";
2. The shareholder's gain is not recognized pursuant to Sections 354 and 356, and
3. The effect of receipt of the stock was "substantially the same as the receipt of a stock dividend."

The Service has held[44] that if the convertible stock is widely held or there is no prearranged plan to have such stock held by the common shareholder, then such stock will not be deemed to constitute "Section 306 stock."

TAX OPTION CORPORATION

A tax-option corporation is one that has elected to have its taxable income or net operating loss passed through to its shareholders. This theory is similar to the conduit theory afforded the tax treatment of partners in a partnership. With the exception of capital gains taxation under Section 1378, it pays no federal income tax. This may not be the case as regards state income taxation. For example, New York State does not recognize tax-option corporations.

The Code imposes requirements which must be adhered to before the favorable tax treatment will be afforded to such shareholders. Among the requirements are the following: (1) there must be less than ten shareholders; (2) the shareholders must be individuals or decedent's estates; (3) it must be a domestic corporation; (4) it must have one class of stock; (5) no nonresident alien may be a shareholder; (6) it may not get over eighty percent of its gross receipts from outside the United States; (7) it may not get more than twenty percent of its gross receipts from interest, dividends, rents, royalties, annuities, and gains from sale or exchange of securities.

A question arises as to whether a corporation can merge with a tax-option corporation. The answer is in the affirmative. The Service has ruled[45] that the effect of a merger between a Subchapter S corporation and a nonelecting corporation was to terminate the taxable year of the tax option effective on the date of the merger. Furthermore, such a merger did not terminate the election retroactive to the beginning of the Subchapter's final taxable year. It would appear that no problem would arise if two Subchapter S corporations were to merge as long as the requirements of the election were met after the merger, that is, one class of stock, less than ten shareholders, and so forth.

The Service recently[46] permitted a consolidation between two Subchapter S Corporations. The newly formed corporation may also elect Subchapter S status, without prior approval, for its first taxable year. The disappearing corporations retained Subchapter S status for their final taxable year.

REVERSE MERGER

Section 368(a)(2)(E) was added to the Code on January 12, 1971 to provide that a controlled subsidiary which uses the stock of its parent in a statutory merger with a third corporation, the surviving corporation, can be the disappearing corporation in a triangular merger—sometimes referred to as a subsidiary merger. Prior to the enactment of this legislative change, the controlled subsidiary had to be the surviving corporation in the triangular merger.

The requirements for consummating a reverse merger are the following:

1. The parent (P) must control subsidiary (S) before the merger.
2. Only the stock of P must be used in the reorganization.
3. The third corporation (X) must own substantially all of the assets of S after the transaction.
4. The former shareholders of X must exchange an amount of X stock which constitutes control of X for P stock.

The effect of this change is that now statutory mergers can be effectuated with a controlled subsidiary being the surviving corporation (subsidiary merger) with a third corporation, or the third corporation can be the surviving corporation (reverse merger).

CONTENTS OF A MERGER AGREEMENT

The following checklist serves as a guide for the items which frequently comprise a typical merger agreement:

1. Name of parties
2. Business purpose of the reorganization
3. Corporate existence of surviving corporation
4. Exchange ratio for conversion of shares
5. Stated capital of surviving corporation
6. Agent for service of process
7. Provision for termination of merger
8. Rights and obligations under the agreement
9. Covenants
10. Conveyances
11. Delivery of stock
12. Assumption of liabilities
13. Opinion of counsel
14. Shareholder approval

15. Rights of minority shareholders
16. Stockholders meeting
17. Stock exchange listing
18. Examination of books and records
19. Miscellaneous provisions
20. Effective date

MERGER CHECKLIST

A. Taxable vs. Tax Free
   1. Advantages and Disadvantages
B. Tax-Free Types
   1. Merger
   2. Consolidation
   3. Subsidiary Mergers vs. Liquidation
   4. Using Stock of Parent
C. Consideration Utilized
   1. Stock
   2. Cash, Notes and Other Property
   3. Boot Problems
   4. Contingent Stock
   5. Relationship to Section 351
   6. Convertible Debentures, Warrants and Section 306 stock
D. Liabilities
E. Regulations Requirements
   1. Business Purpose—form versus substance
   2. Continuity of Interest—stock versus proprietary interest
   3. 50% test
   4. Continuity of Business Enterprise
   5. Step Transaction Doctrine
   6. Record Keeping Requirements
F. Plan of Reorganization
   1. Written versus Oral
   2. Exchange Pursuant to Plan
G. Parties to a Reorganization
   1. Each Corporation
   2. Subsidiary using Stock of Parent
H. Effect on Corporations
   1. Stock or Securities—carryover basis
   2. Boot—gain recognized
   3. Recapture Problems
   4. Carryover Problems
I. Effect on Shareholders
   1. Substituted Basis
   2. Allocation Problems Among Properties Received
   3. Boot Distribution
   4. Dividend versus Capital Gain Problems

FOOTNOTES

[1] Regulations 1.368-2(b).

[2] IRC-1954; Section 368(a)(2)(D).

[3] Ibid; Section 351.

[4] Regulations; 1.351-1 and 1.351-2.

[5] IRC-1954; Section 367.

[6] Ibid; Section 368(c).

[7] Regulations; Section 1.351-3

[8] IRC-1954; Section 358.

[9] Regulations; 1.368-(b).

[10] Gregory v. Helvering; 293 U.S. 465 (1935).

[11] Rev. Proc. 67-1, 1967-1 C.B. 544.

[12] Regulations; 1.368-2(a).

[13] Cortland Specialty Co. v. C.I.R., 60F(2)937 (1932).

[14] Le Tulle v. Scofield, 308 U.S. 415 (1940).

[15] Rev. Proc. 66-348, 1966-2 C.B., 1232.

[16] Ibid.

[17] Rev. Proc. 64-31, 1964-2 C.B. 947.

[18] Rev. Rul. 66-224, 1966-2 C.B. 114.

[19] South Bay v. C.I.R., 145 F(2) 698.

[20] Werner Abegg 50 T.C. 145.

[21] Helvering v. Elkhorn Coal Co., 95F (2) 732.

[22] C.I.R. v. Gordon, 391 U.S. 83.

[23] Casco Products Corp. 49 T.C.-No. 5 (1967).

[24] King Enterprises, Inc. v. C.I.R., 418 F (2) 511.

[25] Regulations; 1.368-3

[26] Regulations; 1.368-2(f).

[27] Regulations; 1.368-2(g).

[28] Regulations; 1.368-3.

[29]IRC-1954; Sec. 381 (c).

[30]Commissioner v. Estate of Bedford, 325 U.S. 283 (1945).

[31]IRC-1954; Sec. 368(a)(2)(A).

[32]Long Island Water Corp., 36 T.C. 377 (1961).

[33]Rev. Rul. 59-296, 1959-1 C.B. 37.

[34]Regulations; 1.322-2(d).

[35]Rev. Rul. 70-223, IRB 1970-19, p.13.

[36]IRC-1954; Section 362 (b).

[37]Rev. Rul. 66-112, 1966-1 C.B. 68; Rev. Proc. 67-13, 1967-1 C.B.

[38]IRC-1954; Section 1223(1).

[39]IRC-1954; Section 1232.

[40]IRC-1954; Section 453.

[41]Helvering v. Southwest Consolidated Corp. 42-1 US7C9248, 315 U.S. 194.

[42]IRC-1954; Section 306.

[43]IRC-1954; Section 306(c)(1)(B).

[44]Rev. Proc 66-34, Section C, 1966-2 C.B. 1232.

[45]Rev. Rul. 64-94, 1964-1 C.B. 317.

[46]Rev. Rul. 70-232, IRB 1970-19.

MAL CORPORATION
Balance Sheet
December 31, 1969
(000's)

ASSETS

Current Assets:

Cash		$ 1,000
Accounts receivable		2,000
Inventories		3,000
Other		4,000
	Total	$10,000
Fixed Assets		20,000
	Total Assets	$30,000

LIABILITIES
AND CAPITAL

Current Liabilities:

Accounts payable		$ 500
Income taxes		2,000
Other		1,000
	Total	$ 3,500

Stockholders' Equity:

Capital stock—$5 par value		$10,000
Capital surplus		6,500
Retained Earnings		10,000
	Total Liabilities and Capital	$30,000

MAL CORPORATION
Income Statement
For The Year Ended
December 31, 1969
(000's)

Net Sales		$12,000
Cost of goods sold		4,000
Selling, general and administration expenses		2,000
Other expenses		1,000
	Total	7,000

Net income before income taxes		5,000
Income taxes—50% rate		2,500
Net income		$ 2,500

Earnings per share — 2,000,000 shares $1.25

JRG CORPORATION

Balance Sheet
December 31, 1969
(000's)

ASSETS

Current Assets:

Cash		$ 500
Accounts receivable		700
Inventories		1,000
Other		1,300
	Total	$ 3,500
Fixed Assets		6,500
	Total Assets	$10,000

LIABILITIES
AND CAPITAL

Current Liabilities:

Accounts payable		$ 200
Income taxes		1,000
Other		800
	Total	$ 2,000

Stockholders' Equity:

Capital stock—$5 par value		$ 5,000
Capital surplus		1,000
Retained earnings		2,000
	Total Liabilities and Capital	$10,000

JRG CORPORATION
Income Statement
For The Year Ended
December 31,1969
(000's)

Net Sales	$4,000
Cost of goods sold	1,000
Selling, general and administration expenses	750
Other expenses	250
Total	$2,000
Net income before income taxes	$2,000
Income taxes—50% rate	1,000
Net Income	$1,000
Earnings per share—1,000,000	$1.00

Purchase Method

Assume that MAL Corporation acquires JRG Corporation on December 31, 1969 for $10,000,000 in notes:

JRG and MAL CORPORATION
Combined Balance Sheet
December 31,1969
(000's)

ASSETS	MAL	JRG	Adjustments	Combined
Current Assets:				
Cash	$ 1,000	$ 500		$ 1,500
Accounts receivable	2,000	700		2,700
Inventories	3,000	1,000		4,000
Other	4,000	1,300		5,300
Total	$10,000	$ 3,500		$13,500
Fixed Assets	20,000	6,500		26,500
Goodwill			$2,000	4,000
Total Assets	$30,000	$10,000	$2,000	$44,000

LIABILITIES
AND CAPITAL

Current Liabilities:

Accounts payable	$ 500	$ 200		700
Income taxes	2,000	1,000		3,000
Other	1,000	800	10,000	11,800
Total	$3,500	$2,000	$10,000	$15,500

Stockholders' Equity:

Capital stock	$10,000	$ 5,000	5,000	10,000
Capital surplus	6,500	1,000	1,000	6,500
Retained earnings	10,000	2,000	2,000	10,000
Total Liabilities and Capital	$30,000	$10,000	$2,000	$42,000

Pooling of Interest Method

Assume that MAL corporation acquires JRG Corporation on December 31, 1969 for an additional $5,000,000 of stock:

JRG and MAL CORPORATION
Combined Balance Sheet
December 31, 1969
(000's)

ASSETS	MAL	JRG	Adjustments	Combined
Current Assets:				
Cash	$1,000	$ 500		$1,500
Accounts receivable	2,000	700		2,700
Inventories	3,000	1,000		4,000
Other	4,000	1,300		5,300
Total	$10,000	$3,500		$13,500
Fixed Assets	20,000	6,500		26,500
Total Assets	$30,000	$10,000		$40,000

LIABILITIES AND
CAPITAL

Current Liabilities:

Accounts payable	$ 500	$ 200		$ 700
Income taxes	2,000	1,000		3,000
Other	1,000	800		1,800
Total	$3,500	$2,000		$5,500

Stockholders' Equity:

Capital stock	$10,000	$ 5,000	$1,000	$14,000
Capital surplus	6,500	1,000	1,000	8,500
Retained earnings	10,000	2,000		12,000
Total Liabilities and Capital	$30,000	$10,000	$	$40,000

MAL and JRG CORPORATION
Combined Income Statement
For the Year Ended
December 31, 1969
(000's)

	MAL	JRG	COMBINED
Net Sales	$12,000	$4,000	$16,000
Cost of Goods Sold	4,000	1,000	5,000
Selling, and General and Administration expenses	2,000	750	2,750
Other expenses	1,000	250	1,250
Total	$ 7,000	$2,000	$ 9,000
Net income before income taxes	$ 5,000	$2,000	$ 7,000
Income taxes—50% rate	2,500	1,000	3,500
Net Income	$ 2,500	$1,000	$ 3,500

ANALYSIS OF THE ILLUSTRATIONS

Income Statements

Under the purchase method, no new income statement has been prepared since earnings are only considered from the date of acquisition.

There has been a small dilution in earnings per share under the pooling of interest method. The earnings per share of the two companies on an individual basis were $2.25, (1.25 + 1.00) while on a combined basis this is approximately $1.17. This is attributable to the additional four million shares being issued to finance the acquisition.

Balance Sheets

Under the purchase method, goodwill in the amount of $2,000 arises from the difference between the notes given in the amount of $10,000,000 for net assets of $8,000,000 ($10,000,000 of assets less liabilities of $2,000,000). The stockholders' equity portion of the balance sheet has been eliminated.

Under the pooling method, the retained earnings of the acquired company are carried forward. In the downward adjustment to reflect the lower number of shares, the capital surplus account was increased. No goodwill appears on the books.

**FORMS TO BE UTILIZED
IN A STATUTORY MERGER**

**WAIVER OF NOTICE OF SPECIAL JOINT MEETING
OF
SHAREHOLDERS AND DIRECTORS
OF
X CORPORATION**

WE, the undersigned, being all of the Shareholders and Directors of X CORPORATION, do hereby waive all notice of a special joint meeting of the Shareholders and Directors of the Corporation, and do consent that the 13th day of October, 1969, at 2:00 P.M. in the afternoon, be and the same hereby is fixed as the time, and the office of the Corporation, as the place for holding the said meeting, and we do hereby consent that all such business may be transacted thereat as may lawfully come before it.

Dated: October 13, 1969.

_____
X Shareholder & Director

_____
Y

AGREEMENT OF MERGER

AGREEMENT OF MERGER dated as of this lst day of August, 1970 pursuant to Article 9 of the Business Corporation Law of the State of New York, among X CORPORATION ("X"), a New York corporation and Y ("Y"), a New York corporation.

WITNESSETH:

WHEREAS, the constituent corporation desires to merge into a single corporation; and

WHEREAS, X was incorporated as a corporation under the laws of the State of Delaware on August 19, 1969, and filed in the office of the Secretary of State on August 19, 1969; has an authorized capital stock of 1,000,000 shares of Common Stock, par value $.05, and which stock 274,000 shares are issued and outstanding; and

WHEREAS, said Y corporation, a corporation organized under the laws of the State of New York, by its Certificate of Incorporation, which was filed in the office of the Secretary of State of New York on April 14, 1970, had an authorized capital stock consisting of 200 Common shares without par value of which ____ shares are now issued and outstanding.

WHEREAS, the office of X in the State of New York is located at_____, New York; and

WHEREAS, the principal office of Y in the State of New York is located at_____, New York.

NOW, THEREFORE, the corporation and the parties to this agreement, in consideration of the mutual covenants, agreements, and provisions hereinafter contained, do hereby prescribe the terms and conditions of said merger and the manner of carrying the same into effect, as follows:

1. X hereby merges into itself Y; and said X shall be, and it hereby is, merged into Y, which shall be the surviving corporation.

2. The Certificate of Incorporation of X as amended, as in effect on the date of the merger, provided for in this agreement, shall continue in full force and effect as the Certificate of Incorporation of the corporation surviving this merger.

Said Certificate of Incorporation, as amended, of Y is annexed hereto, and forms a part hereof.

3. The manner of converting the outstanding shares of Capital Stock of the constituent corporations into the shares or other securities of Y shall be as follows:

(a) Each share of Common Stock of X which shall be outstanding on the effective date of this agreement shall forthwith be changed and converted into 1000 shares of Common Stock of Y.

(b) Each share of Common Stock of X which shall be outstanding on the effective date of this agreement shall forthwith be changed and converted into one share of Common Stock of Y.

(c) After the effective date of this agreement, each holder of outstanding certificates, representing stock of the merged corporations, shall surrender the same to Y and each such holder shall be entitled, upon such surrender, to receive shares of stock of Y on the basis provided herein. Until so surrendered, the outstanding shares of the stock of the merged corporations, to be converted into the stock of Y, as provided for herein, may be treated by Y, for all corporate purposes, as evidencing the ownership of the shares of Y, as though said surrender and exchange had taken place.

(d) No fractional shares shall be issued by Y. If application of the conversion formulae specified in subparagraphs (a) and (b) above, would entitle any shareholder of X to receive a fractional share of any class of stock of Y, Y shall pay to such shareholder in cash the value of such fractional share, as of the date of merger, as provided for in this agreement.

4. The terms and conditions of the merger are as follows:

(a) The By-Laws of X, as they exist on the effective date of this agreement, shall be and remain the By-Laws of Y, until the same shall be altered, amended or repealed, as therein provided.

(b) The directors of X shall be:

A

B

C

and each of them shall continue to hold office as a director until the next annual meeting of shareholders, and until his successor has been elected and qualified.

(c) The officers of Y shall be as follows:

X, President

Vice President

Y, Secretary

Z, Treasurer

and each of them shall hold such office subject to the pleasure of the Board of Directors.

(d) This merger shall become effective upon filing with the Secretary of State of New York. However, for all accounting purposes, the effective date of the merger shall be as of the close of business on July 1, 1970.

(e) Upon the merger becoming effective, all the property, rights, privileges, franchises, patents, trademarks, licenses, registrations and other assets of every kind and description of the merged corporations shall be transferred to, vested in and revolve upon Y without further act or deed, and all property, rights and every other interest of Y and the merged corporations shall be as effectively the property of Y as they were of X and the merged corporations respectively. The merged corporations hereby agree, from time to time, as and when requested by Y or by its successors or assigns, to execute and deliver, or cause to be executed and delivered, all such deeds and instruments, and to take, or cause to be taken, such further or other action, as Y may deem necessary or desirable in order to vest in and confirm to Y title to and possession of any property of the merged corporations acquired, or to be acquired, by reason of, or as a result of, the merger herein provided for, and otherwise to carry out the intent and purposes hereof and the proper officers and directors of the merged corporations, and the proper officers and directors of Y, are fully authorized in the name of the merged corporations or otherwise, to take any and all such action.

(f) Y hereby (i) agrees that it may be served with proceeds in the State of New York in any proceeding for the enforcement of any obligation of X and in any proceeding for the enforcement of the rights of a dissenting shareholder of the merged corporations; (ii) irrevocably appoints the Secretary of State of New York as its agent to accept service of proceeds in any such proceeding; and (iii) agrees that it will promptly pay to dissenting shareholders of the merged corporations the amount, if any, to which they shall be entitled pursuant to the laws of the State of New York.

5. Anything herein or elsewhere to the contrary notwithstanding, this agreement may be terminated and abandoned by the Board of Directors of any constituent corporation at any time prior to the date of filing the agreement with the Secretary of State of the State of New York.

IN WITNESS WHEREOF, the parties to this agreement, pursuant to the approval and authority duly given by their respective Board of Directors, have caused this agreement to be executed and attested, and their respective corporate seals affixed.

X CORPORATION
a New York Corporation

By_____
                    President

ATTEST:

_____
            Secretary

Y CORPORATION
a New York Corporation

By_____
                    President

ATTEST:

_____
            Secretary

WAIVER OF NOTICE OF
SPECIAL COMBINED MEETING OF
THE BOARD OF DIRECTORS AND STOCKHOLDERS
OF Y, INC.

The undersigned, being all of the directors and stockholders of Y, INC., hereby waive notice of a Special Combined Meeting of the Board of Directors and Stockholders to be held at the office of Y, INC., at 4 Main Street, Englewood Cliffs, New Jersey at 2:00 P.M. on the 31st day of August, 1970 for the purpose of discussing and voting upon a merger of this corporation with X CORP., a New York corporation and to conduct any other business which may lawfully come before said meeting.

Dated: August 31, 1970

_____
A

_____
B

_____
C

MINUTES OF A
SPECIAL COMBINED MEETING OF
THE BOARD OF DIRECTORS AND
STOCKHOLDERS OF Y, INC.

A Special Combined Meeting of the Board of Directors and Stockholders of Y, INC. was called to order at 2:00 P.M. on the 31st day of August, 1970 at the office of Y, INC. at 4 Main Street, Englewood Cliffs, New Jersey.

A acted as Chairman of the meeting and B acted as Secretary of the meeting.

The Chairman stated that it was recommended by the accountants to this corporation that it would be desirable for this corporation to merge with X CORP., a New York corporation. In view of the fact that X CORP. no longer had the volume of business which it enjoyed in prior years, and in view of the fact that Y, INC. was engaged in the used automobile business, a merger of the two corporations would be desirable and beneficial both for the corporations and the stockholders thereof. It was pointed out that the stockholders of this corporation and of X CORP. were identical and each stockholder owned a one-third interest in each corporation.

Accordingly, the Plan of Merger was read to those present and upon motion duly made and seconded and after full discussion it was unanimously

RESOLVED, that this corporation merge with X, CORP. as of September 15, 1970, and that the surviving corporation be Y, INC., and it was further

RESOLVED, that each of the stockholders of record of Y, INC. as of July 31, 1970 shall retain two shares of stock originally issued to them by Y, INC. so that there will be a total of six shares of stock issued and outstanding and entitled to vote with respect to the stockholdings of Y, INC. In the event that more than two shares per stockholder have previously been issued by Y, INC. to the stockholders thereof, all shares issued to each of said stockholders of Y, INC. in excess of two shares per stockholder shall be surrendered by each of such stockholders to Y, INC. and cancelled prior to September 15, 1970, and it was further

RESOLVED, that for each .78024 shares of stock of X CORP. issued and outstanding there shall be issued by Y, INC. one share of no par common stock of Y, INC. to the current stockholders of X CORP. as of record as of August 31, 1970, and it was further

RESOLVED, that the valuation of the shares of both X CORP. and Y. INC. shall be made by Joseph R. Guardino & Co., Certified Public Accountants for both X CORP. and for Y, INC. as of the close of business of both corporations on August 31, 1970, and it was further

RESOLVED, that the Plan of Merger shall be effective as of September 15, 1970, and it was further

RESOLVED, that the Plan of Merger shall be consummated upon the approval of all of the stockholders of X CORP. and of Y, INC. at meetings conducted by each of such corporations for that purpose and that upon such approval the Plan of Merger shall not be abandoned, and it was further

RESOLVED, that the officers, directors, accountants and attorneys for the respective corporations be and they hereby are authorized and directed to execute any documents, certificates or other writings and to issue such stock and to consolidate such bank accounts as may be maintained by each corporation and to issue any necessary notices and to do all such other things as may be necessary to effectuate the terms of this merger in an orderly manner, and it was further

RESOLVED, that Y, INC. will designate in the Certificate of Merger the Secretary of State of the State of New York as its agent for the service of process pursuant to the provisions of Section 907 of the Business Corporation Law of the State of New York, and it was further

RESOLVED, that Y, INC. agrees to all of the provisions and requirements set forth in Sections 907, 623 and 306 of the Business Corporation Law of the State of New York.

There being no further business to come before the meeting it was on motion duly seconded unanimously adjourned.

_____

A
Chairman of the Meeting

_____

B
Secretary of the Meeting

WAIVER OF NOTICE OF
SPECIAL COMBINED MEETING OF
THE BOARD OF DIRECTORS AND STOCKHOLDERS
OF X CORPORATION

The undersigned, being all of the directors and stockholders of X CORP. hereby waive notice of a Special Combined Meeting of the Board of Directors and Stockholders to be held at the office of the Corporation at 20 Lexington Avenue, New York, New York at 10:00 A.M. on the 31st day of August, 1970, for the purpose of discussing and voting upon a merger of this corporation with Y, INC. a New Jersey corporation and to conduct any other business which may lawfully come before said meeting.

Dated: August 31, 1970

_____
A

_____
B

_____
C

MINUTES OF A
SPECIAL COMBINED MEETING OF
THE BOARD OF DIRECTORS AND
STOCKHOLDERS OF X CORPORATION

A Special Combined Meeting of the Board of Directors and Stockholders of X CORP. was called to order at 10:00 A.M. on the 31st day of August, 1970 at the office of the corporation at 20 Lexington Avenue, New York, New York.

Mr. A acted as Chairman of the meeting and Mr. B acted as Secretary of the meeting.

The Chairman stated that it was recommended by the accountants to this corporation that it would be desirable for this corporation to merge with Y, INC. a New Jersey corporation. In view of the fact that this corporation no longer had the volume of business which it enjoyed in prior years, a merger of the two corporations would be desirable and beneficial both for the corporations and the stockholders thereof. It was pointed out that the stockholders of this corporation and of Y, INC. were identical and each stockholder owned a one-third interest in each corporation.

Accordingly, the Plan of Merger was read to those present and upon motion duly made and seconded and after full discussion it was unanimously

RESOLVED, that this corporation merge with Y, INC. as of September 15, 1970 and that the surviving corporation be Y, INC., and it was further

RESOLVED, that each of the stockholders of record of Y, INC. as of July 31, 1970, shall retain two shares of stock originally issued to them by Y, INC. so that there will be a total of six shares of stock issued and outstanding and entitled to vote with respect to the stockholdings of Y, INC. In the event that more than two shares per stockholder have previously been issued by Y, INC. to the stockholders thereof, all shares issued to each of said stockholders of Y, INC. in excess of two shares per stockholder shall be surrendered by each of such stockholders to Y, INC. and cancelled prior to September 15, 1970, and it was further

RESOLVED, that for each .78024 shares of stock of X issued and outstanding there shall be issued by Y, INC. one share of no par common stock of Y, INC. to the current stockholders of X CORP. as of record as of August 31, 1970, and it was further

RESOLVED, that the valuation of the shares of both X and Y, INC. shall be made by Joseph R. Guardino & Co., Certified Public Accountants for both X CORP. and for Y, INC. as of the close of business of both corporations on August 31, 1970, and it was further

RESOLVED, that the Plan of Merger shall be effective as of September 15, 1970, and it was further

RESOLVED, that the Plan of Merger shall be consummated upon the approval of all of the stockholders of X CORP. and of Y, INC. at meetings conducted by each of such corporations for that purpose and that upon such approval the Plan of Merger shall not be abandoned, and it was further

RESOLVED, that the officers, directors, accountants and attorneys for the respective corporations be and they hereby are authorized and directed to execute any documents, certificates or other writings and to issue such stock and to consolidate such bank accounts as may be maintained by each corporation and to issue any necessary notices and to do all such other things as may be necessary to effectuate the terms of this merger in an orderly manner, and it was further

RESOLVED, that the accountant to this corporation be and he hereby is authorized and directed to prepare a final tax return for the State of New York so that same may be filed with the New York State Tax Commission in advance of September 15, 1970, so as to enable the attorney for this corporation to obtain the consent of the New York State Tax Commission of any Certificate of Merger to be filed with the Department of State of the State of New York.

There being no further business to come before the meeting it was on motion duly seconded unanimously adjourned.

_____

A
Chairman of the Meeting

_____

B
Secretary of the Meeting

MERGER AGREEMENT

Agreement made as of the 31st day of August, 1970 by and between X CORP., a New York corporation, having a principal place of business at 20 Lexington Avenue, New York, New York and Y, INC., a New Jersey corporation, having its principal place of business at 4 Main Street, Englewood Cliffs, New Jersey.

WHEREAS, the stockholders of X CORP. consist of A, B and C each of whom have a one-third interest in said corporation, and

WHEREAS, the stockholders of Y, INC. consist of A, B and C each of whom have a one-third interest in said corporation, and

WHEREAS, it would be beneficial for Y, INC. and X, CORP. to merge with Y, INC. as the surviving corporation.

NOW, THEREFORE, in consideration of the sum of One ($1.00) Dollar paid by each party to the other receipt of which is hereby acknowledged and in consideration of the mutual promise contained herein it is agreed as follows:

1. That X CORP. (hereinafter referred to as "X") merge with Y, INC. as of September 15, 1970 and that the surviving corporation be Y, INC.

2. That each of the stockholders of record of Y, INC. as of July 31, 1970, shall retain two shares of stock originally issued to them by Y, INC. so that there will be a total of six shares of stock issued and outstanding and entitled to vote with respect to the stockholdings of Y, INC. In the event that more than two shares per stockholder have previously been issued by Y, INC. to the stockholders thereof, all shares issued to each of said stockholders of Y, INC. in excess of two shares per stockholder shall be surrendered by each of such stockholders to Y, INC. and cancelled prior to September 15, 1970.

3. That for each .78024 shares of stock of Y, INC. issued and outstanding there shall be issued by Y, INC. one share of no par common stock of Y, INC. to the current stockholders of _____ as of record as of August 31, 1970.

4. That the valuation of the shares of both Broadway and Y, INC. shall be made by Joseph R. Guardino & Co., Certified Public Accountants for both X and for Y, INC. as of the close of business of both corporations on August 31, 1970.

5. That this Plan of Merger shall be effective as of September 15, 1970.

6. That this Plan of Merger shall be consummated upon the approval of all of the stockholders of X and of Y, INC. at meetings conducted by each of such corporations for such purpose and that upon such approval this Plan of Merger shall not be abandoned.

7. That the officers, directors, accountants and attorneys for the respective corporations shall be authorized and directed to execute any documents, certificates or other writings and to issue such stock and to consolidate such bank

accounts as may be maintained by each corporation and to issue any necessary notices and to do all such other things as may be necessary to effectuate the terms of this merger in an orderly manner.

8. That the accountant to X be authorized and directed to prepare a final tax return for the State of New York so that same may be filed with the New York State Tax Commission in advance of September 15, 1970 so as to enable the attorney for X to obtain the consent of the New York State Tax Commission of any Certificate of Merger to be filed with the Department of State of the State of New York.

9. That Y, INC. will designate in the Certificate of Merger the Secretary of State of the State of New York as its agent for the service of process pursuant to the provisions of Section 907 of the Business Corporation Law of the State of New York.

10. That Y, INC. and X agree to all of the provisions and requirements set forth in Sections 907, 623 and 306 of the Business Corporation Law of the State of New York.

11. The business purpose of this merger is to provide permanent working capital for Y, INC., the surviving corporation.

12. That this agreement shall be deemed to have been made and executed in the State of New York and shall be governed and interpreted under and pursuant to the Laws of the State of New York.

13. This agreement may not be modified orally and may only be changed, amended or modified by a written agreement executed by all of the parties hereto.

14. This agreement shall be binding upon and shall inure to the benefit of the successors, assigns and legal representatives of the parties hereto.

IN WITNESS WHEREOF, the parties have affixed their signatures and seals as of the date above first written.

X CORP.

BY_____

A

Y, INC.

BY_____

B

MINUTES OF A SPECIAL JOINT MEETING
OF
SHAREHOLDERS AND DIRECTORS
OF
X CORPORATION

A special joint meeting of the Shareholders and Directors of X CORPORATION was held at the office of the Corporation on the 13th day of October, 1969, at 2 o'clock in the afternoon.

The following persons were present in person:

X–Shareholder & Director

Y–Shareholder & Director

being all of the shareholders and directors of the Corporation.

X, President of the Corporation, acted as Chairman of the meeting, and Y, Secretary of the Corporation, acted as Secretary of the meeting.

A written waiver of notice of this meeting signed by all of the shareholders and directors, was read by the Secretary and ordered to be placed with the minutes of this meeting.

The Chairman announced that the purpose of the meeting was to discuss and act upon a proposal to liquidate and dissolve the Corporation.

After discussion by the shareholders and directors, and after the President of the Corporation reported on its financial condition, the following resolutions were unanimously adopted:

RESOLVED, that the following plan of liquidation of X CORPORATION be and is hereby adopted;

RESOLVED, that in the judgment of the Board of Directors and Stockholders of the Corporation, it is deemed advisable and for the benefit of the Corporation that it should be liquidated and dissolved;

RESOLVED, that a plan of liquidation be, and it hereby is, formulated to effect such liquidation and dissolution in accordance with the following resolutions;

RESOLVED, that the proper officers of the Corporation be, and they hereby are, authorized to sell or otherwise liquidate any and all of the properties of the Corporation which in their judgment should be sold or liquidated to facilitate the liquidating of the Corporation;

RESOLVED, that the proper officers of the Corporation be, and they hereby are, authorized and directed to file a Certificate of Dissolution pursuant to Section 1003 of the Business Corporation Law of the State of New York with the Secretary of State of the State of New York;

RESOLVED, that the actions provided for in the foregoing resolutions providing for the complete liquidation and the distribution of its assets be commenced as soon as practicable, and that such assets be distributed and the dissolution be completed as soon as practicable, but in no event later than the termination of a twelve-month period commencing with the date of stockholder approval of this plan of complete liquidation; and

RESOLVED, that the proper officers of the Corporation be, and they hereby are authorized and directed to pay all such fees and taxes and to do or cause to be done such other acts and things as they may deem necessary or proper in order to carry out the liquidation and dissolution of the Corporation and to fully effectuate the purposes of the foregoing resolutions.

RESOLVED, that a special meeting of shareholders be called to consider the above resolutions.

There being no further business before the meeting, the same was on motion duly made, seconded and carried, adjourned.

_____

Y

Attest:

_____

X Chairman

CERTIFICATE OF MERGER
OF
X CORPORATION
INTO
Y, INCORPORATED

(Under Section 907 of the Business Corporation Law of the State of New York)

We, the undersigned, A and B being respectively the Secretary and Vice-President of A and B, being respectively the President and Secretary of Y, INC., a corporation organized under the laws of the State of New Jersey, hereby certify:

1. The name of the surviving corporation is Y, INC., and the name of the constituent corporation to be merged is X CORP.

2. The designation and number of authorized shares of each class of Y, INC., the surviving corporation, is 1,000 shares of no par, common stock, of which 6 shares have been issued and are outstanding, and of which 6 shares are entitled to vote. The designations and number of issued and outstanding shares of X CORP., the corporation to be merged, and the number of each class or series entitled to vote and to vote as a class are 1153½ shares of no par, common stock.

3. The effective date of the merger is the 15th day of September, 1970.

4. The merger was authorized by vote of the holders of 100% of all outstanding shares of Y, INC. entitled to vote at a meeting of shareholders in compliance with the applicable provisions of the laws of the State of New Jersey. The laws of the State of New Jersey permit the merger herein effected. The merger was authorized by vote of the holders of 100% of all of the outstanding shares of X CORP. entitled to vote at a meeting of shareholders in compliance with the applicable provisions of the law of the State of New York, which laws permit the merger herein effected.

5. The Certificate of Incorporation of X CORP., a domestic corporation, was filed by the Department of State on April 11, 1956. A Certificate amending the Certificate of Incorporation increasing the total number of shares was filed by the Department of State of New York on February 26, 1960. A Certificate changing the address of the corporation was filed by the Department of State of New York on February 23, 1961. A Certificate amending the Certificate of Incorporation increasing the authorized capital stock of the corporation was filed by the Department of State of New York on April 4, 1961. A Certificate amending the Certificate of Incorporation in order to change the name of the corporation was filed by the Department of the State of New York on August 19, 1965. Y, INC., the surviving corporation, was incorporated under the laws of the State of New Jersey on the 31st day of July, 1970. It has not filed an application for authority to do business in the State of New York and is not to do business in the State of New

York until an application for such authority shall have been filed by the Department of State of the State of New York. There is no present intention of Y, INC. to do business in the State of New York.

6. Y, INC. agrees that it may be served with process in New York in an action or special proceeding for the enforcement of any liability or obligation of any constituent corporation, previously amenable to suit in New York and for the enforcement under the Business Corporation Law, of the right of shareholders of any constituent domestic corporation to receive payment for their shares against the surviving corporation.

7. Y, INC. agrees that subject to the provisions of Section 623 of the Business Corporation Law, it will promptly pay to the shareholders of each constituent New York Corporation the amount, if any, to which they shall be entitled under the provisions of the Business Corporation Law relating to the right of the shareholders to receive payment for their shares.

8. The Secretary of State is designated by the surviving corporation as its agent upon whom process against it may be served in any action or special proceeding. The post office address to which the Secretary of State shall mail a copy of any such process is Y, INC., c/o Joseph R. Guardino, New York, New York.

9. The Plan of Merger has not been abandoned.

Dated, New York, New York
　　September 10, 1970

_____

A, Secretary

_____

B, Vice-President

_____

A, President

_____

B, Secretary

STATE OF NEW YORK
CITY OF NEW YORK } SS.:
COUNTY OF NEW YORK

A, being duly sworn, deposes and says that deponent is the Vice-President of X, CORP., the corporation named in the within Certificate; that deponent has read the foregoing Certificate and knows the contents thereof and that the same is true to deponent's own knowledge, except as to the matters therein stated to be alleged upon information and belief, and as to those matters deponent believes it to be true. This verification is made by deponent because X. CORP. is a corporation. Deponent is an officer thereof, to wit, its Vice President.

Sworn to before me this
11th day of September, 1970.

_____

A

STATE OF NEW YORK
CITY OF NEW YORK } SS.:
COUNTY OF NEW YORK

B, being duly sworn, deposes and says that deponent is the President of Y, INC., the corporation named in the within Certificate; that deponent has read the foregoing Certificate and knows the contents thereof; and that the same is true to deponent's own knowledge, except as to the matters therein stated to be alleged upon information and belief, and as to those matters deponent believes it to be true. This verification is made by deponent because Y, INC. is a corporation. Deponent is an officer thereof, to wit, its President.

Sworn to before me this
11th day of September, 1970.

_____

B

MERGER

Type of Exchanges

Facts

Assume that MAL Corporation is to be merged into JRG Corporation. Each corporation has three shareholders, A, B and C in JRG Corporation and X, Y and Z in MAL Corporation.

There is to be stock of JRG given in exchange for stock of MAL Corporation. The stock of JRG Corporation has a fair market value of $350 per share. The stock of MAL Corporation also has a fair market value of $350 per share. The stock of MAL Corporation also has a fair market value of $350. Assume further that 5,000 shares of stock are given to shareholders of MAL Corporation on December 31, 1970. The book and tax basis are the same.

Tax Consequences

As to the Corporations

Both JRG and MAL Corporations would be parties to the reorganization. If they adopt a plan of reorganization, the exchange would be effectuated tax free.

JRG Corporation would have the same basis for the property acquired from MAL Corporation as in the hands of MAL Corporation.

If assets were acquired for stock in the tax-free merger, JRG Corporation would have the same basis in the assets as in the hands of the transferor.

MAL Corporation who receive the stock from JRG Corporation would have the same basis as in the hands of JRG Corporation.

As to the Shareholders

The shareholders of both JRG and MAL Corporations would retain their tax basis for the stock received. If cash was issued in the tax-free merger, the cash would be taxable as a dividend to the extent of earnings and profits accumulated after February 28, 1913. If other property, such as property is issued to the shareholder, the other property is deemed to be boot and taxed as a dividend.

Liabilities Assumed

If JRG Corporation assumes the liabilities of MAL Corporation, such assumption decreases the transferor's basis for property received in the exchange. The assumption of liabilities of the transferor by the transferee, or taking property subject to transferor's liability, is not treated as giving money or other property and does not ordinarily prevent the exchange from being tax free, unless the purpose was to avoid taxes or the assumption had no valid business purpose.

Accounting Treatment

Books of JRG Corporation Journal Entries

1.

Capital Stock	100,000	
Capital Surplus	400,000	
Capital Stock		500,000

To record the statutory merger effectuated by giving stock for stock pursuant to state law.

2.

Cash	$100,000		
Accounts receivable	70,000		
Inventory	75,000		
Prepaid expenses	10,000		
Machinery & equipment	200,000		
Buildings	100,000		
	555,000		
Allowance for bad debts		5,000	
Accumulated depreciation—machinery & equipment		50,000	
Accumulated depreciation—buildings		50,000	
Notes payable		50,000	
Accounts payable		20,000	
Federal income tax liability		30,000	
Loans payable		100,000	305,000
Capital Stock			100,000
Retained earnings			150,000

To record the assets and liabilities of MAL Corporation.

Books of MAL Corporation

Allowance for bad debts	5,000
Accumulated depreciation—Machinery & equipment	50,000
Accumulated depreciation—buildings	50,000
Notes payable	50,000
Accounts payable	20,000
Federal income tax liability	30,000

Loans payable	100,000	
Capital stock	100,000	
Retained earnings	150,000	
Cash		100,000
Accounts receivable		70,000
Inventory		75,000
Prepaid expenses		10,000
Machinery & equipment		200,000
Buildings		100,000

To record the acquisition of MAL Corporation by JRG Corporation.

Consolidation

The tax treatment would be the same as the A-type transfer with the assets of both corporations being transferred to another new corporation.

Accounting Treatment

Since assets acquired are worth $450,000 and stock with a basis of $500,000 is given, under the pooling treatment, negative goodwill or a write-down of $50,000 would not be recorded.

TAXABLE ASSET TRANSACTION

Assume the same facts except that the requirements of state law were not complied with.

Tax Consequences

As to MAL Corporation

Since the Code requirements are not met, the corporation would recognize gain or loss on the transaction. The gain would be computed as follows:

Fair Market Value of Stock Acquired		$1,750,000
Less: Tax Basis of Assets $450,000		
Less: Liabilities Assumed 200,000		
Net Basis	250,000	
Recognized Gain or Loss		$1,500,000

This gain would be capital gain or loss except for the assets which are subject to depreciation recapture—machinery and equipment and buildings.

As to JRG Corporation

The acquiring corporation receives the assets of the acquired corporation at a tax cost equal to the value of the consideration which it paid for the assets. Here, the consideration exchanged is $1,750,000 which must be allocated among the various assets acquired on the basis of fair market values of the acquired corporation.

As to the Shareholders

There would be no tax consequences to the shareholders of JRG Corporation. This result is not true in the case of the shareholders of MAL Corporation.

They would realize gain or loss and be subject to tax upon receipt of the liquidation proceeds. This results in a double tax, one to the corporation and one to the shareholders. This can be avoided if the sale of the assets (proceeds will be the fair market value of the stock received) takes place in connection with a taxable liquidation of the corporation pursuant to Section 337.

This is the twelve-month liquidation whereby no gain or loss is recognized to a corporation if it adopts a plan of complete liquidation and all assets are sold within a twelve-month period beginning on the date of adoption of the plan. However, there are exceptions to this general rule where inventory items are sold unless to one buyer in a single transaction. Furthermore, there is recapture of depreciation and investment credits previously taken in the past.

The Stock for Stock Reorganization

5

The second type of tax-free reorganization is that of the stock for stock exchange—the B-type. The Code [1] provides that "the acquisition by one corporation, in exchange solely for all or a part of the voting stock (or in exchange solely for all or a part of the voting stock of a corporation which is in control of the acquiring corporation) of stock of another corporation if, immediately after the acquisition, the acquiring corporation has control of such other corporation (whether or not such acquiring corporation had control immediately before the acquisition)" is a B-type tax-free stock exchange. Thus, the B-type involves the acquisition of one corporation in exchange solely for its voting stock or the voting stock of a corporation in control of it, that is, an exchange by a subsidiary for the stock of its parent. The term "control" [2] has the same meaning in a B-type of exchange as that of a statutory merger or consolidation. Control means the ownership of stock possessing at least eighty percent of the total combined voting power of all classes of stock entitled to vote and at least eighty percent of all other classes of stock of the corporation.

A B-type of exchange involves an exchange of stock for voting stock whereas in an A-type of exchange the assets of a company are combined into another company or a newly formed company (consolidation). In a merger the assets of one company are brought together into a single entity pursuant to a stock exchange. The difference between the two types is that a statutory merger or consolidation can only be effectuated pursuant to state law, whereas in a B-type of exchange state law is not required to effectuate such a transaction. After the stock exchange has occurred, a parent-subsidiary relationship exists.

Some of the advantages of the stock for stock exchange are as follows: (1) the approval of shareholders is not required pursuant to state law (no requirement by the New York Stock Exchange); (2) there are no appraisal rights for minority shareholders existing as usually required in a merger under state law; (3) the acquired corporation continues to exist after the stock exchange as a subsidiary.

Among the disadvantages of a stock exchange are: (1) the additional costs attributable to the registration of securities being used pursuant to the 1933 Securities Act; Rule 133 is usually only applicable to the A and C type of reorganization exchanges; (2) the eighty percent stock control after the exchange may present burdensome compliance problems; (3) the only consideration which can be used is voting stock, and the issuance of anything "extra" may disqualify the reorganization in its entirety.

MECHANICS OF THE EXCHANGE

A B-type exchange usually arises when one company exchanges its voting stock for the voting stock of another company. In the alternative, one company, a subsidiary, can acquire the voting stock of another company by using the stock of its parent. This type can be illustrated by the following examples: A Corporation and B Corporation are separate corporations. A corporation exchanges its voting stock for eighty percent of the voting stock of B Corporation with its shareholders. After the exchange, A Corporation is in control of B Corporation. The relationship is that of parent (A Corporation) and subsidiary (B Corporation). A Corporation's stock is distributed to B Corporation's shareholders who transfer their stock to A Corporation. The transaction constitutes a B-type exchange.

Assume that A and B Corporations are parent and subsidiary corporations respectively. C Corporation is an unrelated corporation. B Corporation wishes to acquire control of C Corporation. It uses the stock of its parent, A Corporation, in exchange for eighty percent of the voting stock of C Corporation. After the exchange, B Corporation is in control of C Corporation. In the hierarchy of things, C Corporation is a second tier corporation. The transaction is a B-type reorganization.

If B Corporation, in the first example, received not only voting stock of A, but also nonvoting preferred stock, warrants or debentures, the transaction would not have qualified as a tax-free exchange since the "solely for" voting stock requirement would have been violated.

STOCK B-TYPE EXCHANGE REQUIREMENT

There are requirements both as to the stock being acquired and the consideration being exchanged for it. In transferring stock to the acquired corporation in return for stock of the acquiring corporation, control of the acquired corporation must result. By control is meant the ownership of stock, possessing at least eighty percent of the voting power and at least eighty percent of all other classes of stock. This is the same requirement for the A-type of exchange. For example, if Company A exchanged fifteen percent of its voting stock for at least eighty percent of the voting stock of Company B, and at least eighty percent of all other classes of stock, there is a B-type of reorganization. Corporations A and B would both be parties to the reorganization.

The term "voting stock" means any class of stock which has the inherent right to vote for directors. Thus, common stock is usually voting stock, but preferred stock may have voting rights; however this is usually not the case in actual practice.

The eighty percent control requirement is to be met if the B-type of exchange is to be achieved. If less than eighty percent of stock is acquired, then the reorganization would be taxable in its entirety.

There is no requirement as to the amount of voting stock which the acquiring corporation or its parent by a subsidiary must issue, but it must not give anything else.[3] The "solely for" requirement has been strictly construed by the courts and the Treasury Department. The issuance of cash, nonvoting stock or debt obligations which are convertible into voting stock is fatal to the tax-free nature of the reorganization.

The stock issued by the acquiring corporation must also possess voting rights. If such rights are contingent upon earnings, then the stock received by the acquired corporation is not voting stock. The Service has ruled[4] that voting preferred stock is voting stock when the acquired corporation's shareholders who received such stock were granted the right to participate in the management of the affairs of the acquiring corporation. Furthermore, the Service has ruled[5] that voting preferred and common stock may be used separately or in combination. On the other hand, the issuance of warrants and rights to acquire voting stock have been held not to be voting stock irrespective of the fact that they were exercised.[6] The "solely for" requirement will be satisfied if the acquiring corporation uses its treasury stock.[7]

If one corporation agrees to exchange its stock for voting convertible preferred stock of another corporation, and, in addition, upon conversion, the shareholders of the acquired corporation will have an option to purchase one additional share of common stock, the exchange is not a B-type reorganization. The Service ruled[8] that, because the right to purchase stock constitutes property other than voting stock, the transaction does not qualify as a tax-free reorganization. If the rights were separately issued as part of the consideration along with the convertible preferred stock, it is clear that such rights would constitute property other than voting stock. Whether the rights to purchase stock are issued separately or are incorporated in a stock certificate representing an equity interest, their nature remains the same.

In another ruling,[9] the Service held that the "solely for" requirement was not violated by the distribution of property by a subsidiary corporation to its parent corporation immediately prior to the acquisition of the subsidiary corporation by another corporation. The property distributed by the subsidiary to its parent consisted of rights to amounts receivable by reason of existing claims for refund of federal income taxes. Since only voting stock was utilized as consideration for the exchange, a B-type of exchange was effectuated. The distribution of the refund claim was a taxable dividend distribution.

The Service also ruled[10] that the "solely for" voting stock requirement is not violated when, pursuant to a plan of reorganization, an acquiring corporation substitutes its stock options for the outstanding stock options of the acquired corporation.

The eighty percent control requirement need not be met in one transfer to qualify as a B-type exchange. Hence, it is possible for a corporation to own some stock prior to the acquisition. The important point is that control must exist after the transfer. For example, an acquiring corporation for cash within one year acquires the remaining fifty percent of the stock in exchange for voting stock. The stock exchange is a tax-free B-type of reorganization. This type of transaction of using cash followed by a stock exchange is sometimes referred to as "creeping control." It has its support in the Regulations.[11] The Regulations[12] provide as follows:

> The acquisition of stock of another corporation by the acquiring corporation solely for its voting stock is permitted tax free even though the acquiring corporation already owns some of the stock of the other corporation. Such an acquisition is permitted tax free in a single transaction or in a series of transactions taking place over a relatively short period of time such as twelve months.

Thus, there can be a preconceived plan whereby a number of steps are undertaken with the final transaction resulting in control. These steps must occur in a relatively short period of time; usually one year under the Regulations. Furthermore, it makes no difference whether a shareholder exchanged his shares either before or after the acquiring corporation had its eighty percent controlling. Similarly, it makes no difference that if after it has control, the acquiring corporation issues additional stock in which to eliminate the minority interests of the acquired corporation.

A question usually arising in connection with the control requirement is whether the attribution rules are applicable to a B-type of exchange. The Regulations make no reference to the attribution rules under Section 318. Section 368(c) defines control in terms of direct ownership and not in terms of practical control.[13] The Service has ruled[14] that a stock for stock exchange when only fifty percent control is acquired is not a B-type reorganization exchange although the remaining fifty percent of the acquired corporation's stock was owned by the wholly-owned subsidiary of the acquiring corporation. Thus, the B-type exchange is restricted to only one corporation and not to two corporations. The only apparent exception to this rule is where a subsidiary uses its parent's stock to acquire eighty percent control of another corporation.

USE OF CASH

The use of cash in addition to voting stock would be fatal to the reorganization and, accordingly, gain or loss would be recognized by the shareholders.

But the use of cash in lieu of fractional shares did not destroy the B-type in *Mills*[15] since there was simply a mathematical rounding off for accounting purposes. The cash amounted to less than one-tenth of one percent of the entire value of the transferred voting stock or $27. The Tax Court[16] has previously rejected a *de minimis* rule on the theory that the phrase "solely for voting stock" permitted no cash in a B-type reorganization.

Subsequently, the Service has ruled that it will permit cash to be paid by the acquiring corporation in lieu of fractional share interests.[17]

REDEMPTIONS PRIOR TO
ACQUISITION OF CONTROL

If some stockholders require cash and a B-type is planned, cash can be given to some shareholders to redeem their stock prior to the stock for stock exchange. The Service has ruled[17] that the control requirement was met when eighty percent of the common stock of the acquired corporation was acquired solely for voting stock of the acquiring corporation even though the acquired corporation had a preferred stock that had previously been called for redemption by the acquired corporation. The redemption of the preferred stock had been part of the plan of reorganization. Thus, the ruling indicates that the use of the preferred stock redemption for the purpose of rendering tax free the subsequent stock for stock exchange did not obviate the control test. On the other hand, if the acquiring corporation finances the redemption, either directly or indirectly, such long-term financing would violate the "solely for" voting stock exchange.[18]

EXPENSES INCIDENTAL TO THE REORGANIZATION

A stock for stock exchange may involve incidental expenses such as a finder's fee, legal expenses and stock transfer taxes. These expenses should not be borne by the acquiring corporation but should be paid by the stockholders of the acquired corporation. The Service usually requires that in a request for a ruling in a B-type reorganization, thereby a representation, that the stockholders will pay their own expenses. The Service will treat the payment of these expenses as a constructive dividend to the shareholders of the acquired corporation. The theory underlying shareholders' expenses stems from a case holding that the acquiring corporation may not assume liabilities which arise in a reorganization without disqualifying the transaction.[19] The payment of these expenses may constitute other consideration not within the purview of B-type stock for stock exchange.

REGISTRATION OF SECURITIES

One of the problems arising is that the additional stock given to an acquired corporation may be unregistered stock and the shareholders may be reluctant to take it. Thus, a provision of the contract may require that such stock be registered with the Securities and Exchange Commission.

This raises the problem as to whether the expenses of registering the securities constitutes additional consideration which violate the "solely for" voting stock requirement of the B-type. But the Service has ruled[20] that the payment by the acquiring corporation of the cost to register the stock it has issued to the acquired corporation's shareholders does not disqualify the B-type reorganization. The theory underlying such ruling is that the stock issued in the reorganization will be on a par with and have the same rights regarding transferability as previously issued to outstanding stock. Thus, such expenses do not constitute "boot" received by the acquired corporation's shareholders.

JUDICIAL INTERPRETATIONS

In a single transaction, property or cash is often exchanged for stock. Also, the other shares are often acquired for cash. The Treasury has treated this type of transaction as two separate types. One as being tax free, and the other as taxable as illustrated in the Howard[21] case. In *Howard*, the court made a separation between the two groups, one receiving cash and the other stock. The court held that cash did not destroy the stock-for-stock reorganization. On the other hand, the court in *Turnbow*[22] held that cash destroys a "B" reorganization. The court made a separation by the type of consideration received, since the shareholder received not only a block of stock but also a cash payment. In *Howard,* the transaction was nontaxable for the shareholders who received only stock for stock and taxable for those who received cash in exchange for their stock under Section 356 which provides for the recognition of gain to the extent of both, that is, money and the fair market value of the other property received. The *Turnbow* result seems logical when you consider the fact that it was not even a reorganization. *Turnbow* exchanged seventy percent cash and thirty percent stock rather than complying with the eighty percent requirement of "solely for" voting stock.

One need not be concerned with the adverse decision of *Turnbow* since cash can still be used in a merger and to a limited extent in a C-type reorganization.

USE OF SUBSIDIARY OF ACQUIRING CORPORATION

A variation of the B-type reorganization which is permitted by the Code provides that the voting stock to be given up can be that of a corporation which is in control of the acquiring corporation. Such a corporation is commonly referred to as a parent corporation. Thus, the B-type reorganization adopts a consolidation approach of realizing that a parent corporation and its subsidiary should, in certain instances, be viewed as one. To make the consolidation approach complete, the law also allows the acquiring corporation to transfer the acquired stock to the subsidiary[23] or to a number of controlled subsidiaries.[24]

The use of the stock of the parent by a subsidiary in a B-type reorganization is commonly referred to as a triangular B-type.[25] Accordingly, the parent will be a party to the reorganization.[26]

One point that must be observed carefully is that the stock given up may be that of the corporation or its parent; there cannot be any mixing. The stock given up must be that of the subsidiary corporation or its parent and not the stock of the subsidiary corporation and its parent.[27]

In addition, it should be realized that the transaction will be granted the special treatment only if the block of stock which secures the required control is obtained solely for voting stock of the acquired corporation or its parent. No other consideration is permitted. However, an important point to remember is that there is no minimum amount of voting stock of the acquiring corporation which must be given up.

STEP TRANSACTION DOCTRINE

The step transaction doctrine involved the application of integration rules which combine a number of steps to see what the overall effect would have been. In the area of B-type reorganization, the doctrine is applied to determine whether the solely for voting stock requirement is satisfied.

In the area of a B-type reorganization, the doctrine has been applied to shareholders of the acquired corporation who immediately dispose of their stock in the acquiring corporation. Such disposition violates the continuity of interest requirement, and the reorganization is a taxable exchange. Furthermore the control requirement will also be violated if the eighty percent control of the other classes of stock are subsequently disposed of by the acquiring corporation.

As previously stated, a "creeping type" of acquisition permits the prior acquisitions of stock of the acquired corporation for any property such as cash. Such a prior acquisition for cash is permitted as long as the nonqualifying transaction was independent of the qualifying transaction. If the immediate and previous acquisition are found to be part of a general plan, then all the transactions will be considered together. The requirement of acquiring control solely for voting stock of the corporation will not be met, and the transaction will be taxable. For example, if X Corp. owns fifty percent of the stock of Y Corp. acquired with cash or any other type of consideration, the acquisition of an additional thirty percent in an exchange for stock will qualify as a B-type reorganization. If the fifty percent was acquired with cash and was found to be part of a plan of acquisition which included the additional thirty percent acquired a short time later, the two transactions could be combined under the step transaction doctrine, and the entire transaction could become taxable because it is no longer a solely for voting stock acquisition. However, if the original fifty percent were acquired years before, the doctrine will be inapplicable.

BUSINESS PURPOSE DOCTRINE

The business purpose doctrine must be met even though the statute is literally complied with.[28] Thus, a tax-free acquisition must be prompted primarily by bona fide business considerations, rather than by tax-saving or other motives not evidencing a business or corporate purpose.

CONTINUITY OF INTEREST

The continuity of interest test is based on the concept that the former owners of the acquired corporation must have a continuing interest in the acquiring corporation via an equity interest, rather than a debt interest. There is no problem in the case of a B-type reorganization since the acquiring corporation can only transfer its stock or the voting stock of its parent. Thus, the continuity of interest rules are automatically complied with in a B-type reorganization exchange.

The requirement of continuity of interest applies only to the total consideration involved in the acquisition and not to each shareholder.[29]

The Service has ruled[30] that the continuity of interest rule will be met when fifty percent or more of the consideration received by the shareholders of the acquired corporation is retained by them in the form of an equity interest in the acquiring corporation. This fifty percent rule is determined on the date of the reorganization.

A problem arises when these shareholders immediately dispose of such stock in the acquiring corporation. The continuity rules will be violated and the B-type reorganization's tax-free nature nullified.

CONTINUITY OF BUSINESS ENTERPRISE

The provisions of the regulations permitting tax-free acquisitions contemplate that a reorganization should result in a continuity of the business enterprise under modified corporate form. This requirement will be met even if the acquiring corporation engages in a different business enterprise than previously engaged in by the acquiring corporation.[31]

CONTINGENT STOCK

The use of contingent stock[32] or the "earn-out" has become common in corporate acquisitions as of late, especially with conglomerates. The principal reason for this is that it is usually extremely difficult to value the acquired business for the purpose of determining the number of shares that the acquiring corporation will issue. Furthermore, differences of opinion usually rise as to the future earnings of the acquired corporation. Thus, many corporation acquisitions involve the payment for the stock based upon future earnings to be made in installments over a relatively short period of time, usually five years.

Basically, the requirements of a deferred stock distribution are as follows: (a) delivery of the stock must not be deferred for a period in excess of five years; (b) there must be a valid business reason for the delayed delivery; (c) the maximum number of shares which must be delivered in the future must be stated; (d) at least fifty percent of the maximum number of shares must be delivered at the time of acquisition; (e) the agreement evidencing the right to receive the additional shares must not be assignable; (f) the agreement must grant the shareholders of the acquired corporation the right to receive only stock of the acquiring corporation or its parent.

If payment of part of the purchase price is deferred for more than six months under a contract in which payments are due more than one year after the sale, a portion of each deferred payment will be taxed as interest.[33] In the case of contingent payments, twelve months is the maximum deferral before interest is imposed. If a four percent interest rate is provided for in the contract, no interest will be imputed (otherwise a five percent rate will be imputed).

Deferred payments of voting stock will not disqualify what would otherwise be a tax-free acquisition "solely for" voting stock even if taxed as part of interest.

As it sometimes happens, stock is escrowed, and any dividends paid with respect to the escrowed stock are income to the acquiring corporation. No interest is imputed with respect to the escrowed stock since it is not deemed a deferred payment.

LIQUIDATION OF ACQUIRED CORPORATION IN A B-TYPE REORGANIZATION

The B-type reorganization invariably results in a parent-subsidiary relationship following either the exchange of the parent's stock or the subsidiary utilizing its parent's stock for the stock of the acquired corporation. Subsequently, the acquired corporation may be liquidated with the assets being transferred either to the parent or a newly created subsidiary. The transaction will be tested as an acquisition of assets rather than as an acquisition of stock, which is a C-type reorganization. Similarly, it may be viewed possibly as an A-type since the net effect of both the A and C type is a transfer of assets subject to liabilities. If the liquidation takes place as a separate step, it will be a tax-free intercorporate liquidation under Section 332.

But if the liquidation step is part of the reorganization, the transaction will be viewed as a C-type of exchange, that is, stock for assets, and, possibly tax free under those provisions.[34] There is some case law support for this holding.[35]

MISCELLANEOUS PROBLEMS OF B TYPES OF EXCHANGES

The compliance problems of a B-type of reorganization exchange are the same as those required for a statutory merger or other type of tax-free reorganization exchange.

Section 381 dealing with carryovers in tax-free reorganizations has no application to a B-type of exchange since a parent-subsidiary relationship is created. If any carryovers are to arise, then the rules of Section 332 are to be examined. The only way for carryover rules to arise is if the B-type is deemed to be a C-type of exchange. If this is the case, then all the twenty-two carryover rules are to be applicable.

There are no recapture of depreciation problems in B-type of reorganizations since, by definition, only voting stock can be exchanged in the reorganization. There are two types of depreciation recapture sections.

Section 1245 provides for the recapture of depreciation taken on personal property after December 31, 1961. This has the effect of reducing the capital gains realized upon a sale of personal property to the extent of depreciation taken after December 31, 1961. Such depreciation is taxed as ordinary income.

Section 1250 provides for the recapture of depreciation on real property after December 31, 1963 to the extent that the accelerated method of depreciation exceeds the straight line method. This similarly reduces capital gain by taxing a portion of the gain as ordinary income to the extent that depreciation is recaptured.

If the stock of a Subchapter S Corporation is acquired in a B-type reorganization, the Subchapter S status is terminated along with all its benefits which are subsequently lost in the year of reorganization. Thus, the Subchapter S status is terminated at the close of the taxable year preceding the year of the exchange. The Service has ruled[36] that such would not be the result if the A-type reorganization method is availed upon. In the statutory merger type, the taxable year will terminate in the year of acquisition, and the Subchapter S benefits, such as, net operation losses and undistributed taxable income, will flow through to the shareholders.

It is advisable in every type of reorganization in which the tax-free nature of the transaction is sought that a ruling request be deemed a part of the overall plan. Such a request should be sent to the National Office of the Internal Revenue Service in Washington, D.C.

As stated in the discussion of statutory mergers, preferred stock may be deemed Section 306 stock. This taint may result in dividend treatment upon the subsequent sale.

The Internal Revenue Service has ruled that convertible preferred stock received by a shareholder in a B-type reorganization will not be deemed Section 306 stock if the following two conditions are met: (1) the convertible preferred stock is widely held, or (2) there is no plan whereby the shareholders of the acquired corporation will hold both common and preferred stock.[37]

EFFECT OF B-TYPE REORGANIZATION ON CORPORATIONS

In the case of a tax-free stock acquisition, the acquiring corporation receives the stock of the acquired corporation at a tax cost equal to the tax cost of that stock in the hands of the shareholders of the acquired corporation immediately before the transaction. Thus, there is a carryover tax basis for the stock of the acquired corporation.[38]

The holding period of the acquired corporation's stock in the hands of the acquiring corporation includes the period during which the stock of the acquired corporation was held by those shareholders. A similar rule applies to the stock in the hands of the former stockholders of the acquired corporation.[39]

The exchange of securities between the two corporations must be pursuant to a plan of reorganization between the two corporations to fall within the purview of the tax-free nature of the reorganization exchange.[40]

EFFECT OF REORGANIZATION EXCHANGE ON SHAREHOLDERS

The shareholders of the acquired corporation receive the voting stock of the acquiring corporation at a tax cost equal to their tax cost for the stock of the acquired corporation which they transferred.[41] Thus, the shareholders will obtain a substituted tax basis for the stock of the acquiring corporation which they receive upon the surrender of stock or securities of the acquired corporation. For example, Co. A transfers their stock to Co. B resulting in control. Shareholders X and Y of Co. B have a tax basis of $1,000 and $2,000 for their stock. They receive 100 and 200 shares of Co. A. X and Y will have a basis for Co. A stock of $1,000 and $2,000 respectively.

The boot provisions have no application to the B-type reorganization, since they can only receive voting stock of the acquiring corporation or its parent, and, nothing else.

Thus, no gain or loss is recognized to the acquiring corporation, the acquired corporation or the shareholders of the acquired corporation as a result of the tax-free acquisition of stock.

As it sometimes occurs, an allocation of basis is required because the shareholders may have a different basis for the stock transferred in the reorganization exchange. The Service has ruled[42] that each block of shares are not grouped together but retain their own individual basis. For example, if shareholder has 200 shares with a basis of $10 for 100 shares and $20 for the balance, and he receives 200 shares from the acquiring corporation, then his basis will not be $15 a share ($1000 + 2000÷200) but will be $10 per share for 100 shares and $20 per share for the remaining 100 shares.

If stock is transferred to the acquiring corporation in return for two or more classes of stock, the shares acquired give rise to an allocation of basis pursuant to the fair market values of the classes received.[43]

TAXABLE STOCK ACQUISITIONS

The shareholders of the acquired corporation will recognize a capital gain or loss from their sale of stock of the acquired corporation. On the other hand, the basis of stock of the acquired corporation to the acquiring corporation will be the tax cost equal to the value of the consideration paid for it. The shareholders of the acquired corporation will receive the additional consideration paid by the acquiring corporation at a tax cost equal to its fair market value if consideration other than cash is used. The holding period to the acquiring corporation and the shareholders of the acquired corporation commences at the date of the taxable acquisition.

ACCOUNTING PROBLEMS

The pooling of interest method will be available in a B-type reorganization since the consideration being exchanged can consist only of voting stock. The purchase method of accounting for business combinations would be inapplicable since cash is usually involved which is prohibited in a B-type reorganization.

SECURITIES REGULATIONS

Rule 133 of the Rules and Regulations of the Securities and Exchange has been interpreted to mean that no registration statement is necessary in the case of an A reorganization or C reorganization. This is based upon the theory that the plan of reorganization will be submitted to a vote of the shareholders pursuant to the applicable state law. Thus, this Rule is inapplicable to a B-type of exchange. Accordingly, a registration statement pursuant to Section 5 of the Securities Act will be required.

This rule can be circumvented by a limited number of shareholders of the acquired corporation whose stock control is to be acquired by permitting such exchanging stockholders to take the stock for investment purposes. This is usually referred to as "letter" stock and it is so noted on the stock certificates. Thus, the stockholders who acquire such stock cannot dispose of it for at least two years.

Another method to be utilized to exempt the exchange of such securities in a B-type of exchange from the registration provisions would be under Section 3(a)(10) of the Securities Act. That section exempts from the registration provisions an exchange of securities approved by an official or agency of the United States who is expressly authorized by law to grant such approval. This rule usually applies to State public utility commissions.

LEGAL CHECKLIST

The following checklist is a useful guide as to the type of provisions which are usually found in a stock for stock exchange agreement:

1. Name of parties
2. Business purpose of the reorganization
3. Transfer of shares
4. Valuation of shares
5. Payout, if used
6. Warranties of the shareholders
7. Shareholder approval
8. Covenants
9. Conveyances
10. Exoneration clause
11. Registration of securities
12. Expenses
13. Stock exchange listing
14. Exoneration clause
15. Employment agreements
16. Examination of books and records
17. Opinion of counsel
18. Delivery of stock
19. Miscellaneous provisions
20. Effective date

EXCHANGE OF STOCK FOR STOCK CHECKLIST

A. Taxable vs. Tax Free
    1. Advantages and disadvantages
B. Consideration Utilized
    1. Voting stock
    2. Effect—parent-subsidiary
    3. Other than stock—taxable
    4. Use of stock of parent

     5. Contingent stock
  C. Regulations Requirements
     1. Business purpose—form versus substance
     2. Continuity of interest—stock versus proprietary interest
     3. 50% test
     4. Continuity of business enterprise
     5. Step transaction doctrine
     6. Record keeping requirements
  D. Plan of Reorganization
     1. Written versus oral
     2. Exchange pursuant to plan
  E. Parties to a Reorganization
     1. Each corporation
     2. Subsidiary using stock of parent
  F. Effect on Corporations
     1. Stock or securities—substituted basis
     2. Boot—gain recognized
     3. Recapture problems
     4. Redemptions
     5. Liquidation—may be C type
     6. Carryover problems
  G. Effect on Shareholders
     1. Substituted basis
     2. Allocation problems among properties received
     3. Boot distribution
     4. Dividend
  H. Accounting Problems
     1. Purchase versus pooling of interest
  I. Legal Problems
     1. Negotiations
     2. Board of Directors authorization
     3. Shareholders approval
     4. Stock exchange listing
     5. Internal Revenue Service ruling
     6. Registration statement, if necessary

For additional information relating to any of the following sections, please see the Prentice-Hall Federal Tax Service.

FOOTNOTES

[1] IRC-1954; Section 368(a)(1)(B).

[2] IRC-1954: Section 368(c).

[3] IRC-1954; Section 368(a)(1)(B); 1.368-2(c).

[4] Rev. Rul 63-34, 1963-2 C.B.148.

[5] Ibid.

[6] Helvering v. Southwest Consolidated Corp., 315 U.S. 194 (1942).

[7] Firestone Tire & Rubber Co., 27.C.827 (1943).

[8] Rev. Rul 70-108, I.R.B. 1970-10.

[9] Rev. Rul 70-172, I.R.B. 1970-15,25.

[10] Rev. Rul 70-269, I.R.B.1970-22,7.

[11] Regulations, 1.368-2(c).

[12] Ibid.

[13] Rev. Rul 59-259, 1956-2 C.B. 115.

[14] Rev. Rul 56-613, 1956-2 C.B. 212.

[15] Richard M. Mills, 331F (2) 321 (1964).

[16] 39 T.C. 393 (1962).

[17] Rev. Rul 66-365, 1966-2 C.B. 116.

[18] Rev. Rul 55-446, 1955-2 C.B. 226.

[19] Helvering v. Southwest Consolidated Corp., 315 U.S. 194 (1942).

[20] Rev. Rul 67-275, 1967-2 C.B. 142.

[21] Howard v. C.I.R., 238F (2d) 943 (1957).

[22] Turnbow v. C.I.R., 82 S. Ct. 353 (1962).

[23] IRC-1954; Section 368(a)(2)(C).

[24] Rev. Rul. 58-93, 1958-1 C.B. 188.

[25] IRC-1954; Section 368(a)(1)(B).

[26] IRC-1954; Section 368(b).

[27] Regulations; 1.368-2(d)(1).

[28] Gregory v. Helvering, 293 U.S. 465 (1935).

[29] Rev. Rul 66-224, 1966-2 C.B.114, Rev. Rul. 66-34, 1966-2 C.B. 1232.

[30] Ibid.

[31] Rev. Rul 63-29, 1963-1 C.B. 77.

[32] Rev. Proc. 66-34, 1966-2 C.B. 1232, Rev. Proc 67-13, 1967-1 C.B. 590.

[33] IRC-1954; Sec. 483.

[34] Rev. Rul 67-274; 1967-2 C.B. 141.

[35] C.I.R. v. Dana, 103F(2) 359(1959).

[36] Rev. Rul. 61-94, 1964-1 C.B. 317.

[37] Rev. Rul 66-34, Section 4, 1966-2 C.B. 1232.

[38] IRC-1954; Section 362.

[39] IRC-1954; Section 358.

[40] IRC-1954; Section 354.

[41]IRC-1954; Section 358.

[42]Revenue Ruling 68-23, 1968-1 C.B. 144.

[43]Regulations; 1.358-2(a)(2); 1.358-2(a)(3).

STOCK FOR STOCK EXCHANGE

Facts

Assume that MAL Corporation is to exchange its stock for the stock of JRG Corporation. Each Corporation has three shareholders, A, B and C in JRG Corporation and X, Y and Z in MAL Corporation. After the stock exchange MAL Corporation will be a wholly-owned subsidiary of JRG Corporation.

The stock of JRG Corporation has a fair market value of $350. Assume further that 5,000 shares of voting stock are given to shareholders of MAL Corporation on December 31, 1970. The book and tax basis are the same.

Tax Consequences

Both JRG and MAL Corporations would be parties to the reorganization. If they adopt a plan of reorganization, the exchange would be effectuated tax free.

JRG Corporation would have the same basis for the stock of MAL Corporation as the basis for its stock in the hands of its shareholders, that is, $100 per share. JRG Corporation is exchanging stock having a basis of $500,000 and fair market value of $1,750,000 for stock worth $100,000 and a fair market value of $350,000.

As to the Shareholders

The shareholders of MAL Corporation would have a basis for the stock of JRG Corporation of $100,000, that is, its basis for MAL Corporation stock.

JRG Corporation would have a basis for the stock of MAL Corporation of $500,000.

Accounting Treatment

Journal Entries

Books of MAL Corporation

Capital Stock	100,000	
Capital Stock		100,000

To record the stock for stock exchange.

Books of JRG Corporation

Investment in MAL Corporation	500,000	
Capital Stock		500,000

To record the acquisition by issuing 5,000 shares at $100 par value.

Accounting Treatment
Journal Entries

As to JRG Corporation

Investment in MAL Corporation	1,750,000	
Capital stock		1,750,000

To record the investment of 5,000 shares at $350 per share.

MAL CORPORATION
Balance Sheet
December 31,1970 (Before Merger)

ASSETS		*Per Books*	*Fair Market Value*
Current Assets:			
Cash		$100,000	$100,000
Accounts receivable	$70,000		
Less: Allowance for bad debts	5,000		
Estimated recovery value		65,000	70,000
Inventory		75,000	100,000
Prepaid expenses		10,000	5,000
TOTAL		$250,000	$275,000
Fixed Assets:			
Machinery & equipment	$200,000		
Less: Accumulated depreciation	50,000		
Book value		$150,000	$300,000
Buildings	$100,000		
Less: Accumulated depreciation	50,000		
Book value		50,000	125,000
TOTAL		$200,000	$425,000
TOTAL ASSETS		$450,000	$700,000

LIABILITIES

Current Liabilities:

Notes payable		$50,000

Accounts payable		20,000	
Federal income tax liability		30,000	
TOTAL		$100,000	$100,000

Long-Term Liabilities:

Loans payable	$100,000		$100,000
TOTAL	200,000		200,000

Stockholders' Equity:

Capital Stock—$100 par value

Authorized	1200			·
Unissued	1000			
Issued	1000	100,000		350,000
Retained Earnings		150,000		150,000

Total Liabilities and Stockholders' Equity	$450,000		$700,000

JRG CORPORATION

Balance Sheet

December 31, 1970 (Before Stock Exchange)

ASSETS		*Per Books*	*Fair Market Value*
Current Assets:			
Cash		$1,000,000	$1,000,000
Accounts receivable	$700,000		
Less: Allowance for bad debts	50,000		
Estimated recovery value		650,000	700,000
Inventory		750,000	1,000,000
Prepaid expenses		100,000	50,000
TOTAL		$2,500,000	$2,750,000
Fixed Assets:			
Buildings	$2,000,000		
Less: Accumulated depreciation	500,000		
Book value		$1,500,000	$3,000,000
Machinery & equipment	$1,000,000		
Less: Accumulated depreciation	500,000		
Book value		500,000	1,250,000
TOTAL		$2,000,000	$4,250,000
TOTAL ASSETS		$4,500,000	$7,000,000

LIABILITIES

Current Liabilities:

Notes payable	$500,000	
Accounts payable	200,000	
Federal income tax payable	300,000	
TOTAL	$1,000,000	$1,000,000

Long-Term Liabilities

Loans payable	$1,000,000		$1,000,000
TOTAL	$1,000,000		$1,000,000

Stockholders's Equity:

Capital Stock par value $100

Authorized	20,000		
Unissued	10,000		
Issued	10,000	$1,000,000	$3,500,000
Capital surplus		500,000	500,000
Retained earnings (or deficit)		1,000,000	1,000,000
Total Liabilities and Stockholders' Equity		$4,500,000	$7,000,000

JRG CORPORATION

Balance Sheet
December 31, 1970 (After Stock Exchange)

ASSETS	Per Books	Fair Market Value
Current Assets:		
Cash		$1,110,000
Accounts receivable	$770,000	
Less: Allowance for bad debts	55,000	
Estimated recovery value		715,000
Inventory		825,000
Prepaid expenses		110,000
TOTAL		$2,750,000
Fixed Assets:		
Machinery & equipment	$2,200,000	
Less: Accumulated depreciation	550,000	
Book value		$1,650,000
Buildings	$1,100,000	
Less: Accumulated depreciation	550,000	

Book Value	550,000
TOTAL	$2,200,000
TOTAL ASSETS	$4,950,000

LIABILITIES

Current Liabilities

Notes payable	$ 550,000	
Accounts payable	220,000	
Federal income tax liability	330,000	
TOTAL		$1,100,000

Long-Term Liabilities:

Loans payable	$1,100,000

Stockholders' Equity:

Capital stock par value $100		
Authorized	20,000	
Unissued	5,000	
Issued	15,000	$1,500,000
Capital surplus		100,000
Retained earnings		1,150,000
Total Liabilities and Stockholders' Equity		$4,950,000

Journal Entry
Capital Stock 100,000
Cap. 400,000
Capital Stock 500,000

Shareholders of JRG Corporation

	A	B	C	TOTAL
Number of Shares	3333	3333	3334	10,000

	X	Y	Z	TOTAL
Number of Shares	1667	1667	1666	5,000
Cumulative	5000	5000	5000	15,000

Basis to:	X	Y	Z	TOTAL
Before	33,333	33,333	33,334	100,000
After-Same	33,333	33,333	33,334	100,000

Basis to JRG Corporation	—	$100,000
Basis to MAL Corporation	—	$500,000

JRG CORPORATION
Balance Sheet
December 31, 1970 (After the Exchange)

ASSETS		*Per Books*	*Fair Market Value*
Current Assets:			
Cash		$1,000,000	$1,000,000
Accounts receivable	$700,000		
Less: Allowance for bad debts	50,000		
Estimated recovery value		650,000	700,000
Inventory		750,000	1,000,000
Prepaid expenses		100,000	50,000
TOTAL		$2,500,000	$3,750,000
Fixed Assets:			
Buildings	$2,000,000		
Less: Accumulated depreciation	500,000		
Book value		$1,500,000	$3,000,000
Machinery & equipment	$1,000,000		
Less: Accumulated depreciation	500,000		
Book value		500,000	1,250,000
TOTAL		$2,000,000	$4,250,000
Other Assets:			
Investment in MAL Corporation		500,000	
TOTAL ASSETS		$5,000,000	$7,000,000

LIABILITIES

Current Liabilities:			
Notes payable		$ 500,000	
Accounts payable		200,000	
Federal income tax payable		300,000	
TOTAL		$1,000,000	$1,000,000
Long-Term Liabilities:			
Loans payable	$1,000,000		$1,000,000
TOTAL	$1,000,000		$1,000,000

Stockholders' Equity:

Capital stock par value $100
  Authorized   20,000
  Unissued   5,000

Issued	15,000	$1,500,000	$3,500,000
Capital surplus		500,000	500,000
Retained earnings (or deficit)		1,000,000	1,000,000
Total Liabilities and Stockholders' Equity		$5,000,000	$7,000,000

TAXABLE STOCK EXCHANGE

Assume the same facts except that JRG Corporation acquires only fifty percent control.

Tax Consequences

As to MAL Corporation

Since at least eighty percent control was not met, the entire transaction is taxable.

As to the Shareholders

The shareholders of MAL Corporation would have a recognized gain or loss for the stock they receive as follows:

Fair market value—$350 x 5,000 shares	$1,750,000
Less: Adjusted Basis	500,000
Recognized Gain	$1,250,000

The gain would probably be a dividend on the basis of the Bedford decision.

As to JRG Corporation

JRG Corporation would have a basis for the stock received from the shareholders of MAL Corporation of $1,750,000, that is, the consideration exchanged for the stock.

Accounting Treatment
Journal Entries

As to JRG Corporation

Investment in MAL Corporation	$1,750,000	
Capital Stock		$1,750,000

To record investment of 5,000 shares at $350 per share

JRG CORPORATION
Balance Sheet
December 31, 1970 (After the Exchange)

ASSETS		*Per Books*	*Fair Market Value*
Current Assets:			
Cash		$1,000,000	$1,000,000
Accounts receivable	$700,000		
Less: Allowance for			
bad debt	50,000		
Estimated recovery value		650,000	700,000
Inventory		750,000	1,000,000
Prepaid expenses		100,000	50,000
TOTAL		$2,500,000	$2,750,000
Fixed Assets:			
Buildings	$2,000,000		
Less: Accumulated			
depreciation	500,000		
Book value		$1,500,000	$3,000,000
Machinery & equip-			
ment	$1,000,000		
Less: Accumulated			
depreciation	500,000		
Book value		500,000	1,250,000
Other Assets:			
Investment in MAL Corporation		1,750,000	
TOTAL		3,750,000	$4,250,000
TOTAL ASSETS		$6,250,000	$7,000,000
LIABILITIES			
Current Liabilities:			
Notes payable		$ 500,000	
Accounts payable		200,000	
Federal income tax payable		300,000	
TOTAL		$1,000,000	$1,000,000
Long-Term Liabilities:			
Loans payable	$1,000,000		$1,000,000
TOTAL	$1,000,000		$1,000,000

Stockholders' Equity:

		Per Books	Fair Market Value
Capital stock, par value	$100		
Authorized	20,000		
Unissued	5,000		
Issued	15,000	$1,500,000	$3,500,000
Capital surplus		$1,750,000	500,000
Retained earnings (or deficit)		$1,000,000	1,000,000
Total Liabilities and Stockholders' Equity		$6,250,000	$7,000,000

MAL CORPORATION

Balance Sheet

December 31, 1970 (After the Exchange)

ASSETS		*Per Books*	*Fair Market Value*
Current Assets:			
Cash		$100,000	$100,000
Accounts receivable	$70,000		
Less: Allowance for bad debts	5,000		
Estimated recovery value		65,000	70,000
Inventory		75,000	100,000
Prepaid expenses		10,000	5,000
TOTAL		$250,000	$275,000
Fixed Assets:			
Machinery & equipment	$200,000		
Less: Accumulated depreciation	50,000		
Book value		$150,000	$300,000
Buildings	$100,000		
Less: Accumulated depreciation	50,000		
Book value		50,000	$125,000
TOTAL		$200,000	$425,000
TOTAL ASSETS		$450,000	$700,000

LIABILITIES			
Current Liabilities:			
Notes payable		$ 50,000	
Accounts payable		20,000	
Federal income tax liability		30,000	
TOTAL		$100,000	$100,000

Long-Term Liabilities:

Loans payable	$100,000		$100,000
TOTAL	$200,000		$200,000

Stockholders' Equity:

Capital Stock, $100 par value

Authorized	1,200		
Unissued	1,000		
Issued	1,000	$100,000	$350,000
Retained Earnings		$150,000	$150,000
Total Liabilities and Stockholders' Equity		$450,000	$700,000

The Stock for Assets and Recapitalization Type of Tax-Free Reorganization *6*

The C type of reorganization exchange is defined as "the acquisition by one corporation, in exchange for all or a part of its voting stock (or in exchange solely for all or a part of the voting stock of a corporation which is in control of the acquiring corporation), of substantially all the properties of another corporation."[1] In determining whether the exchange is solely for stock, the assumption by the acquiring corporation of a liability of the other, or the fact that property acquired is subject to a liability shall be disregarded.[2] Basically, a C type of exchange is a stock for assets exchange.

The C type overlaps with both the A and B types of reorganization exchanges. As regards the B type, the similarity is attributable to the fact that they both require the acquiring corporation to exchange or issue solely voting stock, or the voting stock of its parent corporation. In the case of a merger, the similarity arises from the fact that assets are acquired and transferred to the acquiring corporation or a newly issued subsidiary formed to receive it in return for stock. Thus, the assets of the acquired corporation become part of the assets of the acquiring corporation. The C type is usually referred to as a "practical merger" because of its similarity to the A type of exchange. The acquired corporation is usually liquidated after its assets have been acquired since the acquired corporation is only a shell holding stock of the acquiring corporation.

Among the advantages of the C-type of exchange are the following: (1) the assumption of only specific liabilities usually occurs; (2) there is generally an absence of dissenting or minority shareholders' rights like in the A-type; (3) a limited amount of boot is permissible which is impossible in the B-type. Some of the disadvantages of the C-type are the following: (1) state law requires shareholders' approval to dispose of substantially all its assets; (2) the acquired corporation is usually a shell having as its only asset the stock of the acquired corporation. This is usually the case since such corporation may be a personal holding company after the acquisition. This will be discussed later in this chapter.

MECHANICS OF THE EXCHANGE OF VOTING STOCK FOR ASSETS

In order to qualify as a reorganization under the C-type of provisions, one corporation must acquire substantially all the properties of another corporation solely in exchange for all or part of its voting stock. Another way to accomplish such a result is to issue all or a part of the voting stock of another corporation which is in control of the acquiring corporation. This is the triangular C-type of exchange where S, the subsidiary corporation, acquires substantially all the assets of A, the acquired corporation, in exchange for the voting stock of P Corporation received in exchange for voting stock of both corporation P and Corporation S, the transaction is not a C-type of transfer.

The following example will illustrate the basic type of C-type of exchange: Corporation P wishes to acquire X Corporation in a C-type of reorganization. It issues part of its voting stock to X Corporation in exchange for all of X's assets and all of its liabilities. The exchange is a tax-free exchange. Subsequent to the exchange, X Corporation liquidates and distributes the P stock to its stockholders as a liquidating distribution in exchange for the X Corporation stock. The shareholders of X Corporation will similarly receive the stock tax free.

In determining whether the exchange meets the requirements of "solely for voting stock," the assumption by the acquiring corporation of liabilities of the transferor corporation, or the fact that property acquired from the transferor corporation is subject to a liability shall be disregarded. Such an assumption does not prevent an exchange from being solely for voting stock; it may in some cases alter the character of the transaction as to place the transaction outside the C type of tax-free exchange.

The other method of C type of exchange is that one corporation must acquire substantially of the properties of another corporation in such manner that the acquisition would qualify for tax-free treatment if the acquiring corporation exchanges money, or other property in addition to such voting stock, it must acquire, solely for voting stock, the properties of the other corporation having a fair market value which is at least eighty percent of the fair market value of all the properties of the other corporation.[3] The voting stock must be either of the acquiring corporation or of a corporation which is in control of the acquiring corporation. As regards the properties acquired, a liability assumed or to which the properties are subject is considered money paid for the properties. For example, Corporation A has properties with a fair market value of $100,000 and liabilities of $10,000. In exchange for these properties, Corporation Y transfers its own voting stock, assumes the $10,000 liabilities, and pays $8,000 in cash. The transaction is a reorganization even though a part of the properties of Corporation A is acquired for cash. On the other hand, if the properties of Corporation A worth $100,000 were subject to $50,000 in liabilities, an acquisition of all the properties subject to the liabilities, for any consideration other than solely voting stock, would not qualify as a reorganization under this section since the liabilities alone are in excess of twenty percent of the fair market value of the properties.

REQUIREMENTS OF THE C-TYPE OF EXCHANGE

Generally speaking, these are two basic requirements necessary to effectuate a C-type of exchange, namely, (1) the assets acquired from the transferor corporation, and, (2) the consideration being exchanged is limited solely to voting stock given by the acquiring corporation either directly or by its subsidiary.[4]

After the asset acquisition, the acquired corporation is usually liquidated in a complete liquidation under Section 331 of the Internal Revenue Code. As an alternative, it can remain in existence as a holding company for the stock of the acquiring corporation.

One area of flexibility in connection with a C-type of exchange is that the assets may be transferred to either an existing or a newly organized subsidiary, without disqualifying the transaction in part. One ruling[5] permitted some of the assets to be retained by the parent and the balance transferred to several controlled subsidiaries.

In either case, if the parent uses its stock to acquire the assets, or the subsidiary uses the voting stock of its parent, the triangular C, the statutory requirement of "a party to a reorganization," will have been complied with.

One danger in trying to effectuate a C-type exchange could possibly be deemed a divisive D-type reorganization (discussed in a subsequent chapter). If such should be the result, the Code provides that it will be deemed to be a D-type exchange rather than a C-type.[6] The statute requires that substantially all the assets of the transfer or acquired corporation must be acquired in order to meet the C-type exchange requirements. Neither the Code nor the Regulations elaborate on this "substantially all" requirement. Hence, many practical problems arise in utilizing the C-type.

The Treasury's position for ruling purposes was that an operating asset test[7] had to be met to comply with the "substantially all" requirement. By this was meant that all the assets except assets to extinguish its remaining liabilities had to be transferred by the transferor corporation. This test has been replaced by a percentage of asset test.[8] This test provides that a transfer of assets representing at least ninety percent of the fair market value of the net assets *and* at least seventy percent of the fair market value of the gross assets held by the transferor immediately before the transfer. It should be noted that the test is a twofold test as evidenced by the word "and" and lack of the word "or" in the requirement. For example, if T, the transferor corporation, has net assets of $1,500,000 and gross assets of $1,000,000 the transfer of $900,000 of assets will satisfy the "substantially all" test.

It should be noted that this test is only a guide and there is no prohibition against the facts and circumstances of each proposed transaction qualifying as meeting the "substantially all" test.

In the retention of sufficient assets to satisfy liabilities, the Service held (1) that it makes little difference if the transferor transfers all the assets subject to its liabilities which are paid for by the transferee, or (2) if the transferor pays the liabilities prior to the transfer of assets.[9]

On the other hand, if the assets not transferred are used to continue a business, serious doubt exists if the "substantially all" test has been met. If the test is not met, it will be deemed a taxable transaction,[10] unless it meets the D-type reorganization.

If all the operating assets are transferred except cash, the "substantially all" test will be satisfied.[11] The retained assets should not be more than ten percent of its net assets in order to redeem the stock of minority shareholders pursuant to the appraisal rights of state law.[12]

It sometimes happens that only specific assets are desired by the acquiring corporation. Thus, if some assets are retained, it may pose serious problems which could disqualify the C-type exchange. Thus, the acquired corporation may dispose of unwanted assets by way of a sale, distribute them to its shareholders, or use a spin-off of assets.

The effect of a sale to unrelated parties does not pose any problems in effectuating such a C-type reorganization, but no authority exists for this position. The distribution of unwanted assets to the transferor's shareholders in in a taxable distribution will not disqualify the subsequent C-type exchange. If there is a spin-off of unwanted assets, the spin-off would be taxable as a dividend to the shareholders receiving the unwanted assets. The balance of the assets would then be transferred to the acquiring corporation.[13] In one case,[14] the Commissioner was sustained in holding that creation of a new subsidiary with a transfer of the unwanted assets to it was a dividend and the subsequent transfer of assets to the acquiring corporation was not a C-type exchange. It should be noted that a spin-off followed by a statutory merger was taxable in one circuit and tax free[15] in other.

CONSIDERATION OF ACQUIRING CORPORATION

The acquiring corporation must use its own or its parent's voting stock to effect the acquisition. But the C-type exchange is more flexible than the B-type exchange since the acquiring corporation is permitted to use a limited amount of money or other property other than voting stock as consideration. Similarly, the acquiring corporation may assume the liabilities of the acquired corporation or take its liabilities.

Some differences between the A-type and C-type is that deeds and other documents of transfer are not necessary in the A-type, since the assets and liabilities of the acquired corporation pass to the acquiring corporation by operation of law. In a C-type exchange all legal documents are required for conveyance of property. In a C-type exchange, a disposition of unwanted assets may violate the "substantially all" test. This presents no problem in a statutory merger since they can dispose of unwanted assets without affecting the tax-free nature of the exchange.

An exchange is still considered solely for voting stock if, besides giving voting stock, the acquired corporation assumes a liability of the other corporation, or acquires substantially all of the properties of Co. B solely for voting stock and the assumption of a mortgage on the property, the transaction will qualify as a reorganization. If the liabilities are too high a proportion of the consideration given for the property, the reorganization may fail to qualify because of violation of the continuity of interest rules.[16]

If, however, the acquiring corporation gives cash or other property, the total of their value and the value of the assumed liabilities cannot exceed twenty percent of the fair market of the value of the property acquired.[17] Otherwise, there is no reorganization.

USE OF SUBSIDIARY IN C-TYPE EXCHANGE

A C-type reorganization may be effected by exchanging the stock of its parent by a corporation which is in control of the acquiring corporation.[18] This permits a subsidiary to use the stock of its parent to acquire the assets of another corporation. The only restriction is that a mixing of the stock of the parent and subsidiary is prohibited.[19] In other words, the voting stock of either corporation can be used and not the voting stock of the parent and subsidiary corporation. Furthermore, the assets acquired can be transferred to either the parent or subsidiary or both, for example, Corporation Z in exchange for stock of S and stock of P, its parent. Under the

Regulations, S could use either its own stock, or P's stock but not both. On the other hand, if Corporation P acquires substantially all of the assets of corporation Y in exchange for stock of S its subsidiary, this will not qualify as a C-type exchange. There is no authorization for the parent to use voting stock of the subsidiary to acquire the assets, whether or not the parent subsequently transfers the assets to the subsidiary.

LIQUIDATION OF ACQUIRED CORPORATION

The C-type exchange differs from the B-type exchange since "substantially all" the assets must be acquired in one transaction. This must be contrasted to the B-type exchange where once eighty percent of the stock is acquired, subsequent acquisitions will continue to qualify as a B-type reorganization. Furthermore, the prior ownership of stock will not prevent a B-type exchange from being effectuated. The C-type of exchange has no statutory counterpart.

In actual practice, after a B-type of exchange, the acquired corporation, now a subsidiary, is liquidated. The exchange will be viewed by the Internal Revenue Service as a C-type reorganization.[20] If it is to be tax free, the C-type requirements must be met. The liquidation in all probability will be tax free under Section 332 of the Internal Revenue Code.

The most significant case arising in connection with a C-type of exchange has been the Bausch & Lomb decision. The *Bausch & Lomb* decision applies when the acquiring corporation is already a shareholder of transferor and desires to liquidate the transferor. In the case, the acquiring corporation owned 79.9 percent of the transferor's stock and issued its voting stock to the minority shareholders. The court held that the purported C-type exchange was a taxable liquidation, since the acquiring corporation had acquired the assets partly in exchange for its own stock and partly in exchange for the transferor's stock. This case arose under the 1939 Code and has not been overruled to date. Accordingly, its holding could still be used to prevent liquidations when the acquiring corporation is already a stockholder of the transferor corporation. However, the Service has ruled[22] that a transaction qualified as a C-type exchange when the transferor remained in existence solely to hold the stock of the acquiring corporation.

Another way to avoid this result would be for a statutory merger into the acquiring corporation to occur. This is probably the best way from a practical approach.

If a B-type exchange is followed by the liquidation of the acquired corporation, the exchange will be treated as an aborted attempt at a tax-free C-type exchange, because the acquiring corporation held the stock in the acquired corporation prior to the exchange of stock under the Bausch & Lomb decision.

STEP TRANSACTION DOCTRINE

The step transaction doctrine could be used in the C-type exchange to find that the continuity of interest rules were violated if there is no stock distributed to the shareholder of the acquired corporation. Similarly, the doctrine could be invoked to find that the "substantially all" test was not met when assets were used to redeem stock or were disposed of prior to the exchange.

If there is a piecemeal plan to acquire assets over a period of time, the doctrine could be invoked because the C-type exchange provides that "substantially all" the assets must be acquired in one transaction. Furthermore, a redemption occurring prior to an otherwise valid C-type exchange could resurrect the doctrine to find that the acquiring corporation did not acquire substantially all of the assets of the acquired corporation.

THE BUSINESS PURPOSE DOCTRINE

The business purpose doctrine, as previously stated in both the A-type and B-type of exchanges, is applicable to the C-type reorganization. The Service has ruled[23] that any ruling request include a "full statement of the business reasons for the transaction."

CONTINUITY OF INTEREST REQUIREMENT

Since the C-type exchange requires that the voting stock of the acquiring corporation be issued, there are no problems presented since the transaction will automatically comply with the continuity of interest requirements. The problems arise if the stock acquired is subsequently disposed of; then the step transaction may violate the tax-free nature of the exchange.

RULING REQUEST

The safest course of action to pursue in order to insure the tax-free nature of a transaction is to secure a specific ruling, in advance, from the Commissioner stating the tax consequences of the proposed transactions will be tax free. Such a ruling will be respected by the Service as long as the completed transaction is substantially in accordance with the facts stated in the ruling request, and the taxpayer has relied on the ruling in undertaking the transaction.

MISCELLANEOUS CONSIDERATIONS
IN C-TYPE TRANSACTIONS

The Internal Revenue Service has ruled[24] that cash may be used in a C-type of reorganization exchange by an acquiring corporation in lieu of the issuance of fractional shares to the shareholders of the acquired corporation without violating the solely for voting stock rule. The effect of the cash distribution will be treated as a payment in redemption of the fractional share interest under Section 302.

As previously stated in connection with the A-type and B-type of exchanges, the use of contingent stock is permissible. The Service[25] has similarly provided for the use of such stock in C-type exchanges. Any expenses pursuant to the reorganization exchange must be paid for by the acquiring corporation. The expenses of the acquired corporation should be borne by them. If the acquiring corporation pays the expenses of the acquired corporation, the Service could take the position that consideration in addition to the voting stock is being given in exchange for the stock of the acquired corporation. This could result in a disqualification under the C-type of exchange. The effect of the payment of brokerage, legal, accounting and other relevant expenses incurred by the acquired corporation in a C-type reorganization borne by the shareholders are capital expenditures, thereby increasing the basis for their stock. This result is predicated upon a Supreme Court[26] decision holding that an acquired corporation cannot assume liabilities of the acquired corporation arising out of the reorganization itself with the possible exception of the twenty percent rule.

The reporting requirements of the C-type exchanges are the same as required in both the A-type and B-type of exchange.

Section 381 provides that the attributes of the transferor corporation are carried over to the acquiring corporation upon the occurrence of a C-type of exchange. Among the attributes carried over are the following: (1) net operating losses, (2) capital losses, (3) accounting methods, (4) depreciation, and (5) earnings and profits. They will be discussed, along with the other carryover attributes, more fully in a subsequent chapter.

As regards the depreciation recapture rules of tangible personal property and real property, no recapture problems are present. The statute provides that if the "basis of property in the hands of a transferee is determined by reference to its basis in the hands of the transferor by reason of Section 361, then, the amount of gain taken into account by the transferor shall not exceed the amount of gain recognized to the transferor on the transfer of such property."[27] In effect, it means that the transferor who receives only stock or securities from the acquiring corporation will not realize any income attributable to the recapture of depreciation when such "tainted property" is transferred. The converse of the situation will occur when boot is received by the acquiring corporation; then, gain will be recognized to the extent such boot is retained by the acquired corporation. If such boot is distributed to the shareholders when the acquired corporation is liquidated, then no gain shall be recognized to the transferor. Instead, the gain applicable to the boot will be recognized by the shareholders of the acquired corporation.

REORGANIZATION EXCHANGE EFFECT ON CORPORATION

No gain or loss is recognized to a corporation that is a party to a reorganization when it exchanges property solely for stock or securities in another party to the same reorganization.[28] Thus, the acquired corporation would not recognize any gain or loss on the transfer of its assets in exchange for voting stock of the acquiring corporation if it should liquidate.[29] If the corporation is not liquidated, then the basis to the acquiring corporation for the assets received is the basis to the acquired corporation increased by the gain recognized to the acquired corporation. The gain recognized to the acquired corporation is recognized to the extent that the consideration received and retained by it consists of cash or property other than stock or securities of the acquiring corporation or its parent.[30] On the other hand, if such boot is distributed by the transferor corporation to its shareholders, no gain will be recognized to them.[31] If a subsidiary uses the stock of its parent to acquire the assets of another corporation, the tax cost to the parent of the stock in the subsidiary is the basis for the assets acquired. The subsidiary will have a carryover basis for the assets received which is the same as the basis in the hands of the acquired corporation.[32]

EFFECT OF REORGANIZATION EXCHANGE
TO SHAREHOLDERS

No gain or loss will be recognized to shareholders of the acquired corporation so long as the consideration received by them consists of (1) stock of the acquiring corporation or (2) securities of the acquiring corporation not in excess of the principal amount of securities of the acquired corporation surrendered.[33] If cash or property referred to as boot is received by shareholders of the acquired corporation in amounts pro rata to their stock, the gain, if any, is taxable to them as ordinary income.[34] If a shareholder of the acquired corporation receives only cash or property, it should be taxable as capital gain.[35]

The basis for the stock or securities received by the shareholders of the acquired corporation is a substituted basis, that is, the basis for the stock of acquiring corporation is the same as that of the acquired corporation.

Since the liabilities of the transferor corporation have been assumed by the acquiring corporation, the amount of such assumption will be considered boot for other purposes.[36] Consequently, the basis of the voting stock of the acquiring corporation, in the hands of the transferor corporation, will be equal to the basis of the assets transferred less the amount of the liabilities assumed.[37]

TAXABLE STOCK ACQUISITIONS

If the C-type transaction fails to qualify as a tax-free reorganization, then the results will vary depending upon whether it is the acquiring or acquired corporation or shareholders that receive the consideration being exchanged.

The acquiring corporation will have a tax basis equal to the value of the consideration given to acquire those assets. Such consideration paid must be allocated among the various assets acquired on the basis of relative fair market values.[38]

The acquired corporation will have a recognized gain as a result of the disposition of its assets in the taxable transaction. Similarly, any loss would be recognized by the acquired corporation. The fair market value of property or boot is the value of such consideration received.[39]

If the corporation is liquidated, the gain recognized would be taxed to the shareholders for the stock distributed to them. Similarly, the shareholders would be able to deduct any losses recognized on the exchange of their stock in the acquired corporation for stock and other property of the acquiring corporation.

OVERLAP OF C-TYPE AND TAX-FREE INCORPORATION

A problem frequently arising is whether an exchange is a tax-free reorganization or a tax-free incorporation. This situation comes into play when a corporation acquires the assets and assumes the liabilities of another corporation in exchange for the voting stock of an acquiring corporation. In both situations, one might say that such a result is immaterial since no gain or loss is recognized, and the basis of the transferred property in the hands of the transferor carries over to the transferee. But it is important to distinguish between these situations since undesirable results could occur. For example, in a C-type exchange, the accounting methods of the transferee corporation carry over. This result could be sidetracked by the acquiring corporation taking back stock and "boot." Thus, the C-type provisions would be circumvented since the solely voting stock requirement would be violated.

The Service has ruled that a transaction which meets the requirements of both a reorganization and a tax-free incorporation will be treated as a reorganization.[40]

ACCOUNTING REQUIREMENTS

The purchase method rather than the pooling of interest method should be utilized to account for the C-type of business combination. The reason is that assets are being acquired rather than stock, as in a B-type reorganization. The basic problem in an acquisition of assets is one of valuation. It is here that an appraisal would be of substantial value.

SECURITIES REGULATION

The C-type of exchange presents no problem under the 1933 Securities Act. This is attributable to Rule 133 which, in effect, provides that no registration statement is required in a C-type reorganization if, in accordance with state law, the plan of reorganization is submitted to a vote of the shareholders.

PERSONAL HOLDING COMPANY PROBLEMS

One of the traps for the unwary that rises in connection with a stock for assets exchange is the threat of a personal holding company problem. This is attributable to the fact that the acquiring corporation has acquired "substantially all" the assets of the acquired corporation, and the acquired corporation usually is only a holding company with the stock of the acquiring corporation as its principal asset. This problem does not arise when the acquired corporation liquidates tax-free under Section 331.

A personal holding company is one which meets two tests—an income test and a stock ownership test. The penalty for being labeled a personal holding company is that it pays a tax at a seventy percent rate in addition to the normal tax and surtax.[41]

A corporation is a personal holding company when more than sixty percent of its adjusted ordinary gross income for the taxable year is personal holding company income.[42] Personal holding company income[43] is adjusted ordinary gross income from the following items: (1) dividends, interest, royalties and annuities, (2) rent, (3) oil and gas royalties, (4) copyright royalties, (5) payments for the use of corporate property by a shareholder owning, directly or indirectly, twenty-five percent or more in value of the outstanding stock at any time during the tax year, (6) payments under personal service contracts.

Ordinary gross income is gross income less capital gains and Section 1231 gains. From this difference is subtracted rents to the extent of related deductions for property taxes, mortgage interest and depreciation which will result in adjusted ordinary gross income.[44]

Adjusted rent is not personal holding company income if it is at least fifty percent of adjusted ordinary gross income, and any other personal holding company income that exceeds ten percent of ordinary gross income is paid out in dividends.[45]

The stock ownership test must be met even if the income is personal holding company type income. A corporation is not a personal holding company unless more than fifty percent in value of its outstanding stock is owned, directly or indirectly, by or for five or less individuals at any time during the last half of the tax year.[46] The attribution rules are also applied to determine if the stock ownership test is met.[47]

The seventy percent tax is applied[48] to undistributed personal holding company income which is taxable income with certain adjustments such as: (1) federal income taxes accrued, (2) charitable contributions, (3) the excess of net long-term capital gains over short-term capital losses less the applicable taxes and (4) dividends paid deduction. The latter deduction includes: (1) dividends paid during the taxable year, (2) consent dividends when the dividend is picked up by the shareholder in gross income without receiving cash and thus, his basis for the stock investment is increased, (3) dividends paid after the close of the tax year and, (4) dividends carryover.

Thus, it becomes apparent that the tax burden of being labeled a personal holding company can be severe. The way to avoid it is to use the retained assets to generate business type income rather than personal holding company income. A liquidation of the corporation will also forestall such a problem. The last way is to have an unrelated party become a shareholder prior to the consummation of the C-type exchange.

LEGAL PROBLEMS

The approval of the shareholders is required pursuant to state law in a C-type of exchange. In New York, the statute requires approval of both the board of directors and the shareholders. Two-thirds vote of the shareholders is required for there to be a sale or other asset disposition.[49]

If the assets acquired are transferred to a new corporation formed under the same name as the existing corporation, then, upon the expiration of thirty days from the filing of the certificate of incorporation of the new corporation, with the consent of the state tax commission attached, the existing corporation shall be automatically dissolved.[50] The only exception to the foregoing rule is that if such corporation shall change its name within the thirty-day period.[51]

As in the merger, any dissenting shareholders have the right to receive payment for their shares if they perfect their statutory rights. This can be avoided by a triangular C-type of exchange.

In addition, there might have to be an application to the various stock exchanges to list the voting stock being issued to the acquired corporation.

LEGAL CHECKLIST

The following checklist contains the type of provisions usually found in a stock for assets agreement:

1. Name of parties
2. Sale and transfer of assets
3. Consideration for the transfer
4. Instruments of conveyance and transfer
5. Date of closing
6. Change and use of name
7. Representation and warranties by seller and buyer

8. Description of asset
9. Financial statements
10. Tax audit
11. Title to assets
12. Lists of properties, contracts and other data
13. Conditions percedent to buyer's obligations
14. Conditions precedent to seller's obligations
15. Distribution and dissolution
16. Expenses of reorganization
17. Subsidiaries
18. State law controlling
19. Miscellaneous
20. Effective date

STOCK FOR ASSETS EXCHANGE CHECKLIST

A. Taxable vs. Tax Free
    1. Advantages and disadvantages
B. Consideration Utilized
    1. Voting stock
    2. Use of stock of parent
    3. Contingent stock
    4. Other than stock—taxable
    5. Limited amount of boot—20%
C. Regulations Requirements
    1. Business purpose—form versus substance
    2. Continuity of interest—stock versus proprietary interest.
    3. 50% test
    4. Continuity of business enterprise
    5. Step Transaction Doctrine
    6. Record keeping requirement
D. Plan of Reorganization
    1. Written versus oral
    2. Exchange pursuant to plan
E. Parties to a Reorganization
    1. Each corporation
    2. Subsidiary using stock of parent
F. Acquired Corporation
    1. "Substantially all" test
    2. Liquidation problems—tax free
    3. Boot—gain recognized
G. Effect on Corporations
    1. Stock or securities
    2. Boot—gain recognized
    3. Recapture problems
    4. Redemption
    5. Carryover problems

H. Effect on Shareholders
  1. Substituted basis
  2. Allocation problems among properties received
  3. Boot distribution
  4. Dividend
I. Accounting Problems
  1. Purchase
  2. Valuation problems
J. Legal Problems
  1. Negotiations
  2. Board of Directors authorization
  3. Shareholders' approval
  4. Certificate of dissolution
  5. Stock exchange listing
  6. Internal Revenue Service ruling
  7. Rule 133

THE E-TYPE OF REORGANIZATION

Another type of reorganization exchange which is used very sparingly in the business world is recapitalization. This is attributable to the fact that only one corporation is involved.

The E-type of exchange is defined in the Code[52] simply as a recapitalization. Neither the Code nor the Regulations define such a term. Basically, it involves a reshuffling of the capital structure within the framework of an existing corporation.[53]

An E-type of reorganization will occur if there is a rearrangement of equity and debt instruments of a corporation. For example, stocks and bonds will be readjusted as to amount outstanding, dividend rate or interest rate or an agreement between the stockholders and creditors to increase or decrease the capitalization or debts of the corporation or both.[54]

The Regulations[55] illustrate a recapitalization as follows:

1. Corporation X discharges $200,000 par value in outstanding bonds by issuing preferred stock in cancellation thereof.
2. There is surrendered to a corporation for cancellation twenty-five percent of its preferred stock in exchange for no par value common stock.
3. A corporation issues preferred stock, previously authorized but unissued for outstanding common stock.
4. An exchange is made of a corporation's outstanding preferred stock, having certain priorities with reference to the amount and time of payment of dividends and the distribution of the corporate assets upon liquidation, for a new issue of the corporation's common stock having no such rights.
5. A corporation's outstanding preferred stock with dividends in arrears is exchanged for a similar amount of a corporation's preferred stock in addition to the stock (preferred or common) for the dividends in arrears.

Thus, the E-type of reorganization, as illustrated above, indicates that what is usually involved is an exchange of debt instruments for equity securities or an exchange of one form of equity security for another form of equity security, or the exchange of one form of debt security for another form of debt security. Perhaps the major pitfall in such a form of reorganization is that the exchange will constitute a taxable distribution to the shareholders.

PLAN OF REORGANIZATION

There should be a plan of reorganization in order to be afforded the nonrecognition of gain in the recapitalization exchange. Although it is not expressly required under the tax law, it should be assumed that compliance with state corporation laws was met to effectuate a recapitalization.

This will almost always entail an amendment to the corporation's charter which requires approval by shareholders of the corporation.[56] The amended charter will have to be accepted for filing by the Secretary of State of the state of incorporation.[57]

CONTINUITY OF INTEREST DOCTRINE

The continuity of interest requirement is not applicable to a statutory recapitalization since only one corporation is involved. But under Section 354(a)(2), a partial continuity of interest rule can be spelled out since only securities may be distributed tax free under the 1954 Code.

MISCELLANEOUS RECAPITALIZATION PROBLEMS

Since an E-type usually involves only one corporation, no carryover problems are presented.

The taxable year remains the same since only one corporation is involved in the recapitalization exchange.

No accounting problems are presented in a recapitalization exchange since no business combination is involved. Rather, the accounting problems involve the concept of a quasi-reorganization.

A quasi-reorganization involves an adjustment of asset values downward. It gives the corporation a "fresh start" with the expense and other disadvantages attributable to the creation of a new corporate entity. It usually is done to eliminate a deficit.

No legal formalities are necessary to effectuate such a reorganization. It may take the form of offsetting of operating deficits against paid-in surplus which does not affect the net amount legally available for dividends. On the other hand, the change in the capital structure may be such as to necessitate obtaining an amendment of the corporate structure.

It is not necessary that a deficit exist before a quasi-reorganization be effectuated. It may develop as a result of asset write-downs because the fixed assets are overvalued.

The financial statements rendered after the close of the period in which a quasi-reorganization was effectuated must fully disclose all the facts. The retained earnings account, basically, the earnings and profits of the corporation, should be dated for at least a ten-year period.

The Securities and Exchange Commission in Accounting Series Release No. 25 states that "... a quasi-reorganization may not be considered to have been effected unless ... the entire procedure is made known to all persons entitled to vote on matters of general corporate policy and the appropriate consents to the particular transactions are obtained in advance in accordance with the applicable law and charter provisions."

NONTAXABLE EXCHANGE EFFECT ON CORPORATIONS

No gain or loss shall be recognized if stock or securities in a corporation are exchanged solely for stock or securities in such corporation.[58] Thus, the corporation will realize no gain or loss on the exchange. Furthermore, the basis of the stock or securities exchanged will be equal to the basis of the stock or securities received.[59]

REORGANIZATION EXCHANGE EFFECT ON SHAREHOLDERS

In the E-type of exchange, the same rules are applicable to shareholders as previously discussed in the A, B and C types of exchanges along with all its ramifications including the boot provisions.

FOOTNOTES

[1] IRC-1954; Section 368(a)(1)(c).

[2] Ibid.

[3] Regulations; 1.368-2(d)(2)(i) and (ii).

[4] Ibid.

[5] Revenue Ruling 68-261, 1968-1 C.B. 147.

[6] IRC-1954; Section 368(a)(2)(A).

[7] Revenue Ruling 57-518, 1957-2 C.B. 253.

[8] Revenue Procedure 66-34, 1966-2 C.B. 1232.

[9] Revenue Ruling 57-518, 1957-2 C.B. 253.

[10] I.T. 2373, VI-2 C.B. 19(1937).

[11] IRC-1954; Section 368(a)(1)(D).

[12] Gross v. C.I.R., 88 F(2) 567 (1937).

[13] Andrew W. Mellon, 36 T.C. 977 (1937).

[14] Curtis v. U.S. 336 F (2d) 714 (1964).

[15] C.I.R. v. Morris Trust, 367F(2) 794 (1966).

[16] IRC-1954; Section 368(a)(1)(c).

[17] IRC-1954; Section 368(a)(2)(B).

[18] IRC-1954; Section 368(a)(1)(C).

[19] Regulations; 1.368-2(d)(1).

[20] Revenue Ruling 67-274, 1967-2 C.B. 141.

[21]Bausch & Lomb Optical Co. v. C.I.R., 267F(2)75(1959).

[22]Revenue Ruling 68-358, 1968- 2 C.B. 156.

[23]Revenue Procedure 69-1, Sec. 6.02.

[24]Revenue Ruling 66-365, 1966- 2 C.B. 116.

[25]Revenue Procedure 66-34, 1966-1 C.B. 68 and Revenue Procedure 67-13, 1967-1 C.B. 590.

[26]Helvering v. Southwest Consolidated Corp. 315 U.S. 194 (1942).

[27]IRC-1954: Section 1245(b)(3) and Section 1250 (d)(3).

[28]IRC-1954; Section 361.

[29]IRC-1954; Section 1032.

[30]IRC-1954; Section 361(b)(1)(B).

[31]IRC-1954; Section 361(b)(1)(A).

[32]IRC-1954; Section 358(a).

[33]IRC-1054; Section 354(a)(1).

[34]IRC-1954; Section 356(a)(1)(A).

[35]IRC-1954; Section 356(a)(1)(B).

[36]IRC-1954; Section 358(d).

[37]IRC-1954; Section 358(a)(1)(A)(ii).

[38]IRC-1954; Section 356(a)(2).

[39]IRC-1954; Section 354(a)(1).

[40]Revenue Ruling 68-357 1968-2 C.B. 155.

[41]IRC-1954; Section 341.

[42]IRC-1954; Section 542.

[43]IRC-1954; Section 543.

[44]IRC-1954; Section 543(b).

[45]IRC-1954: Section 543(a)(2).

[46]IRC-1954; Section 542(a)(2).

[47]IRC-1954; Section 544(a)(5).

[48]IRC-1954; Section 545.

[49]New York Business Corporation Law; Section 909(a).

[50]New York Business Corporation Law; Section 909(b).

[51]Ibid.

[52]IRC-1954; Section 368(a)(1)(E).

[53]Helvering v. Southwest Consolidated Corp. 315 U.S. 194.

[54]Regulations 1.368-2(e).

[55]Ibid.

[56]New York Business Corporation Law; Section 804.

[57]New York Business Corporation Law; Section 805.

[58]IRC-1954; Section 354(a)(1).

[59]IRC-1954; Section 361.

STOCK FOR ASSETS EXCHANGE

Facts

Assume that MAL Corporation transfers all its assets except cash of $100,000 for 1,000 shares of JRG Corporation.

Tax Consequences

As to MAL Corporation

MAL Corporation after it receives the stock is a shell. It could liquidate tax free pursuant to Section 331 of the Code.

The stock for assets exchange would be tax free since the liabilities are less than fifteen percent ($100,000) of the total fair market value of the assets ($700,000).

As to JRG Corporation

The basis of the property to JRG Corporation is the same as in the hands of MAL Corporation, that is, $350,000 ($450,000-$100,000).

As to the Shareholders

The shareholders would receive the stock of JRG Corporation upon the liquidation of MAL Corporation. No gain or loss would be recognized to them until a subsequent disposition.

The basis for the shares received by the MAL shareholders for the stock of JRG Corporation would be $100,000, their basis for the stock of MAL Corporation.

Accounting Problems

Journal Entries

As to MAL Corporation

1.

Capital Stock–MAL	100,000	
Capital Stock–JRG		100,000
To record the distribution of stock		

2.

Capital stock–JRG	350,000	
Receivables–net		65,000
Inventory		75,000
Prepaid expenses		10,000
Machinery and equipment–net		150,000
Buildings		50,000 350,000
To record the transfer of assets to JRG Corporation		

JRG Corporation

Receivables—net	65,000	
Inventory	75,000	
Prepaid expenses	10,000	
Machinery and		
equipment—net	150,000	
Buildings—net	50,000	
Capital stock		350,000

JRG CORPORATION
Balance Sheet
December 31, 1970 (After Asset Exchange)

ASSETS		Per Books	Fair Market Value
Current Assets:			
Cash		$1,000,000	$1,000,000
Accounts receivable	$770,000		
Less: Allowance for bad			
debts	55,000		
Estimated recovery value		715,000	700,000
Inventory		825,000	1,000,000
Prepaid expenses		110,000	50,000
TOTAL		$2,650,000	$2,750,000
Fixed Assets:			
Buildings	$2,200,000		
Less: Accumulated de-			
preciation	550,000		
Book value		$1,650,000	$3,000,000
Machinery & equipment	$1,100,000		
Less: Accumulated de-			
preciation	550,000		
Book Value		550,000	$1,250,000
TOTAL		$2,200,000	$4,250,000
TOTAL ASSETS		$4,850,000	$7,000,000
LIABILITIES			
Current Liabilities:			
Notes payable		$ 500,000	
Accounts payable		200,000	
Federal income tax payable		300,000	
TOTAL		$1,000,000	$1,000,000
Long-Term Liabilities:			
Loans payable	$1,000,000		$1,000,000
TOTAL	$1,000,000		$1,000,000

Stockholders' Equity:

Capital Stock, par value	$100	
Authorized	20,000	
Unissued	9,000	
Issued	11,000	$1,100,000
Capital surplus		750,000
Retained earnings (or deficit)		1,000,000
Total Liabilities and Stockholders' Equity		$4,850,000

MAL CORPORATION
Balance Sheet
December 31, 1960 (After Asset Exchange)

ASSETS	Per Books
Current Assets:	
Cash	$100,000
Investment in JRG	350,000
TOTAL ASSETS	$450,000

LIABILITIES	
Current Liabilities:	
Notes payable	$ 50,000
Accounts payable	20,000
Federal income tax liability	30,000
TOTAL	$100,000
Long-Term Liabilities:	
Loans payable	$100,000
TOTAL	$200,000

Stockholders' Equity:

Capital stock, $100 par value		
Authorized	1,200	
Unissued	1,000	
Issued	−1,000	$100,000
Retained earnings		$150,000
Total Liabilities and Stockholders' Equity		$450,000

TAXABLE STOCK FOR ASSETS

Assume the same facts except that the only assets acquired were the fixed assets for 1,000 shares of stock.

Tax Consequences

As to MAL CORPORATION

MAL Corporation would have a recognized gain on the disposition of fixed assets determined as follows:

	Fair Market Value	$350,000
Less:	Net Assets Acquired	200,000
	Recognized Gain	150,000
Less:	Depreciation Recapture	100,000
	Section 1231 gain	$ 50,000

As to JRG Corporation

JRG Corporation would have a basis for the assets acquired, or $350,000, the fair market value of the stock exchanged.

Accounting Treatment

As to JRG Corporation

Buildings	$105,000	
Machinery and equipment	245,000	
Capital Stock		$350,000

To record the assets acquired for stock

Asset	Fair Market Value	%	Allocation
Building	125,000	30%	105,000
Machinery	300,000	70%	245,000
TOTAL	$425,000	100%	$350,000

As to MAL Corporation

Accumulated depreciation	50,000	
Accumulated depreciation	50,000	
Investment of Capital stock		
of JRG Corporation	350,000	
Machinery and equipment		200,000
Building		100,000
Retained earnings		150,000

To record the asset disposition

Taxable Exchange

JRG Corporation
Balance Sheet
December 31, 1970

ASSETS		Per Books	Fair Market Value
Current Assets:			
Cash		$1,000,000	$1,000,000
Accounts receivable	$700,000		
Less: Allowance for bad debts	50,000		
Estimated recovery value		650,000	700,000
Inventory		750,000	1,000,000
Prepaid expenses		100,000	50,000
TOTAL		$2,500,000	$2,750,000
Fixed Assets:			
Buildings	$2,105,000		
Less: Accumulated depreciation	500,000		
Book value		$1,605,000	$3,000,000
Machinery & equipment	$1,245,000		
Less: Accumulated depreciation	500,000		
Book value		745,000	1,250,000
TOTAL		$2,000,000	$4,250,000
TOTAL ASSETS		$4,850,000	$7,000,000

LIABILITIES			
Current Liabilities:			
Notes payable		$ 500,000	
Accounts payable		200,000	
Federal income tax payable		300,000	
TOTAL		$1,000,000	$1,000,000
Long-Term Liabilities:			
Loans payable	$1,000,000		$1,000,000
TOTAL	$1,000,000		$1,000,000
Stockholders' Equity:			
Capital Stock, par value	$100		
Authorized	20,000		
Unissued	9,000		
Issued	11,000	$1,100,000	$3,500,000

Capital surplus		750,000	500,000
Retained earnings (or deficit)		1,000,000	1,000,000
Total Liabilities and Stockholders' Equity		$4,850,000	$7,000,000

Taxable Exchange
MAL CORPORATION
Balance Sheet
December 31, 1970

ASSETS		*Per Books*	*Fair Market Value*
Current Assets:			
Cash		$100,000	$100,000
Accounts receivable	$70,000		
Less: Allowance for bad debts	5,000		
Estimated recovery value		65,000	70,000
Inventory		75,000	100,000
Prepaid expenses		10,000	5,000
TOTAL		$250,000	$275,000
Other Assets:			
Investment in JRG Corporation		$350,000	
TOTAL ASSETS		$600,000	

LIABILITIES			
Current Liabilities:			
Notes payable		$ 50,000	
Accounts payable		20,000	
Federal income tax liability		30,000	
TOTAL		$100,000	$100,000
Long-Term Liabilities:			
Loans payable	$100,000		$100,000
TOTAL		$200,000	$200,000
Stockholders' Equity:			
Capital stock, $100 par value			
Authorized	1,200		
Unissued	1,000		
Issued	−1,000	$100,000	$350,000
Retained Earnings		300,000	150,000

Total Liabilities and Stockholders' Equity	$600,000	$700,000

RECAPITALIZATION

Assume the same facts except for the following: the net value of the accounts receivable is $450,000; inventory is $50,000 and there are no prepaid expenses and capital surplus is $1,500,000. Thus, the total assets are $3,500,000. The deficit is $1,000,000 which is eliminated by the offsetting of the operating deficit against such paid-in surplus.

Accounting Entries

1.

Capital surplus	1,100,000	
Retained earnings		1,000,000

To write off the debit balance in retained earnings against the capital surplus.

The financial statements would show a retained earnings account of $100,000 which should be dated for at least ten years.

Tax Problems

There would be no tax consequences to the corporation.

JRG CORPORATION
Balance Sheet
December 31, 1970

ASSETS		Per Books	Fair Market Value
Current Assets:			
Cash		$1,000,000	$1,000,000
Accounts receivable	$500,000		
Less: Allowance for bad debts	50,000		
Estimated recovery value		450,000	700,000
Inventory		50,000	$1,000,000
TOTAL		$1,500,000	$2,700,000
Fixed Assets:			
Buildings	$2,000,000		
Less: Accumulated depreciation	500,000		

Book value		$1,500,000	$3,000,000
Machinery & equipment	$1,000,000		
Less: Accumulated depreciation	500,000		
Book value		$ 500,000	$1,250,000
TOTAL		$2,000,000	$4,250,000
TOTAL ASSETS		$3,500,000	$7,000,000

LIABILITIES

Notes payable		$ 500,000	
Accounts payable		200,000	
Federal income tax payable		300,000	
TOTAL		$1,000,000	$1,000,000

Long-Term Liabilities:

Loans payable	$1,000,000		$1,000,000
TOTAL	$1,000,000		$1,000,000

Stockholders' Equity:

Capital stock, par value	$100		
Authorized	20,000		
Unissued	10,000		
Issued	10,000	$1,000,000	$3,500,000
Capital surplus		400,000	500,000
Retained earnings (attributable to a quasi-reorganization on December 31, 1970)		1,000,000	1,000,000
Total Liabilities and Stockholders' Equity		$3,500,000	$7,000,000

Pitfalls to Avoid in Divisive Reorganizations

7

A divisive or D-type reorganization provides a method for separating an existing business into two or more corporations without the incurrence of any gain or loss being recognized to the corporation or its shareholders. It is the most complicated of all the reorganization provisions with more litigation arising under this section than any other reorganization provision.

The basic requirement of a D-type exchange is that a corporation transfer all or part of its assets to another corporation and, that immediately after such transfer the transferor, or some combination of these, is in control of the transferee.

Among the advantages of this method are the following: (1) a corporation can distribute unwanted assets through a "spin-off"; (2) a single business with two or more divisions can be split up tax free.

Among the disadvantages of this method are the following: (1) the "five-year active business" rule acts as a deterrent in preventing a corporation from using its earnings and profits to acquire a new corporation and then distributing such stock (of newly formed corporation) to its shareholders without the imposition of any tax; (2) the increasing litigation that results in this area.

MECHANICS OF A DIVISIVE REORGANIZATION

There are three types of divisive reorganizations commonly referred to as "split-ups," "split-offs," and "spin-offs." They are referred to as divisive because each type divides what previously was owned in one corporation into two corporations, with the shares of both in the hands of the original stockholder. Section 355 has for its purpose: (1) to permit the tax-free separation of two or more existing businesses; and, (2) to prevent the above three types from being used as a device for the distribution of the earnings and profits of a corporation without any tax consequences.

A split-up[1] results where a corporation is split up into two or more separate corporations. The stock of the new corporations is distributed to the shareholders of the old corporation, who surrender the stock of the old corporation. The parent corporation is then liquidated under Section 331. For example, Corporation A is engaged in the manufacturing of widgets and real estate activities. It distributes the manufacturing activities to a new corporation for its stock which is distributed to the old shareholders for their stock. The real estate activities are transferred to a new corporation for its stock which is similarly transferred to the old shareholders. This is a split-up, and no gain or loss is recognized to the shareholders if the other requirements are met.

A split-off[2] occurs when a corporation transfers part of its assets to a new corporation in exchange for the stock of the new corporation. It then immediately distributes the stock to its shareholders, who surrender part of their stock in the original corporation as part of a stock redemption. Another method used to accomplish a split-off occurs through a distribution by a parent of an existing controlled subsidiary company's stock. For example, Corporation A transfers part of its assets to a newly formed corporation for its stock. Such new stock is distributed to the shareholders who surrender part of their stock in the original corporation.

A spin-off is similar to a split-off with the exception that no stock of the transferor is surrendered by its stockholders upon their receipt of the transferee's stock. For example, Corporation A forms a new corporation by receiving the stock in return for some of A Corporation's assets. The stock of B Corporation is distributed to the shareholders of A Corporation with the result that they now own stock in both Corporations A and B.

STATUTORY REQUIREMENTS

Generally speaking, shareholders who receive only stock or securities on account of stock he owns will not recognize any gain or loss on receipt of such stock or securities. On the other hand, gain or loss will be recognized if the taxpayer receives additional consideration, commonly referred to as boot.

The following requirements must be met before stock or securities of a controlled corporation can be distributed without the imposition of gain or loss being recognized to the shareholders or security holders:

1. The distribution to a shareholder must be with respect to the distributing corporation's stock, while a distribution to a security holder must be in exchange for the distributing corporation's securities.[3]
2. The distribution must be solely stock or securities of a controlled corporation. If anything else is distributed, the "excess" distribution may be taxable as boot.
3. The distribution must not be used principally as a device for the distribution of earnings and profits of the distribution corporation, the controlled corporation, or both.[4]
4. Both corporations must ordinarily have been engaged in a trade or business for at least five years.
5. The distributing corporation must distribute all the stock or securities of the controlled corporation that it held immediately before the distribution, or an amount of stock that constitutes control.[5] If more than one distribution is necessary to meet this requirement, the distributing corporation must commit itself at the time of the first distribution to enough later distributions to divest control.

DISTRIBUTION OF SUBSTANTIALLY
ALL OF THE TRANSFEROR'S ASSETS

The D-type reorganization can be used to transfer the assets of the transferor corporation to a corporation controlled by the transferor and/or its shareholders followed by a complete liquidation of the transferor corporation. This type overlaps with the A-type because in essence there is a merger of the parent into its subsidiary corporation—a downstream merger. Any assets not distributed to the controlled corporation will constitute a boot distribution to the shareholders. Cutting across this is the liquidation-reincorporation problem in which the Treasury has utilized to find the distribution to have the effect of a dividend distribution.

The phrase "substantially all of the assets" has the same meaning as "substantially all the properties" as used in the C-type reorganization.[6] Thus, the "substantially all" requirements of the C-type are to be applied to the D-type not attendant to a corporate separation to determine if the requirements are met. Although there is no statutory requirement that the transferor corporation be dissolved, it is highly probable that the transferor corporation be liquidated as part of the plan of reorganization.

Control is defined as the ownership of eighty percent of the voting power of the corporation and eighty percent of the total number of all nonvoting shares of the corporation.[7] This requirement can be met by either a contribution to the capital of an existing, already controlled corporation or by a transfer of the assets in exchange for the necessary portion of the transferee's stock. For example, Corporation A transfers substantially all its assets to Corporation B, after which A is in control (eighty percent) of B. A then distributes the B stock to A shareholders, followed by a liquidation of A. From the standpoint of Corporation B, this is a transfer of B voting stock in exchange for "substantially all" of the assets of A, which also meets the requirements of a C-type reorganization. Recognizing the overlap in the provisions between both the C- and D-type, Section 368(a)2(A) provides that if a reorganization comes under either section, it will be treated as a D-type reorganization

The requirements of Sections 354 and 355 must be met if there is a change in corporate vehicles. Under these provisions, the transferee controlled corporation must acquire substantially all the assets of the transferor corporation and the transferor corporation must distribute all of its properties, including stock and other property received in the reorganization, in pursuance of the plan of reorganization. The result is a complete liquidation of the transferor, although the Code does not specify this requirement.

MISCELLANEOUS REQUIREMENTS

As discussed in the other types of reorganizations, the requirements of business purpose, continuity of interest, nontaxable exchange effect on both corporations and shareholders, and reporting requirements are also applicable to nondivisive D-type of reorganization. To avoid repetition, they will not be discussed again. The reader is referred to the chapters 4, 5, and 6 for a discussion of these statutory and judicial requirements.

LIQUIDATION-REINCORPORATION PROBLEMS

One of the most litigated areas arising in the reorganization is that of the liquidation-reincorporation technique. A liquidation results in beneficial tax overtones whereby a shareholder can obtain capital gains on the liquidating distribution. The corporation will not recognize any gain or loss on the distribution or upon the sale of assets occurring within a twelve-month period. The Treasury has held[8] that where a corporation liquidates having a substantial amount of undistributed accumulated earnings and profits followed by a reincorporation of the same or substantially the same business, the aforementioned rules are applicable.

The Regulations[9] provide:

> A liquidation which is followed by a transfer to another corporation of all or part of the assets of the liquidating corporation or which is preceded by such a transfer may, however, have the effect of the distribution of a dividend or of a transaction in which no loss is recognized and gain is recognized, only to the extent of "other property."

This technique can arise under the following situations: (1) a liquidation in kind, followed by a retransfer of assets to another corporation; (2) a transfer of operating assets by the corporation to a second corporation, followed by a liquidation of the distributing corporation; or (3) a sale of assets to a related corporation followed by a twelve-month liquidation under Section 337.

The most significant point that will give rise to the Treasury's attack is that the liquidated business is continued in corporation form with substantially the same shareholders.[10] On the other hand, if the business is continued by the same shareholders in the form of a partnership or trust, there will be complete insulation from the liquidation-reincorporation trap.

The factual patterns giving rise to the trap are as follows: (1) Corporation L liquidates under Section 331 with its shareholders transferring some of the assets to a new corporation. (2) Another variation would be to have a subsidiary corporation formed with a transfer of operating assets to New corporation. Old corporation will liquidate and distribute the stock of New to its shareholders. This usually occurs by a merger of the parent into the subsidiary—the downstream merger.

Thus, the shareholders of one corporation will cause it to adopt a twelve-month plan of liquidation, sell all of its operating assets to another corporation controlled by them or newly formed to receive such assets, and then liquidate. The shareholders will receive the corporation's cash and usually nonoperating assets as a liquidating distribution. The shareholders will report capital gains on the transaction since the effect of such a distribution is to avoid the tax-free reorganization provisions. The Internal Revenue Service will hold that such a transaction has the net effect of continuing the business in corporate form while at the same time receiving excess cash and other liquid assets, a bailout of earnings and profits at dividend rates rather than capital gains rates. Consequently, the Service will classify the transaction as a tax-free reorganization in order to have the excess cash and other property taxed as a dividend under the boot provisions of the Code. Such boot will be a dividend to the extent of the corporation's undistributed earnings and profits.[11]

The basic problem is what type of reorganization can be construed to cover the liquidation reincorporation technique. The D-type was used since it consists basically of a transfer of assets from one corporation to another corporation with the transferee in control by the transferor or its shareholders. This fits the reincorporation situation rather well.

The Commissioner has used various approaches to find that a dividend exists. In *Gallagher,*[12] the court held that no bona fide liquidation occurred since the concept of a continuation of an existing business violates the concept that the activities of a business be terminated. But, the continuation of an existing business falls within the purview of the tax-free reorganization provisions. Furthermore, the redemption provisions under Section 302(b)(2) were inapplicable as well as the partial liquidation provisions of Section 346, since such methods will only result in capital gain and not dividend income treatment.

The courts have refused to find that an E-type reorganization could be found since the transaction did not constitute a reshuffling of the capital structure within the framework of an existing corporation as contemplated by the term "recapitalization." Similarly, no F-type reorganization has been found with one exception[13] since the court could not find a "mere change of identity, form, or place of organization" since there would be a change in stock ownership or a shift in proprietary interest.

In *Davant,*[14] the court found an F-type reorganization because of the fact that the corporate business continued uninterrupted except for minor distributions of cash and liquid assets without any shift in the proprietary interests of the shareholders. Thus, the court held that such distributions constituted a dividend taxable under Section 301 rather than Section 356 by holding that the cash distribution and reorganization were separate and unrelated transactions carried on simultaneously. This result is questionable because the step transaction doctrine could be argued by the taxpayer to find that the dividend recognized would be limited to the gain recognized on the exchange under Section 356. Thus, the Regulations under Section 301 were utilized to separate two transactions into one transaction. The Regulations provide that: "A distribution to shareholders with respect to their stock is within the terms of Section 301 although it takes place at the same time as another transaction if the distribution is in substance a separate transaction whether or not connected in a formal sense. This is most likely to occur in the case of a recapitalization, a reincorporation, or a merger of a corporation with a newly organized corporation having substantially no property."

In the latest case[15] involving the liquidation reincorporation area, the District Court held that distributions from a corporation upon liquidation were capital gains, even though the defunct corporation was reincorporated later. There was no preliquidation plan to reincorporate and the transactions did not fall into any of the exceptions for reorganizations under either the D, E or F types.

Briefly, the facts were as follows: Stockton Construction Co., Inc. (Old) distributed it assets to plaintiff and liquidated pursuant to California law. The purpose was for plantiff to avail themselves of the capital gains tax rates pursuant to Section 337 of the Internal Revenue Code of 1954.

Old did not own its operating equipment in its underground pipe construction business. The equipment belonged to the taxpayer as sole proprietor, doing business as Stockton Construction Co. After liquidation, the taxpayer operated as a sole proprietor. He ultimately decided that all his personal assets were subject to claims in subsequent litigation. Therefore he decided to set up a new corporation, also named Stockton Construction Co., Inc. (New).

The court rejected the government's argument that all the steps were part of a single plan, the step transaction doctrine. In fact, each of the steps were mutually exclusive from one another. The liquidation was undertaken for tax avoidance purposes. However, this did not make it any less a bona fide liquidation. The second transaction—the incorporation of the New Stockton—came later and was for business reasons.

The form versus substance doctrine[16] was rejected by the court since there was no "consummation of a preconceived plan." Here, there was no preconceived plan to incorporate again, and the second incorporation was for a nontax business motive.

The F-type reorganization was rejected since the reincorporation was more than a mere change in identity or form. The E-type was rejected since there was no recapitalization despite the partial similarities in capital structure of the two corporations.

Similarly, there was no D-type reorganization because of the absence of an overall plan to transfer the bulk of the operating assets from the "old" to the "new" corporation. Furthermore, the evidence does not show there was a transfer of substantially all the assets, although there was undoubtedly a continuity and identity between the two corporations in the key employees, the goodwill and reputation of the taxpayer, and in some operating equipment rented from the taxpayer, there was nevertheless a significant discontinuity, a failure to transfer the liquid assets of the original corporation. In *Simon,*[17] the court held that failure to transfer liquid assets is necessarily a failure to transfer substantially all the assets. Additionally, a transfer of all the assets is of no consequence if it was not pursuant to a plan of reorganization.

CORPORATE SEPARATIONS

The separation of closely-held business into two or more parts without the recognition of gain or loss is of great importance to such shareholders.

Section 355 provides that only stock or securities of a corporation controlled by the distributing corporation can be used to separate corporate businesses. Before such separation can occur, there must be a group of activities which can be separated and conducted in a controlled subsidiary.

"CONTROLLED SUBSIDIARY"

The activities of a controlled subsidiary can be previously conducted as a branch, division or part of the general operations in an existing corporation. The stock of an existing corporation can be distributed in a tax-free divisive reorganization.[18] On the other hand, a subsidiary can be formed in a tax-free incorporation under Section 351 to be used to provide the divisive type of separation.

In utilizing such a separation, the stock or securities of the controlled corporation may be distributed to the shareholders of the distributing corporation whether or not such shareholders surrender any stock in the exchange.[19]

This corporate separation can be used with both pro rata or non-pro rata distributions. A pro rata distribution occurs when stock in a corporation is spun off to old shareholders in proportion to their holdings in the parent corporation. A non-pro rata distribution is one where the distributions of stock of the controlled corporation is not in the same proportion as their stock in the parent corporation. Furthermore, the nonrecognition of gain or loss is not affected by the fact that there is no surrender of stock, or the distribution is not pursuant to a plan of reorganization.[20]

Thus, if the other requirements are met, the distribution of stock of a subsidiary corporation directly to the shareholders of its parent is tax free whether or not the distribution is proportionate to the parent stock they hold. Similarly, the distribution is tax free whether or not the shareholder surrenders stock in the distributing corporation. This is the usual spin-off type of divisive reorganization.

The chief requirement is that stock representing at least eighty percent control of the controlled corporation is distributed to the shareholders to be afforded tax-free treatment. Thus, not all of the stock or securities of a controlled subsidiary must be distributed. The stock and securities not distributed must establish to the satisfaction of the Commissioner that its retention did not constitute a plan having as one of its purposes the avoidance of federal income taxes.[21]

EFFECT ON SHAREHOLDERS

The shareholders and security holders of the parent corporation may receive either stock or securities of the controlled subsidiary in exchange for their stock and/or securities. Similarly, they could receive both stock and securities.[22]

Generally speaking, securities of a controlled subsidiary distributed in a corporate separation constitute other property and are taxable as boot.[23] An exception[24] is provided whereby a security holder in the parent corporation will not constitute boot if received in exchange for a security of the same or lesser principal amount.[25] If securities in any greater amount are received, the fair market value of the excess is treated as boot.[26] If no securities are surrendered, the fair market value of the securities received is treated as boot or "other property."[27] For example, A, an individual shareholder, exchanged 100 shares of stock and a security in the principal amount of $1,000 for 200 shares of stock and a security in the principal amount of $1,200 with a fair market value on the date of receipt of $1,250. The fair market value of the excess principal amount of $250 is treated as "other property." If the fair market value of the security received was only $900, there would be no excess amount taxable as boot.

If stock is surrendered and boot is recognized, the amount of gain recognized cannot exceed the shareholder's gain from the transaction.[28] If such boot distribution has the effect of a distribution of a dividend, then part or all of the gain would be taxed as a dividend rather than capital gain.[29] This result arises from a case which seems to hold that automatic dividend results in a reorganization having boot problems.[30] The gain recognized as a dividend cannot exceed the shareholders' ratable share of the corporation's undistributed earnings and profits.[31] The balance or remainder of the gain is taxed as capital gain.[32] Loss is not recognized in a divisive reorganization[33] even if the shareholder with a loss receives a distribution of "other property" or boot. If the separation occurs without any exchange or surrender of stock, then the boot received is taxable as a dividend to the extent of the distributing corporation's earnings and profits.[34] The full amount of boot will be taxable as a dividend, depending upon earnings and profits without any limitation on the shareholder's recognized gain rules providing for stock surrender. The basis for this rule is that there is no exchange on which gain can be determined.[35]

BASIS TO DISTRIBUTEE-SHAREHOLDERS

If no boot is involved and the reorganization meets all the requirements of the Code, then the shareholders will have as their basis for the stock received the same basis as the basis of the stock given up.[36]

If no stock is surrendered, but stock of a controlled corporation is received, then the basis of the old and the new stock is determined by allocating the basis of the original stock.[37] If some stock is surrendered for which the stockholder receives more than one class of stock of the controlled corporation, basis must be allocated among the different classes of stock he holds.[38] Thus, the basis of the stock given up in the exchange plus the basis of the stock retained must be reallocated to the retained stock and the newly received stock. The allocations are to be stock and securities held immediately after the distribution.[39]

EFFECT ON DISTRIBUTING CORPORATION

A distributing corporation does not recognize any gain or loss as a result of its distribution of stock or securities of a controlled corporation to its shareholders.[40] Since stock or securities are being distributed, there are no tax consequences for its assets.

A spin-off does result in troublesome problems in connection with the allocation of earnings and profits.[41] The Regulations[42] provide that an allocation of the parent's earnings and profits of its newly created subsidiary is to be made on the basis the distributed assets bears to its retained assets. Another rule which can be utilized is called the net basis rule whereby an allocation of earnings and profits can be made on the "net basis of assets transferred and of assets retained."[43] No allocation can be made where the distributing corporation has a deficit in earnings and profits.[44]

THE EFFECT OF ASSETS RECEIVED
BY CONTROLLED SUBSIDIARY

The basis of assets received by a controlled subsidiary will be the same as the tax basis in the hands of the transferor corporation. Thus, no step-up in basis can occur since there is no purchase of stock as required under Section 334(b)(2).

DEVICE TEST

In order for there to be a tax-free corporate separation, the transaction must not be "used principally as a device for the distribution of earnings and profits of either the distributing corporation, the controlled corporation, or both."[45] This nebulous device requirement has created many troublesome problems in the area of tax planning. Consequently, a ruling is to be requested from the Internal Revenue Service before any such type of corporate separation is to take place resulting in a "clean bill of health" necessary to undertake such transaction.

The purpose of this device clause is to prevent the distribution of a corporation's earnings and profits at capital gains which would normally be taxed as a dividend. It is difficult to perceive how a distribution of a newly formed subsidiary stock is a withdrawal of earnings and profits and, therefore, in violation of the device clause.

If a distributing corporation has no earnings and profits, then any distribution of the stock or securities will not violate the "device clause" with its concomitant dividend consequences to its shareholders. A non-pro rata spin-off should never result in a violation of the device clause, since it will also qualify under the stock redemption provisions of Section 302. Another way in which shareholders can be afforded capital gains treatment is under Section 346 providing for partial liquidation of the business.

THE ACTIVE BUSINESS REQUIREMENT

One of the requirements necessary for a corporation separation to be afforded tax-free treatment is the five-year active business rule. Such rule provides that immediately after the distribution of the stock of the controlled corporation, both the distributing corporation and the controlled corporation are engaged in the active conduct of a trade or business.[46] If the stock of more than one controlled corporation is distributed, each of such corporations must be so engaged.[47]

This affirmative requirement of active business includes a group of activities being carried on with the receipt of income and payment of expenses.[48] The Regulations[49] provide sixteen illustrations as to what would and would not constitute an active trade or business. Basically, the prohibition of this requirement is directed toward passive, investment-type activities which are only incidental to the major activities of the business.[50] An investment or real estate subsidiary[51] are examples of business which are passive in nature. The statute further provides that if the distributing corporation was a holding company, that is, it had no assets other than the stock of the controlled corporation, before distribution, the five-year requirement only applies to the controlled corporation.[52]

The general rule[53] is that a trade or business consists of a specific existing group of activities being carried on for the purpose of earning income or profit from only such group of activities, and the activities included in such group must include every operation which forms a part of, or a step in, the process of earning income or profit from such group. These activities must include income collection and the payment of expenses. There have been rulings from the Internal Revenue Service attempting to clarify the "separate business" issue. One ruling[54] held that a cotton compressing business was a separate business from a fresh fruit cooperative. It was held that this spin-off constituted a nontaxable exchange under Sections 351 and 355 upon the transfer of assets to the new business. Another ruling[55] held that where a business was acquired within two years of the transfer, it did not meet the five-year rule and the distribution of property was taxable under Section 301. The business which was conducted over five years before the transfer of its assets resulted in the nonrecognition of gain under Section 351. The Service's recent pronouncements[56] in the area of spin-offs has not resolved borderline cases.

The rulings have not clarified the issue and the result has been a case holding that the Regulations prohibiting the division of a separate business were invalid. In *Coady*,[57] the issue presented to the court was whether a corporation which presently conducts a single "active business" could separate that business into two corporate segments and distribute the stock of the new corporation to one of its two stockholders. The Tax Court concluded that Section 355(B)(1)(A) and (B)(2) contemplate that where there was only one corporate entity prior to various transfers, immediately subsequent to such transfers, there will be two or more corporations. The Tax Court also believes that the purpose of the active business requirement was to permit separation only of active business assets and further to prevent the tax-free division of an active corporation into active and inactive entities. The Service[58] has conceded to this judicial view. Thus, the Regulations preventing a division of a single business were invalid.

USE OF SPIN-OFF AND OTHER
TAX-FREE REORGANIZATION EXCHANGES

The Internal Revenue Service has conceded that a spin-off can be tax free under Section 355 even if followed by a statutory merger.[59] In the *Morris*[60] case, the court held that a spin-off followed by a merger could be afforded tax-free benefits of the Code since there was a valid business purpose for the spin-off and merger. There were two banks which desired to consolidate. One of the banks placed the assets of an insurance business into a new subsidiary and distributed the subsidiary's stock to its shareholders. The two banks then consolidated. The business reason for such spin-off was that federal banking laws prohibited the surviving entity from carrying on an insurance business. Thus, the active business requirements of Section 355(b)(1)(A) were satisfied even though the distributing corporation immediately after the spin-off merged into another corporation.

The effect of this decision and ruling is to permit unwanted assets to be placed in a new subsidiary under Section 351 and the stock to be distributed tax free to its shareholders. Then the two corporations could effectuate a statutory merger or consolidation. It is also possible that a B-type stock-for-stock or C-type stock-for-assets exchange could be used in conjunction with a spin-off of unwanted assets.

REPORTING REQUIREMENTS

The Regulations[61] provide that "every distributing corporation that makes a distribution of stock or securities of a controlled corporation, as described in Section 355, shall attach to its return for the year of the distribution a detailed statement setting forth such data as may be appropriate in order to show compliance with the provisions of such section."

The Regulations[62] further provide that "every taxpayer who receives a distribution of stock or securities of a corporation that was controlled by a corporation in which he holds stock or securities shall attach to his return for the year in which such distribution is received a detailed statement setting forth such data as may be appropriate in order to show the applicability of Section 355. Such statement shall include, but shall not be limited to, a description of the stock and securities surrendered (if any) and received, and the names and addresses of all the corporations involved in the transaction."

ACCOUNTING PROBLEMS

The purchase and pooling concepts have no application to corporate separations since what is involved is only one corporation, whereas the accounting for business combinations presupposes at least two corporations.

DIVISIVE REORGANIZATION CHECKLIST

A. Types
   1. spin-off
   2. split-up
   3. split-off
B. Advantages and Disadvantages
C. Consideration Utilized
   1. voting stock
   2. assets—substantially all
   3. shareholder exchanges stock—split-off
   4. no exchange of stock by shareholders—spin-off
D. Requirements
   1. exchange of stock
   2. control must be given up
   3. not a device for distributing earnings and profits
   4. five-year active business test
E. Liquidation Reincorporation Problems
F. Corporate Separations
G. Effect on Shareholders
   1. basis
H. Effect on Distributing Corporation
   1. assets received by controlled subsidiary
I. Overlap of "D" type with Other Reorganizations
J. Miscellaneous Problems
   1. accounting
   2. reporting requirements
K. Legal Problems
   1. Board of Directors' authorization
   2. shareholders' approval
   3. Internal Revenue Service ruling

F-TYPE REORGANIZATION

The F reorganization is defined as "a mere change in identity, form, or place or organization, however effected."[63] This type is the simplest of all the reorganization provisions. Generally speaking, it involves very insignificant corporate changes such as a reincorporation in another state. The essential point in such a reorganization is that compliance with state law is necessary if there is to be a change in the name of a corporation or a reincorporation in another state is concerned.

For example, Corporation A, incorporated under the laws of the state of New York, decides to shift its operations entirely to the state of Delaware. Corporation B is formed in Delaware, and all the assets of Corporation A are transferred to Corporation B solely in exchange for B's stock. B's stock is then distributed to A shareholders in the same proportion as their interest before the reorganization. Another illustration would be as follows: Corporation S is the wholly-owned subsidiary of Corporation P. Corporation 2 is formed in another state, and through a statutory consolidation, S and P are merged into Corporation 2.

The foregoing examples indicate that the first example will constitute a C type to Corporation B and a D type to Corporation A, while the second example will constitute a statutory merger. The Internal Revenue Service has rules[64] that if there is an overlap with other types of reorganizations such as A, B, C or D, it will be treated as an F-type reorganization.

CONTINUITY OF INTEREST

The F-type reorganization involves a continuity of interest since the Service has ruled[65] that there should not be any significant change in stock ownership. A one percent de minimis change in the corporation's stockholders did not preclude the finding of an F-type of exchange.[66]

CARRYOVERS

The carryover provisions of Section 381(a) are applicable to an F-type reorganization. Accordingly, the attributes of the predecessor corporation carry over to the successor corporation.

The taxable year of the transferor corporation will not terminate in an F-type exchange as they do in an A, C or D type of exchange. The taxable year remains the same in an E type since only one corporation is involved in the recapitalization adjustment.

EFFECT ON CORPORATION

No gain or loss will be realized by the predecessor corporation in exchange for its property solely for stock or securities of the successor corporation. The successor corporation will not realize any gain on the exchange of its stock or securities for the property of the predecessor corporation.[67] The property received by the successor corporation will have the same basis as in the hands of the predecessor corporation.[68]

EFFECT ON SHAREHOLDERS

The shareholders in an F-type reorganization exchange will not realize any gain or loss upon the giving up of their shares in the predecessor corporation solely for stock or securities in the successor corporation.[69] The basis for the stock received in the successor corporation is the same as that for the stock or securities surrendered in the predecessor corporation.[70]

OVERLAP WITH OTHER REORGANIZATION PROVISIONS

A question that arises when brother-sister corporations merge is whether the reorganization exchange is an A-type or F-type transaction. In one case,[71] the 9th Circuit held that a merger of three corporations qualified as an F-type reorganization exchange since the merger was merely a change is identity or form.

The facts were as follows: The taxpayer was the owner of three separate corporations (brother-sister), one in California, one in New York, and the other in Illinois. Each of the corporations had the same officers and directors, and each filed separate tax returns.

The question to be resolved by the court was whether a loss sustained by the transferee corporation (Stauffer New Mexico) could be carried back to a premerger taxable year of one of three transferor corporations. The Tax Court held that there was a statutory merger, and, accordingly the losses were limited under Regulations 1.381(b)(1)-1(b).

Prior to the consummation of the merger, the Service in a private ruling held that the transaction was a statutory merger.

The Court held that an F-type reorganization need not involve only one corporation. Here there was an F-type reorganization and that portion of the postmerger losses attributable to the California operation could be carried back to a premerger taxable year of that corporation.

In the *Associated Machine*[72] case, the same Court held that the merger of a machine shop business which carried on a sheet metal business was an F-type reorganization since the merger involved nothing more than a mere change in identity or form. Furthermore, an F-type reorganization can involve more than one active corporation. Accordingly, the surviving corporation was entitled to carry back a postmerger loss to the premerger profits of the transferor corporation.

The Service has ruled[73] that it will not follow these decisions. Accordingly, a similar factual pattern will result in the taxpayer having to litigate the same issue again in order to be able to offset postmerger net operation losses against premerger profits of the transferor.

In *Home Construction Corporation of America,*[74] the District Court held that the merger of 123 functionally related corporations into a single Delaware Corporation qualified as an F-type reorganization. After the merger, there was no change in stockholders or their proprietary interests, no change in the ownership, form or location of the corporate assets, no change in the corporate personnel or management, and no change in the type, scope and method of business operations which were previously carried out by the transferor or merged corporations. Accordingly, postmerger losses could be carried back against premerger income of certain of the merged corporations.

FOOTNOTES

[1] IRC-1954; Section 368(a)(1)(D).

[2] IRC-1954; Section 355.

[3] IRC-1954; Section 355(a)(1).

[4] IRC-1954; Section 355(a)(1)(B).

[5] IRC-1954; Section 355(a)(1)(D).

[6] Rev. Proc. 66-34; 1966-2 C.B. 1232.

[7] IRC-1954; Section 368(c).

[8] Regulations 1.331-1(c).

[9] Ibid.

[10]Rev. Rul. 61-156, 1961-1 C.B. 62.

[11]IRC-1954; Section 356(a)(2).

[12]Gallagher, 39 T.C. 144 (1962).

[13]Hyman H. Berghash, 43 T.C. 743, aff'd 361F(2d) 257(1966).

[14]Davant v. Commissioner, 18 AFTR (2) 5523.

[15]Swanson v. United States, 1970-2 USTC 9624.

[16]Gregory v. Helvering, 293 U.S. 465, 35-1 USTC 9043 (1934).

[17]Simon v. United States, 68-2 USTC 9624 (1968).

[18]Regulations; 1.30-1(a).

[19]IRC-1954; Section 355(a)(2)(C).

[20]IRC-1954; Section 355(a)(2)(B).

[21]IRC-1954; Section 355(a)(1)(D)(ii).

[22]Regulations; 1.355-2(d).

[23]IRC-1954; Section 355(a)(1)(A).

[24]IRC-1954; Section 356(d)(1).

[25]IRC-1954; Section 355(a)(1) and (3).

[26]IRC-1954; Section 356(b).

[27]IRC-1954; Section 355(a)(3)(B).

[28]IRC-1954; Section 356(a)(1).

[29]IRC-1954; Section 356(a)(2).

[30]Commissioner v. Bedford's Estate, 325 U.S. 283.

[31]IRC-1954; Section 356(a)(2).

[32]Ibid.

[33]IRC-1954; Section 355(a)(1).

[34]IRC-1954; Section 356(c).

[35]IRC-1954; Section 356(b).

[36]IRC-1954; Section 358(a)(1).

[37]IRC-1954; Section 358(c).

[38]IRC-1954; Section 358(b)(2).

[39]Regulations; 1.358(a)(2)-3.

[40]IRC-1954; Section 311.

[41]IRC-1954; Section 312(c).

[42]Regulations; 1.312-10(a).

[43]Ibid.

[44]Regulations; 1.312-10(c).

[45]IRC-1954; Section 355(a)(1)(B).

[46] IRC-1954; Section 355(a)(1)(C).

[47] IRC-1954; Section 355(b)(1)(A).

[48] Regulations; 1.355-1(C).

[49] Regulations; 1.355-1(D).

[50] Rev. Rul. 66-204, 1966-2 C.B. 113.

[51] Regulations; 1.355-1(d), Example 2.

[52] IRC-1954; Section 355(b)(1)(B).

[53] Regulations; 1.355-1(c).

[54] Rev. Rul. 56-117, 1956-1 C.B. 180.

[55] Rev. Rul. 57-190, 1957-1 C.B. 120.

[56] Rev. Rul. 69-461, 1969-2 C.B. 35.

[57] Edmund P. Coady, 33 T.C. 771, 289F (2d) 490(1961).

[58] Rev. Rul. 64-147, 1964-1 C.B. 136.

[59] Rev. Rul. 69-603, 1968-2 C.B. 148.

[60] C.I.R. v. Mary Archer W. Morris Trust, 367 F(2) 794 (1966).

[61] Regulations; 1.355-5(a).

[62] Regulations; 1.355-5(b).

[63] IRC-1954; Section 368(a)(1)(F).

[64] Rev. Rul. 57-276; 1957-1 C.B. 126.

[65] Rev. Rul. 66-284, 1966 C.B.

[66] Ibid.

[67] IRC-1954; Section 1032(a).

[68] IRC-1954; Section 362(a).

[69] IRC-1954; Section 354(a)(1).

[70] IRC-1954; Section 358(a).

[71] Estate of Stauffer v. Commissioner, 48 T.C. 277, rev'd 403 F.2d 611. 68-2 U.S.T.C. 9634 403F (2d) 622.

[72] Associated Machine, 68-2 USTC 9635.

[73] Rev. Rul. 69-185, 1969-1 C.B. 108.

[74] Home Construction Corporation of America v. United States, 70-1 USTC 9102.

Managing Tax Loss Carryovers with Expertise   *8*

There are various tax attributes such as carryovers which may have a significant bearing on the acquisition of one corporation by another besides the tax types with their manifold accounting, legal and securities regulations problems. These carryovers may determine whether the type of acquisition will be taxable or tax free, and, if the latter method is chosen, then the type to be availed of.

Other tax factors entering into the picture are: (1) the deductibility of legal and accounting fees; (2) use of redemptions in corporate acquisitions; (3) use of corporate liquidations; (4) stock option plans; and (5) consolidated return problems.

CARRYOVERS

Section 381 of the Code lists twenty-three different corporate tax attributes that can be carried over in certain types of acquisitions. The types of acquisitions to which Section 381 are applicable are corporate liquidations under Section 332, the parent-subsidiary liquidation, other than those where the basis of the assets are stepped up,[1] under Section 334(b)(2) and corporate reorganizations of the A, C, D and F types. In effect, the carryover rules permit a successor or continuing corporation to take into effect the tax attributes of a predecessor or acquired corporation. Thus, an acquiring corporation steps into the shoes of the acquired corporation and utilizes all benefits and elections which were available to the predecessor corporation.

The tax attributes which must be carried over in the applicable types of acquisitions are as follows:

1. Net operating loss
2. Earnings and profits or deficits
3. Capital loss
4. Accounting methods
5. Inventory methods
6. Depreciation methods
7. Repealed
8. Unreported income from installment receivables
9. Amortization of bond premium or discount
10. Deferred exploration expenses
11. Unused pension or profit-sharing plan contributions
12. Bad debt recoveries

13. Involuntary conversions
14. Personal holding company dividend carryovers
15. Indebtedness of certain personal holding companies
16. Obligations of distributor or transferor corporation
17. Deficiency dividend of personal holding companies
18. Depletion carryovers
19. Charitable contribution carryovers
20. Carryover of unused pension trust deductions in certain cases
21. Pre-1954 adjustments resulting from change in method of accounting
22. Successor life insurance company attributes
23. The investment credit

The list is not all-inclusive since many tax attributes are covered by other provisions of the Code. For example, foreign tax credit carryover and carryback of excess tax paid is not covered under this section. In addition, depreciation recapture on personal[2] and real property[3] would apply to corporate acquisitions.

WHO IS ENTITLED TO CARRYOVER

The acquiring or successor corporation is entitled to use the tax attributes of the acquired corporation. The term "acquiring corporation" is a word of art referring only to a single corporation.[4] In the case of an intercorporate liquidation, the acquiring corporation would be the parent since it acquires the assets of the subsidiary. As regards a tax-free reorganization, the acquiring corporation is that corporation which, pursuant to the plan of reorganization, ultimately acquires, directly or indirectly, all of the assets transferred by the transferor corporation. If no one corporation ultimately acquires all of the assets transferred by the transferor corporation, that corporation which directly acquires the assets so transferred shall be the acquiring corporation, even though such corporation ultimately retains none of the assets so transferred. Whether a corporation has acquired all of the assets transferred by the transferor corporation is a question of fact to be determined on the basis of all the facts and circumstances.[5]

For example, if a subsidiary corporation used the stock of its parent to acquire the assets of another corporation in a C-type reorganization, the subsidiary corporation would be the acquiring corporation. On the other hand, if the parent corporation in the above example acquired the assets of another corporation solely for its voting stock (C-type), and subsequently transferred the assets to its subsidiary, the subsidiary corporation would be the acquiring corporation. If only part of the assets were transferred to the subsidiary in the above example, the parent corporation would be the acquiring corporation.

The carryover rules are inapplicable to partial liquidations, or divisive reorganizations.[6] The statute provides that carryover rules are applicable to spin-offs and split-offs.[7] If no item or tax attribute is mentioned in the statute, then no inference can be drawn as to whether that item can be taken into account by the successor corporation.[8]

OPERATING RULES APPLICABLE TO CORPORATE ACQUISITION

Generally speaking, the taxable year of the distributor or transferor corporation shall end with the close of the date of distribution or transfer with the exception of the

F type, a mere change in identity or form.[9] In the case of an F-type reorganization, the acquiring corporation shall be treated as the transferor corporation would have been treated if there had been no reorganization. Thus, the taxable year of the transferor corporation shall not end on the date of transfer merely because of the transfer. Any net operating loss of the acquiring corporation for any taxable year ending after the date of transfer shall be carried back three years in computing the taxable income of the transferor corporation for a taxable year ending before the date of transfer; and the tax attributes of the transferor corporation shall be taken into account by the acquiring corporation as if there had been no reorganization.[10]

The date of distribution or transfer shall be that day on which are distributed or transferred all those properties of the distributor or transferor corporation which are to be distributed or transferred pursuant to the liquidation or reorganization. If the distribution or transfer of all such property is not made on one day, then the date of distribution or transfer shall be that day on which the distribution or transfer of all such properties is completed.[11]

The date of distribution or transfer shall be that day as of which (1) substantially all of the properties to be distributed or transferred have been distributed or transferred, and (2) the distributor or transferor corporation has ceased all operations (other than liquidating activities). Such day also shall be the date of distribution or transfer if the completion of the distribution or transfer is unreasonably postponed beyond the date as of which substantially all the properties to be distributed or transferred have been distributed and the transferor corporation has ceased all operations other than liquidating activities. It is permissible for a corporation to retain some money in a reasonable amount to pay outstanding debts after it has transferred substantially all its properties. A corporation shall be considered to have ceased all operations, other than liquidating activities, when it ceases to be a going concern and its activities are merely for the purpose of winding up its affairs, paying its debts, and distributing any remaining monies or other properties to its shareholders. A statement is required which shall specify the day considered to be the date of distribution or transfer of the assets, those not transferred but retained, and the date the transferor corporation ceased all operations other than liquidating activities.[12] Such statement shall be timely filed with the corporation's last income tax return for the period ending on the date of transfer. If the corporation remains in existence after the date of transfer of assets, then another tax return is required to be filed.[13]

NET OPERATING LOSS CARRYOVERS

The acquiring corporation shall succeed to, and take into account the net operating loss carryovers of the transferor corporation. This rule is further subject to the limitations of Section 172 which will permit an acquiring corporation to integrate the acquiring corporation's net operating losses with its own.[14]

Generally speaking, the net operating losses of both the acquiring and acquired corporation are computed separately. The net operating loss sustained by the acquiring corporation after the date of transfer shall not be carried back in computing the taxable income of the transferor corporation,[15] but such loss can be carried back and applied against the acquiring corporation's *own* taxable income. The effect of this rule is to have a loss applied against the income of the corporation that earned it. Another reason is to prevent corporations from being acquired solely for the purpose of utilizing their losses against the acquiring corporation's income.[16] For example, corporation X merged into Y corporation. Y corporation sustained net operating losses after the merger. Such loss cannot be carried back and utilized against X's taxable income, but it may be carried back and applied against its own income. Such loss carryovers available to the transferor corporation as of the close of the date of distribution or transfer shall first be carried to the first taxable year of the acquiring corporation ending after that date. It is immaterial that the date of transfer is on the last day, or any other day, of the acquiring corporation's taxable year. Thus, such loss carryovers will first be used by the acquiring corporation with respect to the computation of its own loss deduction for that first taxable year.[17] The net operating loss carryovers available to the distributor or transferor corporation as of the close of the date of distribution or transfer shall be carried to the acquiring corporation without diminution by reason of the fact that the acquiring corporation does not acquire 100 percent of the assets of the transferor corporation. Thus, if a subsidiary corporation in which the parent owns eighty percent of the stock is liquidated, 100 percent of the subsidiary's loss is available to the parent.[18]

It is possible that a corporation can have two taxable years when it is acquired. This comes about when the date of transfer is not on the last day of the acquiring corporation's taxable year. Thus, the acquiring corporation's taxable year will be subdivided into preacquisition taxable year and postacquisition taxable year. The preacquisition tax year begins with the beginning of the first taxable year of the acquiring corporation and ends with the close of the date of transfer. The postacquisition tax year begins the day following the date of transfer and ends with the close of the taxable year of the acquiring corporation.[19] This has the effect of having the five-year carryforward of net operating losses having to be used up in four years since one taxable period will have two taxable years.

That part of the acquiring corporation's operating loss deduction for its first taxable year ending after the date of transfer, which is attributable to the net operating loss carryovers of the transferor corporation, is limited to an amount equal to the acquiring corporation's postacquisition part-year taxable income. Such postacquisition part-year taxable income is the amount which bears the same ratio to the acquiring corporation's taxable income for the first taxable year ending after the date of distribution or transfer as the number of days in such first taxable year which follows the date of transfer bears to the total number of days in such taxable year.

This limitation applies solely for the purpose of computing the net operating loss deduction of the acquiring corporation for their first taxable year ending after the date of transfer. This limitation is inapplicable to determining the portion of any net operating loss, whether of the distributor, transferor, or acquiring corporation, which may be carried to any taxable year of the acquiring corporation following its first taxable year ending after the date of transfer.[20]

The limitation shall be applied to the aggregate of the allowable net operating loss carryovers of the transferor corporation without reference to the taxable year in which the net operating losses were sustained by such corporation. In those cases in which the assets of two or more transferor corporations were acquired on the same date of transfer, then the limitation provided by Section 381(c)(1)(B) shall be applied to the aggregate of the net operating loss carryovers from all such transferor corporations.[21]

For purposes of illustration, the following two examples from the Regulations are being used: [22]

X Corporation and Y Corporation were organized on January 1, 1956, and make their returns on the calendar year basis. On December 16, 1957, X Corporation transferred all of its assets to Y Corporation in a statutory merger to which Section 361 applies. The net operating losses and taxable income of the two corporations are as follows:

Taxable year	X Corporation (Transferor)	Y Corporation (Acquirer)
1956	$(35,000)	$(5,000)
Ending 12/16/57		
1957	(30,000)	36,500

The aggregate of the net operating loss carryovers of X Corporation under Section 381(c)(1)(A) to Y Corporation's taxable year ending December 31, 1957, is $65,000, but pursuant to Section 381(c)(1)(B), only $1,500 of such aggregate amount ($36,500 x 15/365) may be used in computing the net operating loss deduction of Y Corporation for such taxable year under Section 172(a). This limitation applies even though Y Corporation's own net operating loss carryover to such taxable year is only $5,000, with the result that Y Corporation has taxable income of $30,000, for its taxable year ending December 31, 1957, that is, $36,500 less the sum of $5,000 and $1,500.

X Corporation was organized on January 1, 1954, and Y Corporation was organized on January 1, 1956. Each corporation makes its return on the basis of the calendar year. On December 31, 1956, X Corporation transferred all its assets to Y Corporation in a statutory merger to which Section 361 applies. The net operating losses and the taxable income of the two corporations are as follows:

Taxable year	X Corporation (Transferor)	Y Corporation (Acquirer)
1954	$(5,000)	
1955	(15,000)	
1956	(10,000)	$20,000
1957		40,000

The aggregate of the net operating loss carryovers of X Corporation carried to Y Corporation's taxable year 1957 is $30,000, and the full amount of such carryover is allowed in such taxable year to Y Corporation as a deduction, since such amount does not exceed the limitation ($40,000 x 365/365) for such taxable year.

The purpose of the allocation rules is to limit the net operating loss carryovers of the transferor corporation which can be included in the acquiring corporation's net operating loss deduction for its first taxable year ending after the date of distribution or transfer based upon a ratio of the acquiring corporation's income for that year.

The portion of any net operating loss which is carried back or carried over to any taxable year is the excess, if any, of the amount of the loss over the sum of the taxable income for each of the prior taxable years to which the loss may be carried. The various net operating loss carrybacks and carryovers to such taxable years are considered to be applied in reduction of the taxable income in the order of the taxable years in which the net operating losses are sustained, beginning with the loss for the earliest taxable year. The sequence for the use of loss years remains the same, and the requirement is to begin with the net operating loss of the earliest taxable year, whether or not it is a loss of the distributor, transferor, or acquiring corporation.[23] A net operating loss for a loss year of a distributor or transferor corporation which ends on or before the last day of a loss year of the acquiring corporation shall be considered to be a net operating loss for a year prior to such loss year of the acquiring corporation.[24] In a case where the acquiring corporation has acquired the assets of two or more transferor corporations on the same date of transfer, the loss years of the transferor corporations shall be taken into account in the order in which such loss years terminate; if any one of the loss years of a transferor corporation ends on the same day as the loss year of another transferor corporation, either loss year may be taken into account before the other.[25]

Net operating losses may be carried back three years and carried forward five years. Since the taxable year of the transferor corporation ends with the close of the date of transfer, such taxable year and the first taxable year of the acquiring corporation which ends after that date shall be considered two separate taxable years to which a net operating loss of the transferor corporation for any taxable year ending before that date may be carried over. This rule is applicable irrespective of the fact that the taxable year of the transferor corporation ending on the date of transfer is a period of less than twelve months.[26]

If the date of transfer is not on the last day of the acquiring corporation's taxable year, then a net operating loss of a transferor corporation is carried to the postacquisition part year and then to the acquiring corporation's subsequent taxable years, whereas a net operating loss of the acquiring corporation is carried to the preacquisition part year and then to the postacquisition part year.[27]

In computing the preacquisition part year and postacquisition part year, the allocation required is made in proportion to the number of days in each. After obtaining the taxable income of the preacquisition part year and of the postacquisition part year, a computation is required of the net operating loss deduction for each such part year. The net operating loss deduction for the preacquisition part year is computed without any consideration of the net operating loss of transferor corporation. Consequently, only net operating loss carryovers and carrybacks of the acquiring corporation to the preacquisition part year shall be taken into account in computing the net operating loss deduction for such part year. The net operating loss deduction for the postacquisition part year shall be computed by taking into account all the net operating loss carryovers available to the transferor corporation as of the close of the date of transfer, as well as the carryovers and carrybacks of the acquiring corporation to the postacquisition part year.[28] The taxable income of the preacquisition part year or the postacquisition part year cannot be less than zero.

If the acquiring corporation succeeds to the net operating loss carryovers of two or more transferor corporations on two or more dates of transfer during the same taxable year of the acquiring corporation, and if the amount of the net operating loss carryovers acquired on the first date of transfer equals the postacquisition income, then there will be a limitation which shall be equal to such postacquisition income.[29] That part of the taxable year of the acquiring corporation beginning on the day following the first date of transfer and ending with the close of the taxable year of the acquiring corporation shall be divided into the same number of partial postacquisition years and the number of dates of transfer on which the acquiring corporation succeeds to net operating loss carryovers during its taxable year. The first partial postacquisition year shall begin with the day following the first date of transfer and shall end with the close of the second date of transfer.[30] The second and succeeding partial postacquisition years shall begin with the day following the close of the preceding such partial year and shall end with the close of the succeeding date of transfer, or, if there is no such succeeding date, then with the close of the taxable year of the acquiring corporation. The postacquisition income of the acquiring corporation shall be allocated in proportion to the number of days in each such partial year among the partial postacquisition years.[31]

If the acquiring corporation succeeds to the loss carryovers of two transferor corporations on two dates of transfer during the same taxable year of the acquiring corporation, and if the amount of the loss carryovers acquired on the first date equals or exceeds the income for the first partial postacquisition year, the limitation is the amount of the postacquisition income. If the income for the first partial postacquisition year exceeds the loss carryovers acquired on the first date of transfer, the limitation shall be the amount of the postacquisition income reduced by the amount of the excess.

EARNINGS AND PROFITS (DEFICIT)

The acquiring corporation shall succeed to, and take into account, the earnings and profits, or deficit in earnings and profits, of the transferor corporation as of the close of the date of transfer. If the transferor corporation accumulates earnings and profits, or incurs a deficit in earnings and profits, after the date of transfer and before the completion of the reorganization or liquidation, such accumulation or deficit shall be deemed to have been incurred as of the close of the date of transfer.[32]

The earnings and profits shall be deemed to be received by, and to become a part of the accumulated earnings and profits of, the acquiring corporation as of the date of acquisition. The same rule is applicable to deficits of the transferor corporation. In no event are such earnings or profits, or deficit taken into account in determining earnings and profits of the acquiring corporation for the taxable year during which occurs the date of transfer.[33] This is important in determining whether amounts are available for purposes of dividend distributions. In effect, this provision permits a consolidation of earnings or profits or of deficits as of the date of transfer.[34]

If one corporation has accumulated earnings and profits as of the date of transfer and the other corporation has a deficit in accumulated earnings and profits, then the total of any such deficits shall be used only to offset earnings and profits by the acquiring corporation after the date of transfer. Thus, the acquiring corporation will be deemed to be maintaining two separate earnings and profits accounts after the date of transfer. In effect, this provision prevents an offset of deficits against earnings and profits to reduce the amount available for dividend distributions.[35]

If the date of transfer is a day other than the last day of a taxable year of the acquiring corporation, then the earnings and profits will be deemed to have accumulated as of the close of that date in an amount which bears the same ratio to the undistributed earnings and profits of that corporation for that year as the number of days in the taxable year preceding the date following the date of distribution or transfer bears to the total number of days in the taxable year, and will be deemed to have accumulated after the date of distribution or transfer in an amount which bears the same ratio to the undistributed earnings and profits of the corporation for that year as the number of days in the taxable year following that date bears to the total number of days in the taxable year. Any distributions made during that taxable year shall reduce the undistributed earnings and profits of the acquiring corporation for that year.[36]

In the case of successive acquisitions, a consolidation is required of accounts having earnings and profits and those having a deficit in earnings and profits.[37]

If the transferor corporation distributes boot to its shareholders, then the accumulated earnings and profits of the transferor corporation as of the close of the date of transfer is computed by taking into account the amount of earnings and profits properly applicable to the distribution, regardless of whether this distribution occurs before or after the close of the date of transfer.[38] If there is an intercorporate liquidation occurring without a step up in the basis of assets, and the acquiring corporation receives less than 100 percent of the distributed assets by the liquidating corporation, then the accumulated earnings and profits of the distributor corporation, as of the close of the date of distribution, will be computed by taking into account the amount of earnings and profits applicable to minority shareholders, irrespective of whether these distributions occur before or after the close of the date of distribution.[39] An allocation of earnings and profits is required where part of the assets are transferred to two or more corporations controlled by the acquiring corporation.[40]

The purpose of the allocation rules for earnings and profits is to determine how much of the transferor's corporations earnings and profits are to be recorded by the acquiring corporation for subsequent dividend distributions.

CAPITAL LOSSES

The acquiring corporation succeeds to, and takes into account, the capital loss of the transferor corporation. The capital loss carryovers of the acquiring and transferor corporation are computed without any reference to the capital gains and losses of the other corporation, whether it be the acquiring or transferor corporation.[41]

The capital loss carryover available to the transferor corporation as of the close of the date of transfer shall first be carried to the first taxable year of the acquiring corporation ending after that date, irrespective of whether the date of transfer is on the last day, or any other day, of the acquiring corporation's taxable year.[42] Furthermore, there is no diminution of the capital loss carryover because the acquiring corporation does not acquire 100 percent of the assets of the transferor corporation.[43]

Any capital loss carryover of the transferor corporation which is available to the acquiring corporation as of the close of the date of transfer shall be a short-term capital loss of the acquiring corporation in each of the taxable years to which the net capital loss giving rise to such carryover may be carried. However, in the first taxable year of the acquiring corporation ending after the date of transfer, the total capital loss carryover of the transferor corporation which may be treated in that year as short-term capital losses of the acquiring corporation is limited to an amount which bears the same ratio to the acquiring corporation's net capital gain for such first taxable year as the number of days in such first taxable year which follows the date of transfer bears to the total number of days in such taxable year. Thus, there is no limitation on the amount of carryover if the date of transfer is the last day of the acquiring corporation's taxable year for any short-term capital losses for the first taxable year ending after that date of the acquiring corporation.[44]

This limitation is applied to the aggregate of the capital loss carryovers of the transferor corporation without reference to the taxable years in which the net capital losses giving rise to the carryovers were sustained.[45]

The sequence for applying losses and determining of net capital gains is that such losses can be carried forward five years. The Tax Reform Act of 1969 changed this rule to permit a three-year carryback of such losses. Since the taxable year of a transferor corporation ends with the close of the date of transfer, such taxable year and the first taxable year of the acquiring corporation which ends after that date are considered two separate taxable years to which a net capital loss of the transferor corporation for any taxable year ending before that date shall be carried. This rule is applicable even though the taxable year of the transferor corporation which ends on the date of transfer is a period of less than twelve months. However, this rule is inapplicable to the net capital loss carryforward of the acquiring corporation.[46]

The Regulations[47] provide the following rules in determining the order in which capital loss carryovers of the transferor and acquiring corporations from taxable years ending on or before the date of distribution or transfer are considered to be applied in reducing the net capital gain of the acquiring corporation for any intervening taxable year ending after such date:

> (i)Each taxable year of the distributor or transferor and acquiring corporations which, with respect to the first taxable year of the acquiring corporation ending after the date of distribution or transfer, constitutes a first preceding taxable year, shall be treated as if each such year ended on the same day, whether or not such taxable year actually ends on the same day. In like manner, each taxable year of the distributor or transferor and acquiring corporation which, with respect to such first taxable year of the acquiring corporation ending after the date of distribution or transfer, constitutes a second preceding taxable year, shall be treated as if each such year ended on the same day (whether or not such taxable years actually end on the same day), and a similar rule shall be applied with respect to those taxable years of the distributor or transferor and acquiring corporations which constitute the third, fourth, and fifth preceding taxable years;

> (ii)If in the same preceding taxable years both the distributor or transferor and acquiring corporations incurred a net capital loss which is a carryover to an intervening taxable year of the acquiring corporation ending after the date of distribution or transfer, then in applying such losses in reduction of the net capital gain for such an intervening year, either such loss may be taken into account before the other; and

> (iii)The rules of subdivisions (i) and (ii) of this subparagraph shall apply regardless of the number of distributor or transferor corporations the assets of which are acquired by the acquiring corporation on the same date of distribution or transfer.[47]

If the portion of a net capital loss for any taxable year is carried over to a succeeding taxable year, an intervening taxable year is a taxable year of the acquiring corporation which includes, but does not end on, the date of transfer. The intervening taxable year of the acquiring corporation shall be considered as though it were two taxable years, but only for the purpose of computing capital loss carryovers to subsequent taxable years. The preacquisition part year shall begin with the beginning of such taxable year of the acquiring corporation and end with the close of such taxable year of the acquiring corporation. The postacquisition part year shall begin with the day following the date of transfer and shall end with the close of such taxable year of the acquiring corporation. Though considered as two separate taxable years, the preacquisition part year and the postacquisition part year are treated as one taxable year in determining the carryforward years for a net capital loss. The net capital gain for such intervening taxable year shall be divided between the preacquisition part year and the postacquisition part year in proportion to the number of days in each.[48]

After obtaining the net capital gain of the preacquisition part year and post-acquisition part year, it is necessary to determine the capital loss carryovers which are taken into account with respect to each such part year. With respect to the preacquisition part year, no capital loss carryovers of the transferor corporation shall be taken into account. Only capital loss carryovers of the acquiring corporation shall be considered. As regards the postacquisition part year, capital losses of both the transferor and the acquiring corporation shall be taken into account.

METHODS OF ACCOUNTING

An acquiring corporation shall use the same accounting method as that used by the transferor corporation on the date of transfer unless different methods of accounting were used on that date by several transferor corporations or by a transferor corporation and the acquiring corporation.[49]

The acquiring corporation shall take into account the dollar balances of those accounts. of the transferor corporation representing items of income or deduction which, because of its method of accounting, were not required or permitted to be included or deducted by the distributor or transferor corporation in computing taxable income for taxable years ending on or before the date of transfer. The acquiring corporation shall similarly take into its accounts any reserves in which the transferor corporation has taken a deduction for taxable years ending on or before the date of transfer. Items of income and deduction retain the same character in the hands of the acquiring corporation as they would have had in the hands of the transferor corporation if no transfer had occurred.[50]

If all the parties used the same method of accounting on the date of distribution or transfer, the acquired corporation shall continue to use such method of accounting, unless permission from the Commissioner of Internal Revenue has been secured to change to another method.[51]

If the trades or businesses of the parties to a transaction within this section are operated as separate and distinct trades or businesses, then the method of accounting employed by the parties to the transaction on the date of transfer with respect to each trade or business shall be used by the acquiring corporation unless permission has been procured in order to change the method of accounting. If different methods were employed by the several corporations on the date of transfer, then the acquiring corporation shall adopt the principal method of accounting.[52]

If any of the trades or businesses are not operated as separate and distinct trades or businesses, then, to the extent that the same methods of accounting were employed on the date of distribution or transfer by the parties to the transaction with respect to any trades or businesses which are integrated or are required to be integrated, the acquiring corporation shall continue to employ such methods of accounting. If the businesses are not integrated, then the principal method of accounting shall be applied.[53]

The determination of the principal method of accounting shall be made with respect to each integrated trade or business operated by the acquiring corporation immediately after the date of transfer, except for those items in which only a single method of accounting may be used by any one taxpayer.[54]

The principal overall method of accounting of an integrated trade or business is determined by making a comparison of the total of the adjusted bases of the assets immediately preceding the date of transfer and the gross receipts for a representative period of the component trades or businesses which are integrated or are required to be integrated.[55] If this comparison shows that the one or more component trades or businesses having the greatest total of the adjusted bases of assets also has the greatest amount of gross receipts, then such method shall be the principal overall method of accounting. If this comparison shows that both of the aforementioned tests are not met, then there is no principal overall method of accounting, the acquiring corporation shall request the Commissioner to determine the overall method of accounting for such integrated trade or business.

INVENTORIES

If inventories are received by the acquiring corporation, such inventories shall be taken by the acquiring corporation on the same basis on which such inventories were taken by the transferor corporation, unless different inventory methods were used by the several transferor corporations or a transferor corporation and the acquiring corporation.[56] Method under this provision is applicable to the method of identifying the goods and the method or methods of evaluating the goods.

If all the parties to the transaction used the same method of taking inventories on the date of transfer, the acquiring corporation shall continue to use such method of taking inventories.[57] If the trades or businesses are operated as separate and distinct trades or businesses, the method of taking inventories employed by the parties to the transaction on the date of transfer shall be used by the acquiring corporation.[58] On the other hand, if the trades or businesses are not operated as separate and distinct trades or businesses, then the acquiring corporation shall continue to use such methods of taking inventories for such types of goods unless the acquiring corporation has obtained the consent of the Commissioner to use a different method of taking inventories.[59]

Where the method of taking inventories employed on the date of distribution or transfer is continued, it will be unnecessary for the acquiring corporation to renew any election previously made by it or by the transferor corporation with respect to such method of taking inventories. Similarly, the acquiring corporation is bound by any election made by the transferor corporation with respect to any method of taking inventories as though the transfer has not occurred. [60]

If the acquiring corporation is not permitted to use the same method as employed by the transferor corporation, then the acquiring corporation must use the principal method of taking inventories as long as it clearly reflects income.[61] The principal method of taking inventories shall be made with reference to the particular types of goods of each integrated trade or business operated by the acquiring corporation after the date of distribution or transfer, and with reference to the methods of taking inventories previously employed by the parties with respect to such types of goods of the trades or businesses of such parties which are integrated after the date of transfer.

The fair market value of the particular goods for a representative period shall be compared with the fair market value of comparable goods for such period for other groups of trades or businesses with respect to which another method of taking inventories common to all was employed. The principal method of accounting for inventories to be used is that applicable to the goods for a representative period.[62]

DEPRECIATION METHODS

In the case of a corporation acquiring depreciable property from a distributor or transferor corporation, the acquiring corporation shall compute its depreciation allowance by the same method used by the transferor corporation with respect to such property. Thus, if the transferor corporation used the double declining balance method or the sum of the year's digits method of computing depreciation, the acquiring corporation will continue to use such method in determining the depreciation deduction for the assets acquired. This rule is only applicable with respect to that part or all of the basis of the property in the hands of the acquiring corporation immediately after the date of transfer as does not exceed the basis of the property in the hands of the transferor corporation on the date of transfer.[63]

The acquiring corporation may request permission from the Commissioner to change the method of computing depreciation for the assets acquired.

INSTALLMENT METHOD

If an acquiring corporation acquires installment obligations, the income from which the transferor corporation has elected to report on the installment method under Section 453, then the acquiring corporation shall be treated as the transferor corporation would have been treated had it not distributed the installment obligations.[64] Thus, if a proper election is in effect, the acquiring corporation is required to report the same income as would have been required to be reported by the transferor corporation unless permission to use another method had been procured from the Commissioner of Internal Revenue.[65]

The basis for the installment obligations in the hands of the acquiring corporation shall be the same as in the hands of the transferor corporation.[66]

AMORTIZATION OF BOND PREMIUM OR DISCOUNT

If the acquiring corporation assumes liability for the payment of bonds of a transferor corporation which were issued at a discount or premium, then the acquiring corporation is to be treated as the transferor corporation after the date of transfer for purposes of determining the amount of amortization allowable, or includible, with respect to such discount or premium in computing taxable income.[67] Thus, if an acquiring corporation acquires bonds of a transferor corporation issued at a discount, then the net amount of such discount is deductible in computing taxable income under the amortization methods. On the other hand, if an acquiring corporation assumes bonds of a transferor corporation issued at a premium, the acquiring corporation assuming such bonds is required to amortize the premium into its taxable income under the method of amortization being employed by the transferor corporation.

DEFERRED EXPLORATION AND DEVELOPMENT EXPENDITURES

If any transferor corporation has previously made an election to defer and deduct on a ratable basis any exploration or development expenditures in connection with natural resources, then the acquiring corporation is required to use the same method for such expenditures as if the transfer had not occurred.[68]

CONTRIBUTIONS TO PENSION PLANS, EMPLOYEES' ANNUITY PLANS, AND STOCK BONUS AND PROFIT-SHARING PLANS

The acquiring corporation shall be considered after the date of transfer to be the transferor corporation in determining the amount deductible under Section 404 with respect to any contribution to a pension, profit-sharing, stock bonus or employees' annuity plan.[69] This provision is applicable to any unused deduction or excess contribution carryovers which would have been available to the transferor corporation.[70] The first taxable year of the acquiring corporation in which any amount shall be allowed as a deduction to that corporation because of this section shall be its first taxable year ending after the date of transfer.[71] To be entitled to such deduction, the contribution must be paid to the trust, and such trust must be continued as a separate and distinct trust of its own, or it must be consolidated with that of the acquiring corporation. Another way to obtain such deduction is to establish a comparable trust.[72] If the transferor's plan is terminated by the acquiring corporation, the contributions made shall not be disallowed if there is a consolidation or a comparable plan established for the employees of the transferor corporation.[73]

RECOVERY OF BAD DEBTS, PRIOR TAXES OR DELINQUENCY AMOUNTS

If the acquiring corporation is entitled to a recovery of a bad debt, prior tax, or delinquency amount on account of which a deduction or credit was allowed to a transferor corporation for a prior taxable year, and such debt, tax or amount is recovered by the acquiring corporation after the date of transfer, then the acquiring corporation is required to include in its gross income for the taxable year of recovery the same amount of income attributable to the recovery as the transferor corporation would have been required to include in its income had the transfer not occurred.[74]

INVOLUNTARY CONVERSIONS

The acquiring corporation shall be treated as the transferor corporation for applying the rules relating to involuntary conversions.[75] This rule applies irrespective of the fact that the property similar or related in service or use to the property converted, or the stock of a corporation owning such similar property is purchased by the acquiring corporation after the date of the transfer and is not received from the transferor corporation in an A, C or D-type reorganization or an intercorporate liquidation.[76]

DIVIDEND CARRYOVER TO PERSONAL HOLDING COMPANY

An acquiring corporation shall succeed to and take into account the dividend carryover of a transferor corporation in computing its dividends paid deduction for taxable years ending after the date of transfer for which the acquiring corporation is a personal holding company.[77]

INDEBTEDNESS OF CERTAIN PERSONAL HOLDING COMPANIES

If the acquiring corporation assumes liability for any indebtedness which was qualified indebtedness (as defined in Section 545(c) in the hands of the transferor corporation immediately before the assumption of such indebtedness, then, in computing its undistributed personal holding company income for any taxable year beginning after December 31, 1963, and ending after the date of transfer, the acquiring corporation shall be considered the transferor corporation for such purposes.[78]

OBLIGATIONS OF TRANSFEROR CORPORATION

If the acquiring corporation assumes an obligation of a transferor corporation which gives rise to a liability after the date of transfer and if the transferor corporation would be entitled to deduct such liability in computing its taxable income were it paid or accrued after that date by such corporation, then, the acquiring corporation shall be entitled to deduct such liability as if it were the transferor corporation.[79] However, such rule is inapplicable to an obligation which is reflected in the consideration parted with, such as stock securities, or other property given by the acquiring corporation to the transferor corporation.[80]

DEFICIENCY DIVIDEND OF PERSONAL HOLDING COMPANY

If a transferor corporation is liable for personal holding company tax for any taxable year ending on or before the date of distribution or transfer, then in computing such tax the deduction shall be allowed to such corporation for the amount of deficiency dividends paid by the acquiring corporation with respect to the transferor corporation.[81] A deficiency dividend paid by the acquiring corporation with respect to the transferor corporation is a distribution that would satisfy the definition of a deficiency dividend if paid by the transferor corporation to its own shareholders and shall be paid after the date of transfer and on, or within ninety days after, the date of the determination.[82]

DEPLETION ON WASTING ASSETS

An acquiring corporation shall be considered as though it were the transferor corporation after the date of transfer for determining if it is entitled to an allowance for depletion deduction. Thus, if the transferor corporation was entitled to an allowance for depletion deduction, such deduction can be utilized by the acquiring corporation.[83]

MISCELLANEOUS CARRYOVERS IN CORPORATE ACQUISITIONS

An acquiring corporation shall take into account any charitable contributions made by a transferor corporation during the taxable years ending on the date of transfer, or in immediately preceding years which are in excess of the maximum amount deductible for those taxable years under Section 170(b)(2) relating to contribution carryovers.[84]

Two other adjustments having limited application are: (1) pre-1954 adjustments resulting from changes in accounting methods[85] and (2) successor life insurance company[86] attributes such as operations loss carryovers and the investment yield.

The last attribute having any significance in the carryover of tax attributes is that of the investment credit.[87] The unused investment credit carryovers will be available to the acquiring corporation since such an acquisition does not constitute an early disposition to the acquired corporation.

Such a successor corporation will also acquire the early disposition problems that accompany the credit. Thus, if the successor corporation should dispose of property on which the acquired corporation had taken the seven percent credit, the successor corporation must make the necessary adjustment by increasing its tax in the year of disposition or reduce the credit carryovers.

In certain situations, the unused credit carryover may not be available to the acquired corporation even though the acquisition does not constitute an early disposition. [88] This arises where the assets of a subsidiary are transferred to a new subsidiary. There is no recapture of any investment credit since there is no early disposition. However, unused investment credits of the parent corporation will not be available to the new subsidiary.

Thus, the carryover of tax attributes in certain corporate acquisitions is an extremely complex area, but it must be considered in every successful corporate acquisition.

FOOTNOTES

[1]IRC-1954; Section 334(b)(2).

[2]IRC-1954; Section 1245.

[3]IRC-1954; Section 1250.

[4]Regulations 1.381(a)-1(b)(2).

[5]Ibid.

[6]Regulations; 1.381(a)-1(b)(3).

[7]IRC-1954; Section 381(a)(2).

[8]Regulations; 1.381(a)-1(b)(3).

[9]Regulations; 1.381(b)-1(a)(1).

[10]Regulations; 1.381(b)-1(a)(2).

[11]Regulations; 1.381(b)-1(b)(1).

[12]Regulations; 1.381(b)-1(b)(2).

[13]Regulations; 1.381(c).

[14]Regulations; 1.381(c)(1)-1.

[15]Regulations; 1.381(c)(1)-1(b).

[16]Regulations; 1.381(c)(1)-1(b).

[17]Regulations; 1.381(c)(1)-1(c).

[18]Regulations; 1.381(c)(1)-1(c)(2).

[19]Regulations; 1.381(c)(1)-1(d)(1).

[20]Regulations; 1.381(c)(1)-1(d)(2).

[21]Regulations; 1.381(c)(1)-1(d)(3).

[22]Regulations; 1.381(c)(1)-1(d)(5).

[23]Regulations; 1.381(c)(1)-1(e)(1).

[24]Regulations; 1.381(c)(1)-1(e)(2).

[25]IRC-1954; 172(b)(1).

[26]Regulations; 1.381(c)(1)-(e)(3).

[27]Regulations; 1.381(c)(1)-(b)(2).

[28]Regulations; 1.381(c)(1)-1(f)(6).

[29]Regulations; 1.381(c)(1)-2(b)(1).

[30]Regulations; 1.381(c)(1)-2(b)(2).

[31]Regulations; 1.381(c)(1)-2(b)(3).

[32]Regulations; 1.381(c)(2)-1(a).

[33]Regulations; 1.381(c)(2)-1(a)(2).

[34]Regulations; 1.381(c)(2)-1(a)(4).

[35] Regulations; 1.381(c)(2)-1(a)(5).

[36]Regulations; 1.381(c)(2)-1(a)(6).

[37]Regulations; 1.381(c)(2)-1(b)(1).

[38]Regulations; 1.381(c)(2)-1(c)(1).

[39]Regulations; 1.381(c)(2)-1(c)(2).

[40]Regulations; 1.381(c)(2)-1(d).

[41]Regulations; 1.381(c)(3)-1(a)(2).

[42]Regulations; 1.381(c)(3)-1(a)(2).

[43]Regulations; 1.381(c)(3)-1(b)(2).

[44]Regulations; 1.381(c)(3)-1(c)(1).

[45]Regulations; 1.381(c)(3)-1(c)(2).

[46]Regulations; 1.381(c)(3)-1(d)(3).

[47]Regulations; 1.381(c)(3)-1(d)(1)-(i) & (ii).

[48]Regulations; 1.381(c)(3)-1(e).

[49]Regulations; 1.381(c)(4)-(1).

[50] Regulations; 1.381(c)(4)-(1)(ii).

[51] Regulations; 1.381(c)(4)-(1)(b).

[52] Regulations; 1.381(c)(4)-(1)(b)(2).

[53] Regulations; 1.381(c)(4)-(1)(b)(3).

[54] Regulations; 1.381(c)(4)-(1)(c)(2).

[55] Regulations; 1.381(c)(4)-1(c)(2)(ii)-(a) & (b).

[56] Proposed Regulations; 1.381(c)(5)-1(a)(i).

[57] Proposed Regulations; 1.381(c)(5)-1(b).

[58] Proposed Regulations; 1.381(c)(5)-1(b)(2).

[59] Proposed Regulations; 1.381(c)(5)-1(b)(3).

[60] Proposed Regulations; 1.381(c)(5)-1(b)(a).

[61] Proposed Regulations; 1.381(c)(5)-1(c)(1).

[62] Proposed Regulations; 1.381(c)(5)-1(c)(2).

[63] Regulations; 1.381(c)(6)-1(a)(1) & (2).

[64] Regulations; 1.381(c)(6)-1(e)

[65] Regulations; 1.381(c)(8)-1(a).

[66] Regulations; 1.381(c)(8)-1(b).

[67] Regulations; 1.381(c)(9)-1(a).

[68] Regulations; 1.381(c)(10)-1(a).

[69] Regulations; 1.381(c)(11)-1(a)(1).

[70] Regulations; 1.381(c)(11)-1(b).

[71] Regulations; 1.381(c)(11)-1(c).

[72] Regulations; 1.381(c)(11)-1(d)(4).

[73] Regulations; 1.381(c)(11)-1(e).

[74] Regulations; 1.381(c)(12)-1(a).

[75] Regulations; 1.381(c)(13)-1(a).

[76] Ibid.

[77] Regulations; 1.381(c)(14)-1(a).

[78] Regulations; 1.381(c)(15)-1(a).

[79] Regulations; 1.381(c)(16)-1(a).

[80] Ibid.

[81] Regulations; 1.381-(c)(17)-1(a).

[82] Regulations; 1.381-(c)(17)-1(b).

[83] Regulations; 1.381-(c)(18)-1(a).

[84] Regulations; 1.381-(c)(19)-1(a).

[85] Regulations; 1.381-(c)(21)-1(a).

[86] Regulations; 1.381-(c)(22)-1(a).

[87] IRC-1954; Section 381(c)(23).

[88] IRC-1954; Section 47(b)(2).

Typical Situations Resulting in Reduced Tax Liability 9

One of the most widely used tax devices is the acquisition of a corporation with unused net operating losses for the sole purpose of offsetting such losses against its own or future profits, thereby reducing the tax liability of the acquiring corporation. The Internal Revenue Code presents many obstacles to be overcome before an acquiring corporation can utilize corporate loss carryovers incurred in another business.

Some of the weapons in the Treasury's arsenal to overcome this device are: (1) Section 382, dealing with special limitations on net operating loss carryovers, (2) Section 269, dealing with acquisitions made to evade or avoid taxes, and (3) judicial decisions.

SECTION 382

The net operating loss carryovers of a corporation (hereinafter called a "loss corporation") will be completely eliminated if certain conditions exist. The statute[1] provides that if, at the end of a loss corporation's taxable year, there has been a change since the beginning of such year, or of a prior taxable year, of at least fifty percent in the ownership of the corporation's outstanding stock, and only if the corporation has not continued to carry on substantially the same trade or business as that conducted before such change will such statute apply. Thus, if the statute is applicable, then the entire net operating loss carryovers from prior taxable years of such corporation is disallowed in computing the net operating loss deductions for that year and for all subsequent taxable years. Furthermore, it becomes apparent that the statutory purpose of this section was to eliminate the trafficking in loss corporations.

The circumstances[2] under which Section 382(a) is to be used are:

1. Any one or more of those persons who own, actually and constructively, a percentage of the total fair market value of the outstanding stock of such corporation which is at least fifty percentage points more than such person or persons owned at the beginning of such taxable year or at the beginning of the prior taxable year;
2. The increase in percentage points is attributable to a purchase of such stock or the stock of another corporation owning stock in such loss corporation;
3. The loss corporation has not continued to carry on a trade or business substantially the same as that conducted before any increase in percentage points.

The persons described above shall be the ten persons who own, actually and constructively, the greatest percentage of the fair market value of the outstanding stock of a loss corporation at the end of a taxable year.[3] Thus, this rule is applicable when stockholders of a corporation increase their percentage interest in the corporation by at least fifty percentage points. This is not the same as percentage of increase. For example, if a shareholder owns sixty percent of the outstanding stock of a corporation and he acquires additional shares increasing his interest to seventy-five percent, he has increased his interest by twenty-five percent but has an increase of only fifteen percentage points.

The determination of whether a change of ownership has occurred is made as of the close of the taxable year of a loss corporation. A "change of ownership" has occurred only if the stock ownership of the ten persons has increased at least fifty percentage points at any one time during the taxable year or during the prior taxable year, or may take place in several transactions occurring during such two-year period.[4]

The "change of ownership" must be attributable only to a purchase of stock. There is a purchase of stock only if (1) the basis of such stock is determined solely by reference to its cost to the acquirer thereof, and (2) immediately before its acquisition the ownership of such stock would not be attributed to the acquirer by application of the constructive ownership rules.[5]

This increase in percentage points may be attributable to either an indirect purchase of stock[6] or a decrease in outstanding stock[7] arising from a stock redemption. For example, if X Corporation owns 100 shares of stock of Y Corporation and if A purchases twenty percent in value of the outstanding stock of X Corporation, this will be considered an indirect purchase by A of twenty shares of stock. On the other hand, if A and B each own fifty percent in value of the outstanding stock of X Corporation, a redemption by X Corporation of all of B's stock will increase A's ownership of stock by fifty percentage points.

A change in trade or business will give rise to this section if the loss corporation does not continue to carry on a trade or business substantially the same as that conducted before any increase in stock ownership which is taken into account in determining whether a change of ownership has occurred. The change in trade or business may occur at any time on or after the date of the earliest such increase during the period beginning on the first day of the loss corporation's prior taxable year.[8] All the facts and circumstances shall be taken into account in determining whether a corporation has not continued to carry on a trade or business substantially the same as that conducted before any increase in the ownership of its stock.

A corporation has not continued to carry on a trade or business substantially the same as that conducted before any increase in the ownership of its stock if the corporation is not carrying on an active trade or business at the time of such increase in ownership. Thus, if the corporation is inactive at the time of such an increase and subsequently is reactivated in the same line of business as that originally conducted, the corporation has not continued to carry on a trade or business substantially the same as that conducted before such increase in stock ownership.[9]

If the corporation discontinues more than a minor portion of its business carried on before such increase, the corporation has not continued to carry on a trade or business substantially the same as that conducted before an increase in the ownership of its stock.[10] The word "minor" is really a question of fact with consideration given to whether the discontinuance of the activities has the effect of utilizing loss carryovers to offset gains of a business unrelated to that which produced the losses.

If the corporation continues to carry on its prior business activities substantially undiminished, the addition of a new trade or business does not constitute a failure to carry on substantially the same trade or business.[11] If the location of the business is changed with the result that the business is substantially altered, then the corporation has not continued to carry on a trade or business substantially the same as that conducted before any increase in the ownership of its stock.[12] A similar result occurs when the corporation is primarily engaged in the rendition of services by a particular individual or individuals and, after the increase in ownership, the corporation is primarily engaged in the rendition of services by different individuals.[13]

Section 382(b)(1) provides that if either the transferor corporation or the acquiring corporation has a net operating loss carryover which is a carryover to the first taxable year of the acquiring corporation ending after the date of transfer, the amount of such carryover which may be used by the acquiring corporation is reduced unless the stockholders, immediately before the reorganization, of the corporation possessing the carryover own, immediately after the reorganization at least twenty percent of the fair market value of the outstanding stock of the acquiring corporation.[14] The ownership of at least twenty percent of the fair market value of the stock of the acquiring corporation must result from the ownership of stock in the loss corporation immediately before the reorganization.[15]

The amount of the reduction shall be determined as follows:

> (i) Determine the percentage of the fair market value of the outstanding stock of the acquiring corporation owned, immediately after the reorganization, by the stockholders (immediately before the reorganization) of the loss corporation, which is attributable to their ownership of stock in the loss corporation immediately before the reorganization.
>
> (ii) If the percentage determined under subdivision (i) of the subparagraph is less than twenty percent, compute the difference between such percentage and twenty percent, and multiply such difference by five. The resulting product is the percentage by which the net operating loss carryovers are reduced.[16]

For example, if the shareholders of an acquired corporation own eight percent of the fair market value of the acquiring corporation's outstanding stock after the reorganization, a reduction is required. The difference between eight percent and twenty percent is twelve percent, which when multiplied by five produces sixty percent. Therefore, the amount of the reduction is equal to sixty percent of the net operating loss carryovers from the loss corporation, so that if the net operating loss carryovers amounted to $200,000, the amount of the reduction would be $120,000.

An exception to this reduction is provided if, immediately before the reorganization, the transferor corporation and the acquiring corporation are owned substantially by the same persons in the same proportion. This exception is inapplicable to a statutory consolidation.[17]

In computing the carryovers to subsequent years, the income of the first taxable year that is presumed to have been absorbed in such years, thus reducing the amount of the loss carryover, is to be increased by the amount of the reduction of the total net operating loss.[18]

While Section 382 only covers net operating loss carryovers of loss corporation, there was no prohibition in the Code to prohibit such acquisitions to utilize unused credits and capital losses. The Revenue Act of 1971 enacted Code Section 383 to prevent the acquiring corporation from availing themselves of other tax benefits.

The new provision restricts or eliminates the following carryovers by an acquiring corporation as follows:

1. Investment credit carryover
2. Foreign tax credit carryover
3. Capital loss carryover
4. Work incentive credit carryover

In order for the new provision to apply, either of the two following transactions must have occurred: (1) a change of ownership and business described in Code Section 382(a)(1); (2) a tax-free reorganization in which the former stockholders of the acquired corporation own less than twenty percent of the value of the outstanding stock of the acquiring corporation after the acquisition.

Thus, by incorporating the provisions of Section 382, the acquiring corporation can only utilize a percentage of the acquired corporations's carryovers. This percentage is equivalent to five times the percentage of value of the acquiring corporation's stock owned by the former shareholders of the acquired corporation immediately after the reorganization.

JUDICIAL CONSTRUCTION

The leading case on transfer of losses is *Libson Shops*.[19] This case was decided under the 1939 Code and provides that an operating loss carryover can only be applied to the income from the business which generated the loss. Thus, losses incurred in one business are not available as carryovers to offset the profits of another corporation.

In *Libson,* the taxpayer corporation was organized to provide management services for sixteen sales corporations. The stock of all seventeen corporations was owned, directly or indirectly, by the same individuals in the same proportions. In 1949, the sixteen sales corporations were merged into the taxpayer corporation pursuant to applicable state laws. Prior to the merger, three of the sales corporations had net operating losses which had not been exhausted as carryovers. In the year after the merger, these same three retail units continued to incur losses. However, the taxpayer corporation showed an overall profit. In its return for its first taxable year after the merger, the taxpayer claimed a net operating loss deduction based on carryovers of the premerger losses of the three unprofitable sales corporations. The Commissioner disallowed such deduction and the controversy ultimately reached the Supreme Court.

The Supreme Court sustained the Commissioner because the income against which the offset was claimed was not produced by substantially the same businesses which incurred the losses. Thus, the carryover privilege was not available since there was no continuity of business enterprise.

The Treasury has ruled that the Libson Shop doctrine will not be relied upon for a transaction covered by Section 381(a)[20] which arises in the A- and C-type reorganization. However, they will use the doctrine where a single corporation discontinued a losing operation, acquired a profitable one, and there is a change in ownership.[21] In TIR 773[22] the Service indicated that the Libson Shops rule will not apply unless there is more than a fifty percent change in the benefit of the carryovers plus a change in business under Section 382(a).

In *Maxwell Hardware*,[23] the loss corporation discontinued its hardware business and formed a separate real estate division. The real estate business continued for six years at which time the preferred stock was to be redeemed. The Tax Court held that the Libson Shop doctrine applies and disallowed the loss. The Ninth Circuit held that the Libson Shop doctrine was not applicable under the 1954 Code. The Commissioner has announced that he will not follow this decision.[24] Thus, the effect of this decision was to permit the corporation to utilize a net operating loss carryover and avoid both Section 269 and 382(a).

In the most recent case,[25] the Tax Court denied a carryover to a corporation that ceased doing business during the taxable year after a change in ownership. Some form of business operations must continue subsequent to the change in ownership. Generally speaking, Section 382(a) curtails the use of net operating losses to offset the income of business unrelated to the business which produced the loss. But in the instant case, the income was derived from the same business that produced the operating loss for which a net operating loss carryover was sought. No unrelated business was involved. This is the significance of this case.

Previously, loss carryovers have been disallowed when an active business becomes inactive prior to a change in control followed by reactivation of the same line of business[26] or when an active business experiences a change in control followed by a period of inactivity and then reactivates the old business.[27]

The Service has ruled that a C-type reorganization between brother-sister corporations using their parent's stock for the acquisition is not also an F-type reorganization, therefore the carryback operating losses to prior years of the acquired corporations is not allowable.[28] The reasoning underlying this is that the parent of an acquiring corporation is not a party to a reorganization in an F-type reorganization. In substance, the reorganization is a C-type. On the other hand, the Ninth Circuit held that a merger of brother-sister corporations into a new corporation owned by the same shareholders (A-type) is also an F-type reorganization and allowed carryback of post-merger net operating losses to premerger profitable years of the merged corporation.[29] The Service has refused to follow this decision.[30]

SECTION 269

It is apparent that the Treasury has many weapons at its disposal to prevent the acquisition of a loss corporation by a profitable corporation. Section 269 provides for the disallowance of deductions and credits in the case of acquisitions to evade or avoid income taxes. It is not a corporate reorganization provision and has been used when the provisions of Section 382 are not applicable. Therefore, although a net operating loss carryover may not fall within the prohibition of Section 382 because the same trade or business is carried on after a change of ownership, the carryover may be disallowed under Section 269 if the principal purpose of the change in ownership is to evade or avoid income tax. The application of this section depends upon the motive for the acquisition which is basically a factual question.

Section 269 provides that: (1) any person or persons acquired, directly or indirectly, control of a corporation, or (2) any corporation acquires, directly or indirectly, property of another corporation, the basis of which property in the hands of the acquiring corporation is determined by reference to the basis in the hands of the transferor corporation, the Commissioner may disallow any deduction, credit, or other allowance if the principal purpose of the acquisition was to secure such a benefit which otherwise would not be enjoyed. "Control" means the ownership of stock possessing at least fifty percent of the total combined voting power of all classes of stock entitled to vote or at least fifty percent of the total value of shares of all classes of stock of the corporation.

It applies to the postacquisition losses as well as the preacquisition losses as long as the principal purpose of the acquisition was the evasion or avoidance of tax by securing the benefit of these losses.[31] The disallowance can refer to deductions of both the acquiring and acquired corporation.[32] It has been availed of in the so-called downstream acquisition, when a loss corporation acquires a profitable corporation[33] since the acquiring corporation secures the benefit of a loss it would not otherwise have enjoyed.

SECTION 482

Section 482 provides that:

> In any case of two or more organizations, trades, or businesses (whether or not incorporated, whether or not organized in the United States, and whether or not affiliated) owned or controlled directly or indirectly by the same interests, the secretary or his delegate may distribute, apportion, or allocate gross income, deductions, credits, or allowances between or among such organizations, trades or businesses, if he determines that such distribution, apportionment, or allocation is necessary in order to prevent evasion of taxes or clearly to reflect the income of any of such organizations, trades, or businesses.

In *Maxwell Hardware*,[34] the court held by way of dictum that Section 482 may be used to deny a corporation a net operating loss carryover.

CONSOLIDATED RETURNS

The consolidated return regulations are an attempt by the Internal Revenue Service to reflect the accounting principle that members of a group of corporations which are controlled by one corporation should eliminate income realized on transactions between members of the group. The basis for such rule is that no income has been earned by the group until there has been a transfer of goods and services outside the group.

Another method to utilize losses of affiliated companies is to file consolidated returns. But there must be a business purpose for a corporation to file consolidated returns apart from the offsetting of net operating losses against taxable income of other profitable affiliated companies. In *Elko Realty Co.*[35] and *American Pipe and Steel Corp.*,[36] the court used Section 269 to deny affiliated companies from deducting the net operating losses of an acquired corporation when the principal purpose of tax evasion or avoidance was present.

The consolidated return regulations provide limitations on the availability of net operating losses. Some of the limitations provided are: (1) separate return limitation year (SRLY); (2) consolidated return change of ownership (CRCOO) and (3) built-in deductions.

A separate return limitation year in effect provides that prior losses can only be used to offset income by the company generating the loss, provided there is no consolidated net operating loss for the year of the affiliated group.[37]

This can raise an interesting tax planning possibility in the case of A-C type reorganizations. The assets of the acquired company should be placed within the most profitable member's corporate structure. The SRLY concept will then be limited to the combined results of operations of the entity acquired and the member into which the assets of the acquired entity were placed.

If a company acquired in a B-type reorganization has desirable carryover attributes, it might be advisable to cast the transaction as a C-type reorganization by a subsequent liquidation of the acquired company to reach the same result as described above. If the stock of a company having carryover attributes is purchased, a later liquidation or merger of the acquired company into one most likely to absorb the carryovers will similarly reduce the effect of the SRLY rules. Of course, the liquidation or merger must be planned to avoid the application of Section 334(b)(2) of the Code.

The consolidated return change of ownership rules similarly limit the carryover of net operating losses. It does not apply to a carryback to a consolidated return year. This rule is similar to the change of ownership rule of Section 382(a) without the discontinuance of trade or business requirement. It has the effect of preventing operating losses of members incurred prior to the year of acquisition of being applied to the profits of new members.[38]

The built-in deduction rules provide[39] that deductions or losses which were economically accrued in a separate return limitation year are not deductible, such as depreciation or capital losses.

It is interesting to note that while the limitations concerned with SRLY's, CRCO's and built-in deductions are, in fact, limitations, the Section 382(a) provisions result in complete disallowance.

TRANSFEREE LIABILITY

Section 6901 provides that there may be assessed against the transferee the Federal income taxes of the corporate distributor when there has been a corporate liquidation or reorganization. In order to hold a transferee of assets liable for the transferor's taxes, the Commissioner must prove that the transfer caused insolvency. A transfer for adequate consideration does not result in transferee liability since the assets given in consideration take the place of the transferred assets in the hands of the transferor.

The term "transferee" includes shareholders of dissolved corporations, successor corporations which are parties to a reorganization within Section 368, and all other distributees.[40] Insolvency occurs when the transfer results in a lack of assets by the transferor to satisfy its tax liabilities. Prior to the Commissioner collecting or attempting to collect from the transferee, the Commissioner must exhaust his remedies against the transferor.

A transferee who agrees to assume the debts of a transferor can be subject to transferee liability.[41] In the case of a successor corporation, the general rule is that when one corporation sells or otherwise transfers all its assets to another corporation, the latter is not liable for the debts and liabilities of the transferor. Four exceptions are as follows: (1) when the purchaser expressly or impliedly agrees to assume such debts; (2) when the transaction amounts to a consolidation or merger; (3) when the purchaser corporation is merely a continuation of the selling corporation; and (4) when the transaction is fraudulent.[42]

A new corporation is organized to take over the assets of another corporation for stock of the new company. Since the new company was a reincorporation of the old having the same assets, the new corporation was a transferee of the old.[43]

LIQUIDATION AND REORGANIZATION EXPENSES

The general rule is that expenses incurred in connection with corporate reorganizations are capital expenditures and are not deductible as business expenses or losses. Such amounts include fees and expenses in connection with statutory mergers and consolidations, recapitalizations of an existing corporation, and other changes in a corporation's capital structure. If the proposed merger or reorganization is abandoned, then such expenses are deductible.

The courts have refused a corporate deduction for legal and accounting fees and professional services and expenses in connection with corporation mergers.[44] The theory is that a merged, consolidated or reorganized corporation has transferred its rights, powers, liabilities and obligations to the surviving entity and that they have continuing benefits to the survivor. On the other hand, such expenses have been allowed to a liquidating corporation in a "practical merger," that is a C-type reorganization.[45]

Thus, expenses of reorganizing a corporation have been required to be capitalized and, like organizational expenditures, are deductible only upon dissolution. They differ from organizational expenditures in that they may not be treated as deferred expenses under Section 248 of the Code permitting amortization over a sixty-month period.

Legal fees incurred for tax advice as to merger, followed by stock split and proposed stock redemptions, have to be capitalized. But if the proposed redemption is abandoned, then fees attributable to the stock redemption are deductible in the year of abandonment.[46]

In the case of a liquidation and dissolution, the expenses incurred are deductible as ordinary and necessary business expenses. Any expenses incurred in connection with a twelve-month liquidation are capital expenditures which are proper to offset to capital gains.[47]

Partial liquidations have given the courts more difficulty since such transaction involves both a liquidation and distribution of business assets, the expenses of which are ordinarily deductible, and a change in the corporation's capital structure which should be allowed. In one case,[48] the court held that no part of the expenses allowed in connection with a partial liquidation was considered to be a recapitalization. In another case,[49] a deduction was allowed a corporation for expenses incurred in its plan for partial liquidation to separate a nonbanking business into another corporation. However, no expenses were permitted to change the corporate name since it involved acquisition of capital asset and therefore was capital expenditure.

Professional expenses incurred in connection with a cash purchase of asset would involve the allocation of same among the assets acquired. Thus, to the extent they are allocable to tangible assets, they may be deducted over the useful life of such assets.[50] The seller of such business would offset such fees against the purchase price and thus reduce the gain or increase the loss on sale.

If the stock is acquired for cash, the professional fees will be treated as part of the cost of the stock.[51] If the acquired corporation is liquidated in a transaction to which Section 334(b)(2) applies, the fees are to be allocated among the assets acquired. On the other hand, if the step-up in basis is not met, then the fees become part of the basis of the subsidiary's stock.[52]

STAMP, SALES TAX,
SOCIAL SECURITY AND FILING REQUIREMENTS

There is no longer any Federal Documentary Stamp Tax to be imposed on the issuance or transfer of stock or certificates of indebtedness in a reorganization. Such tax was repealed by the Excise Tax Reduction Act of 1965.[53]

In New York State, the Tax Law imposes a stock transfer tax[54] upon the sale or transfer of stock.

No sales tax is imposed upon transfers to a corporation for stock in a merger or reorganization or upon property distributions as a liquidating dividend.[55]

A corporation in existence during any portion of a taxable year is required to file a return.[56] It must report its taxable income or loss for the portion of year it was in existence. When an existing corporation reincorporates under the law of another state and merges into the newly organized corporation under state merger statutes, the transaction constitutes an F-type reorganization. Under Code Section 381(b), the part of the taxable year before reorganization, as well as the part after reorganization, constitutes a single taxable year of the acquiring corporation.[57]

As regards social security taxes, only the first $9,000 of wages an employee receives during the calendar year is subject to tax.[58] In figuring the wage limitation, a successor employer who acquires a business can count the wages paid by the predecessor to the employees who continue in the employ of the successor employer.[59]

In the area of qualified stock options, restricted stock options and stock purchase plans, the substitution of a new option for an old option or when such option is assumed by a new corporation, the rights and privileges of the optionee are preserved.[60] Thus, there would be no disposition of such option resulting in the immediate recognition of income.

This rule includes mergers, consolidation, purchase or acquisition of stock or property or liquidation. The change may result from a taxable acquisition of stock or property for cash or a tax-free reorganization or when an acquiring corporation makes the substitution or assumption or when made by a new parent or subsidiary.

The conditions giving rise to the aforementioned rules require the following conditions: (1) the aggregate spread between the option price and value of the stock after the substitution or assumption is not greater than the spread before the substitution or assumption; (2) the new option or the assumption of the old option does not give the employee additional benefits which he did not have under the old option.[61]

EFFECT OF CORPORATE
REORGANIZATIONS ON PENSION PLANS

A pension plan is a program established by a corporate employer for the accumulation of funds to be disbursed to its employees at retirement. The employer usually funds the program through periodic contributions, although the employees may make some voluntary contributions.

A pension plan is a form of deferred compensation to employees with favorable tax advantages if the plan meets the statutory requirements.[62] The corporation is entitled to a corporate deduction for such contributions subject to certain limitations.[63] Such payments are not currently taxable to the corporate employees.

An analysis of any existing pension plan is required when a company is being acquired or merged. Such action may have a bearing with various tax consequences to the employer, employee or the trust fund itself. The applicable tax treatment depends upon the type of acquisition being contemplated. The acquiring corporation may not have a plan or, if it has one, it may desire to extend its plan to cover the employees of the acquired company. Thus, the predecessor's plan may be terminated and distributions made from the plan. In any event, amendments are usually required to one or both companies' pension plans, often prior to the consummation of the reorganization.

If the plan is terminated, all the benefits must vest in the participants.[64] The beneficiaries will be afforded long-term capital gains on amounts paid on account of separation from service, if such payments are made within one of the distributee's taxable years.[65] The keynote of the problem is the phrase "separation from service." Thus, if there has been such a separation from service, then capital gains are to be afforded to the beneficiaries. In the area of tax-free reorganizations, many problems have arisen with conflicting authority.

In an A-type reorganization, there is normally a separation from service for the employees of the merged corporation. However, no such separation exists as regards the employees of the surviving corporation. The Court in one case[66] held that there was a separation of services for the employees of the acquired corporation and qualified for long-term capital gains treatment. The case involved a C-type reorganization in which the May Company acquired the assets of the Strouss-Mirshberg Company in exchange solely for shares of voting stock. These shares were distributed to the shareholders of the Strouss-Mirshberg Company in cancellation of their outstanding shares. Pursuant to the reorganization, the acquired company's retirement plan was terminated and distribution was made to the participants. Thus, there was a separation from service even though the employees continued to work for the acquiring company. The same result was held by the court in another case.[67] The Service subsequently held[68] that distributions within one taxable year of the total amount standing to the credit of the participants under the predecessor company's qualified plan, which is terminated by reason of the reorganization, are accorded long-term capital gain treatment.

In a B-type reorganization, the Service[69] has held that an exchange of stock for stock followed by a statutory merger pursuant to the same plan results in a separation of service for the employees of the acquired corporation. In effect, what in substance really occurred was an acquisition of assets for stock. The inference is that in a B-type reorganization, no separation of service would necessarily have occurred. The Tax Court[70] has also held that a plan terminated in a B-type reorganization did not result in a separation of service.

A C-type reorganization involves the exchange of stock for assets, and it has the effect of a separation from service. The Service has ruled that there was a separation from service when pursuant to a reorganization in which all of the assets and liabilities of a company were turned over to a corporation in exchange for its voting stock. There is also a separation from service when such corporation in turn makes a transfer to its wholly-owned subsidiary and receives the common stock of the subsidiary so that the business of the original company is then owned and operated by such subsidiary, which also takes over the employees.

A recent case[71] has caused many problems in the separation from service issue. In the case, Ford Corporation acquired the assets of Philco Corporation in exchange for stock under 368(a)(1)(c). The assets of Philco and their liabilities were transferred to a new subsidiary entitled Philco-Del. The old corporation was liquidated. The new subsidiary adopted the profit-sharing plan of the old corporation. The employees were given the option to take a lump-sum distribution or to defer benefits until death or other separation from service. The taxpayer continued in the employ of the company. The Court held that the lump-sum distribution did not qualify for capital gains treatment since there was no separation from the service of his employer, since there was no change in the makeup of the employees.

In neither the E-type nor F-type reorganization, no capital gains' treatment would be afforded the beneficiaries since no separation of service has occurred.

The Service has ruled[72] that a complete liquidation of a corporation will result in a separation from service. This rule is inapplicable to intercorporate liquidations resulting in a step-up in the basis of assets.[73]

TAX REFORM ACT OF 1969

Congress has recently passed the most significant tax law since the enactment of the 1954 Code. Some of the changes affect reorganizations when the consideration involved is indebtedness. Other changes enacted concern pension plans, use of installment sales and minimum tax on preferences.

The original proposal directed against conglomerate mergers was the Mills Bill.[74] It proposed that if one corporation acquires stock of another corporation, and more than thirty-five percent of the consideration involved for the stock acquired consists of evidence of indebtedness of the acquiring corporation, then part of the interest deduction is disallowed. It proposed that the interest deduction would be allowed in full only up to thirty-five percent of the total consideration. The higher the debt used to acquire a company, the lower the interest deduction.

The new law[75] as enacted limits the deductibility of interest on "corporate acquisition indebtedness" used to finance acquisitions when such interest exceeds five million dollars per year. This five million dollar exemption is further reduced by interest incurred on indebtedness issued after 1967 used to acquire either corporate stock or operating assets (excluding cash). These are not corporate acquisition indebtedness because of the effective date of this Section or the failure to meet the three tests discussed below. For example, indebtedness incurred in 1968 would reduce the five million dollar exemption if such indebtedness qualified as corporate acquisition indebtedness or if after October 10, 1969.

The term "corporate acquisition indebtedness"[76] includes: (1) obligations used to provide consideration for the acquisition of stock in another corporation if the acquiring corporation owns five percent of the stock of the acquired corporation at any time after October 9, 1969, (2) obligations used to provide consideration for the assets of another corporation pursuant to a plan under which at least two-thirds in value of all assets (excluding cash) used in trades or businesses of such other corporation are acquired.

The types of indebtedness to which the above rules apply are obligations which meet the three tests: (1) the subordination test, (2) the convertibility test, and (3) the interest or debt equity test.[77]

The subordination test is met if the debt instruments issued are either subordinate to the claims of the issuing corporation's general creditors or to any substantial amount of the corporation's unsecured indebtedness. It makes no difference if such indebtedness is outstanding or subsequently issued. A debt instrument is considered subordinated whether the terms of the subordination are provided in the obligation itself or in a separate agreement. The subordination must relate to either interest or principal or both.

The convertibility test is met when the debt instrument provides that it is convertible, directly or indirectly, into the stock of the issuing corporation. Furthermore, the convertibility test includes debt instruments which are part of an investment unit which includes an option to acquire, directly or indirectly, stock of the issuing corporation.

The debt-to-equity test is the last requirement for falling within the purview of this prohibition. The debt instrument test is applied as of the last day of the year in which the obligation is issued to acquire another corporation's stock or operating assets. The debt to equity test must be in excess of two to one. This ratio is determined by subtracting the corporation's total indebtedness from the net value of all its assets. This is basically the working capital of a corporation. This amount is then compared with the corporation's total indebtedness. If it exceeds the two to one ratio, the test is met.[78]

Another way of meeting the debt-to-equity ratio is the earnings test.[79] The earnings test is determined, on the last day of the taxable year, by comparing the projected earning of the issuing corporation with its annual interest cost on its total outstanding indebtedness. Average annual earnings[80] is the annual average for a three-year period ending with the last day of a taxable year computed without reduction for interest paid or incurred, depreciation or amortization, dividends paid and federal tax liability.

All of the aforementioned tests must be met before any interest can be disallowed. Assuming the tests are met, the interest is disallowed only for the taxable year in which the debt instrument becomes corporate acquisition indebtedness, and for all subsequent taxable years.[81] If control is subsequently acquired, and, if the earnings test is then met on a combined basis, then the interest will be disallowed as a deduction.

INSTALLMENT METHOD

The use of the installment sales method has been used frequently when debentures and other readily marketable securities were issued. To curtail such use, the Code[82] was amended to provide that a registered coupon, or readily marketable bond or other evidence of indebtedness issued by a corporation or payable on demand must be taken into account in determining whether payments in the year of the sale were less than the thirty percent rule. Thus, many debt securities, along with other forms of consideration received by the shareholders of the acquired corporation, are to be aggregated in determining whether the installment sales election can be made. This change in the reporting rules applies only to sales or other dispositions made after May 27, 1969.

EMPLOYEE PLANS

As previously stated, lump-sum distributions from employee plans will qualify for capital gains treatment by the employee if received within one year. The Tax Reform Act amended the Code to provide that lump-sum distributions from employee plans will not qualify for capital gains treatment by the employee to the extent they are attributable to employer contributions for years beginning after 1969. Furthermore, employer contributions will include amounts which are forfeited and allocated among employees. Such ordinary income portion of a qualified lump-sum distribution will qualify for a seven-year averaging rule.[83] This special rule provides that the tax is limited to seven times the increase in tax which would result from including fourteen and two-sevenths percent of the net lump-sum distribution in gross income in the year received.

FOOTNOTES

[1] Glover Packing Company of Texas vs. United States 328F(2)342(1969).

[2] Regulations; 1.382(a)-1(b).

[3] Regulations; 1.382(a)-1(c).

[4] Regulations; 1.382(a)-1(d).

[5] Regulations; 1.382(a)-1(e).

[6] Regulations; 1.382(a)-1(f).

[7] Regulations; 1.382(a)-1(g).

[8] Regulations; 1.382(a)-1(h).

[9] Regulations; 1.382(a)-1(h)(6).

[10] Regulations; 1.382(a)-1(h)(7).

[11] Regulations; 1.382(a)-1(h)(8).

[12] Regulations; 1.382(a)-1(h)(9).

[13] Regulations; 1.382(a)-1(h)(10).

[14] Regulations; 1.382(b)-1(a)(1).

[15] Regulations; 1.382(b)-1(a)(2).

[16] Regulations; 1.382(b)-1(b)(1)(i) & (ii) a.

[17] Regulations; 1.382(b)-1(d)(1).

[18] Regulations; 1.382(b)-1(e).

[19] Libson Shops Inc. v. Koehler, 353 U.S. 382 (1957).

[20] Rev. Rul 58-603, 1958-2 C.B. 147.

[21] Rev. Rul. 63-40; 1963-1 C.B. 46.

[22] T.I.R. 713, 10/13/65.

[23] Maxwell Hardware, 343F(2)713(1965).

[24] T.I.R. 777 10/13/65.

[25] S.F.H. Inc. 33 T.C. No. 5 (1969).

[26] Glover Packing Co. of Texas v. U.S. 328 F(2)342 (1964).

[27] C.I.R. v. Barclay Jewelry. Inc. 367F(2)193(1966).

[28] Rev. Rul. 69-413, IRB 1969-31, p. 8.

[29] Estate of Stauffer v. C.I.R. 403F(2)611(1968).

[30] Rev. Rul. 69-413, IRB 1969-31, p.8.

[31] R.P. Collins & Co. v. U.S. 303F(2)142(1962).

[32] James Realty Company v. U.S. 280F(2)394(1960).

[33] F.C. Publications Corp. v. C.I.R., 304F(2)779(1962).

[34] Maxwell Hardware Co. v. C.I.R. 343F(2d)713(1965).

[35] 29T.C. 1012(1958).

[36] 243 F(2)115.

[37] Regulations; 1.1502-21(c).

[38] Regulations; 1.1502-21(d).

[39] Regulations; 1502-15(b)(4).

[40] Regulations; 301.6901-1(b).

[41] Kamen Soap Products Co., Inc. v. C.I.R. 230F(2)565.

[42] West Texas Refining & Development Co. v. C.I.R., 13AFTR457.

[43] Waterproofed Products Co., 25BTA648.

[44] Motion Pictures Capital Corp, 32BTA339, 80F(2)872.

[45] Kingsford Company, 41TC646(1964).

[46] Rev. Rul. 67-125,1967-1 C.B. 3.

[47] Mountain States Mixed Feed Co. v. U.S., 65-2UST(955).

[48] Mills Estate Inc. v. C.I.R. 206F(2)244.

[49] U.S. v. General Bancshares Corp. 21 AFTR(2)352.

[50] IRC-1954; Section 1012.

[51] Firemen's Insurance Co. v. C.I.R., 30BTA 1004 (1934).

[52] Regulations; 1.334-1(b).

[53] IRC-1954; Section 3301.

[54] NY Tax Law, Section 270.

[55] New York Tax Law, Section 1101(b)(4)(ii)(A).

[56] Regulations 1.6022-2(a)(2).

[57] Rev. Rul 57-276, 1957-1 C.B. 126.

[58] IRC-1954; Section 3121(a).

[59] IRC-1954; Section 3121(a)(1).

[60] Regulations; 1.425-1(1)(a).

[61] Regulations; 1.425-1(a)(1).

[62] IRC-1954; Section 401(a).

[63] IRC-1954; Section 404(a).

[64] IRC-1954; Section 401(a)(17).

[65] IRC-1954; Section 402(a)(2).

[66] Mary Miller, 227C293, aff'd 226F(2)618, acq. 1958-1 C.B. 5).

[67] Lester B. Martin, 26 T.C. 100(1956).

[68] Rev. Rul. 58-94, 1958-1 C.B. 194.

[69] Rev. Rul. 58-383, 1958-2 C.B. 149.

[70] Robert E. Beaulieu, 24TCM 1670(1965).

[71] Victor S. Gittens, 49 T.C. No. 44(1968).

[72] Rev. Rul. 58-96, 1958-1 C.B. 200.

[73] Ibid.

[74] T.R. 7489(1969).

[75] IRC-1954; Section 279.

[76] IRC-1954; Section 279(b)(1).

[77] IRC-1954; Section 279(b)(2).

[78] IRC-1954; Section 279(c)(1) & (2).

[79] IRC-1954; Section 279(c)(3).

[80] IRC-1954; Section 279(c)(3)(b).

[81] IRC-1954; Section 279(d).

[82] IRC-1954; Section 453(c)(3).

[83] Tax Reform Act, Section 515 Amending Sec. 402(a), 403(a)(2).

Corporate Redemptions and Liquidations

10

DIVIDENDS

The term "dividend" means any distribution of property made by a corporation to its shareholders out of earnings and profits accumulated after February 28, 1913, or out of its earnings and profits of the taxable year (computed without diminution of any distributions made during the taxable year) without regard to the amount of the earnings and profits at the time the distributions were made.[1] Generally speaking, every distribution is made out of earnings and profits to the extent thereof, and from the most recently accumulated earnings and profits.

The phrase "earnings and profits" is frequently used in the Tax Code, but it has not been defined anywhere. It is not synonymous with the accountant's concept of retained earnings, nor is it the same as taxable income, although this is usually the starting point in making such determination. Earnings and profits are usually taxable income or loss with adjustments. Some of the adjustments to increase earnings and profits are: tax exempt interest and proceeds of life insurance. An adjustment that decreases earnings and profits is the excess of accelerated methods of depreciation over straight-line depreciation.

By using various methods, such as the accelerated methods, for tax purposes, as distinguished from the straight-line depreciation method and financial reporting, corporations have been able to distribute tax-free dividends. The Tax Reform Act of 1969[2] provides that for purposes of computing earnings and profits, not of taxable income, for taxable years beginning after June 30, 1972, a corporation is required to deduct depreciation on the straight-line method. This change is similar to one requiring that cost depletion rather than percentage depletion be used in computing earnings and profits.[3]

The term "property"[4] means money, securities and any other property, except stock of the distributing corporations or rights to acquire stock of the distributing corporation.

PROPERTY DIVIDENDS

Noncorporate shareholders must include in gross income the fair market value at the date of the dividend of property received as a dividend.[5] When the dividend is in both cash and property, the amount reported in gross income is the amount of cash received plus the fair market value of the property at the date of the dividend.[6] The dividend is to be reduced by the amount of any liability of the corporation assumed by the shareholder in connection with the distribution or the amount of liability to which the property is subject immediately before, and immediately after, the distribution.[7] In no case is the dividend to be reduced below zero. The basis of property received as a dividend is the fair market value at the date of distribution.[8]

In the case of corporate shareholders, the amount of any distribution is the amount of money received, plus the lower of the fair market value of the property received or the adjusted basis of the other property received increased by the gain recognized to the distributing corporation on LIFO (last in-first out) inventory and liability in excess of basis.[9] That portion of the distribution which is a dividend is included in gross income. That portion of the distribution which is not a dividend shall be applied against and reduce the adjusted basis of the stock.[10] After the basis is recovered, the excess is treated as a gain from the sale or exchange of property.[11] The basis to the corporation is the lower of the fair market value of such property or the adjusted basis.[12]

A corporate distribution to a shareholder with respect to his stock is within the purview of Section 301, although it takes place at the same time as another transaction, if the distribution is in substance a separate transaction, whether or not connected in a formal sense. This is the step transaction doctrine, and is most likely to occur in the case of a recapitalization, a reincorporation, or a merger of a corporation with a newly organized corporation having substantially no property.[13]

STOCK REDEMPTIONS

Stock shall be treated as redeemed by a corporation if the corporation acquires its stock from a shareholder in exchange for property, whether or not the stock so acquired is cancelled, retired or held as treasury stock.[14] The redemption will be treated as a distribution in part or full payment in exchange for the stock.

Such redemption will be treated as exchange if any of the following tests are met: (1) the redemption is not essentially equivalent to a dividend, (2) the distribution is substantially disproportionate with respect to the stockholder and the stockholder owns (immediately after the redemption) less than fifty percent of the entire voting stock, (3) the redemption is in complete redemption of all of the stock of the corporation owned by the stockholder, (4) the redemption is of stock issued by a railroad corporation pursuant to a plan of reorganization under Section 77 of the Bankruptcy Act.[15]

A distribution will be deemed to be substantially disproportionate with respect to a shareholder only if the ratio which the voting stock owned by the shareholder immediately before the redemption bears to all of the voting stock of the corporation at such time. This test applies only to common stock, whether or not it is voting stock. If there is more than one class of common stock, the test is based on the fair market value. The aforementioned provisions are inapplicable to any redemptions made pursuant to a plan, the effect of which is a series of redemptions which are not substantially disproportionate with respect to the stockholder.[16] For purposes of illustration, assume the following data:

Share-holders	Number of Shares Before Redemption	Shares Redeemed	After Redemption	Percentage of Ownership Before	After
A	100	55	45	25%	15%
B	100	25	75	25%	25%
C	100	20	80	25%	26-2/3%
D	100	0	100	25%	33-1/3%
	400	300	300	100%	100%

In order to meet the substantially disproportionate test, such shareholder must own after the redemption less than twenty percent (80% x 25%) of the then outstanding shares. Only shareholder A would meet the test and be afforded the capital gains treatment on the distribution. The other shareholders would have to report dividend income on the distribution.

The constructive ownership rules would apply to a redemption when the corporation is closely held. The rule[17] provides that in case of a complete redemption of all of the stock of a corporation owned by the shareholder, the attribution rules do not apply if: (1) immediately after the distribution the distributee has no interest in the corporation (including an interest as an officer, director or employee) other than an interest as a creditor, (2) the distributee does not acquire any such interest (other than stock acquired by bequest or inheritance) within ten years from the date of such distribution, and (3) the distributee files an agreement to notify the Commissioner of any acquisition. This is often referred to the ten-year "look back" or "look forward" rule and gives the Commissioner an additional one year to assess additional taxes.

The aforementioned rules do not apply if:

1. Any portion of the stock redeemed was acquired, directly or indirectly, within the ten-year period ending on the date of the distribution by the distributee from a person, the ownership of whose stock would be attributable to the distributee under the constructive ownership rules, or,
2. Any person owns (at the time of the distribution) stock, the ownership of which is attributable to the distributee under Section 318(a); and if such person acquired any stock in the corporation, directly or indirectly, from the distributee within the ten-year period ending on the date of distribution, unless such stock so acquired from the distributee is redeemed in the same transaction.

Corporations in the past have used appreciated property to redeem their stock without any tax being imposed upon the appreciation. Section 311, prior to the 1969 Tax Reform Act, provided that no gain or loss is recognized to a corporation if it distributes property with respect to its stock. The new section[18] provides that if a corporation distributes appreciated property to a shareholder in redemption of all or part of his stock, then such gain is recognized to the corporation to the extent that the fair market value exceeds its adjusted basis. It is immaterial that the redemption proceeds are to be treated as dividend income. Some exceptions to this new provision are: (1) complete or partial liquidation of a corporation, (2) a distribution in complete termination of the interest of a shareholder owning at least ten percent of the stock, (3) distribution of stock of a fifty percent or more owned subsidiary.

PREFERRED STOCK BAIL-OUTS

If a shareholder sells or otherwise disposes of Section 306 stock, which disposition is not a redemption within Section 317(b), then the amount realized is treated as ordinary income to the extent of the stock's ratable share of earnings and profits of the issuing corporation at the time of its distribution. Any excess is treated as capital gain to the extent it exceeds the adjusted basis.[19] No loss is recognized. Thus, if such disposition is a redemption, then the amount realized is treated as a dividend.[20] For example, a common stock shareholder receives preferred stock as a nontaxable dividend. The preferred stock is treated as Section 306 stock, and upon a subsequent sale or other disposition, the entire sales proceeds will be a dividend.

Section 306 stock means stock which is not common stock, and which was received by the shareholder in pursuance of a plan of reorganization and with respect to which no gain or loss was recognized.[21] Section 306 stock includes convertible stock.[22]

The exceptions to the taint of Section 306 stock includes: (1) complete termination of shareholder's interest, (2) if "Section 306 stock" is redeemed in a distribution in part or complete liquidation, (3) when gain or loss is not recognized, (4) transactions not in pursuance of a plan having as one of its principal purposes the avoidance of federal income tax.

Preferred stock received in connection with a merger is "Section 306 stock." The proceeds or the disposition of preferred stock which is issued in a merger is not tainted stock unless such disposition is in anticipation of a redemption after issuance of the stock.

CORPORATE LIQUIDATIONS

The 1954 Code provides various methods of liquidating a corporation, each with adverse tax consequences. Some of the methods may provide a stepped-up basis for the assets acquired, a tax-free liquidation, or avoidance of a double tax on the sale of the assets.

The statute sets the rules for taxing distributions in complete or partial liquidation of a corporation.[23] As a general rule, there will be no recognized gain or loss to the corporation since the amounts distributed in complete liquidation are considered as received in full payment for the stock, that is, if the stockholder in a sale or exchange gave up his stock and received the distribution in exchange. Gain will be recognized to the extent that the amount of distribution (liquidating distribution) exceeds the basis for the stock. It is taxed at favorable capital gains rates.[24] On the other hand, if the liquidating distribution is less than the basis of the stock, it will result in a capital loss. There are two exceptions to the rule: (1) installment obligations received when the corporate assets are sold and distributed to the shareholders as a liquidating dividend,[25] (2) in the area of collapsible corporations, when the proceeds are taxed as ordinary income.[26]

The various types of liquidation are:

1. Any ordinary complete liquidation of the corporate business.
2. The liquidation of the subsidiary by the parent or as it is often called, intercorporate liquidation.
3. The one-month corporate liquidation in which the shareholders can avoid tax on unrealized appreciation of corporate assets at the price of paying the ordinary income tax on accumulated earnings received in liquidation.
4. The "twelve-month" liquidation whereby the double tax is avoided on the sale of a corporate business.
5. A partial liquidation in which distributions may be received as capital gains provided statutory conditions are met or a bona fide contraction of the business can be demonstrated.

If the rules are adhered to, there will be a capital gains tax upon the liquidating distributions, whether in cash or property received by the shareholders. No tax will be imposed upon the corporation when the assets are sold.

THE ORDINARY LIQUIDATION

The term "complete liquidation" is not defined either in the Code or the applicable Regulations. Some of the confusion concerning liquidations arise in the legal concept of dissolution. The terms "liquidation" and "dissolution" are not synonymous. The former involves the winding up of a corporate business, while the latter involves the termination of the legal entity. It thus becomes apparent that both steps are required for the "death-blow" to a corporation.

The keynote of all statutory liquidations is that there must be a plan of liquidation adopted by the shareholders. In the absence of such a resolution authorizing a liquidation, the courts take the position that it is not by itself controlling or determinative.[27] The Regulations state that the date of the adoption of a plan of complete liquidation is the date of adoption by the shareholders of a corporate resolution authorizing the distribution of all the corporate assets in redemption of all its stock. The fact that assets are segregated in order to meet unascertained or contingent liabilities will not disqualify the liquidation.

A liquidation takes place when a corporation winds up its affairs and distributes its assets, either in one or a series of distributions. Generally, the steps involved are:

1. Shareholders' resolution authorizes dissolution, and a plan of liquidation is adopted;
2. Information return (Form 966) is filed within thirty days after the adoption of the plan;
3. Corporate affairs are wound up, debts paid, assets distributed, and the corporation dissolved;
4. Income tax returns are filed up to the date of dissolution along with a request for prompt assessment within eighteen months, and;
5. Information returns (Forms 1096 and 1099L) for $600 or more liquidating dividends paid any of the stockholders are filed by February 28 of the following year.

Gain is realized by the shareholders in the year the distributions are received. If there is a series of distributions, the shareholders will be able to defer their gain until there has been a recovery of the cost basis of their stock. This is because there is no Code requirement that a liquidation be completed within any prescribed time.

Such a method could be utilized effectively in tax planning when a corporation has appreciated property which stockholders want to operate in their own names at a stepped-up basis (recoverable by depreciation methods) at a cost of a capital gains tax. Similarly, Section 331 could be utilized when a corporation has accumulated earnings over a period of years that stockholders want to take out at capital gains rates.

INTERCORPORATE LIQUIDATIONS

Section 332 deals exclusively with the liquidation of a subsidiary by a parent corporation. It is never applicable to the liquidation of a corporation owned by individuals. The general rule provides that no gain or loss is recognized to a parent corporation that receives property distributed in complete liquidation, if all of the following conditions are met:

1. That there is a plan of liquidation and the parent plan need not be written or formal, but since a certified copy must be filed, it should be in writing.
2. The parent was the owner of stock of the subsidiary of at least eighty percent of the total combined voting power of all classes of voting stock, and the owner of at least eighty percent of the total number of shares of all other classes of stock at the time of the adoption of the plan and also during all the time intervening between the adoption of the plan and the receipt of the property. The 1966 Foreign Investors Tax Act amended the statute so that stock purchased from the fifty percent controlled subsidiary can be used in meeting the eighty percent requirement if the controlling interest in the subsidiary was acquired within the twelve-month period.
3. The distribution of the property by the subsidiary is in complete cancellation or redemption of all its stock and the property is all transferred within one taxable year, or, the distribution of property is one of a series of distributions in complete cancellation or stock redemption, and is made in accordance with a plan of liquidation under which the liquidation is to be completed within three years from the end of the year in which the first distribution is made. This is the so-called "four-year rule."

The purpose of this Section is to provide simplification of corporate structures without incurring immediate tax liability on any gains. The Section also provides that the transfer of property by a liquidating subsidiary to its parent in satisfaction of a debt, which was outstanding as of the date of the adoption of the plan of liquidation, does not result in any gain or loss being recognized to the subsidiary. The basis of the property received by the parent is the same as it was in the hands of the subsidiary, namely, a substituted basis.[28]

This Section also requires, like other liquidation provisions, that there must be a plan of liquidation.[29] But in the case of a subsidiary and its parent, the plan must be adopted by both corporations.[30]

TAX-FREE ACQUISITION OF ASSETS OR STOCK

An interesting device can be utilized due to the interplay of Sections 332 and

334(b)(2), whereby the parent can achieve a stepped-up basis for the assets equal to the purchase price of the stock. The rule provides that if:

1. An acquiring corporation owns eighty percent of the stock of another corporation and
2. Such stock was purchased within a twelve-month period, and
3. A plan of liquidation is adopted by the acquired corporation within twenty-four months after the stock acquisition, then
4. The tax basis of the assets acquired in the liquidation shall be the same as the adjusted cost of the stock.

The *Kimbell Diamond* case[31] was responsible for the rule being incorporated in the 1954 Code. The rule as enunciated by the court holds that a corporation purchaser could get a stepped-up basis for the subsidiary's assets in liquidation when it could not buy the assets and the only way to acquire the corporation was by a purchase of the stock and immediately thereafter the subsidiary would be liquidated. This judicially evolved principle is an exception to the general rule that the basis of the property received is equal to the basis of property given up.

Thus, if the amount of consideration paid exceeds the basis of the subsidiary's assets, it may be desirable to liquidate the subsidiary promptly to obtain the "stepped-up" basis. Conversely, it is deemed advisable to postpone liquidation for more than a two-year period, if the basis of the subsidiary's assets is more than the consideration paid for the stock by the parent.

THE ONE MONTH OR LESS LIQUIDATION

Section 333 is a relief Section resulting in nonrecognition of gain under certain conditions. It is a relief provision which must be strictly adhered to in order to obtain the result in the corporation which owns assets that have appreciated in value, does not have a large earned surplus, and wishes to liquidate.

There are two tax treatments afforded to the shareholders depending upon whether it is an individual or a corporate shareholder.

A noncorporate shareholder is taxed as follows:

1. The amount of gain realized by him on the transaction is the maximum amount which can be taxed.
2. Dividend income is recognized to the shareholder to the extent that the shareholder's gain does not exceed his ratable share of the earnings and profits of the corporation accumulated after February 28, 1913.
3. The balance of the gain, if any, is taxed only to the extent that the value of the securities acquired by the distributing corporation after December 31, 1953, plus the cash received by the shareholder, exceeds the amount taxed as a dividend. This excess is taxed as a capital gain.

A corporate shareholder is taxed only upon any gain realized at capital gains rates to the extent of the greater of: (1) the shareholder's share of earnings and profits accumulated after February 28, 1913, or (2) the value of securities acquired by the distributing corporation after December 31, 1953, plus cash received by the shareholder. No dividend income will accrue to an electing shareholder. This is due to the eighty-five percent corporate deduction for dividends received by a corporation who would pay a tax of 7.2 percent (85 x 48), rather than the twenty-five percent capital gains tax. The basis of the assets received is the basis of the stock surrendered, minus the cash received, plus the gain recognized on the exchange (including the portion taxed as a dividend), plus the amount of the unsecured liabilities assumed. This total basis is apportioned among the assets in the ratio of the market value of the respective assets on the date of the distribution.[32]

It is advisable to use Section 333 when the corporation has little or no earnings and profits, or no cash or securities. A subsequent sale by the shareholders can then be an installment sale. On the contrary, a corporation which has a potential accumulated earnings problem would be foolhardy to utilize this method.

TWELVE-MONTH LIQUIDATION

Section 337 contains provisions added by the 1954 Code, designed to meet the problems involved in the *Court-Holding* and *Cumberland* cases.[33] Under pre-1954 law, if a corporation sold assets that had appreciated in value, it realized a gain, ordinary or capital, depending on the character of the assets. If it distributed the proceeds to its shareholders, then the distribution was taxed again to the stockholders as an ordinary or liquidating dividend. One tax, therefore, was saved when the corporation, instead of selling its assets and distributing the proceeds, distributed its assets in kind and allowed the stockholders to dispose of them.

As a practical matter, stockholders were often reluctant to accept assets in kind unless they were certain they could readily dispose of them. Thus, in many cases, negotiations by the corporation for the sale of the assets were well advanced or actually concluded before the distribution. In such a case, for example, the *Court-Holding Company* case, the Supreme Court held that the sale was made by and taxable to the corporation. In the later *Cumberland* case, the stockholders, in negotiations with the prospective purchasers, had offered to obtain the assets by liquidating the corporation and to then sell the assets. The Supreme Court held that there was no tax to the corporation since there was a genuine liquidation and dissolution prior to the sale.

The Section[34] provides that, if a corporation adopts a plan of complete liquidation and pursuant to it distributes within the following twelve months all assets not required to meet claims, then no gain or loss will be recognized to the corporation on any sales or exchanges made by it within such twelve-month period. Thus, it remains only for the courts to decide whether a sale was made by the corporation or the shareholders. Two exceptions to the aforementioned rule are engrafted in the Code. One exception is for stock in trade, inventory and property held for sale to customers in the ordinary course of business. It provides that gain or loss will be recognized to the corporation on the sale or exchange if such property is sold to one person in one transaction. Thus, there is an exception to the exception in case of a bulk transfer or sale. The other exception relates to gain being recognized to the corporation upon the distribution of certain installment obligations.

The philosophical basis for the *Court Holding-Cumberland* situations has been "It ain't what you do, it's the way that you do it." Thus, the law states that there should be no tax consequences to the shareholders whether the sale precedes or is subsequent to the liquidation.

Two tax traps to avoid are, first, selling depreciable property at a loss before adopting a plan of liquidation. There the losses will not be recognized even if the corporation does not plan to liquidate within the purview of Section 337.

The second tax trap is that all the corporate assets may be distributed after a plan of liquidation is adopted, but more than twelve months after there was a loss upon a sale of some of its property. But if the loss sale is held to be the date of the adoption of the plan, then all subsequent gain would be taxable to the corporation.

Under two enacted Code Sections, ordinary income may be realized by a corporation selling its property in a Section 337 liquidation to the extent of the "recovery" of prior depreciation deductions after December 31, 1963. Section 1245 provides for ordinary income treatment upon the sale of personal property. Section 1250 deals with the "recovery" of depreciation upon the sale of real property after December 31, 1963, to the extent that accelerated methods of depreciation resulted in a larger deduction than straight-line depreciation. The Tax Reform Act amended the recapture of depreciation[35] on real property to provide for the recapture of all post-1969 excess depreciation. This post-1969 excess depreciation will be recaptured before pre-1970 excess depreciation. The limit on the recapture is the gain on the sale. Then, if there is any gain left, the pre-1970 depreciation is recaptured as follows: all depreciation is recaptured if the property has been held for less than twenty months. This recapture percentage decreases by one percent for each full month the property has been held over twenty months. There is no recapture after it has been held for more than ten years. If the property is held for less than one year, all the depreciation is recaptured.

PARTIAL LIQUIDATIONS

The provisions dealing with partial liquidation show the interrelationship of both liquidations and redemptions. There is an interrelationship between Sections 302 and 346. The former deals with redemptions on the shareholder's level, while the latter deals with redemptions at the corporate level. There is a provision in the Section which states that with respect to a shareholder, if a distribution qualifies under Section 302(b), it shall not be taken into account in determining whether the distribution, with respect to such shareholder, is also a distribution in partial liquidation of the corporation.[36] It is this provision which makes for effective tax planning with regard to redemptions and, also the fact that the constructive ownership rules are not applicable to partial liquidations.

Section 346 defines a partial liquidation and Sections 331(a)(1) and 336 set forth the tax consequences. Section 331(a)(2) provides that amounts distributed in partial liquidation are treated as in part or full payment in exchange for the stock.[37] It further states that the application of Section 301, with its predisposition to dividends, is expressly excluded.[38] This is another reason for qualifying stock redemptions under the partial liquidation rules. Section 336 provides that no gain or loss is to be recognized to a corporation upon the distribution of its property in a partial liquidation.

A corporate distribution can qualify[39] as a partial liquidation when:

1. The distribution is one of a series of distributions in redemption of all of the stock of the corporation pursuant to a plan; or

2. The distribution is "not essentially equivalent to a dividend" and is in redemption of a part of the stock of a corporation pursuant to a plan; or

3. The distribution is attributable to the termination of a business conducted by a corporation and is in redemption of a part of the stock of the corporation.

There is an additional requirement in regard to partial liquidations which necessitate that for redemption to occur, another requirement which must be taken into consideration is the termination of business rule. The rule states that the distribution must relate to the corporation's ceasing to conduct, or consist of the assets of, a trade or business which has been actively conducted throughout the five-year period. Immediately preceding the distribution, the liquidating corporation must be actively engaged in a trade or business which was actively conducted throughout the five-year period ending on the date of the distribution. This is the so-called five-year active business rule, and its importance is in connection with the divisive type of reorganization whereby a corporation splits up its business into two or more corporate businesses and, were it not for the five-year requirement, the transaction would be tax free.

The Regulations[40] set forth certain criteria for determining if a certain activity constitutes a trade or business.

In order for a liquidation to occur, there must be a contraction or business curtailment. This is the contraction theory of business splitting. These terms are used interchangeably in certain cases without the courts defining those terms. The keynote of the partial liquidation section is business contraction. If there is no contraction, then the distribution will be taxable under the "dividend equivalency" test.

This becomes obvious upon the examination of certain rulings dealing with the problem. The Service held[41] that a redemption occurred when certain amounts are distributed on a pro rata basis in a stock redemption because of a genuine contraction of business, that is, the termination of one of two separate businesses, one dealing in bread, cake and bakery goods. In another ruling[42] a corporation owned three distinct parcels of real estate, A, B and C, which it operated as rental properties. Buildings A and B were acquired more than five years before the described transaction, but building C was purchased only four and one-half years before it. Building A was distributed by the corporation in exchange for the shareholders' stock. The Service held that this was a genuine contraction of the business. If building C were distributed, the result probably would be a dividend because the five-year active business requirement would not have been met.

Certain relationships occur under Sections 302 and 346. As previously mentioned, it is better to qualify under the partial liquidation rules because there the transaction will always result in capital gain, whereas, under stock redemptions, the transaction may result in "dividend equivalence." There are other reasons for qualifying under this Section, such as attribution rules are not applicable and a stockholder may reacquire an interest in the corporation within the ten-year period, regardless of the fact that the transaction would have produced ordinary income under Section 302.

An interesting problem arises in connection with the divisive types of reorganizations and the partial liquidation provisions. There is a close relationship between the two Sections since both involve the splitting of a corporate enterprise. Under Section 355, the gain, if any, is deferred to a subsequent sale, which under Section 346, the gain is recognized and taxed at capital gains rates.

There is yet another type of partial liquidation. When a complete liquidation is attempted in a series of distributions, each distribution is a partial liquidation under Section 331. Hence, when the complete liquidation is in steps, and the total term of liquidation extends beyond one taxable period of the stockholder, each step is itself a partial liquidation.

Distributions may be made in kind in a partial liquidation. Hence, a stockholder may take over the termination business in redemption of his stock. If property of a liquidating corporation has appreciated in value, it would be advantageous to make a distribution in kind. A distribution in partial liquidation is a capital transaction, and need not be made pro rata.

The Regulations[43] place a restriction on the distribution in partial liquidation of inventory or the proceeds of the sale of inventory. The inventory can be distributed only if it is substantially the same kind and quantity as was regularly on hand during the previous five years. The proceeds from the sale of inventory in bulk can be distributed, but not if the inventory was sold in the ordinary course of business.

In conclusion, a partial liquidation can be used by a corporation with more than one active business if it sells or discontinues one of its businesses, and wants to distribute assets or proceeds to its stockholders. The distribution qualifies for capital gains treatment, instead of dividend treatment. To avoid double tax, distribute assets which stockholders can then sell, rather than sell first and then distribute.

ILLUSTRATIONS

By now it is apparent that the Sections dealing with liquidations result in favorable tax benefits if the provisions of the statute are adhered to. The best way, as previously stated, to determine which of the liquidations should be chosen is to illustrate the various results flowing from the method selected. This can be demonstrated by the following illustrations:

MAL Corporation
Balance Sheet
December 31, 1966

ASSETS		Per Books	Fair Market Value
Cash		$ 25,000	$ 25,000
Accounts receivable	$300,000		
Less: Allowance for bad debts	15,000	285,000	200,000
Inventory		$180,000	$180,000
Land		125,000	200,000
Building	$750,000		1,000,000
Less: Allowance for depreciation	150,000	600,000	
Machinery	400,000		500,000

Less: Allowance for depreciation	180,000	220,000	
TOTAL		$1,435,000	$2,105,000

LIABILITIES AND
STOCKHOLDERS' EQUITY

Accounts payable		$300,000
Mortgage payable		500,000
Notes payable		100,000
Capital stock		300,000
Capital surplus		90,000
Earned surplus	$115,000	
Net Income to 12/31/66	30,000	145,000
TOTAL		$1,435,000

MAL Corporation has four equal shareholders, MAL, KAL, Trudel and JG.

The gain to be recognized on the liquidation would be computed as follows in the complete liquidation:

Total fair market value of the assets			$2,105,000
Less:	Liabilities		
	Accounts payable	$300,000	
	Mortgage payable	500,000	
	Notes payable	100,000	900,000
	Net fair market value		$1,205,000
	Less: Capital stock and surplus		390,000
	Recognized gain on liquidation		$ 815,000

The gain to be recognized to each shareholder would be as follows:

Stockholders	Net Fair Market Value	Capital Stock and Surplus	Recognized Gain
MAL	$301,250	$97,500	$203,750
Trudel	301,250	97,500	203,750
KAL	301,250	97,500	203,750
JG	301,250	97,500	203,750
TOTAL	$1,205,000	$390,000	$815,000

The corporation would file a final corporation income tax return for the year 1966 indicating a net profit of $30,000. The balance sheet will only show the assets at the beginning of the year, January 1, 1966. No assets or liabilities will be shown at the end of the taxable year. The final return should be filed within two and a half months after the date of dissolution. This gain to each of the shareholders would be long-term capital gain (assuming the statutory holding period of six months is met), subject to the depreciation recapture rules relating to both tangible real and personal property. The fair market values would be reported on Form 1099 and given to each of the shareholders with a copy sent to the Internal Revenue Service.

Calendar Month Liquidation—Section 333

Assume the same fact pattern as in the previous illustration with one change—instead of "inventory" on the balance sheet, let's call it "marketable securities" with the same book and fair market value.

Computation of Recognized
Gain on Liquidation

Stockholders' Distribution	MAL	KAL	TRUDEL	JG	TOTAL
Money	$6250	$6250	$6250	$6250	$6250
Securities acquired after 12/31/53	50,000	50,000	50,000	50,000	200,000
Other Assets	470,000	470,000	470,000	470,000	1,980,000
	$526,250	526,250	526,250	526,250	2,105,000
Basis of Stockholders' Stock	$ 75,000	75,000	75,000	75,000	300,000
Actual Gain	$451,250	451,250	451,250	451,250	1,805,000
Earned Surplus	$ 36,250	36,250	36,250	36,250	145,000

Section 333

Ordinary Dividend	36,250	36,250	36,250	36,250	145,000
Long-Term Capital Gain	20,000	20,000	20,000	20,000	80,000
Nonrecognized Gain	370,000	370,000	370,000	370,000	1,180,000

Computation of Basis of Other Assets

Adjusted Basis of Stock	$300,000	
Less: Money Received	25,000	
Balance	$275,000	
Add: Liabilities assumed		
Accounts Payable	$300,000	
Mortgage payable—lien	500,000	
Gain recognized—ordinary & capital	205,000	1,005,000
Basis of Assets to Be Apportioned		$1,280,000
Less: Specific Liens Against Property		300,000
Basis Apportionable		$ 780,000

Twelve-Month Liquidation—Section 337

Assuming the same facts, the assets were realized at the fair market value. Thus, the realized gain of $670,000 ($2,105,000 - 1,435,000) would be nontaxable to the corporation. The gain to the stockholders would be as follows:

Liquidating Dividend	MAL	KAL	TRUDEL	JG	TOTAL
Cash	$500,000	500,000	500,000	500,000	$2,000,000
Less: Capital Stock	75,000	75,000	75,000	75,000	300,000
Recognized Gain	$425,000	425,000	425,000	425,000	$1,700,000

Each shareholder would have a recognized gain of $425,000 which would be part ordinary income equal to the depreciation recapture on personal property after 1962 and real property after 1964. The balance would be long-term capital gain.

The balance of the cash $105,000 ($2,105,000-$2,000,000 distributed) could be retained to meet unascertained and contingent liabilities plus taxes for the final return filed.

Section 334(b)(2)—Stepped-Up Basis

Assume that the stock of the Trudel Corporation was purchased by Baby-Hully Corporation, and then it is liquidated within two years. The purchase price is $1,980,000.

Basis of Stock to Be Spread Over the Assets Acquired

Cost of Stock		$1,980,000
Unsecured Liabilities		
Accounts payable	$300,000	
Notes Payable	100,000	400,000
		$2,380,000
Less: Cash and Equivalent		
Cash		25,000
Adjusted Basis of Stock		$2,355,000

This basis would be spread as follows:

Assets	New Fair Market Value	% of Total*	Share of Basis
Accounts Receivable	$200,000	12.5	$294,375
Inventory	180,000	13.0	306,150
Land	200,000	12.5	294,375
Building (1,000,000- 500,000)	500,000	31.0	730,050
Machinery	500,000	31.0	730,050
TOTAL	$1,580,000	100.0	$2,355,000

*rounded off to even numbers

The last adjustment to the basis would be adding the $150,000 mortgage to the building. Thus, the total basis for the building would be $880,050 ($730,050 + 150,000). Each of the shareholders would have a long-term capital gain of $420,000 ($1,980,000 ÷ 4) - 300,000 ÷ 4).

Intercorporate Liquidation

If the shareholders of MAL Corporation were another corporation, so that a parent-subsidiary relationship existed, then the property would have a carryover basis to the parent. If the subsidiary was indebted to the parent, upon the cancellation of debt, no gain or loss would incur to either the parent or subsidiary.

Comparative Summary of Liquidation Alternatives

Shareholders	Ordinary Liquidation	Calendar Month Liquidation		Twelve-Month Liquidation	Sale of Stock
MAL	203,750	36,250	Div		
		20,000	LTCG	425,000	420,000
KAL	203,750	36,250	Div		
		20,000	LTCG	425,000	420,000
Trudel	203,750	36,250	Div		
		20,000	LTCG	425,000	420,000
JG	203,750	36,250	Div		
		20,000	LTCG	425,000	420,000

From the foregoing, it can readily be seen that a sale of stock under Section 334(b)(2) will produce the best results. Of the $420,000 gain, fifty percent would be excluded under the long-term capital gains deduction. Under the other methods of liquidation, a part of the gain would be ordinary income due to the recapture provisions of the Code. The calendar month liquidation appears to be the least desirable method due to the dividend income being recognized because of the large earned surplus.

THE PROBLEM OF UNMERGING CORPORATIONS

Since not all marriages are made in heaven, it invariably arises that amalgamated corporations may wish to unmerge. This can arise because of liquidity problems, unprofitability of acquired corporation, breach of contract and/or warranty or governmental antitrust action.

The mechanics of unmerging may have been originally provided for in the original contract. Another way is to sell assets for cash or stock or to effectuate another merger or consolidation.

Generally speaking, the tax consequences of unmerging will be a taxable transaction since the amount of the value of return stock or assets will exceed the original basis of acquired corporation's shareholders in stock of acquired corporation. Thus, the undoing of corporate acquisition cannot be achieved under the tax-free provisions of the A, B or C type of reorganization exchanges. However, it may be possible to accomplish the de-merging as a tax-free spin-off under Section 355. To accomplish this, it is necessary that after spin-off, the distributing and the spun-off corporation must each have been engaged in conduct of a business which was actively conducted for the preceding five-year period and was not the subject of a taxable transaction during that period.

FOOTNOTES

[1] IRC-1954; Sec. 316(a).

[2] IRC-1954; Sec. 312(m).

[3] Regulations; 1.312-6(c)(1).

[4] IRC-1954; Sec. 317(a).

[5] IRC-1954; Sec. 301(b)(1)(A).

[6] IRC-1954; Sec. 301(b)(2) & (3).

[7] IRC-1954; Sec. 301(c).

[8] IRC-1954; Sec. 301(d).

[9] IRC-1954; Sec. 301(b)(1)(B).

[10] IRC-1954; Sec. 301(c)(2).

[11] IRC-1954; Sec. 301(c)(3).

[12] IRC-1954; Sec. 301(d)(2)(A) & (B).

[13] Regulations; 1.301-1(1).

[14] IRC-1954; Sec. 317(b).

[15] IRC-1954; Sec. 302(b).

[16] IRC-1954; Sec. 302(b)(1)(D).

[17] IRC-1954; Sec. 302(c).

[18] IRC-1954; Sec. 311(d).

[19] IRC-1954; Sec. 306(a)(1)(1A) & (B).

[20] IRC-1954; Sec. 306(a)(2).

[21] IRC-1954; Sec. 306(c).

[22] IRC-1954; Sec. 306(e).

[23] IRC-1954; Sec. 331(a).

[24] IRC-1954; Sec. 1001(a).

[25] IRC-1954; Sec. 453(b).

[26] IRC-1954; Sec. 341.

[27] Rev. Rul 57-140; 1957-1 C.B. 118

[28] IRC-1954; Sec. 334(b)(1).

[29] IRC-1954; Sec. 332(b).

[30] Reg., 1.332-6(a).

[31] Kimbell Diamond Milling Co. v. C.I.R. 187F(2) 718(1950).

[32] IRC-1954; Sec. 333.

[33] United States v. Cumberland Public Service Co. 338 U.S. 451 (1950).

[34]Court Holding Co. v. C.I.R. 324 U.S. 331 (1945).

[35]IRC-1954; Sec. 337.

[36]Tax Reform Act; Sec. 521 (b) and (d).

[37]IRC-1954; Sec. 346(c).

[38]IRC-1954; Sec. 346(b).

[39]IRC-1954; Sec. 346(b).

[40]Regulations; 1.355-1(c).

[41]Rev. Rul. 56-613; 1956-2C.B. 91.

[42]Rev. Rul. 57-334, 1957-2 C.B. 240.

[43]Regulations; 1.346-1(b).

Appendix A

PLAN OF REORGANIZATION AND AGREEMENT

Plan of Reorganization and Agreement dated this day
of   , 1971, by and between

organized and existing under the laws of the United States, with an office at

(the "COMPANY"); a corporation organized and existing under the laws of the
State of New York with offices at

(the "PURCHASER");
residing at

and   residing at

WHEREAS, the PURCHASER, by its Certificate of Incorporation, as
amended, filed in the Department of State of the State of New York on
and
has authorized capital stock consisting of   shares of Common Stock,
par value $.10 per share, of which   shares are issued and outstanding
(hereinafter shares of the PURCHASER's Common Stock is sometimes referred to
as the "Common Stock").

WHEREAS, the COMPANY

are now issued and outstanding and owned by

WHEREAS, the parties hereto desire to adopt a Plan of Reorganization
(the "PLAN OF REORGANIZATION") pursuant to Section 368(1)(B) of the
Internal Revenue Code of 1954, as amended.

WHEREAS, the COMPANY and the PURCHASER believe that through
the combination of the facilities and personnel of the COMPANY and the

PURCHASER many efficiencies and economies can be accomplished and that the acquisition by the PURCHASER of the aforesaid shares of the COMPANY's stock will facilitate such combination and will promote the continued expansion of the business and operations presently conducted by the COMPANY and the PUR-CHASER.

NOW, THEREFORE, in consideration of the foregoing and the mutual agreements hereinafter set forth, the parties hereto agree as follows:

1. Adoption of Plan of Reorganization

The parties hereto hereby adopt the Plan of Reorganization which will comprise the acquisition by the PURCHASER of 100% of the outstanding stock of the COMPANY solely in exchange for voting shares of the Common Stock, par value $.01 per share (the "Common Stock") of the PUR-CHASER, upon and subject to the terms and conditions of this PLAN of REORGANIZATION as hereinafter set forth. The parties hereto will promptly take such legal and corporate action as in the opinion of their respective counsel may be necessary or desirable to effect such PLAN of REORGANIZATION.

2. Manner of Exchange of Shares

2.1 Subject to the terms and conditions of this PLAN of RE-ORGANIZATION and AGREEMENT, the manner of exchange of the outstanding shares of the Common Stock of the COMPANY for the shares of the PURCHASER shall be as follows:

2.1.1   each agree to assign, transfer and deliver   shares of Common Stock of the COMPANY owned by them (constituting 100% of the outstanding shares of the COMPANY and free and clear of all liens, pledges, charges and encumbrances of every kind, nature and description) to the PURCHASER on the closing (as hereinafter defined) in exchange for the shares of the PURCHASER referred to in paragraph 2.1.2 pursuant to the PLAN of REORGANIZATION and AGREEMENT.

2.1.2 On the Closing Date, the PURCHASER hereby agrees to assign, transfer and deliver to the SHAREHOLDERS   shares of the Common Stock,

2.1.3 (a) In addition to the shares to be delivered to the SHAREHOLDERS pursuant to paragraph 2.1.2 hereof, the PURCHASER hereby agrees to assign, transfer and deliver to the SHAREHOLDERS the following:

(i) On or before   such number of shares of Common Stock as shall equal in value (as hereinafter defined) five times the net profits (as hereinafter defined) of the COMPANY for the period from   to and including   1972;

(ii) On or before   such number of shares of Common Stock as shall equal in value (as hereinafter defined) five times the net profits (as hereinafter defined) of the COMPANY for the period from   to and including   1973;

(iii) On or before   such number of shares of Common Stock as shall equal in value (as hereinafter defined) five times the net profits (as hereinafter defined) of the COMPANY for the period from   to and including   1974;

(iv) On or before   such number of shares of Common Stock as shall equal in value (as hereinafter defined) five times the net profits (as hereinafter defined) of the COMPANY for the period from   to and including   1975;

(v) On or before   such number of shares of Common Stock as shall equal in value (as hereinafter defined) five times the net profits (as hereinafter defined) of the COMPANY for the period from   to and including

(b) The term "net profits" as used in this paragraph shall mean the net profits of the COMPANY before taking into consideration any provisions or payments of any income taxes which may become due or which are accruable and shall include all income of the COMPANY before taking into consideration any provisions or payments of any income taxes which may become due or which are accruable and shall include all income of the COMPANY, whether or not arising in the ordinary course of business, including but not limited to, income from the sale or disposition of capital assets and after the deduction of necessary and proper expenses.

In determining net profits of the COMPANY, the following principles shall be applicable:

(1) Interest attributable to loans obtained by the PURCHASER and provided to the COMPANY as working capital shall be deducted.

(2) Travel and other direct reimbursable out-of-pocket expenses incurred by the PURCHASER's personnel which actually engaged in the COMPANY's business at the COMPANY's request shall be deducted.

(3) Depreciation on a straight-line basis computed over the reasonable or normal life expectancy of the assets to be depreciated shall be deducted.

(4) Overhead and administrative expenses of the PURCHASER which are chargeable to the COMPANY shall not be deducted.

(5) Expenses incident to this PLAN of REORGANIZATION and AGREEMENT shall not be deducted.

(6) Expenses incurred in connection with the filing of any proxy material including but not limited to the costs of printing of notices of meetings and exhibits thereto, the annual report of the PURCHASER, legal fees and fees for certified public accountants, shall not be deducted.

Net profits shall be determined by the independent certified public accountants of the COMPANY in accordance with generally accepted accounting principles applied on a consistent basis and subject to the provisions of this paragraph.

Such determination of net profits shall be made separately for each of the periods enumerated above in subparagraph (a) and neither net profits nor net losses of each period shall be offset against the net profits or net losses of another period for the purposes of determining the number of shares of Common Stock, if any, to which the SHAREHOLDERS may become entitled under the provisions of this paragraph.

(c) The shares of Common Stock to be issued to the SHARE-HOLDERS pursuant to the provisions of this paragraph 2.1.3 shall be valued at $ per share.

2.1.4 Notwithstanding anything herein to the contrary, the PUR-CHASER shall not be obligated to issue more than   shares of Common Stock pursuant to the provisions of paragraph 2.1.3; provided, however, that the number of shares to be issued to the SHAREHOLDERS of the COMPANY pursuant to the provisions of 2.1.3 shall be adjusted proportionately in the event that at any time after the date of this Agreement and prior to the time the number of shares of the PURCHASER to which the SHAREHOLDERS may be entitled shall be finally determined, the PURCHASER shall subdivide its outstanding Common Stock or declare a stock dividend thereon, the total number of the PURCHASER's Common shares issuable to the SHAREHOLDERS at the Closing or from time to time thereafter, as the case may be, shall be adjusted upward to prevent dilution by increasing the relative number of the PURCHASER's shares issuable to the SHAREHOLDERS in proportion to the increase in the number of outstanding shares of the PURCHASER resulting from such subdivision or stock dividend; conversely, if any combination of the PURCHASER's shares should occur during such period, a downward adjustment shall be made in the number of shares of the PURCHASER's Common Stock at any time issuable to the SHAREHOLDERS hereunder so as to decrease such number in proportion to the decrease in the number of outstanding shares of the PURCHASER. In case of any capital reorganization, consolidation, merger of the PURCHASER, or the sale of the assets of the PURCHASER as, or substantially as, an entirety to any other corporation, the SHAREHOLDERS shall be entitled to receive from time to time thereafter under this PLAN of REORGANIZATION and AGREEMENT the kind and number of shares of voting stock of the PURCHASER or of the corporation resulting from such consolidation or surviving such merger or to which such sale of assets may be made, as the case may be, as shall be equivalent to the Common Stock to which the SHAREHOLDERS would have been entitled at the Closing of this Agreement or at any time thereafter in the absence of such capital reorganization, consolidation, merger or sale of assets, as the case may be.

3. Closing

The Closing provided for in this Agreement shall take place at the offices of Joseph R. Guardino,   New York, New York, or at such other place as the parties shall mutually agree upon on the earlier date to occur of either (1) ten days after the shareholders of the PURCHASER shall have approved the transaction contemplated herein, or (2) at such other time as the parties shall mutually agree (the "Closing").

4. Schedules of Properties, Contracts and Personnel Data to be Delivered by the PURCHASER Prior to the Closing

The COMPANY shall deliver to the PURCHASER, as soon as practicable after the execution hereof but in no event later than accurate lists and summary descriptions, certified correct by authorized officers of the COMPANY, of the following:

4.1 *Real Property*—All real property owned of record or beneficially or leased by the COMPANY and a brief description of all buildings and structures located thereon ("Schedule 4.1"), accompanied by the original or certified copies of the deeds, title insurance policies and other title documents relating to such real property as is owned.

4.2 *Inventories*—Inventories of materials, merchandise, machinery, equipment, furniture and fixtures, as recorded in the books of account and recorded of the COMPANY as of   ("Schedule 4.2").

4.3 *Patents, Trademarks, Etc.*—All patents, patent applications, trademarks, trade-mark registrations and applications therefor, trade names, copy rights, copyright registration and applications therefore, patent licenses, contracts with employees or others relating in whole or in part to disclosure, assignment or patenting of any inventions, discoveries, improvements, processes, formulae or other know-how, and all other agreements relating in whole or in part to any item in any of the categories referred to herein presently owned, in whole or in part, by the COMPANY ("Schedule 4.3"), accompanied by the originals or certified copies thereof, all of which patents, trademarks and copyrights, to the best of the COMPANY's knowledge and belief, are valid and in good standing and all of which licenses, contracts and other agreements are valid and enforceable in accordance with their terms and all are assignable, or proper consents to the assignment thereof have been, or, prior to the Closing Date, will be obtained; and all patent or trademark licenses granted by the COMPANY to others and in force accompanied by the originals or certified copies thereof.

4.4 *Automobiles and Trucks*—A schedule of all automobiles and trucks owned or leased by the COMPANY ("Schedule 4.4").

4.5 *Insurance Policies*—A schedule of all policies of insurance with respect to the COMPANY and covering its properties, buildings, machinery, equipment, furniture, fixtures and operations, all of which are in force ("Schedule 4.5"), accompanied by the originals or certified copies thereof.

4.6 *Leases and Contracts*—Each presently existing lease of personal property, contract or other commitment of the COMPANY involving an aggregate payment by the COMPANY of more than $10,000 or extending beyond

December 31, 1971, or otherwise materially affecting the COMPANY's business ("Schedule 4.6"), accompanied by the originals or certified copies thereof.

4.7 *Certain Salaried Employees*—The names and current salary rates of all the COMPANY's present directors, officers and employees whose current annual salary rate is equivalent to $15,000 (U.S.) or more, together with a summary of the bonuses, additional compensation and other like benefits, if any, paid or payable to such persons for the calendar year 1971 ("Schedule 4.7").

4.8 *Pension Arrangements*—The pension arrangements for the COMPANY's employees, both salaried and nonsalaried, including any formal or informal plans, and the funding arrangements in regard thereto ("Schedule 4.8").

4.9 *Banks*—The name of each bank in which the COMPANY has an account or safe deposit box, the amount of deposit therein, and the names of all persons authorized to draw thereon or have access thereto ("Schedule 4.9").

4.10 *Powers of Attorney*—The names of all persons, if any, holding powers of attorney from the COMPANY ("Schedule 4.10").

4.11 *Stock Optionees*—The names of all optionees holding outstanding options under any stock option plan of the COMPANY, the date of grant of each such option, the expiration date thereof, the number of shares of the COMPANY's capital stock subject thereto, and the option price, accompanied by copies of the agreements evidencing such options ("Schedule 4.11").

4.12 *Loan and Credit Agreements, etc.*—All mortgages, deeds of trust, loan or credit agreements and similar instruments to which the COMPANY is a party, and all amendments or modifications of any thereof ("Schedule 4.12"), accompanied by originals or certified copies thereof.

4.13 *Government Authorizations, Licenses or Registrations*—All authorizations, licenses or registrations and applications therefor not otherwise covered in this paragraph 4 presently issued to, registered in the name of, necessary for the conduct of the business of the COMPANY ("Schedule 4.13"), accompanied by the originals or certified copies thereof.

5. Schedules of Properties, Contracts and Personnel Data to be Delivered by the PURCHASER Prior to the Closing

---

The PURCHASER shall deliver to the COMPANY as soon as practicable after the execution hereof but in no event later than   , 1971, accurate lists and summary descriptions, certified correct by authorized officers of the PURCHASER, of the following:

5.1 *Real Property*—All real property owned of record or beneficially or leased by the PURCHASER, and a brief description of all buildings and structures located thereon ("Schedule 4.1"), accompanied by the original or certified copies of the deeds, title insurance policies and other title documents relating to such real property as is owned.

5.2 *Inventories*–Inventories of materials, merchandise, machinery, equipment, furniture and fixtures, as recorded in the books of account and records of the PURCHASER, as of   , 1971 ("Schedule 5.2").

5.3 *Patents, Trademarks, etc.*–All patents, patent applications, trademarks, trade-mark registrations and applications therefor, trade names, copyrights, copyright registrations and applications therefore, patent licenses, contracts with employees or others relating in whole or in part to disclosure, assignment or patenting of any inventions, discoveries, improvements, processes, formulae or other know-how, and all other agreements relating in whole or in part to any item in any of the categories referred to herein presently owned, in whole or in part, by the PURCHASER ("Schedule 5.3"), accompanied by the originals or certified copies thereof, all of which patents, trademarks and copyrights, to the best of the PURCHASER's knowledge and belief, are valid and in good standing and all of which licenses, contracts and other agreements are valid and enforceable in accordance with their terms and all are assignable, or proper consents to the assignment thereof, have been, or prior to the Closing Date, will be obtained; and all patent or trademark licenses granted by the PURCHASER to others and in force accompanied by the originals or certified copies thereof.

5.4 *Automobiles and Trucks*–A schedule of all automobiles and trucks owned or leased by the PURCHASER ("Schedule 5.4").

5.5 *Insurance Policies*–A schedule of all policies of insurance with respect to the PURCHASER and covering its properties, buildings, machinery, equipment, furniture, fixtures and operations, all of which are in force ("Schedule 5.5") accompanied by the originals or certified copies thereof.

5.6 *Leases and Contracts*–Each presently existing lease of personal property, contract or other commitment of the PURCHASER involving an aggregate payment by the PURCHASER of more than $5,000 or extending beyond December 31, 1971, or otherwise materially affecting the PURCHASER's business ("Schedule 5.6"), accompanied by the originals or certified copies thereof.

5.7 *Certain Salaried Employees*–The names and current salary rates of all the PURCHASER's present directors, officers and employees whose current annual salary rate is $10,000 or more, together with a summary of the bonuses, additional compensation and other like benefits, if any, paid or payable to such persons for the calendar year 1971 ("Schedule 5.7").

5.8 *Pension Arrangements*–The pension arrangements for the PURCHASER's employees, both salaried and nonsalaried, including any formal or informal plans, and the funding arrangements in regard thereto ("Schedule 5.8").

5.9 *Banks*–The name of each bank in which the PURCHASER has an account or safe deposit box, and the names of all persons authorized to draw thereon or have access thereto ("Schedule 5.9").

5.10 *Powers of Attorney*–The names of all persons, if any, holding powers of attorney from the PURCHASER ("Schedule 5.10").

5.11 *Stock Optionees*—The names of all optionees holding outstanding options under any stock option plan of the PURCHASER, the date of grant of each such option, the expiration date thereof, the number of shares of the PURCHASER's Common Stock subject thereto, and the option price, accompanied by copies of the agreements evidencing such options ("Schedule 5.11").

5.12 *Loan and Credit Agreements, etc.*—All mortgage, deeds of trust, loans or credit agreements and similar instruments to which the PURCHASER is a party, and all amendments or modifications of any thereof ("Schedule 5.12"), accompanied by originals or certified copies thereof.

5.13 *Government Authorizations, Licenses or Registrations*

All authorizations, licenses or registrations, and applications therefor not otherwise covered in this paragraph 5 presently issued to, registered in the name of, necessary for the conduct of the business of the PURCHASER ("Schedule 5.13"), accompanied by the originals or certified copies thereof.

6. Documents to be delivered to the
PURCHASER by the COMPANY at the Closing

6.1 At the Closing, the COMPANY and/or the SHAREHOLDERS shall deliver to the PURCHASER the following:

6.1.1 Certificates representing all of the outstanding shares of stock of the COMPANY, all of which shall be duly endorsed in blank, or, in the alternative, with stock powers affixed thereto, in proper form for transfer, with transfer taxes with respect to such shares, if applicable, paid, or a check for the necessary costs thereof delivered.

6.1.2 Evidence reasonably satisfactory to the PURCHASER and its attorney demonstrating that the COMPANY,   have taken all necessary corporate and other action to make this Plan of Reorganization and Agreement and the obligations of the COMPANY hereunder binding and enforceable legal obligations of the COMPANY.

6.1.3 The minute book, stock certificate book and ledger and other similar corporate records, including all items listed in Schedules 4.1 to 4.13, together with all books, records, tax returns and other similar items necessary or convenient to the conduct of the business of the COMPANY.

6.1.4 A favorable opinion of Joseph R. Guardino, counsel for the COMPANY, dated as of the Closing, stating that:

6.1.4.1 The COMPANY is a corporation duly organized and validly existing and in good standing under the laws of the United States with the corporate power to own its own properties and to carry on its business as now being conducted and is duly qualified to do business and is in good standing in every jurisdiction in which the character of the property owned by or the nature of the business conducted by it makes such qualifications necessary.

6.1.4.2 The COMPANY's shares delivered to the PURCHASER by the SHAREHOLDERS are legally and validly issued and fully paid and nonassessable.

6.1.4.3 That this Plan of Reorganization and Agreement is a valid and binding obligation of the COMPANY enforceable in accordance with its terms and that all proceedings required by law or the provisions of this Agreement to be taken by the COMPANY on or prior to the Closing have been taken.

6.1.4.4 That the instruments executed and delivered by under this Plan of Reorganization and Agreement have been properly executed and are valid and enforceable in accordance with their terms.

6.1.4.5 That such counsel has no knowledge of any litigation pending or threatened against or adversely affecting the COMPANY not disclosed herein, or which questions the validity of this Plan of Reorganization and Agreement or of any other action taken or to be taken by the COMPANY pursuant to or in connection with the provisions of this Plan of Reorganization and Agreement; nor does such counsel know or have any reasonable grounds to know of any basis for any such action, suit or proceeding.

6.1.4.6 In connection with the above opinion, counsel for the COMPANY shall have the right to rely upon American Counsel as to matters of the law of the United States.

6.1.5 The certificate required by paragraph 8.1.1 hereof.

6.1.6 Any and all other documents or instruments necessary to effectuate the terms of this Plan of Reorganization and Agreement.

7. Documents to be Delivered by the
   PURCHASER to the COMPANY of the
   SHAREHOLDERS at the Closing

7.1 At the Closing, the PURCHASER will deliver to a certificate or certificates representing the number of shares of the Common Stock to which   are entitled pursuant to the provisions of paragraph 2.1.2 hereof, with transfer taxes with respect to such shares, if applicable, paid, or a check for the necessary costs thereof delivered.

7.2 At the Closing, the PURCHASER will deliver to the COMPANY the following:

7.2.1 A certificate dated as of the Closing signed by a duly authorized officer of the PURCHASER which shall provide in substance the following:

7.2.1.1 That at a duly convened meeting of the Board of Directors of the PURCHASER, resolutions were adopted authorizing the PURCHASER to enter into this Plan of Reorganization and Agreement and to consummate the transaction provided for herein;

7.2.1.2 That at a duly convened meeting of the SHARE-HOLDERS of the PURCHASER resolutions were adopted authorizing the PUR-CHASER to increase the number of authorized shares of Common Stock of the PURCHASER, par value $.10 per share, from   to 5,000,000 shares and to enter into this Plan of Reorganization and Agreement and to consummate the transactions provided for herein; and that none of such resolutions has been rescinded or amended; or, if amended, the text of each such amendment, resolution or resolutions shall be furnished.

7.2.2 Evidence reasonably satisfactory to the COMPANY, and their attorney demonstrating that the PURCHASER has taken all necessary corporate and other action to make this Plan of Reorganization and Agreement and the obligations of the PURCHASER hereunder binding and enforceable legal obligations of the PURCHASER.

7.2.3 Copies of all items listed in Schedules 5.1 to 5.13, together with copies of all books, records, tax returns and other similar items necessary or convenient to the conduct of the business of the PURCHASER.

7.2.4 A favorable opinion of   , counsel for the PUR-CHASER, dated as of the Closing, stating that:

7.2.4.1 The PURCHASER is a corporation duly organized and validly existing and in good standing under the laws of the state of New York with the corporate power to own its own properties and to carry on its business as now being conducted, and is duly qualified to do business and is in good standing in every jurisdiction in which the character of the property owned by or the nature of the business conducted by it makes such qualification necessary.

7.2.4.2 The PURCHASER's shares delivered to the SHARE-HOLDERS are legally and validly issued and fully paid and nonassessable.

7.2.4.3 That this Plan of Reorganization and Agreement is a valid and binding obligation of the PURCHASER enforceable in accordance with its terms and that all proceedings required by law or the provisions of this Plan of Reorganization and Agreement to be taken by the PURCHASER on or prior to the Closing have been taken.

7.2.4.4 That the instruments executed and delivered by the PURCHASER under this Plan of Reorganization and Agreement have been properly executed and are valid and enforceable in accordance with their terms.

7.2.4.5 Such counsel has no knowledge of any litigation pending or threatened against or adversely affecting the PURCHASER not disclosed herein or which questions the validity of this Plan of Reorganization or of any other action taken or to be taken by the PURCHASER pursuant to or in connection with the provisions of this Plan of Reorganization and Agreement; nor does such counsel know or have any reasonable grounds to know of any basis for any such action, suit or proceeding.

7.2.5 The certificate required by paragraph 9.1.1 hereof.

7.2.6 Any and all other documents or instruments necessary to effectuate the terms of this Plan of Reorganization and Agreement.

8. Conditions Precedent to the Closing by the PURCHASER

8.1 The obligations of the PURCHASER under this Plan of Reorganization and Agreement are, at the option of the PURCHASER, subject to the conditions that at or before the Closing:

8.1.1 The representations and warranties made by the COMPANY and the SHAREHOLDERS shall be true and correct on and as of the Closing with the same force and effect as though such representations and warranties were made at the Closing and the COMPANY shall have delivered a certificate to such effect signed by a duly authorized officer of the COMPANY.

8.1.2 The PURCHASER shall have received all of the outstanding shares of the COMPANY from the SHAREHOLDERS.

8.1.3 The PURCHASER shall have received a certified financial statement of the COMPANY as of   prepared by independent certified public accountants for the COMPANY, which shall reflect a minimum net worth of the COMPANY of

8.1.4 The PURCHASER shall have received the favorable opinion of the attorneys for the COMPANY referred to in 6.1.4.

8.1.5 All the terms, covenants and conditions of the Plan or Reorganization and Agreement to be complied with and performed by the COMPANY and the SHAREHOLDERS on or before the Closing shall have been duly complied with and performed.

8.1.6 Since   , 1971, the business, properties, operation and condition, financial and otherwise, of the COMPANY shall not have been adversely affected in any material way by any cause whatsoever and there shall have been no material adverse changes in said business, properties, operations or conditions of the COMPANY.

9. Conditions Precedent to the Closing by the COMPANY and the SHAREHOLDERS

9.1 The obligations of the COMPANY and the SHAREHOLDERS under this Plan of Reorganization and Agreement are, at the option of the COMPANY and the SHAREHOLDERS, subject to the conditions that at or before the closing:

9.1.1 The representations and warranties made by the PURCHASER shall be true and correct on and as of the Closing with the same force and effect as though such representations and warranties were made at the Closing, and the PURCHASER shall have delivered to the COMPANY and the SHARE-HOLDERS a certificate to such effect signed by a duly authorized officer of the PURCHASER.

9.1.2 The SHAREHOLDERS shall have received all of the shares of the PURCHASER required to be delivered to them at the Closing hereunder.

9.1.3 At a duly convened meeting the SHAREHOLDERS of the PURCHASER shall authorize the PURCHASER to increase the number of authorized shares of Common Stock of the PURCHASER, par value from $.10 per share, as provided herein, and to enter into this Plan of Reorganization and Agreement and consummate the transaction provided for herein.

9.1.4 At a duly convened meeting the Board of Directors of the PURCHASER shall authorize the PURCHASER to enter into this Plan of Reorganization and Agreement and consummate the transactions provided for herein.

9.1.5 The COMPANY shall have received a certified financial statement of the PURCHASER as at   prepared by independent certified public accountants for the PURCHASER, in accordance with generally accepted accounting principles applied on a consistent basis.

10. Warranties of the PURCHASER

10.1 The PURCHASER represents, warrants and covenants that:

10.1.1 The PURCHASER is a corporation duly organized and existing and in good standing under the laws of the state of New York and with full authority and licenses wherever required in order to conduct its business as presently being carried on and with full power and authority to carry out the transactions contemplated under this Plan of Reorganization and Agreement.

10.1.2 The Common Stock of the PURCHASER to be delivered hereunder are, and will be, validly issued, fully paid and nonassessable, and that such shares are and shall be free and clear of all liens, pledges, charges, options, calls, agreements and encumbrances of every kind, nature and description.

10.1.3 All corporate and other proceedings required to be taken by or on its part to authorize it to carry out this Plan of Reorganization and Agreement have been duly and properly taken and this Agreement is a valid and binding obligation of the PURCHASER enforceable in accordance with its terms.

10.1.4 Copies of the Certificate of Incorporation of the PUR-CHASER and all amendments to date certified by the Secretary of State of the state of New York and the By-Laws of the PURCHASER, as amended, to date certified by the Secretary of the PURCHASER, as amended, to date, certified by the Secretary of the PURCHASER, all of which are annexed hereto as Exhibit "A," are correct and complete.

10.1.5 The PURCHASER has no investment or interest in any other corporation, partnership, joint venture or other business entity except for the corporations, partnerships, joint ventures and business entities listed on Exhibit "B" annexed hereto.

10.1.5.1 With respect to any such corporation, partnership, joint venture, or other business entity in which the PURCHASER's interest is 25% or more, the PURCHASER further represents and warrants that such corporation, partnership, joint venture, or other business entity is duly organized, existing and in good standing under the laws of the jurisdiction in which it is organized and with full authority and licenses wherever required in order to conduct its business as presently being carried on and that all representations and warranties made below with respect to the PURCHASER are also made by the PURCHASER with respect to such corporation, partnerships, joint ventures and other business entities.

10.1.6 The PURCHASER has an authorized capital stock consisting of _____ shares of Common Stock, par value $.10 per share, of which _____ shares are issued and outstanding.

10.1.7 The shares of the PURCHASER to be delivered to the SHAREHOLDERS will on the Closing be validly issued and outstanding, fully paid and nonassessable, and there are no outstanding subscriptions, options, or other agreements or commitments obligating the PURCHASER to issue any additional shares of its capital stock of any class or any options or rights with respect thereto, except as set forth on Exhibit "C." The Common shares of the PURCHASER to be issued to the SHAREHOLDERS on the Closing will, when issued, constitute not less than _____ % of the issued and outstanding shares of the PURCHASER.

10.1.8 Annexed hereto as Exhibit "D" are Balance Sheets and Statement of Income, Profit or Loss of the PURCHASER as at _____ and _____ , and for the periods ending _____ and _____ and fairly present the financial condition of the PURCHASER as of _____ and _____ and the results of its operations for each of such periods, in conformity with generally accepted accounting principles applied on a consistent basis.

10.1.9 The PURCHASER shall have delivered to the COMPANY and the SHAREHOLDERS prior to _____ financial statements prepared by independent certified public accountants, for the period ending _____ which will be true and correct and present fairly the financial condition of the PURCHASER as at _____ and the results of its operations for such period, in conformity with generally accepted accounting principles applied on a consistent basis.

10.1.10 Since _____ , there has been no material adverse change in the condition, financial or otherwise, of the PURCHASER from that set forth in the balance sheets as at _____ and the PURCHASER has no liabilities or obligations, absolute or contingent, except those disclosed on the Balance Sheet as at _____ attached hereto as Exhibit "E" or incurred in the normal course of business since _____

10.1.11 All accounts payable of the PURCHASER are reflected on the books of the PURCHASER and all accounts receivable of the PURCHASER are bona fide, current and collectible, except to the extent reserved against on the balance sheets of the PURCHASER as shown on Exhibit "E."

10.1.12 The PURCHASER is not a party to any written or oral, express or implied contract, except as set forth in Schedules 5.3, 5.4, 5.5, 5.6, 5.7, 5.11 and 5.12 annexed hereto, including but not limited to any (i) contract made in the ordinary course of business; (ii) employment contract not terminable without penalty or liability at the will of the PURCHASER; (iii) contract with any labor union or association; (iv) bonus, pension, profit-sharing, retirement, stock purchase, deferred compensation hospitalization, insurance or similar plan or practice; (v) lease, mortgage, pledge, security agreement, conditional sales contract, factoring agreement, or other similar agreement with respect to any real or personal property, whether as lessor, lessee, or otherwise; (vi) continuing contract for the future purchase of materials, supplies or equipment in excess of the normal requirements of its business or for normal operating inventories; (vii) contract or commitment for capital expenditures in excess of $1,000 in the aggregate; (viii) forward sales agreement or other contract continuing over a period of more than six months from its date; or (ix) guarantee, subordination or any other similar or related type of agreement; (x) contract or commitment with respect to the merger, consolidation, purchase or sale of all or substantially all the assets or similar transactions between the PURCHASER and any other person, firm or corporation.

10.1.13 The PURCHASER has in all respects performed all obligations required to be performed by it to date and is not in default under any agreement, lease or other instrument to which it is a party, except as set forth in Exhibit "F."

10.1.14 Neither the execution and delivery of this Agreement nor the consummation and transaction contemplated herein will conflict with or result in the breach of or accelerate the performance required by any terms of any agreement to which the PURCHASER is now a party, or constitute default thereunder, or result in the enforcement or imposition of any liens, charges or encumbrances against or upon any of the properties or assets of the PURCHASER.

10.1.15 There are no actions, suits, proceedings or investigations (whether or not purportedly on behalf of the PURCHASER pending or to the knowledge of the PURCHASER threatened against or affecting the PURCHASER or its properties or business, at law, or in equity, or before or by any federal, state, municipal or other governmental department, commission, board, bureau, agency or instrumentality, domestic or foreign except as set forth in Exhibit "G" annexed hereto.

10.1.16 The PURCHASER is not in default with respect to any order, writ, injunction or decree of any court of federal, state, municipal or other governmental department, commission, board, bureau, agency or instrumentality, domestic or foreign.

10.1.17 The PURCHASER has complied in all material respects with all laws, regulations and judicial or administrative tribunal orders applicable to its business now being conducted by it, except as set forth in Exhibit "H" annexed hereto.

10.1.18 All federal, state and local tax returns required to be filed by the PURCHASER have been duly filed when due and all such returns and reports have been prepared on the same basis as those of previous years. All federal, state, city, profits, franchises, sales, use, occupation, property, excise or other taxes due have been duly paid or adequately reserved for upon the books of the PURCHASER.

10.1.19 The information contained in the Schedules to be delivered to the COMPANY pursuant to Article 5 hereof will be true and correct as at the Closing Date.

10.1.20 The PURCHASER owns outright all other assets and properties reflected in the balance sheet of the PURCHASER as at   or acquired after said date other than such assets or properties sold or otherwise disposed of in the ordinary course of business subsequent to said date, in each case free and clear of all mortgages, liens, charges or encumbrances of any nature whatsoever. The equipment owned by the PURCHASER is in good operating condition and repair subject to usual wear and tear from normal use thereof, and all other properties and assets owned by the PURCHASER are in good and usable condition.

10.1.21 In the opinion of the PURCHASER, the properties and business of the PURCHASER of an insurable nature are adequately insured under such policies to the extent usually insured by corporations engaged in the same or similar businesses against loss or damage of the kind customarily insured against by such corporations.

10.1.22 Since   there have been and to the Closing Date there will be no material adverse changes in the business, properties or condition, financial or otherwise, of the PURCHASER, except changes arising from transactions in the ordinary course of its business.

10.1.23 Except as otherwise set forth in any Exhibits or Schedules annexed hereto, since   the PURCHASER has not and will not between the date hereof and Closing: incur any obligation or liability (absolute or contingent) except nonsubstantial obligations or liabilities incurred in the ordinary course of its business; discharge or satisfy any lien, charge or encumbrance or pay any obligation or liability (absolute or contingent) other than liabilities shown or reserved against on its Balance Sheet attached hereto as Exhibit "E" and current liabilities incurred since that date in the ordinary course of its business; declare or make in payment or distribution to shareholders or purchase or redeem any of its shares; issue or sell or grant any option to purchase any of its stock bonds or other corporate securities except as set forth in Exhibit "I"; mortgage, pledge or subject to lien or any other charge or encumbrance, any of its assets tangible or intangible, sell, assign, or transfer any of its tangible or intangible assets or cancel any debts or claims, except in each case in the ordinary course of its business; sustain any net operating losses or extraordinary losses, enter into any transaction other than in the ordinary course of its business; incur any loss, damage or destruction, whether or not covered by insurance, of any of its assets or properties; increase the compensation payable or to become payable to any of its officers, employees or to others, waive any right of substantial value.

10.2 No representations or warranty by the PURCHASER in this Plan of Reorganization and Agreement or in any document delivered pursuant to the terms hereof or in connection with the consummation of the transactions contemplated hereby will contain any untrue statement of a material fact or omit to state a material fact necessary to make the statements contained therein not misleading.

10.3 The representations and warranties of the PURCHASER contained herein shall be true and as of the Closing with the same effect as though all such representations and warranties had been made on and as of that date.

11. Warranties of the COMPANY and the SHAREHOLDERS

11.1 The COMPANY and the SHAREHOLDERS represent, warrant and covenant that:

11.1.1 The COMPANY is a

with full authority and licenses wherever required in order to conduct its business as presently being carried on and with full power and authority to carry out the transactions contemplated under this Plan of Reorganization and Agreement.

11.1.2 The Common Stock of the COMPANY to be delivered hereunder has been validly issued, fully paid and nonassessable, and that such shares are, and shall be, free and clear of all liens, pledges, charges, options, calls, agreements and encumbrances of every kind, nature and description.

11.1.3 All corporate and other proceedings required to be taken by or on its part to authorize it to carry out this Plan of Reorganization and Agreement have been duly and properly taken and this Plan of Reorganization and Agreement is a valid and binding obligation of the COMPANY and the SHARE-HOLDERS and enforceable in accordance with its terms.

11.1.4 Copies of the Certificate of Incorporation of the COM-PANY and all amendments to date certified by the   and the By-Laws of the COMPANY, as amended to date, certified by the Secretary of the COMPANY, all of which are annexed hereto as Exhibit "AA" are correct and complete.

11.1.5 The COMPANY has no investment or interest in any other corporation, partnership, joint venture or other business entity except for the corporations, partnerships, joint ventures and business entities listed on Exhibit "BB" annexed hereto.

11.1.5.1 With respect to any such corporation, partnership, joint venture, or other business entity in which the COMPANY's interest is 25% or more, the COMPANY further represents and warrants that such corporations, partnerships, joint venture or other business entity is duly organized, existing and in good standing under the laws of the jurisdiction in which it is organized and with full authority and licenses wherever required in order to conduct its business as presently being carried on and that all representations and warranties made below with respect to the COMPANY are also made by the COMPANY with respect to such corporations, partnerships, joint ventures and other business entities.

11.1.6 The COMPANY has an authorized capital stock consisting of　　shares of Common Stock, par value $　　per share, of which　　shares are issued and outstanding.

11.1.7 The shares of the COMPANY to be delivered to the PURCHASER will on the Closing Date be validly issued and outstanding, fully paid and nonassessable, and there are no outstanding subscriptions, options, or other agreements or commitments obligating the COMPANY or the SHAREHOLDERS to issue any additional shares of its Capital Stock of any class or any options or rights with respect thereto, except as set forth on Exhibit "CC" annexed hereto.

11.1.8 The COMPANY shall deliver to the PURCHASER a Balance Sheet and Statement of Profit and Loss as at　　, for the period ending　　annexed hereto as Exhibit "DD," which are true and correct in all material respects and will represent fairly the financial condition of the COMPANY as of such date, and the results of its operations for such period, in conformity with generally accepted accounting principles applied on a consistent basis.

11.1.9 The COMPANY has no material liabilities or obligations except those disclosed on the Balance Sheet attached hereto as Exhibit "EE" or incurred in the normal and regular conduct of its business since the date of the aforesaid Balance Sheet.

11.1.10 The financial statements of the COMPANY to be delivered to the PURCHASER pursuant to paragraph 11.1.8 hereof will reflect a net worth of not less than $　　.

11.1.11 The normal and regular conduct of the business of the COMPANY

11.1.12 The COMPANY is not a party to any written or oral, express or implied contract, except as required to be set forth in Schedules 4.3, 4.4, 4.5, 4.6, 4.7, 4.11 and 4.12 annexed hereto, including but not limited to any (i) contract not made in the ordinary course of business; (ii) employment contract not terminable without penalty or liability at the will of the PURCHASER; (iii) contract with any labor union or association; (iv) bonus, pension, profit-sharing, retirement, stock purchase, deferred compensation, hospitalization, insurance, or similar plan or practice; (v) lease, mortgage, pledge, security agreement, conditional sales contract, factoring agreement or other similar agreement with respect to any real or personal property, whether as lessor, lessee, or otherwise; (vi) continuing contract for the future purchase of materials, supplies or equipment in excess of the normal requirements of its business or for normal operating inventories; (vii) contract or commitment for capital expenditures in excess of $10,000 in the aggregate; (viii) forward sales agreement or other contract continuing over a period of more than six months from its date; or (ix) guarantee, subordination, or any other similar or related type of agreement; (x) contract or commitment with respect to the merger, consolidation, purchase or sale of all or substantially all the assets or similar transaction between the COMPANY and any other person, firm or corporation.

11.1.13 The COMPANY has in all respects performed all obligations required to be performed by it to date and is not in default under any agreement lease, or other instrument of which it is a party.

11.1.14 Neither the execution and delivery of this Plan of Reorganization and Agreement nor the consummation of the transaction contemplated herein will conflict with or result in the breach of or accelerate the performance required by any terms of any agreement to which the COMPANY or the SHAREHOLDERS are now a party, or constitute default thereunder, or result in the enforcement or imposition of any liens, charges or encumbrances against or upon any of the properties or assets of the COMPANY.

11.1.15 There are no actions, suits, proceedings or investigations (whether or not purportedly on behalf of the COMPANY) pending or to the knowledge of the COMPANY, threatened against or affecting the COMPANY or its properties or business, at law, or in equity, or before or by any federal, state, municipal or other governmental department, commission, board, bureau, agency or instrumentality, domestic or foreign except as set forth in Exhibit "EE" annexed hereto.

11.1.16 The COMPANY is not in default with respect to any order, writ, injunction, or decree of any court or federal, state, municipal or other governmental department commission, board, bureau, agency or instrumentality, domestic or foreign.

11.1.17 The COMPANY has complied in all material respects with all laws, regulations and juridical or administrative tribunal orders applicable to its business and the COMPANY holds all licenses or permits required to conduct the business now being conducted by it.

11.1.18 All federal, state and local tax returns required to be filed by the COMPANY have been duly filed due and all such returns and reports have been prepared on the same basis as those of previous years. All federal, state, city, profits, franchises, sales, use, occupation, property, excise or other taxes due have been duly paid or adequately reserved for upon the books of the COMPANY.

11.1.19 The COMPANY owns outright all assets and properties reflected in the balance sheet of the COMPANY as at   or acquired after said date other than such assets or properties sold or otherwise disposed of in the ordinary course of business subsequent to said date, in each case free and clear of all mortgages, liens, charges or encumbrances of any nature whatsoever or except as set forth in Exhibit "FF" annexed hereto. The equipment owned by the COMPANY is in good operating condition and repair, subject to usual wear and tear from normal use thereof, and all other properties and assets owned by the COMPANY are in good usable condition.

11.1.20 In the opinion of the COMPANY, the properties and business of the COMPANY of an insurable nature are adequately insured under such policies to the extent usually insured by corporations engaged in the same or similar businesses against loss or damage of the kind customarily insured against by such corporations.

11.1.21 Since   there has not been:

11.1.21.1 Any material change from the conditions shown on the Balance Sheet and Statement of Profit or Loss of the COMPANY as at   in the COMPANY's financial condition, assets, liabilities, operations or business other than changes in the ordinary course of business, none of which has been materially adverse.

11.1.21.2 Any declaration, setting aside, or payment of any dividend or other distribution in respect of the COMPANY's Capital Stock or any direct or indirect redemption, purchase or other acquisition of any such stock.

11.1.21.3 Any increase in the compensation payable or to become payable by the COMPANY to any of its officers, employees or agents or any bonus payment, deferred compensation, profit-sharing, retirement arrangement, insurance or other benefit plan made to or with any of them, except as set forth in Exhibit "GG" annexed hereto.

11.1.21.4 Any litigation or proceeding pending or to the COMPANY's knowledge threatened against or relating to the COMPANY, its properties or business, nor does the COMPANY know or have reasonable grounds to know of any basis for such action or of any government investigation relative to the COMPANY, its properties or business:

11.2 No representation or warranty by the COMPANY or the SHAREHOLDERS in this Plan of Reorganization and Agreement or in any document delivered pursuant to the terms hereof or in connection with the consummation of the transaction contemplated hereby will contain any untrue statement of a material fact or omit to state a material fact necessary to make the statement contained therein not misleading.

11.3 The representations and warranties of the COMPANY and the SHAREHOLDERS contained herein shall be true and as of the Closing with the same effect as though all such representations and warranties had been made on and as of that date.

12. Conduct of Business Prior to Closing

12.1 On and after the date hereof until the date of Closing, the PURCHASER agrees that:

12.1.1 The PURCHASER will continue to operate its business in the same manner as heretofore conducted by it, it being expressly agreed that the PURCHASER will not undertake any commitments or enter into any obligations without the express prior written consent of the COMPANY and in this connection, the PURCHASER agrees that it will use its best efforts to maintain its assets and its good will.

12.1.2 The PURCHASER will not, except upon the prior written consent of the COMPANY or except as permitted by this Plan of Reorganization and Agreement:

(i) amend its Certificate of Incorporation or By-Laws;

(ii) issue or sell, or grant any option to purchase any of its stock, bonds or other corporate securities;

(iii) incur any obligations or liability (absolute or contingent), except current obligations and liabilities incurred in the ordinary course of business;

(iv) declare or make any payment or distribution to its stockholders or purchase or redeem any shares of its stock;

(v) make any wage or salary increases or pay any bonuses;

(vi) mortgage, pledge or subject to lien or any other encumbrance, any of its assets, tangible or intangible;

(vii) sell or transfer any of its tangible assets or cancel any debts or claims;

(viii) sell, assign or transfer any patents, trademarks, trade names, copyrights, licenses or other intangible assets;

(ix) waive any right or any substantial value; or

(x) enter into (a) any agreement of a type set forth in paragraph 10.1.12 hereof or required to be listed in any Exhibit or Schedule annexed hereto or (b) any transaction other than in the ordinary course of business.

13. Investment Purpose

13.1 The SHAREHOLDERS each represent that he is acquiring the Common Stock to be issued to him pursuant to this Plan of Reorganization and Agreement for investment and not with a view to, or for sale in connection with any distribution thereof and that he has no present intention of selling or distributing the Common Stock. The SHAREHOLDERS each understand that the Common Stock to be acquired by him pursuant to this Plan of Reorganization and Agreement have not been registered under the Securities Act of 1933, as amended (the "Act"), and agrees that in the absence of an effective registration statement under the Act covering the Common Stock he will not offer, sell, transfer, or otherwise dispose of any of the Common Stock without first obtaining an opinion of counsel to the PURCHASER that such disposition may be made without registration of the Common Stock under the Act or obtaining a letter from the Division of Corporation Finance of the Securities and Exchange Commission (the "Commission") that it will recommend no action against the SHAREHOLDERS if the Common Stock to be disposed of are so disposed of without registration.

14. Registration of the Common Stock

14.1 If the PURCHASER shall at any time register any securities for its own account or for the account of others upon the Act on Form S-1 or any comparable form, the PURCHASER will give the SHAREHOLDERS timely notice of such registration (either prior to or upon the filing of a registration statement in respect thereof) and, promptly after receipt of a written request made by the SHAREHOLDERS within twenty (20) days after the giving of such notice, the PURCHASER at its sole cost and expense, will register under such Act all or part of the Common Stock held by the SHAREHOLDERS and covered by any such request; provided that the offering of such Common Stock may be deferred for a period not exceeding forty (40) days from the effective date of such registration statement if the underwriter for securities to be sold by the PURCHASER is of the opinion that a simultaneous offering of such Common Stock would adversely interfere with the sale of such securities.

14.2 In connection with any registration or filing made pursuant to paragraph 14.1:

14.2.1 The PURCHASER will use its best efforts to have the registration statement or other filing become effective in accordance with the Act in compliance in all respects with the Act and the rules and regulations of the Commission thereunder, and will take such action as may be necessary to permit the sale of the Common Stock in such states as the SHAREHOLDERS shall reasonably designate.

14.2.2 The PURCHASER will make generally available to its security holders, as soon as practicable but in no event later than fifteen (15) months after that effective date of the registration statement, an earnings statement (which need not be audited) covering a period of at least twelve (12) months, beginning after the effective date of the registration statement, which earnings statement will satisfy the provisions of Section 11(a) of the Act.

14.2.3 The SHAREHOLDERS agree to furnish in writing to the PURCHASER such information regarding themselves and their proposed distribution of the Common Stock as the PURCHASER shall request in order to effect such registration.

14.2.4 The PURCHASER, at its sole cost and expense, will furnish to the SHAREHOLDERS a prospectus (in such reasonable quantities as such SHAREHOLDERS shall request) containing certified financial statements and other information meeting the requirements of the Act and the rules and regulations thereunder and relating to the Common Stock.

14.2.5 The Company will keep any registration statement filed pursuant to paragraph 14.1 hereof relating to the Common Stock, effective for the period required by the Act and the rules and regulations thereunder so as to enable the SHAREHOLDERS to freely dispose thereof; and the expense therefor shall be borne by the PURCHASER.

14.3 The PURCHASER will indemnify and hold harmless the SHAREHOLDERS, each underwriter, if any, for any such SHAREHOLDER and each person, if any, who controls any such SHAREHOLDER or underwriter within the meaning of the Act, against any losses, claims, damages or liabilities, joint or several, to which they or any of them may become subject under the Act or otherwise insofar as such losses, claims, damages or liabilities (or actions in respect thereof) arise out of or are based upon, any untrue statements or alleged untrue statements of any material fact contained in any registration statement filed pursuant to paragraph 14.1 hereof, or any preliminary prospectus or final prospectus contained therein or any amendment or supplement thereto, or arise out of or are based upon the omission or alleged omission to state therein a material fact required to be stated therein or necessary to make the statements therein not misleading; and will reimburse each such SHAREHOLDER, underwriter and controlling person for any legal or other expenses reasonably incurred by any of them in connection with investigating, defending or settling any such loss, claim, damage, liability or action; provided, however, that the PURCHASER will not be liable in any such case to the extent that any such loss, claim, damage, liability or expense arises out of or is based upon an untrue statement or alleged untrue statement or omission or alleged omission made in any such registration statement or any preliminary prospectus or final prospectus contained therein or in any amendment or supplement thereto, in reliance and in conformity with written information furnished to the PURCHASER by such SHAREHOLDER, underwriter or controlling person specifically for use in the preparation thereof. Promptly after receipt by an indemnified party under this paragraph 14.3 of notice of the commencement of any action, such indemnified party shall, if a claim in respect thereof is to be made against an indemnifying party, give written notice to such indemnifying party of the commencement thereof; but the omission so to notify the indemnifying party will not relieve it from any liability which it may have to any indemnified party otherwise than pursuant to this Plan of Reorganization and Agreement. In case any such action is brought against any indemnified party, and it notifies an indemnifying party of the commencement thereof, the indemnifying party will be entitled to participate in, and, to the extent that it may wish, jointly with any other indemnifying party similarly notified, so assume the defense thereof, with counsel satisfactory to such indemnified party to its election so to assume the defense thereof, the indemnifying party will not be liable to such indemnified party under this paragraph 14.3 for any legal or other expenses subsequently incurred by such indemnified party in connection with the defense thereof other than reasonable cost of investigation.

14.4 The SHAREHOLDERS agree in the same manner and to the same extent as set forth in paragraph 14.3 hereof to indemnify and hold harmless the PURCHASER, the directors of the PURCHASER, the officers of the PURCHASER who shall have signed any registration statement which includes the Common Stock and each person, if any, who controls the PURCHASER within the meaning of Section 15 of the Act with respect to any statement in or omission from the registration statement or any posteffective amendment thereto, or any prospectus (as amended or as supplemented). If such statement or omission was made in reliance upon information peculiarly within the knowledge of the SHAREHOLDERS and furnished as herein stated or in writing to the PURCHASER by the SHAREHOLDERS specifically for use in connection with the preparation of any registration statement or any prospectus or any such amendment thereof or supplement thereto. The SHAREHOLDERS shall not be liable for amounts paid in settlement of any such litigation if such settlement was effected without their consent. In case of the commencement of any action, in respect of which indemnity may be sought from the SHAREHOLDERS on account of the indemnity agreement contained in this paragraph 14.4, each person agreed to be indemnified by the SHAREHOLDERS shall have the same obligation to notify the SHAREHOLDERS as the SHAREHOLDERS have toward the PURCHASER in paragraph 14.3 above, subject to the same loss of indemnity in the event such notice is not given and the SHAREHOLDERS shall have the same right to participate in (and, to the extent that they shall wish, to direct) the defense of such action as their own expenses, but such defense shall be conducted by counsel of recognized standing and reasonably satisfactory to the PURCHASER. The SHAREHOLDERS agree to notify the PURCHASER promptly of the commencement of any litigation or proceeding against them or against any such controlling person, of which it may be advised, in connection with the issue and sale of any of the securities of the PURCHASER and to furnish to the PURCHASER at its request, copies of all pleadings therein and permit them to be observers therein and apprise them of all developments therein, at the SHAREHOLDERS' expense.

14.5 Insofar as the foregoing indemnity agreements may permit indemnification for liabilities under the Act, the PURCHASER has been advised that in the opinion of the Securities and Exchange Commission such a provision may be broad enough to contravene federal public policy as expressed in the Act. In the event that a claim for indemnification under this Plan of Reorganization and Agreement for any such liabilities is asserted by such a person, the PURCHASER will submit to a court of appropriate jurisdiction (unless in the opinion of counsel for the PURCHASER the matter has already been adjudicated by such a court) the question of whether or not indemnification by it for such liabilities is against public policy as expressed in the Act and therefore unenforceable and the PURCHASER will be governed by the final adjudication of such issue.

15. Survival of Representations

All representations, warranties and agreement of the parties hereunder shall survive the Closing.

16. Assigns

All of the terms and provisions of this Plan of Reorganization and Agreement shall be binding upon and inure to the benefit of and be enforceable by the individual parties hereto and their respective executors, administrators, heirs, successors and assigns, and the corporate parties hereto and their respective successors and assigns.

17. Brokerage

Each of the parties represents that he or it, as the case may be, had no dealings in the connection with this transaction with any finder or broker and that no third party brought about this transaction, except for who represented the PURCHASER and   who represented the COMPANY and the SHAREHOLDERS. Therefore, the SHAREHOLDERS and the PURCHASER and the COMPANY agree to indemnify and hold the other harmless from any and all liabilities (including, without limitation, costs of counsel) to any other persons claiming brokerage commissions or finders' fees on account of services purportedly rendered on behalf of the indemnifying party in connection with this Plan of Reorganization and Agreement, or the transaction contemplated hereby.

18. Expenses

In connection with this Plan of Reorganization and Agreement and the transactions contemplated hereby, the COMPANY and the SHAREHOLDERS shall pay their own expenses and costs and the PURCHASER shall pay its own expenses and costs.

19. Books and Records

19.1 From the date hereof until the Closing, the COMPANY agrees that the PURCHASER or its designated representatives, shall have the right to examine during business hours on reasonable notice, all of the books, records and files of the COMPANY relative to the matters covered by this transaction.

19.2 From the date hereof until the Closing, the PURCHASER agrees that the COMPANY and the SHAREHOLDERS and their designated representatives shall have the right to examine during business hours on reasonable notice all of the books, records and files of the PURCHASER relative to the matters covered by this transaction.

20. Further Assurances

Each of the parties hereto will, at any time and from time to time, before and after the Closing, upon request of another party so to do, execute, acknowledge, and deliver all such further acts, deeds, assignments transfers, conveyances, powers of attorney and assurances as may be required to carry out the provisions of this Agreement.

21. Notices

21.1 Any notice, offer, acceptance, request, demand, instruction or other document to be given hereunder or pursuant hereto to any party shall be in writing and delivered personally or sent by certified or registered mail, return receipt requested, as follows:

If to the PURCHASER, to

If to the SHAREHOLDERS of the COMPANY, to

21.2 Any party may change its or his address for purposes of this paragraph by giving written notice of such change to the other parties in the manner herein provided for giving notice. Unless and until such written notice is received, the last address and addresses stated by written notice or provided herein if no written notice of change has been sent and received, shall be deemed to continue in effect for all purposes hereunder.

22. Governing Law

The parties hereto agree that this agreement has been executed and delivered in the state of New York and that the laws of the state of New York shall govern the interpretation of this Plan of Reorganization and Agreement.

23. Amendments and Counterparts

This instrument contains the entire agreement between the parties and may not be altered, amended or terminated except in writing signed by all parties. This Plan of Reorganization and Agreement may be executed in one or more counterparts, each of which shall be deemed to be an original, but all of which together shall constitute one and the same instrument.

IN WITNESS WHEREOF, the parties hereto have caused this Plan of Reorganization and Agreement to be duly executed as of the day and year first above written.

By————————————————————————————————
                                                        President

————————————————————————————————

————————————————————————————————

By————————————————————————————————
                                                        President

Appendix B

MODEL AGREEMENTS FOR SPECIAL SITUATIONS

SALE OF ASSETS

AGREEMENT, made this   day of 1971, between
and
with principal offices at
(hereinafter sometimes referred to as the "Sellers"), parties of the first part;
          as Agent for the Sellers, with principal office at   New York,
(hereinafter referred to as the "Agent");   a New York corporation with
an office at   , New York, (hereinafter referred to as the "Buyer"), party
of the second part; and   of   , (hereinafter referred to as "Party
of the Third Part");

The Sellers and Buyer agree as follows:

I.   SALE OF ASSETS—PRICE

A. The Sellers, jointly and severally agree to sell their respective assets hereinafter described, and the Buyer agrees to buy and pay therefor the sum hereinafter described:

B. The Sellers, jointly and severally, agree to sell the assets hereinafter described which are owned by them respectively at the date of closing, and the Buyer agrees to pay therefor the amounts hereinafter set forth, namely:

1. All trade accounts receivable which are owing from customers who are being serviced by the Sellers or any of them at the date of title closing (other than intercorporate accounts receivable among the Sellers) for which

the Buyer shall pay the entire unpaid balance of each such account at the date of title closing, which such accounts receivable for all of the Sellers is estimated to be in the sum of \$.

2. All loans or notes receivable from customers who are being serviced by the Sellers (other than intercompany loans or notes receivable among Sellers), or any of them, and all loans and notes receivable from employees of the Sellers, at the date of title closing for which the Buyer shall pay the entire unpaid balance of each said loan or note receivable at the date of title closing, which said loans receivable, for all of the Sellers, as set forth in the Schedule of Loans and Notes Receivable from Customers hereto annexed, is hereby fixed at the sum of \$.

3. All inventory of   , whether or not in unopened or original containers for which the Buyer shall pay the Sellers the last delivery cost thereof, minus all sales or use taxes, and, in the case of obsolete and damaged merchandise, the marked-down price thereof as shown on the Sellers' inventory count sheets disclosed to Buyer, which said inventory of   in the inventory of both of the Sellers is hereby estimated at \$.

C. The purchase price shall be adjusted:

(1) By adding thereto the pro rata portion attributable to the period after the closing date of all prepaid items, including, without limitation, premiums on policies of insurance accepted by an assignment to the Buyer, utility bills, deposits with utility companies and others, prepayments on service contracts, estimated at \$.

(2) By adding thereto the amount paid by the Sellers, or any of them, for all items of any fixed assets as set forth in Schedule "A" hereof delivered from   , to the date of closing inclusive, less the value of items traded in against such acquisitions, which net amount paid by the Sellers is hereby fixed at \$

D. Payment of the purchase price shall be made as follows:

(1) To   , as Agent for the Sellers for their assets listed in Paragraph (a), (b) and (c) hereof.

(a) At Closing, \$ by Buyer making, executing and delivering its installment promissory note, in writing, to the order of   , as Agent for

dated as of the date of title closing, bearing interest at the rate of 6% per annum on all of the unpaid installments of principal. Interest at the rate of 6% per annum upon the unpaid principal balance of said note shall be due and payable on the last days of March, June, September and December of each year, beginning   .

The said note and the installments of principal and interest thereon shall be due and payable at The   Bank,   .

The first installment of principal shall be due and payable on the last day of   . The remaining principal installments, together with interest on the unpaid principal balance of said note, owing on the due date of each said installment of principal shall be due and payable quarter-annually thereafter on the last days of June, September, December and March in each year through   . Each of said installments of principal shall be for 1/   of the principal face amount of the promissory note. All of said installments of principal shall be in equal amounts, except that the first installment shall reflect breakage. The said promissory note shall bear the following legend on its face:

In the event that any installment of principal or any payment of interest shall not be paid when due and such default continue for a period of thirty (30) days thereafter, then all of the remaining unpaid installments then owing, together with interest thereon, shall, at the option of any holder of this note, forthwith become due and payable.

The payment of principal and interest on this note is subordinated to the payment of certain indebtedness to the Bank of   , Bank of   , Bank of   , and Bank of   , to the extent as set forth in a Subordination Agreement dated   , between the payee of this note and the said banks.

The prepayment of all or any principal installment, together with interest thereon, if applicable, to the date of such prepayment, may be made at the option of the maker, at any time after the date hereof without premium or penalty. Prepayment on account of the principal of this note shall be applied in payment of any installment determined by the maker in a notice given to the holder at the time of making said payment.

(b) By certified check at closing to the order of   , as Agent for

$

(c) By assumption by the Buyer of the liability on the restrictive agreements of the Sellers, (estimated), $.

With reference to the purchase price payable to the Sellers hereunder, adjustments in connection with the following items shall be made:

(i) In cash:

Free service adjustments;

Gratuities adjustment;

Prepaid service adjustment;

(ii) Against the Note:

Vacation pay and sick leave adjustments;

New goods adjustment;

Customers' loan adjustment;

Accounts receivable adjustment;

Trade discount adjustment

affecting accounts receivable
assigned to Buyer.

Any vacation pay or sick leave adjustment allowed to Buyer and not paid out by it shall be readjusted to Sellers.

The following adjustments shall be made by the assumption of the payment of the purchase price therefor, provided Sellers have not paid the purchase price. If Sellers have paid the purchase price, the adjustment shall be made in cash.

Additions to fixed assets as set forth in Schedule "A" hereof

The parties agree that promptly after the closing they will proceed to compute the purchase price for the assets set forth in Paragraph "B" hereof, and the adjustments referred to in Paragraph "C" hereof. If the purchase price so computed shall exceed the payments theretofore made by the Buyer to the Sellers under said Paragraph "D," the difference shall be added to the amount of the said note and each of the installments payable under said note shall be increased by one- (1/ th) of the amount of said reduction. The said adjustment shall be made within five (5) days after the completion of the computation. All payments to be made by the Buyer under this Agreement shall be made in Certified or Bank Cashier's checks in New York Clearing House funds. At the closing each of the Sellers shall execute and deliver to the Buyer a Bill of Sale substantially in form set forth in Schedule "B" hereof.

II.   SELLERS' CONTRACTS AND ASSUMPTION OF LIABILITY THEREFOR

The Sellers hereby assign to the Buyer all of their right, title and interest in and to their respective:

(1) Purchase orders, agreements and other obligations to purchase materials, supplies, equipment, facilities, or services and leases or equipment or fixtures, entered into in the ordinary course of business of the Sellers or any of them;

(2) Leases of real property and other agreements to pay rent as set forth in Schedule "C" thereof;

(3) Agreements with public utilities;

(4) Agreements and arrangements with employees entered into in the ordinary course of the business of the Sellers, or any of them, it being further agreed that the Sellers have no employment contracts which do not terminate or cannot be terminated within one year without liability to the Buyer;

(5) Contracts, agreements and arrangements to sell goods

or services, including, but not limited to contracts, agreements or arrangements with customers for discounts, gratuities, concessions, allowances or free services;

(6) Loans and notes receivable from existing customers of the business and from employees, set forth in the Schedule of Loans and Notes Receivable from Customers. At the time of title closing the Seller shall deliver to the Buyer all instruments executed by the borrowers evidencing said loans.

(7) All trade accounts receivable owing to the Sellers from existing customers of the said businesses as at the date of title closing, provided, however, that there shall be excluded from the foregoing all intercompany contracts, agreements, orders, commitments and arrangements among the Sellers; and provided, further, that to the extent any of the foregoing are assignable, Sellers severally agree, at Sellers' expense, to do whatever Buyer reasonably requests in order to enable the Buyer to obtain the benefit of such rights.

The Buyer assumes and agrees to perform all covenants and obligations which are by the Sellers to be observed and performed on and after the date hereof, of said orders, contracts, agreements, leases, commitments and arrangements (other than said intercompany items) set forth in this Article "II" and agrees to assume, pay, satisfy and discharge all of said indebtednesses but only to the extent disclosed to Buyer and the liabilities of the Sellers, and each of them, of any and every kind, direct or contingent, by reason thereof, and to indemnify and save harmless the Sellers and each of them from all liability with respect thereto and from all liability of the Sellers, or any of them, with respect to vacation pay, customers' deposits, and future free service commitments to customers.

III. SELLERS' INDEMNITY FOR CLAIMS OF CREDITORS

Except to the extent of the assumption of liabilities by the Buyer under the provisions of this agreement, the Sellers jointly and severally agree to satisfy all valid claims of their respective creditors and to indemnify and save the Buyer harmless from all claims of Sellers' said respective creditors existing at the time of the closing and from all liens, franchise taxes, sales and use tax, other than such taxes specifically required to be paid by the Buyer under Subparagraph (c) of Article "V" hereof.

IV. REPRESENTATIONS BY SELLERS

The Sellers, jointly and severally, represent and warrant as follows:

(a) Each of the Sellers is a corporation duly organized, validly existing and in good standing under the laws of the State of its incorporation, and are duly qualified to do business in the areas in which they operate where required by law.

(b) Each conveyance, assignment, transfer or other transaction contemplated hereunder to be performed by Sellers has been or will be duly authorized by the Sellers' Boards of Directors, and, to the extent required by law, by the Sellers' stockholders.

(c) Since the closing of business   , the business of each of the Sellers has been conducted only in its ordinary course and the Sellers shall continue so to conduct their business until the closing of title hereunder.   (d) The average weekly net sales, net of all trade discounts and allowances of   sold by the Sellers to their customers as reflected on their books of account for the calendar year,   , was not less than the sum of $

(e) There is no litigation or proceeding pending, or, to the knowledge of the Sellers and/or the Third Parties, threatened against the Sellers, their properties or businesses, except claims which are fully insured against, nor do the Sellers know of any basis for any such action or of any governmental investigation relative to Sellers, their properties or businesses.

(f) The Sellers and the Third Parties, and each of them will, at the request of the Buyer, execute such further documents as may be necessary to effect the sale of the assets herein sold and transferred and will cooperate with the Buyer in its efforts to obtain the Sellers' present telephone numbers.

(g) Each of the Sellers will, at the time of closing, furnish the Buyer with duly certified copies of the resolutions adopted or to be adopted by its Board of Directors and by its stockholders, as required by Paragraph (b), Article "IV" hereof.

(h) That no commitments have been made by the Sellers, or any of them, to any of their customers for free service, gratuities, or for the receipt from the Sellers by any of said customers of anything of value which is to take effect after the date hereof, except as is set forth in the Schedule of Free Service which shall be furnished to the Buyer by each Seller within one week after title closing.

(i) That none of the Sellers' customers have prepaid for any service, except as set forth in the Schedule of Prepaid Service which shall be furnished to the Buyer by each Seller within one week after title closing.

(j) That each of the trade accounts receivable owing to the Sellers are valid and subsisting accounts receivable, justly due and owing to each of them, and that there are no offsets or defenses thereto or counter-claims existing against any thereof.

(k) That all of the loans and notes receivable which have been assigned to the Buyer are owing by the customers and employees who are presently customers and employees of the Sellers; that all of said borrowers have been making regular amortization payments on said loans in each case where the loans are to be amortized in accordance with each of their agreements therefor with the Sellers, and said borrowers are not in arrears of their payments thereon, except as disclosed by Sellers to Buyer.

(l) That they have not received from any of the customers of their businesses any notice that any of said customers intend to discontinue or curtail their service to take effect either before or after the closing of title or to be effective against the Buyer after title closing.

(m) That   is the duly appointed and qualified Agent of each of the Sellers for the purpose of receiving all checks and promissory notes which are to be delivered to the Sellers hereunder and that said checks and promissory notes shall be **made** payable to the order of the said   as Agent, for three (3) Sellers.

V. REPRESENTATIONS BY BUYER

The Buyer represents and warrants as follows:

(a) The Buyer is a corporation duly organized and existing and in good standing under the laws of the state of New York.

(b) The execution of this agreement by Buyer and the execution of all other instruments contemplated hereunder to be executed by Buyer have been or will be duly authorized by its Board of Directors, and, to the extent required by law, by its Stockholders.

(c) Buyer will pay or satisfy, and will hold the Sellers, and each of them, harmless from any and all liability for sales and use taxes levied by any state, county, city, municipality or governmental authority, and which may be payable by reason of the transactions covered by this agreement.

(d) The Buyer will, at the time of closing, furnish each of the Sellers with duly certified copies of the resolutions adopted or to be adopted, by its Board of Directors as required by Subparagraph (b) of this Article "V" and by the Executive Committee of   , a Delaware corporation, authorizing the execution of an Agreement of Guaranty, a copy of which is hereto annexed and made a part hereof and called "Guaranty."

VI. UNDERTAKINGS BY THE SELLERS

(a) In connection with all of the trade accounts receivable assigned by the Sellers to the Buyer, pursuant to the terms of this Agreement, the Sellers and each of them, undertake that they will accept a reassignment of all or any portions thereof at any time on·or prior to   , and credit the face amount thereof in reduction of the first installment or installments then owing on the promissory note executed by the Buyer to the order of the Sellers, provided, however, that all sums received from customers who are indebted to Sellers on said trade accounts receivable, when collected by Buyer, shall have been credited on a first-in, first-out basis in payment of said assigned accounts receivable, unless said payment was specifically earmarked for an account receivable owing to the Buyer, or for any other obligation owing by said customer to the Buyer.

(b) In connection with all of the loans and notes receivable from customers and employees which are assigned by the Sellers to the Buyer, pursuant to the terms of this agreement, the Sellers agree that they will accept a reassignment of any said loan or so much thereof as remains unpaid, at any time within sixty (60) days after the occurrence of any default in payment of any installment of principal or interest owing on any of said loans by any borrower. In the event of such reassignment by the Buyer of any of such loans or notes receivable to the Sellers, the Sellers shall credit the unpaid balance owing on said notes or loans receivable, as the case may be, in reduction of the first installment or installments owing on the promissory note executed by the Buyer to the order of the Sellers.

(c) The Sellers shall be entitled to take any action at law or otherwise to effect collection of any trade accounts receivable reassigned to them by the Buyer pursuant to the provisions of Subparagraphs (a) and (b) hereof.

(d) The Agent for the Sellers, and the Sellers, jointly and severally, shall execute Subordination Agreements in form and substance as set forth in the exhibit labeled "Subordination Agreement," hereto annexed and made part hereof, wherein and whereby they shall subordinate the payment of any and all installment promissory notes made to their order to the obligation of the Buyer to   Bank of   and   and in pursuance of the provisions of said Subordination Agreement, each and all of said promissory notes made, executed and delivered by the Buyer to the order of the Agent of the Sellers and/or the Sellers, shall have endorsed on the face thereof the following legend:

The payment of principal and interest on this note is subordinated to the payment of certain indebtedness to the   Bank of

, to the extent as set forth in between the payee of this note and said Banks.

(e) The Sellers hereby guarantee that the combined sum of accounts and loans receivable owing to the Seller from customers and employees of the business (as described in Article "I", Paragraph "B", "1" and "2" hereof), plus the amount of the   (as described in Article "I", Paragraph "C", (1) after making all adjustments thereof provided on Page "6" of this Agreement shall amount to no less than $. In the event that the amount thereof is less than $, the purchase price thereof shall be reduced by a sum equal to the difference between $ and the sum thereof so determined. If the sum thereof is greater than $, the Buyer shall pay the full amount thereof, but the purchase price hereinbefore fixed for the good will shall be reduced by a sum equal to the difference between the amount thereof and $

VII.   BOOKS AND RECORDS

The Sellers, jointly and severally, agree that at the closing they will deliver to the Buyer all of their respective books, records, documents and papers, excluding their general journals and general ledgers, stock ledgers, minutes books, and other records relating to their capital stock and corporate organization. The Buyer agrees that it will, at all reasonable times during business hours subsequent to the closing, permit the Sellers, or their respective authorized representatives to have access to all such books and records delivered to Buyer by the Sellers, and that Buyer will keep and preserve said books and records for a period of at least six (6) years after the closing unless otherwise permitted by the Sellers in writing.

VIII.   CHANGE OF NAMES OF SELLERS

The Sellers agree promptly after the closing of title to change their names to different and unsimilar names by filing with the Secretary of State of the state of New York a Certificate of Change of Name. Simultaneously with the filing of said Certificate, the Buyers will file Certificates of Incorporation covering the incorporation of new corporations with names similar to the names of the Sellers prior to the change. The Sellers agree to execute any and all instruments necessary or desirable to effectuate the intent of this provision.

IX.   AGREEMENTS NOT TO COMPETE

The Sellers, jointly and severally, agree to obtain and deliver to the Buyer, at the closing, agreements not to compete in form as set forth in Schedule "D" hereto annexed, executed by   and by the respective Sellers.

X.   AGREEMENTS WITH SELLERS' EMPLOYEES

The Sellers, jointly and severally, agree with the Buyer that they have entered into negative and restrictive covenant employment agreements with all of their present and past employees who have had contact with any of the customers of the Sellers' businesses during a period of two (2) years last past. Said negative and restrictive covenant employment agreements are in form and substance as set forth in the forms hereto annexed and made a part hereof comprising Schedule "E." The Sellers agree to assign all of said negative and restrictive covenant employment agreements to the Buyer at the time of closing.

XI.   CONSEQUENCES OF NONFRAUDULENT
        MISREPRESENTATIONS

After the closing, neither Buyer nor Sellers shall be entitled to rescind the transaction by reason of any nonfraudulent misrepresentation. In no event shall either Buyer or Sellers be entitled to recover damages from the others by reason of any nonfraudulent misrepresentations unless a proceeding in arbitration to recover such damages is commenced prior to   . Nothing herein contained shall be deemed to affect any of the indemnification provisions of this agreement.

XII.   CONSEQUENCES OF FIRE, ETC .

In the event that any of the property of the Sellers subject to this sale shall be partially or totally destroyed by fire or by any other hazard, this contract shall remain in full force and effect except that Sellers shall turn over to Buyer the proceeds of any insurance collected by the Sellers in connection with such casualty. Sellers will keep the policies of insurance existing on   , in force until the date of closing.

XIII.   CLOSING

The closing of sale shall take place at the office of
at   on

XIV.   ARBITRATION

All controversies arising under or in connection with or relating to any alleged breach of this agreement shall be settled by arbitration in the City of New York, State of New York.   is hereby nominated as the sole arbitrator and any decision or award rendered by him shall be final and binding upon all the parties hereto and judgment upon any such award rendered may be entered in any court having jurisdiction. In the event of the failure, refusal or inability of the arbitrator named herein to act, or in the event of the said arbitrator's incapacity or death, the parties hereto agree that all of the said controversies arising under or in connection with or relating to any alleged breach of this agreement shall be disposed of by arbitration, pursuant to the rules of the American Arbitration Association, in the City of New York, and the decision of any arbitrator or arbitrators appointed pursuant to the said rules of the said Association shall constitute a final award and shall be binding upon all of the parties hereto and judgment upon any such award rendered may be entered in any court having jurisdiction. The provisions of the Article shall not apply to any controversy arising under or in connection with the agreement referred to in Article "IX."

XV. INDEMNIFICATION BY PARTIES OF THE THIRD PART

The Parties of the Third Part hereby jointly and severally agree to indemnify and save harmless the Buyer from all loss or damage arising out of any misrepresentation made to Buyer by the Sellers, or any of them, in this agreement, or in any of the exhibits thereto, or from any breach by the Sellers, or any of them, of any obligation to be performed by the Sellers, or any of them, pursuant to the provisions of this agreement or the exhibits thereto; provided, however, that in no event shall the Buyer be entitled to recover damages from the Parties of the Third Party by reason of any nonfraudulent misrepresentation unless a proceeding in arbitration to recover such damages is commenced against the Sellers and/or Third Parties prior to

XVI. CONSTRUCTION

This agreement shall be construed and enforced in accordance with the laws of the state of New York and may not be changed or terminated orally.

XVII. SURVIVAL OF REPRESENTATIONS AND WARRANTIES

All representations, warranties, agreements and indemnities made by the Sellers, or any of them, or by the Buyer, respectively, in this agreement or pursuant thereto, shall survive the closing hereunder.

This agreement shall be binding upon and inure to the benefit of the respective successors and assigns of the parties hereto.

IN WITNESS WHEREOF, the parties hereto have caused their hands and seals to be hereunto affixed the day and year first above written.

By:_____
                                    President

By:_____
                                    President

By:_____
                                    President

_____
                                    individually
and as agent.

_____

By:_____
                                        President

_____

SCHEDULE B
BILL OF SALE

That

having offices and places of business at

parties of the first part, for and in consideration of the purchase prices hereinafter set forth, to them in hand paid, at or before the ensealing and delivery of these presents, by   a New York corporation have an office and place of business at   party of the second part, the receipt whereof is hereby acknowledged, have bargained and sold, and by these presents do grant and convey unto the said party of the second part, its successors and assigns, all of the tangible personal property owned by the parties of the first part and/or used by the parties of the first part in the operation and conduct of their businesses, no matter where located, as follows:

(1) All of the good will of the parties of the first part herein in the operation of their routes, all of its rights to do business with their customers, all of their trade names, including, without limitation, all service contracts with their customers, all trade routes, all of its rights to do business with their customers, all of their trade names, including their corporate names, all lists of their customers, and the negative and restrictive covenant employment agreement which they have heretofore entered into with their employees,

The parties of the first part are the sole owners of the property described in this Bill of Sale, and each and every part thereof, and have the full right to sell and transfer the same; that the said property, and each and every part thereof is free and clear of any and all liens, mortgages, and other encumbrances or claims of whatsoever kind or nature.

TO HAVE AND TO HOLD the same unto the said party of the second part, its successors and assigns forever; and the parties of the first part do, for themselves, their successors and assigns, covenant and agree to and with said party of the second part to warrant and defend the sale of said property hereby sold unto the said party of the second part, its successors and assigns, against all and every person and persons whomsoever.

IN WITNESS WHEREOF, the parties of the first part have caused this Bill of Sale to be executed by their officers thereunto duly authorized and their corporate seals to be hereunto affixed and attested, this   day of   , 1971.

(SEAL)

ATTEST: By:

                                                    _____
                                                                President

(SEAL)

ATTEST: By:

                                                    _____
                                                                President

(SEAL)

ATTEST: By:

                                                    _____

_____
            Secretary

PURCHASE OF STOCK

PURCHASE AGREEMENT

AGREEMENT, made this   day of November, 19 , by and between_____ and _____, residing at _____ ("Sellers") and _____, a _____ corporation having its principal offices located at _____("Buyer").

W I T N E S S E T H :

WHEREAS, Sellers are the owners of all of the issued and outstanding shares of _____, a New York corporation having offices at _____, _____ (hereinafter referred to as "ABC"); and

WHEREAS, Buyer desires to acquire from ABC certain specific assets of ABC, including all of its supply contracts with various European suppliers of wines, champagnes and fortified wines, subject only to specific liabilities, and ABC is unwilling to sell such assets; and

WHEREAS, Sellers are willing to sell to Buyer, and Buyer desires to purchase from Sellers, all of the shares of ABC for the purpose of enabling Buyer to acquire the assets (including supply contracts) hereinafter specified, subject to the liabilities hereinafter specified, on the terms and conditions hereinafter set forth, Buyer having the intention of liquidating ABC so as to acquire the rights and assets specified;

NOW, THEREFORE, in consideration of the foregoing and of the mutual promises, covenants and conditions hereinafter set forth, the parties hereto agree as follows:

1. *Sale of Shares.* On the terms and subject to the conditions hereinafter set forth, Sellers agree to sell, assign and transfer to Buyer, and Buyer agrees to purchase, on the Closing Date (as hereinafter defined), all of the shares of ABC owned by Sellers and consisting, as at the date hereof, of 212 shares of Common Stock, _____ par value. Simultaneously with the Closing, Sellers will cause ABC to redeem a portion of their shares in exchange for those specified assets which Buyer does not wish to acquire and which Sellers wish to retain, all as set forth on Exhibit A hereto, subject only to those liabilities listed on Exhibit A, which redemption shall constitute a part of the transactions contemplated hereby, so that Buyer can ultimately acquire only those specified assets, subject to specific liabilities, as hereinafter set forth, which it desires to purchase.

2. *Purchase Price; Payment.* The total purchase price for the shares to be sold hereunder, allocated *pro rata* between the Sellers, is $750,000, of which $200,000 shall be paid to Sellers at the Closing and $50,000 shall be paid on January 15, 1972, in each case by check, subject to collection. The balance of the purchase price, in the amount of $500,000, shall be paid to Sellers in quarterly installments on the fifteenth day of January, April, July and October of each year, over a period of ten years commencing January 15, 1972, in accordance with the following schedule, with interest on each installment calculated from the Closing Date at the rate of 2% per annum:

Year of Payment	Amount of Annual Payment	Amount of Quarterly Installment
1972	$25,000	$ 6,250.00
1973	25,000	6,250.00
1974	56,250	14,062.50
1975	56,250	14,062.50
1976	56,250	14,062.50
1977	56,250	14,062.50
1978	56,250	14,062.50
1979	56,250	14,062.50
1980	56,250	14,062.50
1981	56,250	14,062.50

3. *Representations of Sellers.* In order to induce Buyer to enter into this Agreement, Sellers hereby represent and warrant to Buyer as follows:

(a) The shares to be sold by Sellers hereunder, after the redemption described in Paragraph 1 hereof, will constitute all of the issued and outstanding shares of capital stock of ABC as of the Closing Date (hereinafter referred to as the "Shares").

(b) As of the Closing Date, Sellers will have good and valid title to the Shares, free and clear of any and all liens, charges, encumbrances and claims of others of any nature whatsoever, and there will be no existing impediment to the sale and transfer thereof to Buyer hereunder.

(c) Sellers have the right, power, legal capacity and authority to enter into this Agreement and to sell and deliver the Shares as herein provided, and this Agreement shall, when executed, constitute a valid and binding obligation of the Sellers.

(d) ABC is a corporation duly organized, validly existing and in good standing under the laws of the State of New York. Sellers have delivered to Buyer a certified copy of the Certificate of Incorporation of ABC, with all amendments thereto through the Closing Date, receipt of which is hereby acknowledged by Buyer.

(e) Attached hereto as Exhibit B is a list of all existing contracts between ABC and European suppliers with respect to the supply of wines, champagnes and fortified wines, which contracts constitute assets of ABC which Buyer will acquire upon the liquidation of ABC following the sale of the Shares hereunder. Sellers have delivered to Buyer, receipt of which is hereby acknowledged by Buyer, lists and schedules setting forth gross sales with respect to each of such supply contracts over the last three years. The purchase price for the Shares to be sold hereunder has been reached as a result of arm's length negotiations, and is equal to the amount that Buyer would have been willing to pay to ABC and ABC would have been willing to accept for the supply contracts and other specific assets referred to herein. Sellers make no specific representation with respect to future sales or commissions under any of the supply contracts, and Buyer specifically acknowledges that it has obtained independent appraisals with respect to each of such contracts and has relied on such appraisals and its own business judgment in determining the price it would be willing to pay for each of such contracts alone.

(f) ABC presently occupies leased premises located at_____
_____, under a lease or leases providing for an aggregate rental of $_____ per year, expiring November 30, 1972. Copies of this lease or leases have been delivered to Buyer, which hereby acknowledges receipt thereof. The right to occupy such premises under such lease or leases is among the assets which Buyer will acquire upon the liquidation of ABC.

(g) Sellers have delivered to Buyer an unaudited balance sheet of ABC, as at August 12, 1971, prepared by the regular independent accountants of ABC, setting forth, on an accrual basis, all assets and all liabilities, whether actual, contingent or accrued, of ABC as of the date thereof. Such balance sheet (hereinafter the "Balance Sheet") has been prepared in accordance with generally accepted accounting principles, applied on a consistent basis, and is true and correct as of the date thereof. As of the Closing Date, subsequent to the redemption referred to in Paragraph 1 above, ABC shall own and retain the fixed assets, consisting of office furniture and fixtures, supplies and other assets set forth in the Balance Sheet, as well as security and deposits, and trademarks listed on the Balance Sheet. These specified assets, which will be acquired by Buyer upon the liquidation of ABC, have the values, subject to allowance for depreciation, ascribed to them in the Balance Sheet.

(h) As at August 12, 1971, there were no liabilities of ABC, whether actual, contingent or otherwise, including provision for all taxes of ABC based upon earnings and operations of ABC through that date, other than as set forth on the Balance Sheet. Since August 12, 1971, ABC has incurred no liabilities or obligations other than liabilities and obligations arising out of the ordinary course of the business of ABC, except such liabilities as are expressly set forth or disclosed herein or in the Exhibits hereto, or in the financial statements of ABC previously delivered to Buyer. Buyer specifically acknowledges receipt of unaudited balance sheets and income statements of ABC as at and for the periods ended September 30, 1971 and October 31, 1971. Such financial statements are true and correct on and as of the date thereof, and there has been no material adverse change in the business or operations of ABC since October 30, 1971.

(i) It is the basic understanding of Sellers and Buyer hereunder that all earnings and profits of ABC subsequent to August 12, 1971, subject to the liabilities of ABC incurred in the normal course of business since that date, have been and are for the account of Buyer, while any earnings and profits, subject to any and all liabilities, arising prior to August 12, 1971, shall inure to and remain the obligation of Sellers. Accordingly, any commission income realized on purchase orders received by ABC subsequent to August 12, 1971, shall remain as a part of the assets of ABC upon the Closing Date, while all commission income on purchase orders received by ABC prior to August 12, 1971, subject to any and all liabilities of ABC as of that date, shall be delivered to Sellers in redemption of a portion of their shares of ABC, as contemplated by Paragraph 1 hereof. The method of the allocation contemplated hereby is the Balance Sheet, as at August 12, 1971, it being understood that the net amount of all assets, including cash and accounts receivable allocable to Sellers in accordance with this subparagraph, but excluding those specific assets to be retained by ABC as referred to herein, after provision for any and all liabilities of ABC as at August 12, 1971, shall be delivered to Sellers in redemption of their shares simultaneously with the Closing hereunder.

(j) ABC presently has all necessary state and local licenses required for it to continue conducting the business in which it is presently engaged, and all such licenses or permits are valid and in effect. It is an express condition to the Closing hereunder that Buyer shall obtain any necessary license renewals or transfers, or any necessary approval of the transactions contemplated hereby by appropriate licensing authorities.

(k) There is no suit, proceeding or litigation pending or, to the knowledge of Sellers, threatened against or relating to ABC or its property or business.

(l) ABC has filed all tax reports and returns and all related information required to be filed prior to the date hereof and all payments reported or required to be reported on such returns as due from ABC have been paid in full. Any deficiency assessments, with interest and penalties thereon, levied against ABC for all periods to August 12, 1971, shall be indemnified by Sellers in accordance with Paragraph 7 below. The tax returns of ABC were last audited by the federal government for the period ended _____.

(m) Attached hereto as Exhibit C is a list of all unfilled purchase orders received by ABC, which list is current as of November __, 1971. Except as disclosed in Exhibit C or as otherwise disclosed herein or in the Exhibits hereto, or n the Balance Sheet or any other financial statements delivered to Buyer and referred to herein, ABC is not a party to any leases, contracts, commitments or other agreements.

(n) Neither this Agreement nor any statement or Exhibit or other document furnished or to be furnished to Buyer pursuant to or in connection with this Agreement contains or will contain any untrue statement of a material fact or omits or will omit to state a material fact necessary in order to make the statements herein and therein, in light of the circumstances in which they are made, not misleading.

4. *Representations and Acknowledgments of Buyer*. In order to induce Sellers to enter into this Agreement, Buyer hereby represents, warrants and acknowledges to Sellers as follows:

(a) Buyer is a corporation duly organized, validly existing and in good standing under the laws of the State of _____, and has full right, power and authority to enter into this Agreement and to carry out its obligations as contemplated hereby, and this Agreement shall, when executed, constitute a valid and binding obligation of Buyer.

(b) Buyer hereby acknowledges that it knows the value of the business and assets of ABC to be retained by ABC subsequent to the Closing hereunder. Buyer further acknowledges that no representation has been made to it, by Sellers or by ABC or any of its officers or directors, as to any matters other than those specifically set forth in this Agreement. Buyer agrees specifically that Sellers shall retain no responsibility for any obligations or liabilities of ABC arising or incurred in the normal course of business subsequent to August 12, 1971, it being understood that Sellers have in effect conducted the business of ABC on behalf of Buyer since that date.

5. *Covenants of Buyer.*

(a) Buyer hereby covenants and agrees with Sellers that, subsequent to the Closing Date, Sellers and their accountants, agents or representatives shall have reasonable access to the relevant books and records of ABC, at reasonable times and upon reasonable notice duly given, in connection with any tax examination for any periods ending prior to the Closing Date or any other matter for which Sellers may remain liable pursuant to the terms hereof and for which such access may be necessary.

(b) In the event Buyer shall default on any payment required to be made by it to Sellers pursuant to Paragraph 2 hereof for a period of more than 30 days after the date of written notice from Sellers, or if Buyer shall default in the performance of any other obligation owing to Sellers or to either of them, whether under this Agreement or under the Employment Agreement of even date herewith between Buyer and_____, for a period of more than 20 days after the date of written notice from Sellers, Buyer shall promptly, at the request of Sellers, return all of the issued and outstanding stock of ABC to Sellers and, in such event, Buyer shall have no further right, title or interest in such stock or the business of ABC, Sellers shall retain any and all payments previously received from Buyer, and Buyer shall have no further obligations under this Agreement; provided, however, that if Buyer can demonstrate to Seller that delay in payment of any such obligation is a direct result of failure or delay in delivery of products from Europe because of strike, embargo, hurricane, tornado, or other Act of God or force majeure beyond the control of Buyer or of ABC, which failure or delay in delivery has a material adverse effect on the business of ABC, and if Buyer and ABC are unable, after using reasonable efforts, to obtain substitute delivery from other suppliers to replace any such products, then and in such event, but only in such event, Buyer shall have the right, temporarily, to suspend payment of any such amount due and owing to Sellers, or either of them, until termination of the event or situation causing the failure or delay in delivery, whereupon the full amount due shall become payable within ten days of termination.

6. *Closing.* The Closing hereunder shall take place on December___, 1971, or on such other date, not later than December 31, 1971, as the parties shall mutually agree, after fulfillment of any closing conditions hereunder, at the offices of_____, New York. The date of the Closing is referred to in this Agreement as the Closing Date.

(a) At the Closing, Sellers shall deliver to Buyer the following:

(i) A certificate or certificates representing the Shares to be sold hereunder, duly endorsed in blank, or with stock powers affixed thereto, in proper form for transfer, with stock transfer stamps affixed thereto or funds therefor;

(ii) The written resignations of the officers and directors of ABC, dated and effective as of the Closing Date;

(iii) A general release in favor of ABC, excluding only those obligations recognized or created by this Agreement;

(iv) All of the stock books, minute books and stock transfer ledgers of ABC, and all other corporate books and records of ABC; and

(v) An opinion of_____, counsel to Sellers, dated the Closing Date, to the effect that ABC is duly organized, validly existing and in good standing under the laws of the state of New York; that, except as otherwise disclosed herein or in any Exhibits or other documents delivered hereunder, they do not know of any litigation pending or threatened against or relating to ABC; that, to the best of their knowledge, Sellers have full right, power and authority to enter into this Agreement and to sell, assign, transfer and deliver the Shares hereunder, free and clear of all liens, charges and encumbrances; and that this Agreement is valid and binding upon the Sellers and enforceable in accordance with its terms.

(b) At the Closing, Buyer shall deliver to Sellers the following:

(i) A check or checks in the aggregate amount of $200,000, as required by Paragraph 2 hereof;

(ii) An Employment Agreement between Buyer and_____
_____, in the form of Exhibit D attached hereto; and

(iii) An Opinion Letter of_____, counsel to Buyer, dated the Closing Date, to the effect that Buyer is a corporation duly incorporated, validly existing and in good standing under the laws of the state of _____; that this Agreement has been duly authorized, executed and delivered by Buyer, which has full power and authority to take all actions required to be taken by it pursuant to the provisions hereof; that this Agreement is valid and binding upon Buyer and is enforceable in accordance with its terms.

7. *Survival of Representations; Indemnification.* Sellers hereby covenant that all representations, warranties, covenants and agreements made by them in this agreement or pursuant hereto shall be true and correct when made and at and as of the time of closing, and shall be deemed and construed to be continuing representations, warranties, covenants and agreements which shall survive the Closing and the execution and delivery of all instruments and documents provided herein. Sellers hereby jointly and severally agree to indemnify and hold Buyer harmless from and against any loss (net of tax benefit, if any) that Buyer of ABC may incur arising out of (a) any misrepresentation or breach of warranty contained in this Agreement or in any Exhibit furnished or to be furnished to Buyer by Sellers hereunder; and (b) all actions, suits, or proceedings, demands, assessments, judgments, costs and expenses, including reasonable legal fees, incident to the foregoing. The extent of Sellers' aggregate liabilities shall be limited to the aggregate amount received by Sellers for the Shares sold hereunder, and Buyer shall have the right to offset claims under this Paragraph 7 against any future installments of the purchase price owing to Sellers pursuant to Paragraph 2 hereof, it being understood that any such offset shall constitute only a mechanical method by which Sellers may pay the amount of such claims and shall not be deemed to constitute a reduction in the total purchase price for the Shares to be sold hereunder. Buyer agrees to give Sellers prompt written notice of the assertion of any claim of which it has knowledge which is covered by this indemnity and to afford Sellers an opportunity to be represented by counsel of their choice, at their own expense, and to defend, contest, litigate, negotiate, settle or otherwise deal with any such claim. If Sellers elect not to participate to the defense of any such claim, Buyer shall have the right to dispose of such claim in such manner as it deems advisable and, for the purposes hereof, such disposition shall have the same effect as though the disposition had been made by Sellers. Deduction by Buyer of the amount of any loss claimed by Buyer hereunder against any installments of purchase price payable under Paragraph 2 hereof shall not constitute an admission by Sellers of the validity of any such claim.

8. *Restrictive Covenant of Sellers.* Sellers agree that for a period of ten (10) years from the Closing Date they will not, directly or indirectly, engage or participate in or become employed by or render advisory or other services in the United States, Puerto Rico or the U.S. Virgin Islands, in connection with any business activity competitive with that of ABC and will not make any financial investment, directly or indirectly, in any firm, corporation or business enterprise competitive in any way with the business or activities of ABC. Nothing herein, however, shall restrict Sellers from making any investments in any company whose stock is listed on any national securities exchange or actively traded in the over-the-counter market, so long as such investment does not give Sellers the right to control or influence the policy decisions of any such business or enterprise which is or might be in competition with the business of ABC. Nothing herein shall prevent Sellers from engaging in any activities, whether inside or outside the United States, so long as no such activities involve the import, sale or distribution of wines,

fortified wines or champagnes into or within the United States, Puerto Rico or the U.S. Virgin Islands. Without limitation upon the foregoing, and anything herein to the contrary notwithstanding, it is expressly understood and agreed that Sellers shall have the right to import, distribute, sell and otherwise deal in dehydrated or other soups and chateau-bottled European wine within the United States, Puerto Rico or the U.S. Virgin Islands shall either be effected through ABC or Buyer, or ABC or Buyer shall receive a commission of five percent of the sales price on any direct sales by Sellers within the prescribed area. The restrictive covenant set forth within this Paragraph 8 shall terminate and shall be of no further force or effect in the event of a material breach of the obligations of Buyer hereunder or under the Employment Agreement, of even date herewith, between Buyer and_____ _____. It is expressly understood by Buyer and Sellers that no portion of the purchase price is to be allocated to the covenant contained herein, it being understood that the terms of the Employment Agreement between Buyer and_____ _____, in providing basic salary and bonus compensation to_____ _____ or, in certain instances, to_____, constitute the total compensation and consideration for such covenant.

9. *Notices.* All notices, requests and other communications required or permitted to be given hereunder shall be in writing and shall be deemed to have been duly given if mailed, first class, postage prepaid, by registered or certified mail, return receipt requested, to either party at the address set forth at the beginning of this Agreement. Either party may change the address to which such communications are to be directed by giving written notice to the other party of such change in the manner hereinabove provided.

10. *Expenses.* Each of the parties hereto shall pay his or its own costs and expenses, in connection with this Agreement and the transactions contemplated hereby.

11. *General.* This Agreement shall be governed by and construed and enforced in accordance with the laws of the state of New York from time to time obtaining. All of the terms, covenants, representations, warranties and conditions of this Agreement shall be binding upon, and shall inure to the benefit of and be enforceable by, the parties hereto and their respective heirs, representatives, successors and assigns. This Agreement may not be amended, modified, superseded or cancelled and none of the terms or conditions hereof may be waived, except by a written instrument executed by the parties hereto or, in the case of a waiver, by the party waiving compliance. This Agreement contains the entire understanding of the parties hereto with respect to the transactions contemplated hereby, and supersedes and cancels any prior agreements or understandings with respect thereto.

12. *Counterparts.* This Agreement may be executed in one or more counterparts, each of which shall be deemed to be an original and all of which shall constitute one and the same instrument of the parties hereto.

IN WITNESS WHEREOF, the parties hereto have duly executed this Agreement as of the day and year first above written.

By_____

_____

_____

EMPLOYMENT AGREEMENT

AGREEMENT made this ___ day of December ___, 19 be-
tween_____, a_____ corporation
with offices located at _____
_____ (hereinafter called the "Corporation"), and _____, residing
at_____ (here-
inafter referred to as "Employee").

WITNESSETH:

In consideration of the mutual promises herein contained, the parties
hereto agree as follows:

1. *Employment.* Corporation agrees to employ Employee and Employee agrees to serve Corporation upon the terms and conditions hereinafter set
forth.

2. *Term of Employment.* The employment of Employee hereunder
shall commence on January 1, 19—, and shall continue for a period of three (3)
years thereafter, unless sooner terminated pursuant to the provisions of this
agreement.

3. *Duties of Employee.* Employee agrees to serve Corporation faithfully
and to the best of his ability under the direction of the Board of Directors of
Corporation. It is the intention of the parties that Employee shall serve Corporation
specifically in connection with European purchases of wines, champagnes and
fortified wines. Employee shall also render such executive, purchasing, selling and
other duties, whether within or without the United States, as Corporation may
from time to time require of him, including such business trips in the United States
and in Europe as may be necessary in the fulfillment of his duties hereunder.

4. *Compensation.* Corporation agrees to pay, or cause to be paid, to
Employee, and Employee agrees to accept, as compensation for the services
to be rendered by Employee hereunder, a minimum salary of $20,000 per
annum, payable in equal monthly installments, or in such other installments
as the parties hereto shall mutually agree. Corporation shall reimburse Employee
for all reasonable business expenses incurred by Employee on behalf of Corporation
including the expenses of any business trips in the United States and in Europe
undertaken in connection with employment hereunder.

(a) In the event of the death of Employee during the term of this
agreement, or in the event of termination of employment hereunder for any other
reason, Employee or his personal representatives or designee, as the case may be,

shall be entitled to receive, in the manner provided herein, the basic salary set forth above up to the end of the month in which death or termination occurs.

(b) In the event that Employee shall become incapacitated by reason of mental or physical disability or otherwise during the term of this agreement, so that he is prevented from performing his principal duties and services hereunder for a period of four (4) consecutive months, or the equivalent of six consecutive months during any twelve (12) month period, Corporation shall have the right to terminate this agreement by sending written notice of termination to Employee, and thereupon his employment hereunder shall terminate at the end of the month in which such notice is sent.

5. *Restrictive Covenant of Employee.* Employee agrees that during the entire term of this agreement and, in any event, for a minimum period of ten (10) years from the date hereof, he will not, directly or indirectly, engage or participate in or become employed by or render advisory or other services in the United States, Puerto Rico or the U.S. Virgin Islands, in connection with any business activity competitive with that of Corporation and will not make any financial investment, directly or indirectly, in any firm, corporation or business enterprise competitive in any way with the business or activities of Corporation. Nothing herein, however, shall restrict Employee from making any investments in any company whose stock is listed on a national securities exchange or actively traded in the over-the-counter market, so long as such investment does not give Employee the right to control or influence the policy decisions of any such business or enterprise which is or might be in competition with the business of Corporation. Nothing herein shall prevent Employee from engaging in any activities, whether inside or outside the United States, so long as no such activities involve the import, sale or distribution of wines, fortified wines or champagnes into or within the United States, Puerto Rico or the U.S. Virgin Islands. Without limitation upon the foregoing, and anything herein to the contrary notwithstanding, it is expressly understood and agreed that Employee shall have the right to import, distribute, sell and otherwise deal in dehydrated or other soups and chateau-bottled European wines; provided, however, that any sale of chateau-bottled European wines within the United States, Puerto Rico or the U.S. Virgin Islands shall either be effected through the Corporation or the Corporation shall receive a commission of 5% of the sales price on any direct sales by Employee within the prescribed area. The restrictive covenant set forth in this Paragraph 5 shall terminate and be of no further force or effect in the event of a material breach of the obligations of Corporation hereunder or under a Purchase Agreement of even date herewith between Corporation, as Buyer, and Employee and_____, as Sellers.

6. *Consulting Services.* Upon termination of Employee's employment hereunder for any reason other than his death, whether prior to or after the initial term of employment provided herein, Employee shall continue to serve Corporation on a part-time basis as an adviser and consultant with respect to the purchase

and distribution of European wines, fortified wines and champagnes, and shall be available to the Corporation, at reasonable times and upon reasonable notice, to render such advisory and consulting services. Employee agrees to render the services provided in this Paragraph 6 for a period not to end later than seven and one-half (7 1/2) years from the commencement of employment hereunder, at no additional compensation other than the bonus compensation provided in Paragraph 7 below, so long as Corporation shall not be in material breach of any of its obligations hereunder or under the Purchase Agreement referred to in Paragraph 5 above.

7. *Bonus Compensation.* In addition to the basic salary and compensation provided in Paragraph 4 above, Corporation shall pay to Employee in consideration for his employment as well as the consulting services to be rendered by him pursuant to Paragraph 6 above, bonus compensation calculated in accordance with this Paragraph 7 for a period of seven and one-half (7-1/2) years. Bonus compensation shall be based upon gross commissions (including over prices, if any) received by the Corporation on all sales of wines, champagnes, fortified wines, distilled products and cordials (excluding only sales of distilled products and cordials for which Employee is not directly responsible) calculated on an annual basis for a period of seven (7) years, and on a six-month basis for the last payment, beginning with the year ending December 31, 19——. Bonus compensation shall be equal to ten (10%) percent of the aggregate amount of all such gross commissions in excess of $200,000 during each year (or in excess of $100,000 during six months, for the last payment), calculated separately for each year (or six months), and shall be paid to Employee or, in the case of his death, to_____, within thirty (30) days of the close of each such year (or six months). In the event of the death of the survivor of Employee and_____ before final payment of all bonus compensation provided hereunder, such compensation shall be reduced to six (6%) percent of gross commissions in excess of $200,000 (or such lesser amount, depending upon the portion of any year remaining) effective with the date of such death, and remaining payments, at such reduced rate, shall be paid to the heirs or personal representatives of Employee, in accordance with the terms hereof.

8. *Notices.* All notices, requests, demands and other communications hereunder shall be in writing and shall be delivered personally or sent by Registered or Certified Mail, return receipt requested, to the parties hereto at their respective addresses as set forth at the beginning of this agreement. Any party may change the address to which notices, requests, demands and other communications hereunder shall be sent by sending written notice of such change of address to the other parties.

9. *Assignment.* This agreement is personal as to Employee and shall not be assignable by Employee, except that the advisory and consulting services to be provided by Employee hereunder shall be provided by_____ in the event of Employee's death, and any payments of bonus compensation payable

under Paragraph 7 shall, in the event of Employee's death, be paid to_____ _____ or to Employee's heirs or personal representatives in accordance with such Paragraph. This Agreement may be assigned by Corporation to any corporation which may acquire all or substantially all of the assets and business of Corporation or with or into which Corporation may be consolidated or merged.

10. *Binding Effect.* All of the terms and provisions of this agreement shall be binding upon and shall inure to the benefit of and be enforceable by the parties hereto and their respective heirs, executors, administrators, successors and assigns.

11. *Complete Understanding.* This agreement constitutes the complete understanding between the parties and no statement, representation, warranty or covenant has been made by either party except as expressly set forth herein. This agreement shall not be altered, modified, amended or terminated orally, but may be altered, modified amended or terminated by written instrument signed by both of the parties hereto.

IN WITNESS WHEREOF, the parties hereto have duly executed this agreement, intending to be legally bound thereby, the corporate party by a corporate officer thereunto duly authorized, as of the day and year first above written.

_____

By_____

REVENUE RULING

In re: (1) _____
(2) _____

Dear Mr. _____ :

This is in reply to a letter dated November 20, 1970, requesting a ruling as to the Federal income tax consequences of a proposed transaction. Additional information was submitted in letters dated January 27 and February 4, 1971. The relevant facts submitted are summarized below.

Y Corporation is a Delaware Corporation engaged, through its subsidiaries, in the record communications business. As of June 30, 1970, Y had outstanding 9,030,487 shares of $2.50 par value common stock, 370,788 shares of $100 par value 4.6 percent series voting cumulative convertible preferred stock, and 200,697 shares of $100 par value 4.9 percent series voting cumulative convertible preferred stock. Y's stock is listed on the New York Stock Exchange and is widely held.

X Corporation is an Ohio corporation engaged in the business of rendering on-line real time electronic tele-data-processing services and certain off-line data processing services for companies engaged in the wholesale distribution of various products. As of November 20, 1970, X had 300 shares of Class A no-par-value voting common stock outstanding and ninety shares of Class B no-par-value nonvoting common stock which were owned as follows:

Shareholders	Shares held	
	Class A	Class B
A	125	35
B	125	35
C	25	10
D	25	10

The only distinction between the Class A and Class B common stock is the voting rights.

In order to obtain the type of business which X has to offer as a leader in its field, a share exchange agreement and plan of reorganization was entered into on October 30, 1970, whereby Y proposes to acquire all the outstanding stock of X in exchange for voting common stock of Y. The shareholders of X will receive 93 shares of common stock of Y for each share of Class A and Class B common stock of X held by them as of the effective date of the exchange. The exchange will be subject to antidilution provisions until the effective date. At the first closing, which is scheduled for March 1, 1971, the X shareholders will receive, in the aggregate, 36,270 Y shares of stock. There will be no fractional shares resulting from the exchange.

In addition to the 36,270 shares to be received at the first closing, an additional number of Y voting common shares, not exceeding 36,230 shares, may be issued to the X shareholders at a date no later than March 1, 1974, based on a formula of one additional Y share for each $4.14 of X's pretax earnings for a period of four consecutive calendar quarters during the time period commencing April 1, 1971, and ending December 31, 1973.

It is represented that the operations of X will be continued on a relatively unchanged basis. The shareholders of X have no present intention to sell the stock of Y to be received in the transaction and have not entered into any negotiations with respect to such a potential sale. Y does not presently intend to liquidate X.

Under the agreement, all shareholders' costs incurred in the transaction will be paid by the shareholders, and all of Y's costs incurred in the transaction will be paid by Y.

Mr. A. will become president of X and has entered into an employment contract with X. It is represented that none of the Y shares received by Mr. A. in the proposed transaction will be in consideration for the employment contract.

Based solely on the information submitted, it is held as follows:

(1) The acquisition by Y of all the outstanding stock of X in exchange solely for Y voting common stock, as described above, will qualify as a reorganization within the meaning of section 368(a)(1)(B) of the Internal Revenue Code of 1954. Both Y and X will be parties to the reorganization within the meaning of section 368(b).

(2) No gain or loss will be recognized to the shareholders of X upon the exchange of their Y stock in X for voting common stock of Y (including any additional shares that may be received but excluding any shares that may be received as interest) (section 354(a)(1)).

(3) The basis of the stock of Y (including any additional shares that may be received but excluding any shares that may be received as interest) received by the shareholders of X will be the same as the basis of the stock of X surrendered in exchange therefor (section 358(a)(1)).

(4) The holding period of the Y voting common stock (including any additional shares that may be received but excluding any shares that may be received as interest) received by the X shareholders will include the holding period of the X stock surrendered in exchange therefor provided that the X stock is a capital asset in the hands of the X shareholders on the date of the exchange (section 1223(1)).

No opinion is expressed as to the tax treatment of the transaction under the provisions of any other section of the Code and Regulations which may also be applicable thereto or to the tax treatment of any condition existing at the time of, or effects resulting from, the transaction which are not specifically covered by the above rulings.

A copy of this letter should be attached to the Federal income tax returns of the taxpayers involved for the taxable year in which the transaction covered by this ruling letter is consummated.

Sincerely yours,

Chief, Reorganization Branch

REORGANIZATION AGREEMENT

REORGANIZATION AGREEMENT dated as of ＿＿＿＿＿＿ 19＿＿, between X Inc., a New York corporation (hereinafter called Buyer), and A, B, C, and D (the Sellers), each for himself, severally and not jointly, except as otherwise expressly provided.

The Sellers desire to transfer to Buyer, and Buyer desires to acquire from the Sellers, all the issued and outstanding stock of A Corporation, Inc., B Corporation, C Corporation, and D Corporation, all New York corporations, all upon the terms and subject to the conditions hereinafter set forth.

Accordingly, the parties hereto agree as follows:

1. *Terms of Exchange.* (a) On the Closing Date referred to below, and upon the terms and subject to the conditions set forth in this Agreement, each of the Sellers hereby agrees to transfer, assign and deliver to Buyer, and Buyer agrees to acquire and accept from each of the Sellers, the number of shares of Common Stock of each of the A Companies set forth below under the name of such A Company and opposite the name of such Seller, free and clear of all liens, pledges and encumbrances:

	Number of Shares of Common Stock of			
Name of Seller	A Corp.	B Corp.	C Corp.	D Corp.
A	50	5	10	10
B	50	5	10	10
C	50	––	––	––
D	50	––	––	––
TOTAL	200	10	20	20

(b) On the Closing Date each of the Sellers will deliver to Buyer certificates representing the number of shares of Common Stock of each of the A Companies set forth under the name of such A Company and opposite the name of such Seller in Section 1(a) hereof, duly endorsed in blank for transfer, or with appropriate stock powers in blank attached, with all necessary state transfer tax stamps affixed or provided for.

(c) In exchange for all the issued and outstanding stock of the A Companies, Buyer shall issue and deliver to Sellers:

(i) ＿＿＿＿＿ shares of Convertible Preferred Stock Series C (hereinafter called Series C Stock) of Buyer which shall be a series of the Preferred Stock which Buyer is now authorized to issue and which shall have the relative rights, preferences and limitations set forth in the form of resolutions of the Board of Directors of Buyer attached hereto as Annex I; and

(ii) ＿＿＿＿＿ shares of Common Stock of Buyer.

2. *Time of Exchange and Escrow Arrangement.* (a) On the Closing Date Buyer shall deliver certificates for shares of its Series C Stock and of its Common Stock to the Sellers as follows:

Name of Seller	Number of Shares of Series C Stock	Number of Shares of Common Stock
A	18,427	11,256
B	18,426	11,256
C	2,108	1,860
D	666	588

(b) On the Closing Date Buyer and A and B shall execute and deliver an Escrow Agreement in substantially the form of Annex II hereto (hereinafter called the Escrow Agreement) with the Escrow Agent named therein and, in addition to the Certificates required to be delivered under Section 2(a), Buyer shall deliver to A and B, and each of A and B shall immediately thereafter deliver to said Escrow Agent a certificate for 5,000 shares of Common Stock of Buyer registered in his name to be held by said Escrow Agent in accordance with the terms of said Escrow Agreement. Each of A and B shall deliver to the Escrow Agent blank stock powers executed by him.

3. *Access to Plants, Properties and Records.* From and after the date of this Agreement, the Sellers shall cause each of the A Companies to afford to the officers, attorneys, accountants and other authorized representatives of Buyer, free and full access to all its offices, properties, books and records in order that Buyer may have full opportunity to make such further investigation as it shall desire to make of its affairs, and Buyer shall be permitted to make extracts from, or copies of, such books and records; and the Sellers shall furnish to Buyer such financial and operating data and other information as to the business and properties of each of the A Companies as Buyer shall request. Any such financial and operating data so furnished to Buyer shall constitute additional representations and warranties of A and B. In the event that the transaction described herein is not consummated, then all information obtained by the Buyer concerning the A Companies shall be and remain confidential information and all documents furnished to the Buyer concerning them shall be turned over to the Sellers.

4. *The Closing Date.* (a) The exchange provided for in this Agreement shall take place at the offices of _____, Inc., _____, New York, New York, at 10:00 a.m., on _____, 19___, or such other date as Sellers and Buyer may mutually agree upon (herein called the Closing Date).

(b) On the Closing Date, the Sellers shall deliver to Buyer in addition to the stock certificates referred to in Section 1 hereof, all such certificates, signed by Sellers, in form and substance satisfactory to Buyer, as Buyer shall reasonably request to evidence the compliance with the terms and satisfaction of the conditions of this Agreement by the Sellers as of the Closing Date. As a covenant of further assurance and to perfect to Buyer all the stock issued by any of A Companies which is held by, or on behalf of, Sellers, the Sellers hereby agree from and after the Closing to sign all such stock certificates and other documents and instruments as may be necessary or appropriate in connection with the foregoing.

(c) On the Closing Date, the Sellers shall deliver to Buyer duly signed resignations of such of the officers and directors (other than A and B) of each of the A Companies as shall have been requested in writing by Buyer for presentation at a special meeting of the Board of Directors of each of the A Companies, duly called to be held at the same time and place at which the closing hereunder is to be held.

(d) Seller hereby agrees to cooperate in all respects with Buyer in continuing the business of each of the A Companies.

(e) At the request of Buyer, the Sellers agree to use their best efforts to persuade employees of each of the A Companies to continue as such employees following the Closing Date.

5. *Representations of Sellers.* Each of the Sellers represents and warrants that he now is, and will continue to be up through the closing on the Closing Date, the lawful owner of the number of shares of Common Stock of each of the A Companies set forth under the name of such A Company and opposite his name in Section 1(a) hereof and that he now has and will continue to have good and marketable title to said shares and the absolute right to sell, assign, transfer and deliver the same to Buyer pursuant to this Agreement, free and clear of all liens, pledges, encumbrances, options, rights of first

refusal or other claims of any nature whatsoever. Upon consummation of the exchange provided for in this Agreement, Buyer will have good and marketable title to and own all the issued and outstanding stock of each of the A Companies, free and clear of all liens, pledges, encumbrances, options, rights of first refusal and other claims of any nature whatsoever, and such shares will be fully paid and nonassessable. Sellers other than A and B do not make any representations or warranties except as set forth in this Section 5 and Section 11 hereof.

6. *Representations of A and B.* Each of A and B, jointly and severally, represents, warrants and agrees as follows:

(a) Each of the A Companies is a corporation duly organized and validly existing under the laws of the state of New York and has the corporate power and is entitled and has qualified as a foreign corporation to carry on its business and to own or lease its properties as and in the places where such business is now substantially conducted and such properties are now owned, leased or operated. None of the A Companies has any subsidiaries or owns any stock in any other corporation, firm, person or interest.

(b) None of the A Companies has outstanding any warrants, rights, options or other obligation (whether or not evidenced by securities) with respect to its capital stock and the authorized and outstanding capital stock of each of the A Companies is as follows:

Name of A Company	Authorized Stock	Outstanding
A	20,000 shares of Common Stock, $1 par value per share	10,000 shares
B	200 shares of Common Stock, without par value	20 shares
C	200 shares of Common Stock, without par value	100 shares
D	100 shares of Common Stock, without par value	100 shares

(c) Annexed hereto as Exhibit A are the following financial statements: (i) audited balance sheets of each of the A Companies as at December 31, 19___, and related statements of earnings and of capital and earned surplus (x) for the five years then ended for C and D (and its predecessor) and (y) for the three years then ended for C and D, together, in each case, with the related report of _____, independent certified public accountants, (ii) audited combined balance sheet of the A Companies as at December 31, 19___, and related combined statements of earnings and of capital and earned surplus for the five years then ended, together with the related report of _____, independent certified public accountants; (iii) unaudited statements of earnings of each of B, Inc., and C for the five years ended December 31, 19___; (iv) unaudited combined statement of earnings for the five years ended December 31, 19___, of the A Company, B Company, and C Company; (v) unaudited balance sheets of each of the A Companies as at April 30, 19___, and 19___, and related unaudited statements of earnings for the respective three-month periods then ended; (vi) unaudited combined balance sheets of the A Companies as at April 30, 19___, and 19___, and related unaudited combined statement of earnings for the respective three-month periods then ended and (vii) unaudited statements of earnings of each of B Company and C Company for the three months ended April 30, 19___. The financial statements constituting Exhibit A are in accordance with the books of each of the B Company, C Company, Inc., and D Company, Inc., are correct and complete in all material respects, have been prepared in conformity with generally accepted accounting principles applied on a consistent basis and present fairly the financial position at the respective dates of said balance sheets and results of operations for the periods indicated in said statements of earnings. The combined financial statements and the financial statements of B (and its predecessor) have been restated to reflect accrual of all corporate income taxes; since its organization, B has been an electing small business corporation within the meaning of the Internal Revenue Code and prior thereto its predecessor operated as a partnership.

"Merchandise inventory" was based (i) in the case of audited financial statements, on a physical inventory as at December 31, 19___, consistent as to exclusions and inclusions with inventory count as at December 31, 19___, priced at the lower of cost (first in, first out method, except where impracticable, in which case average cost was used) or market; and (ii) in the case of unaudited financial statements on a physical inventory taken by the A Company as at April 30, 19___, which was priced at cost and on computed inventories as at January 31, 19___, April 30, 19___, and January 31, 19___. Such computations were made as follows: (a) at January 31, 19___, and January 31, 19___-applied gross profit percentage for the period January 1 to March 31 to January sales (actual inventories were available for March 31, 19___, and March 31, 19___); (b) at April 30, 19___-applied gross profit percentage as computed above to sales from February 1, 19___, to April 30, 19___. "Market" for this purpose was the lower of replacement cost or net realizable value (estimated selling price, less trade discounts, freight out and selling expenses and less estimated cost of completion for work in process). "Cost" for this purpose was (i) with respect to raw materials and the material content of goods in process and finished goods, the price paid for the raw materials, less any trade discounts and plus transportation charges, throwing costs, import duties and expenses and purchase commissions and (ii) with respect to work in process, material, trimmings and cutting labor. The "cost" of piece goods purchased included the invoice price of the merchandise purchased, less trade discounts, plus transportation charges. The "cost" of finished goods manufactured included cost of materials, plus cost of direct labor, including outside contracted _____ labor and estimated factory overhead. Obsolete, slow-moving and irregular stock was valued at the estimated amount to be realized, less disposal cost. In the combined financial statements, there was not eliminated from total inventories the net amount of intercompany profits between the combined companies. However, such intercompany profits were not in excess of $15,000 at the end of any fiscal period for which income statements have been supplied as part of Exhibit A for all the A Companies. There are not any purchase commitments over the fair market value of such goods at December 31, 19___. There are not any anticipated losses on forward sales contracts for merchandise undelivered at December 31, 19___.

Each of the A Companies has filed all Federal income and other tax returns which are required to be filed. The Internal Revenue Service has examined Federal income tax returns of A and B. For all past fiscal years to and including the fiscal year ended December 31, 19___; and all deficiencies proposed as a result of such examinations have been paid or settled. The Internal Revenue Service has not examined any Federal income tax returns for C or D. The amounts set up as provisions for taxes on the balance sheets of each of the A Companies other than B Corporation as at December 31, 19___, are sufficient for the payment of all accrued and unpaid Federal, state, county and local taxes of each of the A Companies other than B Corporation, respectively, for the year ended on said date and for all years prior thereto. With respect to B Corp., there were not and are not any Federal income taxes due for the year ended December 31, 19___, or for any prior periods and the provision for Federal (other than income), state, county and local taxes on the balance sheet of B Corp. as at December 31, 19___, is sufficient for the payment of all such taxes which were accrued and unpaid for the year ended on said date and for all years prior thereto. Each of the A Companies owns outright all the assets and properties reflected in its balance sheet as at December 31, 19___, or acquired by any of them after said date, other than inventory or equipment sold or otherwise disposed of in the ordinary course of business subsequent to said date, in each case free and clear of all mortgages, liens, charges or encumbrances of any nature whatsoever, except as stated in said Exhibit A. The premises, fixtures and equipment of each of the A Companies and all other tangible properties and assets reflected in its balance sheet as at December 31, 19___, or thereafter acquired, are in good operating condition and have been maintained and repaired on a regular basis so as to preserve their utility and value.

(d) At December 31, 19___, the A Companies did not have any liabilities, absolute or contingent, which are not shown or provided for on their balance sheets (or the notes thereto) attached hereto as part of Exhibit A, except (i) those listed or referred to in the other Exhibits hereto, and (ii) obligations under contracts entered into in the ordinary course of business. None of the A Companies has any material unrealized or anticipated losses or any material unfavorable commitments or contracts not adequately provided for in such balance sheets.

(e) All accounts receivable and other receivables of the A Companies constitute bona fide receivables the amount of which is actually due and payable to one of the A Companies in the ordinary course of business. Taken as a whole, the books of each of the A Companies fairly state the facts stated therein and the balances due thereon. The documents and instruments evidencing and securing the accounts receivable and other receivables, and any insurance policies, certificates and coverages relating thereto, conform in all material respects with all applicable laws, rules, regulations and ordinances, and are true, valid, genuine, complete in all respects and enforceable in accordance with their terms, subject to no defense, claim of disability, counterclaim or offset. All payments reflected on said books as having been made on such accounts receivable and other receivables were made by the respective account debtors and not directly or indirectly by any of the officers, directors, employees or agents of any of the A Companies.

(f) Annexed hereto as Exhibit B is a list of all real property owned and all premises occupied by any of the A Companies and of all properties, real or personal, leased to or by any of the A Companies together with, in each case, a brief description of the property owned, the premises occupied and the properties leased to or by any of the A Companies. The A Companies have legal and valid occupancy permits and other required licenses or governmental approvals for each of the properties and premises listed on Exhibit B. None of the A Companies owns any real property except as listed on Exhibit B. Except as listed on Exhibit B, the A Companies have good and marketable title in fee simple, to all real property shown on Exhibit B as being owned, free and clear of all mortgages, liens, charges, restrictions (whether zoning or otherwise) or encumbrances of any nature whatsoever except for liens for taxes not yet due and minor easements, minor zoning restrictions and other minor encumbrances which in the aggregate do not materially lessen the value of such real property and do not prevent or impair the intended use thereof. Except as listed on Exhibit B, the A Companies own outright all fixtures and equipment located in the properties owned by any of them, in each case free and clear of all mortgages, liens, charges or encumbrances of any nature whatsoever. With respect to all leases listed on Exhibit B, the description thereof includes the annual rental, the lessor of such property, and the expiration date of such leases. All such leases are valid as between the parties thereto and the A Companies are tenants or possessors in good standing thereunder, free of any material default or breach whatsoever by the A Companies; all rental and other payments due thereunder have been duly made. On and immediately after the Closing Date and the acquisition by Buyer of all the issued and outstanding stock of each of the A Companies, the A Companies shall have the legal right (without the consent or other approval of any lessor) to possess and quietly enjoy said premises and personal property under said leases and agreements. The A Companies are the owners and holders of all the leasehold estates purported to be granted by the leases described in Exhibit B and own outright all fixtures and equipment located in the leased premises, in each case free and clear of all mortgages, liens, charges or encumbrances of any nature whatsoever except as listed on Exhibit B.

(g) Annexed hereto as Exhibit C is a list and brief description of all patents, patent applications and trademark registrations owned by or registered in the name of any of the A Companies or in which any of them has any rights, and in each case a brief description of the nature of such rights. None of the A Companies is a licensor or licensee in respect of any patents, trademarks, trade names, copyrights or applications therefor, except as stated in Exhibit C. The A Companies own, or possess adequate licenses or other rights to use, all patents, trademarks, trade names or copyrights necessary to conduct their businesses as now operated, and within the three years immediately past have not received any notice of conflict with the asserted rights of others.

(h) Annexed hereto as Exhibit D is a list and brief description (including name of insurer, agent, premium, coverage and expiration date) of all policies of liability, burglary, theft, fidelity, life, fire and other forms of insurance held by the A Companies. Such policies are in amounts deemed by Sellers to be adequate and policies in such amounts will be outstanding and duly in force at the Closing Date.

(i) Except in each case as listed in Exhibit E annexed hereto, none of the A Companies is a party to any written or oral (i) contract or commitment for the employment of any officer or individual employee; (ii) contract or commitment with any labor union; (iii) continuing contract for the future purchase of materials, supplies or equipment at an aggregate price of more than $25,000 or which is in excess of its requirements for normal operating inventories or for business now booked; (iv) sales order or commitment for $50,000 or more or for a price less than prices now quoted; (v) contract continuing over a period of more than one year from its date; (vi) distributor or sales agency contract or advertising contract; (vii) lease under which it is lessor or lessee, other than a lease listed on Exhibit B; (viii) contract with any subcontractor; (ix) bonus, pension, profit sharing, retirement, severance or termination pay, stock purchase, stock option, hospitalization, insurance or similar plan or practice, formal or informal, in effect with respect to its employees or others; (x) contract or commitment for the borrowing of money or other agreement or arrangement for a line of credit; (xi) contract or commitment of any other nature with any current or former director, officer or employee of one of the A Companies; (xii) contract or commitment for charitable contributions aggregating in excess of $1,000 for all such contracts or commitments; (xiii) contract or commitment for capital expenditures; or (xiv) contract not made in the ordinary course of business. Each of the A Companies has performed all obligations required to be performed by it, to date, and is not in default under any contract, agreement, lease or other document to which·it is a party. Also set forth on Exhibit E is a list of all cars, apartments and other facilities owned or operated by one of the A Companies for executive, administrative or sales purposes and a list of all country club and other club memberships owned or paid for by one of the A Companies. At April 30, 19___, the sales order backlog of the A Companies was approximately _____, which was in excess of the backlog at April 30, 19___.

(j) At the date hereof, there are not any accrued or unpaid liabilities for completion of capital projects undertaken or authorized by one of the A Companies. Since December 31, 19___, there has not been any material change in the position, financial or otherwise as shown in the balance sheets as at such date, of any of the A Companies other than changes occurring in the ordinary course of business, which changes have not adversely affected its business, properties or financial position. None of the A Companies is party to a representation or labor agreement except those listed on Exhibit E and no claim has been made that any of such companies is in breach of, or has not properly complied with, the provisions of any such contract. None of such companies has received notice from any other labor union that it represents, or intends to represent, any of its employees. Such companies do not have reason to believe that any strike or work interruption by any of their employees is threatened or imminent. None of such companies or the Sellers have made any loan to or given anything of value to any representative of any labor union.

(k) Except in each case as listed and described in Exhibit F annexed hereto, there are no actions, suits, proceedings or investigations (whether or not purportedly on behalf of any of the A Companies) pending or threatened against or affecting any of the A Companies, at law, or in equity or admiralty, or before or by any Federal, state, municipal or other governmental department, commission, board, bureau, agency or instrumentality, domestic or foreign, which (x) relate to the operation or any business location of any of the A Companies, (y) involve the likelihood of any judgment or liability, not fully covered by insurance, in excess of $1,000 in any one case or $10,000 in the aggregate, or (z) may result in any material adverse change in the business, operations, properties or assets or in the condition, financial or otherwise, of any of the A Companies. None of the A Companies is in default with respect to any order, writ, injunction or decree of any court or Federal, state, municipal or other governmental department, commission, board, bureau, agency or instrumentality, domestic or foreign. Also set forth on Exhibit F is a description of all actions brought or presently intended to be brought on behalf of any of the A Companies, except collection actions each involving less than $1,000.

(l) Each of the A Companies has complied in all material respects with all laws, licensing requirements, regulations and orders applicable to its business (including, without limitation, Federal wage and hour requirements and labeling requirements) and has filed with the proper authorities all statements and reports required by all applicable laws, rules, regulations and orders applicable to its business (including, without limitation, Federal wage and hour requirements and labeling requirements) and has filed with the proper authorities all statements and reports required by all applicable laws, rules, regulations and ordinances.

(m) Except in each case as listed and described in Exhibit G annexed hereto, since December 31, 19___, none of the A Companies has (i) issued any stock, stock options, bonds or other corporate securities; (ii) incurred any obligation or liability (absolute or contingent) except current liabilities incurred, and obligations under contracts entered into, in the ordinary course of business; (iii) discharged or satisfied any lien or encumbrance or paid any obligation or liability (absolute or contingent) other than current liabilities and current portions of long-term liabilities shown on its balance sheet as at December 31, 19___, and current liabilities incurred since such date in the ordinary course of business; (iv) declared or made any payment or distribution to stockholders or purchased or redeemed any shares of its capital stock; (v) mortgaged, pledged or subjected to lien, charge or any other encumbrance, any of its assets, tangible or intangible; (vi) sold or transferred any of its tangible assets or canceled any debts or claims, except in each case in the ordinary course of business; (vii) sold, assigned or transferred any patents, trademarks, trade names, copyrights or other intangible assets; (viii) suffered any extraordinary loss or waived any right of substantial value; (ix) made any change in employee, officer or director compensation, except in the ordinary course of business, and, except for decreases, none of such changes related to a person whose current rate of annual compensation exceeds \$10,000; (x) made any charitable contribution or commitment or pledge therefor in excess of \$1,000 in the aggregate, or incurred any other nonbusiness expense (other than payment of amounts accrued on its balance sheet as at December 31, 19___); or (xi) entered into any transaction other than in the ordinary course of business; except in each case as listed and described in Exhibit E.

(n) Except as set forth on Exhibit H, none of the A Companies is a party to any lease, contract or commitment with any former or current director or officer of one of the A Companies or with any record or beneficial owner of capital stock of one of the A Companies or with any entity which is owned, in part or in whole, directly or indirectly, by one of the Sellers or any associate of one of the Sellers.

(o) The execution and carrying out of this Agreement and of the Escrow Agreement and compliance with the provisions hereof and thereof by each of the Sellers does not violate any provision of law or conflict with or result in any breach of any of the terms, conditions or provisions of, or constitute a default under, the Certificate of Incorporation or bylaws of any of the A Companies, or any indenture, mortgage, agreement or other instrument to which any of the Sellers or any of the A Companies is a party or by which it is bound or affected.

7. *Conditions of Obligations of Buyer.* The obligations of Buyer under this Agreement are, at the option of Buyer, subject to the conditions that:

(a) All the terms, covenants and conditions of this Agreement to be complied with and performed by each of the Sellers on or before the Closing Date shall have been fully complied with and performed and A and B shall have entered into employment agreements with A Company, Inc., in substantially the form of Annex III hereto.

(b) The representations and warranties made herein or pursuant hereto by (i) Sellers and (ii) A and B shall be true and correct on and as of the Closing Date, with the same force and effect as though such representations and warranties had been made on and as of the Closing Date and Buyer shall have received certificates to those effects signed by (i) Sellers and (ii) A and B, respectively.

(c) The business and properties of each of the A Companies, at the Closing Date, shall not have been adversely affected as the result of any fire, accident or other casualty or any labor disturbance or act of God or the public enemy and the value of such business and properties shall not have been adversely affected by any force majeure. There shall not have been any changes in the net income, business, properties or prospects of any of the A Companies since April 30, 19___, which would have a material adverse effect on the value of the business of any of the A Companies.

(d) All actions, proceedings, instruments and documents required to carry out this Agreement or incidental thereto and all other related legal matters shall have been approved by Joseph Richard Guardino, counsel for Buyer.

(e) All Common Stock of Buyer to be issued on the Closing Date to Sellers, or upon conversion of the Series C Stock, shall have been duly approved for listing by the New York Stock Exchange.

(f) Buyer shall have received an opinion of Louis Lawyer, counsel for Sellers, dated the Closing Date, in form and substance satisfactory to Buyer and its counsel, to the effect that:

(i) each of the A Companies is a corporation duly organized and validly existing under the laws of the state of New York and has the corporate power and is entitled and has qualified as a foreign corporation to carry on its business and to own or lease its properties as and in the places where such business is now conducted and such properties are owned, leased or operated;

(ii) the execution and carrying out of this Agreement and of the Escrow Agreement and compliance with the provisions hereof and thereof by each of the Sellers has not violated any provision of law or conflicted with or resulted in any breach of any of the terms, conditions or provisions of, or constituted a default under, the Certificate of Incorporation or bylaws of any of the A Companies, or any indenture, mortgage, agreement or other instrument to which any of the Sellers or any of the A Companies is a party or by which any of them is bound or affected;

(iii) the duly authorized capital stock of each of the A Companies is as set forth in Section 6(b) hereof, of which the shares of Common Stock of each of them shown in Section 1(a) have been validly issued and are outstanding, fully paid and nonassessable and under the laws of the state of New York no liability attaches to the holders thereof (subject to Section 630 of the New York Business Corporation Law providing, in certain circumstances, for liability for wages); Buyer has acquired good and marketable title to all the issued and outstanding shares of Common Stock of each of the A Companies, free and clear of all liens, pledges, encumbrances, options, rights of first refusal, or other claims of any nature whatsoever; and

(iv) this Agreement has been duly executed and delivered by or on behalf of each stockholder of record of each of the A Companies on the date of this Agreement and on the Closing Date and the Escrow Agreement has been duly executed and delivered by each of A and B, and this Agreement is the legal, valid and binding obligation of each of the Sellers in accordance with its terms and the Escrow Agreement is the legal, valid and binding obligation of each of A and B in accordance with its terms.

(g) Buyer shall have received a letter from _____, dated the Closing Date, stating that, on the basis of (i) reading the latest available unaudited interim combining and combined financial statements of the A Companies, (ii) consultation with and inquiries of officials of the A Companies (who to their knowledge have primary responsibility for financial and accounting matters), (iii) review of the minutes of meetings of the stockholders and Board of Directors of each of the A Companies, and (iv) making other specified inquiries, nothing came to their attention which would cause them to believe that, during the period from December 31, 19___, to a date not more than five days prior to the Closing Date, there has been (x) any material change in the current or long-term liabilities of any of the A Companies, (y) any material adverse change in the cash, working capital or financial condition of any of the A Companies from that set forth in the audited financial statements as at December 31, 19___, or (z) any material adverse change in the results of operations of the A Companies as compared with their results of operations for the corresponding period of the preceding year. In addition, such letter shall state that _____ have been independent public accountants in accordance with the standards under the Securities Act of 1933 and the rules and regulations thereunder with respect to (i) B and C Corp. and its predecessor during the period from December 31, 19___, to the date of such letter and (ii) each of B Company, Inc. and C Company, Inc. during the period from its date of organization to the date of such letter.

(h) The persons designated by Buyer shall have been elected as Directors of each of the A Companies.

If any Seller or Sellers shall default in his or their obligations hereunder, then Buyer may elect to acquire from the nondefaulting Sellers the shares of stock of the A Companies held by such nondefaulting Sellers. Nothing herein shall relieve a defaulting

Seller of his liability to Buyer for damages occasioned by his default hereunder or shall limit the right of Buyer to seek specific performance of the obligations of any defaulting Seller.

8. *Representations of Buyer.* Buyer represents, warrants and agrees as follows:

(a) Buyer is a corporation duly organized and validly existing under the laws of the state of New York.

(b) This Agreement has been duly authorized by the Board of Directors of Buyer. Subject to compliance with the condition set forth in Section 7(e), the execution and carrying out of this Agreement and compliance with the provisions hereof by Buyer will not violate any provision of law and will not conflict with or result in any breach of any of the terms, conditions or provisions of, or constitute a default under, its Certificate of Incorporation or bylaws, or any indenture, mortgage, agreement or other instrument to which Buyer is a party or by which it is bound or affected.

(c) All shares of Common Stock and of Series C Stock of Buyer, when delivered pursuant to this Agreement, shall be duly authorized, validly issued, fully paid and nonassessable.

(d) Buyer has furnished to Sellers copies of its 19___ annual report containing an audited consolidated balance sheet of Buyer and subsidiaries as at _____, 19___, and the related statements of income, retained earnings and capital surplus for the year then ended, together with the related report of _____, independent public accountants. Such financial statements are in accordance with the books of Buyer, have been prepared in conformity with generally accepted accounting principles applied on a consistent basis and present fairly the consolidated financial condition and the related results of operations of Buyer and subsidiaries as at the date of said balance sheet and for the year then ended.

9. *Conditions to Obligations of Sellers.* The obligations of Sellers under this Agreement are, at Seller's option (which, if exercised, must be exercised by all Sellers), subject to the conditions that:

(a) All the terms, covenants and conditions of this Agreement to be complied with and performed by Buyer on or before the Closing Date shall have been fully complied with and performed.

(b) The representations and warranties made by Buyer herein shall be correct, on and as of the Closing Date, with the same force and effect as though such representations and warranties had been made initially on and as of the Closing Date.

(c) On the Closing Date, Sellers shall have received an opinion of Joseph Richard Guardino, counsel for Buyer, to the effect that (i) Buyer is a corporation duly organized and validly existing under the laws of the state of New York; (ii) the execution, delivery and performance of this Agreement by Buyer has been duly authorized by all requisite corporate action; (iii) this Agreement has been duly executed and delivered by Buyer and constitutes a legal, valid and binding obligation of Buyer in accordance with its terms; and (iv) the shares of Common Stock and of Series C Stock of Buyer deliverable pursuant to Section 2 hereof have been duly authorized for issuance by the Board of Directors of Buyer and upon execution and delivery on behalf of the Company of certificates therefor pursuant to this Agreement such shares shall be validly issued, fully paid and nonassessable (subject to Section 630 of the New York Business Corporation Law providing, in certain circumstances, for debts for wages).

10. *Additional Undertakings of Sellers.* (a) Sellers agree that from the date hereof through the Closing Date the business of each of the A Companies will be operated in the regular and ordinary course of business and none of the A Companies will, without the written consent of Buyer, do any of the things listed in Section 6(m) of this Agreement.

Each of the A Companies will use its best efforts to collect the accounts receivable and other receivables owed to it, which are due and payable on or prior to the Closing Date, and will follow its past practices with respect to the extension (or renewal) of any credit prior to the Closing Date.

(b) Sellers agree to cause each of the A Companies to use its best efforts to preserve its business organization, to keep available the services of present employees, and to preserve the good will of customers and others having business relations with it.

(c) Each of A and B agrees that he will not, without the written consent of Buyer, for a period of five (5) years after the Closing Date, directly or indirectly, do any of the following and that such undertaking shall inure to the benefit of, and be enforceable by, Buyer and each of the A Companies: engage, directly or indirectly, in any business of designing, manufacturing or selling products similar to those produced by any of the A Companies during the period of his employment by any of the A Companies (except on behalf of one of the A Companies or Buyer) either (i) as an individual, (ii) as a director, officer, employee, consultant, independent contractor or any other similar capacity, (iii) by acting through or with any other person, firm or corporation, or (iv) by owning any stock or having any other interest in such a business other than a corporation whose shares are listed on a national securities exchange or regularly traded over-the-counter, and in which he owns less than 1% of the outstanding stock.

(d) Each Seller will not employ or otherwise encourage the resignation of any person who now or prior to the Closing Date is employed by any of the A Companies. Each Seller agrees not to interfere in any way with the good will of the A Companies.

11. *Securities Act Registration.* (a) Each of the Sellers represents that the shares of Common Stock and of Series C Stock (and any shares of Common Stock issuable upon conversion thereof) of Buyer to be delivered hereunder for the account of each such Seller will be acquired for his own account for investment and not with a view to the sale or distribution thereof.

(b) If, at any time prior to three years after the Closing Date, and while any of the Sellers is an owner of shares of Common Stock of Buyer (consisting either of shares of Common Stock delivered pursuant to Section 2 hereof or on conversion of shares of Series C Stock delivered pursuant to Section 2 hereof), Buyer shall determine, or shall be required pursuant to any agreement with another stockholder of Buyer, to make application to register any of its Common Stock under the Securities Act of 1933 on Form S-1 or other similar applicable form for public underwritten offering, Buyer will, promptly thereafter, give Sellers written notice thereof. If any Seller, within three weeks after receipt of such notice so requests in writing, Buyer will, at the time of making such application, also endeavor to register shares of Common Stock of Buyer as requested by any such Seller (but Buyer shall not be required to endeavor to register less than 10,000 shares for either A or B, or less than the entire amount owned by any other Seller) under such Act and will use its best efforts to cause (a) the shares so registered to be included in any underwritten public offering and (b) such registration to remain effective for the lesser of (i) a period of three months, or (ii) the period of time required to complete the distribution of such shares; provided, however, that Buyer shall have the right to select the underwriters who shall make such offering and provided, further, that, if the underwriters selected by Buyer shall determine that it is inadvisable to attempt to sell the total number of shares of Common Stock of Buyer proposed to be sold by Buyer, Sellers and any other person entitled to join in any such registration statement and public underwritten offering, Sellers agree that the number of shares to be sold by them may be reduced to that number of shares which is equal to the number of shares which Sellers shall have requested in accordance with this Section 11(b) be included in such registration statement and public underwritten sale multiplied by a fraction, the numerator of which shall be the total number of shares which such underwriters shall determine it is advisable to sell and the denominator of which shall be the total number of shares originally proposed to be sold by Buyer, Sellers and any other person entitled to join in such registration statement and public underwritten offering. If Buyer shall give Sellers the written notice specified in the first sentence of this Section 11(b) within one year from the Closing Date, then A and B agree that, at the request of Buyer, they will sell not less than 20,000 shares of Common Stock of Buyer as part of the public underwritten offering specified in such written notice and, in the absence of an agreement among them, each of them will sell 10,000 shares of Common Stock. All legal, accounting and printing costs and all other expenses of Buyer in connection therewith (whether or not the offering shall be consummated) shall be paid by the Buyer.

(c) At the joint written request of A and B made not more than 90 days after the conclusion of any fiscal year of Buyer, Buyer will, promptly after receipt of such request, proceed to make application to register under the Securities Act of 1933 on Form S-1 or other similar applicable form for public underwritten offering the number of shares of Common Stock of Buyer which they shall request be so registered for public under-written offering. Buyer will use its best efforts to cause such registration to remain effective for the lesser of (i) a period of three months, or (ii) the period of time required to complete the distribution of such shares. Buyer shall have the right to select the underwriters who shall make such offering. All legal, accounting and printing costs and all other expenses of Buyer in connection with a registration pursuant to this Section 11(c) (whether or not the offering shall be consummated) shall be paid by A and B.

(d) In connection with any registration statement being effected by Buyer as described in Section 11(b) or 11(c) hereof, if any stop order shall be issued by the Securities and Exchange Commission, Buyer shall use its best efforts to obtain its removal. At the time of filing of any such registration statement, the Sellers participating therein and Buyer shall enter into a mutually satisfactory cross-indemnity agreement. In no event shall Buyer be required to make more than one application for registration under Section 11(c) hereof.

(e) Each Seller agrees that he will not sell any shares of Common Stock or of Series C Stock of Buyer received pursuant to this Agreement or any shares of Common Stock received on conversion of such Series C Stock unless (i) a registration statement under the Securities Act of 1933 shall be in effect with respect thereto and he shall have complied with the provisions of said Act and all applicable rules and regulations issued pursuant thereto, (ii) he shall have previously advised Buyer in writing of the proposed sale and, if Buyer shall have so requested, he shall have delivered to Buyer an opinion of Joseph Richard Guardino, or other counsel mutually satisfactory to him and Buyer, that registration under said Act is not required, or (iii) a "no action" letter with respect to such proposed sale shall have been obtained from the Securities and Exchange Commission.

(f) Each certificate for shares of Common Stock issued pursuant to this Agreement to A, B, or C, and each certificate for shares of Common Stock initially issued on the conversion of shares of Series C Stock to any of such persons, and each certificate for shares of Common Stock issued to any transferee of any such certificate (except for certificates for shares of Common Stock which have been registered under the Securities Act of 1933), shall be stamped or otherwise imprinted with a legend in substantially the following form:

The shares represented by this certificate have not been registered under the Securities Act of 1933 and may not be sold except in accordance with the provisions of the Reorganization Agreement dated as of _____, 19___, between _____ and _____.

Each certificate for shares of Series C Stock issued pursuant to this Agreement to A, B, or C, and each certificate for shares of Series C Stock issued to any transferee of any such certificate, shall be stamped or otherwise imprinted with a legend in substantially the following form:

> The shares represented by this certificate and the shares of Common Stock into which such shares are convertible have not been registered under the Securities Act of 1933 and may not be sold except in accordance with the provisions of the Reorganization Agreement dated as of _____, 19___, between _____ and
> _____ .

(g) Each of the Sellers shall indemnify Buyer from and against any liability incurred by Buyer (or its transfer agent) (y) as a result of sale by such Seller, or any transferee, of any shares of Common Stock or of Series C Stock of Buyer in violation of the Securities Act of 1933 or any similar statute or law or (z) as a result of refusing to recognize any transfer which Buyer (or its transfer agent) believes in good faith may have been made in violation of the provisions of this Agreement.

12. *Survival of Representations.* All representations, warranties and covenants contained in this Agreement by Sellers and Buyer, respectively, are true and correct as of the date hereof, shall be true and effective on the Closing Date, shall survive thereafter and shall be fully applicable and effective whether or not the other party relies in fact thereon or has knowledge, acquired either before or after the date hereof or the Closing Date, of any fact at variance with, or of any breach of, any representation, warranty or covenant. Each of the Sellers agrees to indemnify and defend and hold Buyer harmless from any and against all liability, loss, damage or injury, together with all reasonable costs and expenses relating thereto, including legal and accounting fees and expenses arising out of any misrepresentation or breach of representation (whether due to commissions, omissions or otherwise), warranty or covenant of each such Seller set forth herein or made a part of transactions contemplated hereby. A and B, jointly and severally, agree to indemnify and defend and hold Buyer harmless (to the extent hereinafter provided) from any and against all liability, loss, damage or injury, together with all reasonable costs and expenses directly relating thereto, including legal and accounting fees and expenses, (i) arising out of any substantial misrepresentation or breach of representation (whether due to commissions, omissions, or otherwise), warranty or covenant of Sellers set forth herein or made a part of transactions contemplated hereby or (ii) as the result of a final determination that any of the A Companies owes additional amounts for taxes on or based on income for any fiscal year or period ending on or prior to December 31,19___. Buyer will notify A and B of any proposed determination by the Internal Revenue Service that any of A Companies owes additional amounts for Federal income taxes, and A and B shall have the right to direct all further proceedings or litigation of any such proposed determination with counsel and accountants of their own choosing and shall have the sole right to settle any such proceeding or litigation on such terms as they may see fit. In the event A and B shall elect to direct any such proceedings or litigation, Buyer or the A Company involved shall have the right to participate with counsel or accountants of its own choosing, but shall not be entitled to receive indemnification hereunder for the fees and expenses of such counsel or accountants relating to services rendered after Buyer shall have been notified of such election.

Buyer shall not have any claim for breach, default or violation of any of the representations, warranties or covenants set forth in Section 6 hereof to the extent: (i) of the first $40,000 of the aggregate of any such claim or claims (it being understood that such $40,000 cushion is not a separate amount for each of A and B but an aggregate for both of them); (ii) that any liability of any of the A Companies for taxes on or based on income as a result of adjustments of income actually results in a corresponding net tax benefit (computed with discounted interest factor at a rate of 6% compounded annually) to such A Company for any period after December 31, 19___; and (iii) that any such claim or claims may be reduced by applicable proceeds of any policy of insurance or other offsets for amounts received from third parties.

The obligations of the Sellers hereunder shall survive the dissolution and liquidation of any and all the A Companies and shall bind the legal representatives and successors of each of the Sellers.

13. *Expenses.* Sellers and Buyer shall each pay their own expenses in connection with this Agreement and the transactions contemplated hereby. If the transactions contemplated by this Agreement shall be consummated, the taxes and expenses of Sellers in connection with preparing this Agreement and consummating such transactions (including, without limitation, all counsel and auditing fees and sales, use and transfer taxes) shall be paid by Sellers, and none of such expenses shall be paid by any of the A Companies or by Buyer. If all of any part of the transactions herein contemplated shall not be carried out for any reason other than the willful default of any of the parties hereto, no party shall be liable to any other for any damages hereunder, and in such event each of the parties shall pay its own expenses in connection with this Agreement and the transactions covered herein.

14. *Reclassification of Shares of Buyer.* If after the date hereof and prior to the Closing Date the shares of Common Stock of Buyer shall be reclassified into a different number of shares or a stock dividend thereon shall be declared with a record date within such period, the number of shares of Common Stock of Buyer to be delivered to Sellers as herein provided and the provisions relating to conversion of shares of Series C Stock into shares of Common Stock of Buyer shall be correspondingly adjusted.

15. *Assignment by Buyers.* Buyer may assign its rights hereunder to one or more wholly owned subsidiaries of Buyer. Any such assignment shall not relieve Buyer of its obligations hereunder and Buyer shall retain a primary obligation to the Sellers. Upon any such assignment by Buyer, there shall automatically inure to the direct benefit of Buyer and each such assignee all representations, warranties and covenants of Sellers made herein and all undertakings and covenants of the Sellers made herein and all instruments of transfer and certificates, opinions and other instruments provided for herein shall be in the name of Buyer or such assignee as Buyer shall direct.

16. *Miscellaneous.* (a) Each party represents and warrants that there are no claims for brokerage commissions or finders' fees in connection with the transactions contemplated by this Agreement resulting from any action taken by it except that Sellers are obligated to pay a fee in an amount to be determined to _____. Sellers agree to indemnify and hold Buyer harmless in respect of any claim by _____arising out of this Agreement or the transactions contemplated hereby. Each of the parties agrees to exonerate, indemnify, and hold harmless the other in respect of any and all losses sustained by the other as a result of liability to any other broker or finder on the basis of any arrangement or agreement made by or on behalf of such party.

(b) This Agreement cannot be orally changed, amended or terminated.

(c) This Agreement shall be binding upon and inure to the benefit of the parties hereto and their respective successors and assigns, provided that neither party shall assign any of its rights or privileges hereunder without the prior written consent of the others.

(d) This instrument and the Annexes and Exhibits attached hereto and made a part hereof contain the entire agreement between the parties hereto with respect to the transactions contemplated herein and supersede all prior agreements made by the parties with respect thereto. This Agreement shall be governed by the internal law of the state of New York.

IN WITNESS WHEREOF, the parties hereto have caused this Agreement to be duly executed and their respective seals to be affixed hereto, all as of the day and year first above written.

SELLERS

_____
_____
_____
_____

BUYER

by _____

Attest:

_____
Secretary

ESCROW AGREEMENT

Annex I

ESCROW AGREEMENT dated June____, 19____,
among A and B (the Principal Sellers), X COMPANY, INC.,
a New York corporation and BANK AND TRUST COM-
PANY, a New York trust company (the Escrow Agent).

Pursuant to a Reorganization Agreement dated as of June 3, 19____ (the Reorganization Agreement), between X Corporation and the Principal Sellers, _____
_____, under a Trust Agreement dated December 27, 19____
_____, (the principal Sellers and the other persons to the
Reorganization Agreement except for X Corporation are hereinafter sometimes collectively
called the Sellers), X Corporation has acquired all the issued and outstanding capital stock of
A Companies, B Company, C Company, Inc., and D Company, Inc., all New York
corporations (hereinafter called the A Companies) in exchange for _____ shares of
Convertible Preferred Stock Series D and _____ shares of Common Stock of X
Corporation.

X Corporation and the Principal Sellers have agreed that there shall be deposited
with the Escrow Agent _____ shares of Common Stock of X Corporation, Inc. in order
to secure the obligations of Sellers to indemnify and defend and hold X Corporation
harmless as contemplated by the Reorganization Agreement.

Accordingly, the parties hereto agree as follows:

1. *Other Agreements Not Limited by This Agreement.* This Escrow Agreement and
the deposit of the Escrowed Property (as defined in Section 2 hereof) with the Escrow
Agent hereunder are without prejudice to, and are not in limitation of, any obligations of
the Sellers to X Corporation in respect of any of the representations, warranties or
covenants of any of the Sellers contained in the Reorganization Agreement, except that X
Corporation, Inc. shall have recourse against the Principal Sellers only if and to the extent
that the Escrowed Shares deposited hereunder shall be insufficient to remedy and hold X
Corporation, Inc. harmless from any breach of such representations, warranties or
covenants.

2. *Deposit of Escrowed Shares.* On the date hereof, _____ shares of Common
Stock of X Corporation were delivered to the Escrow Agent for deposit in escrow
pursuant to the provisions hereof. Each of the Principal Sellers delivered a certificate
representing _____ such shares registered in his name and accompanied by blank stock
powers executed by him. Said _____ shares of Common Stock of X Corporation
deposited hereunder and any other property substituted therefor is hereinafter referred to
as the Escrowed Property.

3. *Liabilities Covered.* This Escrow Agreement has been executed and the deposit of
the Escrowed Property hereunder has been made for the purpose of indemnifying and
defending and holding X Corporation harmless from any and against all liability, loss,
damage or injury, together with all reasonable costs and expenses directly relating
thereto, including legal and accounting fees and expenses, arising out of any substantial
misrepresentations or breaches of representations (whether due to commissions, omis-

sions, or otherwise) warranties or covenants of Sellers made in the Reorganization Agreement or in connection with transactions contemplated thereby.

4. *Settlement of Liabilities or Obligations.* X Corporation will give to the Principal Sellers notice prior to settling or adjusting any liability or obligation in respect of which X Corporation would be entitled to receive any Escrowed Property under this Agreement. In the case of any suit, action or other legal proceeding which might result in a liability, obligation, loss or expense of the nature referred to in Section 3 hereof, the Principal Sellers shall be entitled to participate, at their own expense, with X Corporation, Inc. in the defense of such suit, action or proceeding, with counsel approved by X Corporation, Inc., which approval shall not be unreasonably withheld.

5. *Delivery of Escrowed Property to X Corporation.* Whenever there shall be delivered to the Escrow Agent either

(i) a certificate signed on behalf of X Corporation and the Principal Sellers certifying, or

(ii) a certified copy of a final judgment of a court of competent jurisdiction determining that X Corporation, Inc. has incurred liability, loss, damage or injury on account of which X Corporation, Inc. shall be entitled to receive Escrowed Property under this Agreement and specifying the amount of the liability, loss, damage or injury so incurred and of all reasonable costs and expenses directly relating thereto, including legal and accounting fees and expenses, the Escrow Agent shall, to the extent that the Escrowed Property then held by it shall be sufficient for the purpose, transfer, assign and deliver to X Corporation, Inc. Escrowed Property equal in value to the amount of the liability, loss, damage or expense so incurred and of all reasonable costs and expenses directly relating thereto, including legal and accounting fees and expenses. The value of Escrowed Property shall be the average of the high and low sales prices as reported in the Eastern Edition of *The Wall Street Journal* of the Escrowed Property (adjusted, to the extent required, for all interest payments, dividends, stock splits or other distributions on such Escrowed Property) on the last trading day prior to delivery by the Escrow Agent to X Corporation of such Escrowed Property.

6. *Delivery of Escrowed Property.* Three years after the date hereof the Escrow Agent shall deliver to the Principal Sellers (or, in the case of the death of one of them, to his legal representative) the Escrowed Property registered in their respective names then held by the Escrow Agent hereunder; *provided, however,* that if at said date any liabilities of any of the A Companies for Federal taxes for a fiscal year or period ending prior to the date hereof shall not have been finally determined (whether because the Statute of Limitations relating thereto shall not then have expired or because any such A Company shall have waived the Statute of Limitations) and all amounts due shall not have been paid, or if at said date there shall be pending or threatened any claim in respect of any other liability against which the Escrowed Property has been deposited as indemnity, and if X Corporation, Inc. shall deliver a certificate to that effect to the Escrow Agent, the Escrowed Property shall not without the written consent of X Corporation, Inc. be delivered to them pursuant to this Section until such liabilities or claims shall have been finally determined and disposed of and X Corporation, Inc. shall have so certified in writing to the Escrow Agent.

7. *No Transfer of Escrowed Property.* While any Escrowed Property shall continue to be held by the Escrow Agent, neither of the Principal Sellers will transfer, sell, pledge or otherwise dispose of his rights to any Escrowed Property, except that (i) such rights may be transferred by him in the event of death, by will or the laws of descent and distribution, in each case subject to the provisions of this Escrow Agreement and (ii)

either Principal Seller may request delivery to him of Escrowed Property registered in his name upon delivery of cash or high grade investment securities registered in his name, accompanied by appropriate blank transfer powers, to the Escrow Agent equal in value to the Escrowed Property to be delivered to him, the valuation in each case to be based on the average of the high and low sales prices as reported in the Eastern Edition of *The Wall Street Journal* (adjusted, to the extent required, for all interest payments, dividends, stock splits or other distributions) on the last trading day prior to the request by a Principal Seller.

8. *Notices.* Any and all notices or other instruments or papers to be sent to any party hereto by any other party hereto pursuant to this Agreement shall be delivered or sent by registered mail to the following respective addresses:

9. *Escrow Agent's Liability.* The Escrow Agent may act upon any instrument or other writing believed by it in good faith to be genuine, and to be signed or presented by the proper person, and shall not be liable in connection with the performance by it of its duties pursuant to the provisions of this Escrow Agreement, except for its own willful default or gross negligence.

10. *Delivery of Stock Powers.* Each of the Principal Sellers shall execute and deliver to the Escrow Agent such additional blank stock powers as it shall from time to time reasonably request in connection with delivery of Escrowed Property to X Corporation, Inc. pursuant to this Agreement.

11. *Instructions.* Any provision herein contained to the contrary notwithstanding, the Escrow Agent shall at any time and from time to time take such action hereunder with respect to the Escrowed Property as shall be agreed to in writing by X Corporation, Inc. and by the Principal Sellers, provided that the Escrow Agent shall first be indemnified to its satisfaction with respect to any of its costs or expenses which might be involved.

12. *Escrow Agent's Fees.* X Corporation, Inc. shall pay for the services rendered by the Escrow Agent pursuant to the provisions of this Escrow Agreement, and will reimburse the Escrow Agent for its reasonable expenses incurred in connection with the performance by it of such services.

13. *Successors.* The obligations imposed and the rights conferred by this Escrow Agreement shall be binding upon and inure to the benefit of the respective successors and assigns of X Corporation, Inc., the Principal Sellers and the Escrow Agent.

14. *Governing Law.* This Escrow Agreement shall be governed by and construed in accordance with the laws of New York.

15. *Agreement of Escrow Agent.* The Escrow Agent hereby agrees to act as escrow agent under this Agreement.

16. *Entire Agreement.* This Agreement contains the entire agreement between the parties hereto with respect to the transactions contemplated herein.

17. *Amendment.* This Agreement cannot be terminated, altered or amended except pursuant to an instrument in writing signed by all the parties hereto.

IN WITNESS WHEREOF, the parties hereto have caused this Escrow Agreement to be signed the day and year first above written.

BUYER

by _____

Vice President

[Corporate Seal]
Attest:

———————————————————————
Secretary

SELLER
by ———————————————————————
Vice President

EMPLOYMENT AGREEMENT

Annex II

EMPLOYMENT AGREEMENT dated as of _____ between X CORPORATION, INC. (hereinafter called the Employee) and A COMPANY, INC. (hereinafter called the Corporation).

WHEREAS the Employee has been serving the Corporation for many years as a key employee during which time he has acquired unique experience and knowledge of its operations; and

WHEREAS X Corporation, Inc. (hereinafter called X Corporation), is acquiring all the issued and outstanding stock of the Corporation from the Employee and the other Sellers named in a Reorganization Agreement dated as of _____ between X Corporation and such Sellers and X Corporation and the Corporation desire to assure themselves of the continued services of Employee.

NOW, THEREFORE, in consideration of the premises and of the mutual covenants hereinafter set forth, the parties hereto agree and do hereby mutually agree as follows:

1. (a) The Corporation agrees to employ the Employee and the Employee agrees to work for the Corporation in a senior executive capacity with such title as may be designated by the Board of Directors of the Corporation and to perform such services and duties of a senior executive character for the Corporation and any subsidiary or affiliate thereof as shall be assigned to him from time to time by the Board of Directors of the Corporation during the Employment Period as hereinafter defined, such services to be performed principally in the metropolitan New York area.

For purposes of this Agreement, the term "Employment Period" shall mean the period commencing _____ and ending _____ or on the last day of the month during which the Employee shall die, or, in the opinion of the Board of Directors of the Corporation, shall become mentally or physically incapacitated to continue to render services hereunder, whichever date shall be the earliest to occur.

(b) In addition to the provisions of paragraph 6 hereof, Employee agrees, during the Employment Period, to devote his entire time during regular business hours of the Corporation, best efforts, attention and skill (reasonable vacations, periods of temporary leave and sick leave excepted) to the business of the Corporation and its subsidiaries and affiliates, and will not engage or be otherwise directly or indirectly interested in any way in any business competing with or of a nature similar to the business of the Corporation and its subsidiaries and affiliates (except as an investor in securities issued by any corporation listed on the New York Stock Exchange, American Stock Exchange or other registered national securities exchange and in which the Employee, directly or indirectly, owns less than 1% of the value of its outstanding stock). Employee further agrees that during the Employment Period and thereafter without limit, he will not, except to the Corporation and its subsidiaries and affiliates, communicate or divulge to any person, firm or corporation, either directly or indirectly, any information (except that which is generally known to the public) relating to the business, customers and suppliers, or other affairs of the Corporation or its subsidiaries or affiliates.

2. The Corporation agrees to pay to the Employee during the Employment Period as compensation for the services to be rendered by the Employee:

(a) a current salary at the rate of $_____ per annum, payable in equal monthly installments on or before the last day of each month during the Employment Period; and

(b) in respect of each year of the Employment Period, such bonus, if any, as the Board of Directors of the Corporation shall determine.

3. Nothing herein contained shall affect the right of the Employee to participate in and receive benefits under and in accordance with the provisions of any present or future pension plan, insurance plan, stock option plan, plan of deferred compensation or other similar plan or policy of the Corporation for the benefit of its employees.

4. The Employee will submit to the Corporation periodic reports of traveling and other expenses in connection with his employment hereunder, in such form and at such times as may reasonably be required by the Corporation. Such traveling and other expenses will be subject to approval by the Corporation and the Employee will be reimbursed for such expenses as are approved by the Corporation.

5. In the event that the Corporation shall at any time be merged or consolidated with any other corporation or corporations or shall sell or otherwise transfer a substantial portion of its assets to another corporation or entity, the provisions of this Agreement shall be binding upon and inure to the benefit of the Corporation or entity surviving or resulting from such merger or consolidation or to which such assets shall be so sold or transferred. Except as provided in the preceding sentence, this Agreement shall not be assignable by the Employee or the Corporation.

6. The Employee agrees that until five years after termination of his employment by the Corporation (and, in any case, until five years after termination of the Employment Period) he will not, without the express written approval in each case of the Board of Directors of the Corporation (or any corporation succeeding to a substantial portion of its assets), engage, or be otherwise directly or indirectly interested, in any _____ manufacturing business in the United States (including Puerto Rico) either (i) as an individual, (ii) as a director, officer, employee, consultant, independent contractor or other similar capacity, (iii) by acting through or with any other person, firm or corporation or (iv) by owning any stock or having any other interest in such a business other than a corporation listed on a national securities exchange in which the Employee owns less than 1% of the outstanding stock.

7. For purposes of this Agreement, the term "affiliate" shall mean any person, firm or corporation controlling, controlled by or under common control with, the Corporation. The term "control" shall mean the power to direct the affairs of any person, firm or corporation by reason of ownership of voting stock, by contract or otherwise.

8. Any notice or other communication provided for or permitted herein shall be deemed to be fully given if in writing and mailed by registered or certified mail, return receipt requested, to such party at the addresses shown below; if to the Corporation, care of the following:

if to the Employee, then to the following:

Each party may change its or his respective address by written notice as described above.

9. This Agreement constitutes the full and complete understanding and agreement of the parties, supersedes all prior understandings and agreements as to the employment of the Employee and cannot be amended, changed, modified or terminated without the consent in writing of X Corporation.

10. The waiver by either party of a breach of any provision of this Agreement shall not operate or be construed as a waiver of any subsequent breach thereof.

11. This Agreement shall be executed in several counterparts, each of which shall be deemed to be an original.

12. This Agreement shall be governed by and construed according to the laws of the state of New York.

IN WITNESS WHEREOF, the Corporation has caused this Agreement to be executed in its corporate name and its corporate seal to be hereunto affixed and attested by its proper officers, and the Employee has hereunto affixed his hand and seal, all as of the day and year first above written.

_____ [L.S.]

Employee

A COMPANY, INC.

ATTEST:

by

_____

_____

Secretary

TABLE OF CODES

TABLE OF CASES

Casco Products Corp.	49 T.C. No. 5 (1967)
Coady	33 T.C. 771, rev'd 289 F (2) 490 (1961)
R.P. Collins & Co. v. U.S.	303 F (2) 142 (1962)
Cortland Specialty Co. v. C.I.R.	60 F (2) 937 (1932)
Court Holding Co. v. C.I.R.	324 U.S. 331 (1945)
United States v. Cumberland Public Service Co.	338 U.S. 451 (1950)
Curtis v. U.S.	336 F (2) 714 (1964)
Commissioner v. Dana	103 F (2) 359 (1959)
Davant v. C.I.R.	18 A.F.T.R. (2) 5527
F.C. Publications Corp. v. C.I.R.	304 F (2) 779 (1962)
Glober Packing Company of Texas v. U.S.	328 F (2) 342 (1969)
Helvering v. Elkhorn Coal Co.	95 F (2) 732
Fireboard Paper Products v. N.L.R.B.	379 U.S. 203 (1964)
Firemen's Insurance Co. v. C.I.R.	30 B.T.A. 1004 (1934)
Firestone Tire & Rubber Co.	27 T.C. 827 (1943)
Gallagher	39 T.C. 144 (1962)
General Banc Shares Corp.	388 F (2) 184; 21 A.F.T.R. (2) 352
Gittens	49 T.C. No. 44 (1968)
C.I.R. v. Gordon	391 U.S. 83
Gross v. C.I.R.	88 F (2) 567 (1937)
Hackney Iron and Steel Co.	182 N.L.R.B. No. 52
Home Construction Corporation of America v. U.S.	34 F Supp. 830 (1969)
Howard v. C.I.R.	238 F (2d) 943 (1957)
James Realty Company v. U.S.	280 F (2) 394 (1960)
Kamen Soap Products Co. Inc. v. C.I.R.	230 F (2) 565
Kimbell Diamond Milling Co. v. C.I.R.	187 F (2) 718 (1950)
King Enterprises, Inc. v. C.I.R.	418 F (2) 511
Kingsford Company	41 T.C. 646 (1964)
Kota Division of Dura Corporation	182 N.L.R.B. No. 41
Le Tulle v. Scofield	308 U.S. 415 (1940)
Libson Shops Inc. v. Koehler	353 U.S. 382 (1957)
Long Island Water Corp.	36 T.C. 377 (1961)
Lester B. Martin	26 T.C. 100 (1956)
Maxwell Hardware	343 F (2) 713 (1965)
Andrew W. Mellon	36 T.C. 977 (1937)
Mary Miller	22 T.C. 293, aff'd 226 F (2) 618, acq. 1958–I.C.B.5
Richard M. Mills	331 F (2) 321 (1964)
Mills Estate Inc. v. C.I.R.	206 F (2) 244
C.I.R. v. Morris Trust	367 F (2) 794 (1966)
Motion Pictures Capital Corp.	32 B.T.A. 399
Mountain States Mixed Feed Co. v. U.S.	365 Fed (2) 244
U.S. v. Pabst Brewing Co.	384 U.S. 349 (1966)
S.F.M. Inc.	33 T.C. No, 5 (1969)
Simon Trust v. U.S.	402 F (2) 272; 68-2 U.S.T.C. 9624
South Bay v. C.I.R.	145 F (2) 698
Southwest Consolidated Corp.	315 U.S. 194 (1942)
Estate of Stauffer v. C.I.R.	48 T.C. 277, rev'd 403 F (2) 611
Swanson v. U.S.	319 Fed. Supp. 959, 1970–2U.S.T.C. 9624
Travelodge Corporation	182 N.L.R.B. No. 52 (1970)
Turnbow v. C.I.R.	82 S. Ct. 353 (1962)
Wackenhut Corp. v. International Union	332 F (2) 954 (1964)
Waterproofed Products Co.	25 B.T.A. 648
West Texas Refining & Development Co. v. C.I.R.	13 A.F.T.R. 457
John Wiley & Sons v. Livingston	376 U.S. 543 (1964)

TABLE OF PROPOSED REGULATIONS

1.381 (c) (5) - 1 (a) (i)
1.381 (c) (5) - 1 (b)
1.381 (c) (5) - 1 (b) (2)
1.381 (c) (5) - 1 (b) (3)
1.381 (c) (5) - 1 (b) (a)
1.381 (c) (5) - 1 (c) (1)
1.381 (c) (5) - 1 (c) (2)

TABLE OF REGULATIONS

TABLE OF REVENUE RULINGS AND PROCEDURES

Revenue Rulings (Rev. Rul.)

59-259, 1959 -2 C.B. 115	67-275, 1967 -2 C.B. 141
59-296, 1959 -1 C.B. 37	67-275, 1967 -2 C.B. 142
61-156, 1961 -1 C.B. 62	68-23, 1968 -1 C.B. 144
63-34, 1963 -2 C.B. 148	68-261, 1968 -1 C.B. 147
63-40, 1963 -1 C.B. 46	68-257, 1968 -2 C.B. 155
64-94, 1964 -1 C.B. 317	68-358, 1968 -2 C.B. 156
64-147, 1964 -1 C.B. 136	69-185, 1969 -1 C.B. 108
66-34, 1966 -2 C.B. 1232	69-413, 1961 -2 C.B. 55
66-112, 1966 -1 C.B. 68	69-603, 1968 -2 C.B. 7
66-204, 1966 -2 C.B. 113	70-108, 1970 -1 C.B. 78
66-224, 1966 -2 C.B. 114	70-172, 1970 -1 C.B. 77
66-284, 1966	70-223, 1970 -1 C.B. 79
66-365, 1966 -2 C.B. 116	70-232, 1970 -1 C.B. 177
67-125, 1967 -1 C.B. 3	70-269, 1970 -1 C.B. 82

T.I.R.

713	10/13/65
777	10/13/65

Revenue Procedure (Rev. Proc.)

64-31,	1964 -2 C.B. 947
66-34,	1966 -2 C.B. 1232
67-1,	1967 -1 C.B. 544
67-23,	1967 -1 C.B. 590
69-1,	1969 -1 C.B. 381

New York Business Corporation Law (BCL)

Sec. 623	Sec. 906 (b) (3)
Sec. 623 (b) (4)	Sec. 907 (a)
Sec. 804	Sec. 907 (b)
Sec. 805	Sec. 907 (d)
Sec. 901 (a) (1)	Sec. 907 (f)
Sec. 901 (a) (2)	Sec. 909
Sec. 901 (b) (3)	Sec. 909 (a) and (b)
Sec. 901 (b) (4)	Sec. 910
Sec. 901 (b) (5)	Sec. 910 (a) (1) (A)
Sec. 902	Sec. 910 (a) (1) (B)
Sec. 903	Sec. 910 (a) (1) (A) (i)
Sec. 904	Sec. 910 (a) (1) (A) (ii)
Sec. 905	Sec. 1001
Sec. 906 (b) (1)	Sec. 1002
Sec. 906 (b) (2)	Sec. 1007

New York Executive Law

Sec. 96 (9) (b)

New York General Business Law

Sec. 359 (e)
Sec. 359 (f)
Sec. 359 (2)

New York Tax Law

Sec. 180
Sec. 270
Sec. 293
Sec. 203 (a)
Sec. 1101 (b) (4) (ii) (A)

Securities Act of 1933

Sec. 8
Sec. 2 (3)
Sec. 3 (a) (9)
Sec. 4
Rule 405

Securities Exchange Act of 1934

Sec. 12 (b)
Sec. 13
Sec. 14
Rule 15d-11

Uniform Commercial Code   Sec. 6-102
                                                       Sec. 6-103
                                                       Sec. 6-103 (7)
                                                       Sec. 9-111

Revenue Rulings

69 - 413	1969 - 2 CB 55
69 - 460	1969 - 2 CB 51
69 - 185	1969 - 1 CB 108
69 - 603	1969 - 2 CB 7
70 - 108	1970 - 1 CB 78
70 - 172	1970 - 1 CB 77
70 - 223	1970 - 1 CB 79
70 - 232	1970 - 1 CB 177
70 - 269	1970 - 1 CB 82

Index